Sm0000+763

'4/01

L.95

TOP

(an)

The Reality of Aid
2000

✓

109

1853 83 6613

The Reality of Aid 2000

An Independent Review of Poverty Reduction and Development Assistance

The Reality of Aid Project

Edited by Judith Randel, Tony German
and Deborah Ewing
Development Initiatives

Earthscan Publications Ltd, London

First published in the UK in 2000 by
Earthscan Publications Ltd

A catalogue record for this book is available from the British Library

ISBN: 1 85383 661 3

Page design by Paul Sands Design
Additional page design, typesetting and figures by PCS Mapping & DTP, Newcastle upon Tyne
Printed and bound by Thanet Press Ltd, Margate, Kent
Cover design by Andrew Corbett
Cover photos © Samfoto (top) and Elin Høyland (bottom)

For a full list of publications please contact:

Earthscan Publications Ltd
120 Pentonville Road
London, N1 9JN, UK
Tel: +44 (0)171 278 0433
Fax: +44 (0)171 278 1142
Email: earthinfo@earthscan.co.uk
http://www.earthscan.co.uk

Earthscan is an editorially independent subsidiary of Kogan Page Limited and publishes in association with WWF-UK and the International Institute for Environment and Development

This book is printed on elemental chlorine-free paper

Contents

Contents

Boxes and Tables

Boxes

Tables

Boxes and Tables

Acknowledgements

The Reality of Aid Management Group is chaired by Elin Enge (NPA). Its members are Simon Stocker (EUROSTEP), Mariano Valderrama (ALOP) Brian Tomlinson (Canadian Council for International Cooperation), the Project Manager Gunhild Ørstavik (NPA) and the editors of *The Reality of Aid* Tony German, Judith Randel and Deborah Ewing (Development Initiatives).

The Reality of Aid is funded by the participating NGOs and by a generous grant from the Ford Foundation. We would like to thank the many people who have supported the work of The Reality of Aid. In particular we would like to thank the Ford Foundation, the Development Cooperation Directorate of the Organisation for Economic Co-operation and Development (OECD) and the many individuals in governments, aid agencies and the research community who have generously contributed their knowledge and advice.

A detail from the letter written by Yaguine Koita, 15, and Fodé Tounkara, 16, who froze to death in the landing gear of a plane in August 1999, in an attempt to reach Europe and seek help for the children and young people of Africa. The two stowaways from Guninea lost consciousness without losing hold of their letter appealing to European leaders. Extracts from their plea are also inset

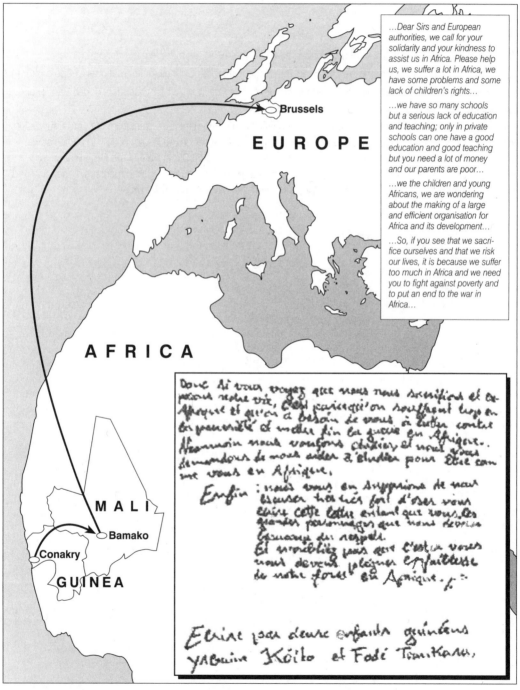

...Dear Sirs and European authorities, we call for your solidarity and your kindness to assist us in Africa. Please help us, we suffer a lot in Africa, we have some problems and some lack of children's rights...

...we have so many schools but a serious lack of education and teaching; only in private schools can one have a good education and good teaching but you need a lot of money and our parents are poor...

...we the children and young Africans, we are wondering about the making of a large and efficient organisation for Africa and its development...

...So, if you see that we sacrifice ourselves and that we risk our lives, it is because we suffer too much in Africa and we need you to fight against poverty and to put an end to the war in Africa...

Foreword

The tragic deaths of Yaguine Koita and Fodé Tounkara in August 1999 moved the hearts and surely the consciences of people around the world who read of their desperate journey to escape hardships in Guinea, West Africa (see detail from their handwritten letter, opposite). They did not, however, move many budget lines. Perhaps we should not expect otherwise: crises in Angola, Somalia and Central America have cost thousands of lives in the past year without provoking essential shifts in the volume and nature of aid. That the financial crisis in Asia generated such a swift and significant response indicates that aid continues to be more of a political than a humanitarian tool.

The World Bank has declared the Asian crisis over but its social impact, both within and beyond the region, is deepening. Worldwide, poverty is getting worse, despite economic recovery and growth in some areas. Some countries have fallen two decades behind in development; and, even in the richest countries, the poorest people are becoming poorer.

Most major agencies have conceded that the previous, growth-driven model of aid and development has proved inadequate. The proposition that economic growth alone will solve long-term needs and emergency programmes will fill the gaps in the short-term has been widely acknowledged as false. It is agreed that the strategy for poverty eradication and aid must be reviewed. Growth is a necessary but insufficient condition for poverty reduction and the same is true of aid. However, little has been done put a new model in place and urgent, creative engagement on this is needed by all involved.

During the past year, most donor governments have made *Shaping the 21st Century* (S21C), and its goal of poverty eradication, the centre of their aid policy. Many have taken steps towards a more coherent and transparent policy on aid, improved monitoring of aid flows and impact, and have pledged to make aid more effective. However, the rhetoric around this has not been matched by contributions at a level that can realise the S21C goals.

For example, throughout the 1990s, donors have stressed their commitment to Basic Education as a crucial tool for overcoming poverty. Yet while the international community may have shifted its rhetorical goals in education, it has clearly failed to provide its share of the US$7 to US$8 billion in annual investment necessary to achieve them.

In any event, the focus on S21C has tended to usurp the responsibility of donors to address seriously the broader agenda for achieving global social development, set out at the Copenhagen Social Summit. The follow-up by donor countries to the Social Summit needs to ensure that S21C is an integral part of, not an alternative to that broader agenda.

While making aid more effective is important, it is a relative concept. Aid is merely one element in a poverty eradication strategy and its effectiveness depends on other contextual factors – trade, investment and fulfilment of human rights among others. The bigger picture is enabling governments and people directly affected by poverty to solve the problems that cause it.

This requires a redistribution of wealth and changed power-structures within the poor countries and between North and South. The concept of development and its objectives need to be challenged, discussed and reshaped. A clarification of where the agenda is set and by whom is important to ensure transparency and allocate responsibility.

Foreword

Development strategies need to be linked first and foremost to ensuring basic human rights – including dignity – creating employment and livelihood opportunities. They also need to be linked to genuine efforts to shift decision-making and responsibility – and the resources to make these meaningful – to the countries and the people experiencing the worst effects of poverty. The multilateral donors, governments and NGOs alike need to ask themselves: Do marginalised people really feature in the development process – or only in funding proposals? Is true partnership achievable when large segments of society suffer exclusion due to their poverty, ethnic origin or gender? Whose definition of development counts?

Donor and recipient country governments alike have signed up to the global commitments to eradicate poverty. Both need to be held accountable for this. Yet 'partnership' is hardly possible in the face of growing inequity, with developing country governments being asked to sign up to conditions rather than consensus. In this climate, an honest dialogue about a new poverty eradication model might be more realistic than a false partnership in the old one.

The reality of aid on the threshold of a new millennium is that it is not helping to eliminate poverty – more than four million children born in the year 2000 will die before they reach the age of five.

The fact that more than a billion people are living and dying in poverty is not a tragic twist of fate but a deliberate turning of heads. The goal of absolute poverty elimination remains affordable and within reach. Most governments have committed themselves to this goal. If it is to become reality, there is an urgent need for a concerted and creative approach to replacing the old donor-driven model of aid. This must involve governments, civil society and donors. It must include channelling adequate resources to practical poverty eradication efforts. Above all, however, it must focus on ensuring that people living in poverty have the power to challenge the forces that create poverty.

Elin Enge
Chair, The Reality of Aid Management Committee

The Reality of Aid Project

The Reality of Aid Project exists to promote national and international policies that will lead to poverty eradication. It is a collaborative, not-for-profit project, which reports on the performance of aid donors from the perspective of non-governmental organisations (NGOs). This year sees the publication of the seventh edition in a series of annual reports.

The Reality of Aid report is produced by European Solidarity Towards Equal Participation of People (EUROSTEP), Latin American Association of Development Organisations (ALOP) and a coalition of NGOs from the non-European Development Assistance Committee donor countries. The NGO Norwegian People's Aid (NPA) is the lead agency.

During the last two years, The Reality of Aid Project has strengthened Southern involvement in the assessment of efforts to eradicate poverty and the debate around aid issues. This process will continue over the next two years with a view to achieving a balanced participation between Northern and Southern NGOs on an individual basis and through networks.

The Reality of Aid is a collaborative project, implemented and managed by NGOs. Every effort is made to ensure that the information supplied in the report is accurate and that the interpretation is fair. Corrections to any errors of fact or interpretation would be welcome. The views expressed in *The Reality of Aid* are those of the individual chapter authors and do not necessarily reflect the views of EUROSTEP, ALOP, NPA or Development Initiatives.

EUROSTEP

Established in 1990, European Solidarity Towards Equal Participation of People (EUROSTEP) is an international association of European NGOs working for justice and equal opportunities for people North and South. EUROSTEP seeks to improve the development cooperation policies and practices of the European Union (EU) and its Member States. It draws on the experiences of its members and its partners in the South in establishing its positions and messages and provides coordination in the approaches of its member organisations on policy at the European level.

EUROSTEP
115 rue Stevin
1000 Brussels
Belgium
Tel + 322 231 1659
Fax + 322 230 3780
email: eurostep@eurostep.org

ALOP

La Asociación Latinoamericana de Organizaciones de Promoción (ALOP) has members in Argentina, Bolivia, Brazil, Chile, Ecuador, Guatemala, Nicaragua, Paraguay, Peru, Uruguay, and Venezuela. Its activities include evaluation of new trends in international cooperation in Latin America drawn from the perspective of civil society and analysis of the impact of global trends on development in Latin American countries.

ALOP
Casilla Postal 265 1350
San Jose
Costa Rica
Tel + 506 283 2122
Fax + 506 283 5898
email: info@alop.or.cr
www.rcp.net.pe/cti

The Reality of Aid Project

Norwegian People's Aid

Norwegian People's Aid (NPA) was founded in 1939, and is the humanitarian organisation of the Norwegian labour movement. NPA's basic principles of value are solidarity, human dignity, unity, peace and freedom.

NPA has approximately 15,000 individual members and works in Norway and internationally. NPA has several hundred projects in 34 countries, where the work is carried out in close cooperation with local partners. NPA is primarily involved in long-term development assistance, but also in short-term emergency aid. NPA is a key organisation in world-wide humanitarian action to ban landmines.

Norwegian People's Aid
PO Box 8844 Youngstorget
N-0028 Oslo
Norway
Tel + 47 22 03 77 43
Fax + 47 22 17 70 82
email: Gunhild.Oerstavik@npaid.org

Development Initiatives

Development Initiatives is an independent research and information organisation working on aid and poverty policy, NGO-government relations, advocacy, evaluation and information for development. It produces a quarterly bulletin, Development Information Update, and edits a number of global reports on international development issues.

Development Initiatives
Old Westbrook Farm
Evercreech
Somerset BA4 6DS
United Kingdom
Tel: + 44 1749 831141
Fax + 44 870 0548727
email: di@devinit.org
www.devinit.org

Part I
The Reality of Aid versus the Reality of Poverty

World aid at a glance

Percentage of national income spent on aid: a 30-year picture

How much aid does the DAC give?

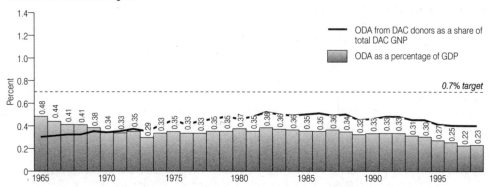

Legend:
— ODA from DAC donors as a share of total DAC GNP
▨ ODA as a percentage of GDP

0.7% target

Values shown on bars: 0.48, 0.44, 0.41, 0.41, 0.38, 0.34, 0.33, 0.35, 0.29, 0.33, 0.35, 0.33, 0.33, 0.35, 0.35, 0.37, 0.35, 0.38, 0.36, 0.35, 0.35, 0.36, 0.34, 0.32, 0.33, 0.33, 0.33, 0.31, 0.30, 0.27, 0.25, 0.22, 0.23

Where is DAC aid spent?

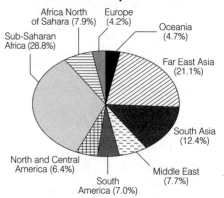

- Africa North of Sahara (7.9%)
- Europe (4.2%)
- Oceania (4.7%)
- Far East Asia (21.1%)
- Sub-Saharan Africa (28.8%)
- South Asia (12.4%)
- North and Central America (6.4%)
- South America (7.0%)
- Middle East (7.7%)

How much of DAC aid is spent through multilateral organisations?

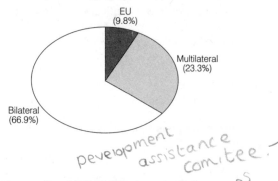

- EU (9.8%)
- Multilateral (23.3%)
- Bilateral (66.9%)

development assistance comitee – produces statistics on aid.

What is DAC aid spent on?

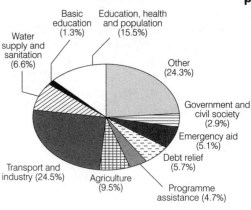

- Basic education (1.3%)
- Education, health and population (15.5%)
- Water supply and sanitation (6.6%)
- Other (24.3%)
- Government and civil society (2.9%)
- Emergency aid (5.1%)
- Debt relief (5.7%)
- Programme assistance (4.7%)
- Agriculture (9.5%)
- Transport and industry (24.5%)

How much of DAC aid goes to the poorest countries?

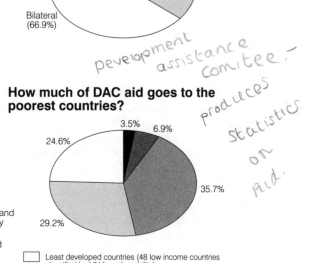

Values: 3.5%, 6.9%, 24.6%, 35.7%, 29.2%

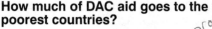
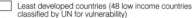

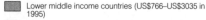
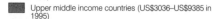

- ☐ Least developed countries (48 low income countries classified by UN for vulnerability)
- Low income countries (<US$765 annual income per capita in 1995)
- Lower middle income countries (US$766–US$3035 in 1995)
- Upper middle income countries (US$3036–US$9385 in 1995)
- ■ High income countries (>US$9385 per capita in 1995)

For notes on data and sources see page 286

World aid at a glance

Box 1 World aid at a glance

How much aid do the 21 OECD donors give?

The donors gave	US$51,521 million in 1998[*]
that was	0.23% of their total GNP
and	0.59% of combined total government expenditure
which meant	US$63 per person in 1998

Is it going up or down?

In 1998 aid	rose by US$3,197 million, a real-terms rise of 8.9%
8 donors	were less generous, reducing the proportion of GNP allocated to development assistance
10 donors	were more generous
Private flows	amounted to US$100.2 billion in 1998, a decrease of US$142.3 billion over 1997, but still nearly twice the volume of ODA

What proportion of bilateral aid goes to basic education and basic health?

In 1997 17 countries[**] reported their bilateral aid committed to basic education, basic health, and population and reproductive health. Their combined commitments were:

Basic education	1.44% of combined bilateral ODA – an average country effort of 2.1%
Basic health	1.72% of bilateral ODA – an average country effort of 2.9%
Population and reproductive health	1.24% of bilateral ODA – an average country effort of 0.8%

How much goes to the poorest countries?

Just over half	of DAC ODA (50.7%) was spent in low income countries with an average per capita income of US$2 a day in 1997

How much OECD aid is tied to purchases from the donor country?

Just over a quarter	of DAC bilateral aid (26.5%) is given on the condition it is used only to purchase goods and services from the donor country. This excludes Technical Cooperation which is mostly tied to services from the donor and which amounted to 40% of bilateral ODA in 1997

[*] This total will rise to US$51,780 million when ODA from Portugal is included (see notes on page 287)
[**] Those not reporting are: France, Ireland, New Zealand and Switzerland

World aid at a glance

ODA Volume DAC donors 1998 (US$ millions)

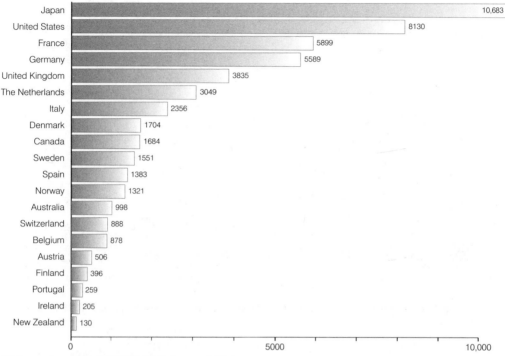

Japan	10,683
United States	8130
France	5899
Germany	5589
United Kingdom	3835
The Netherlands	3049
Italy	2356
Denmark	1704
Canada	1684
Sweden	1551
Spain	1383
Norway	1321
Australia	998
Switzerland	888
Belgium	878
Austria	506
Finland	396
Portugal	259
Ireland	205
New Zealand	130

ODA as a percentage of ODA DAC donors GNP 1998

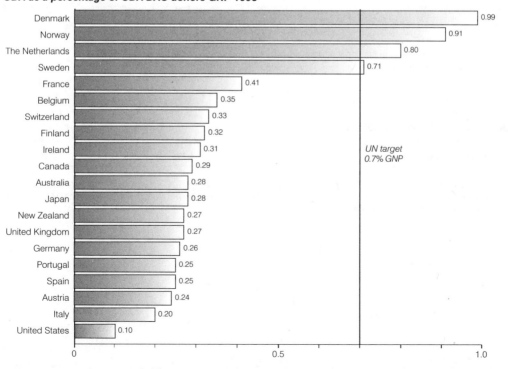

Denmark	0.99
Norway	0.91
The Netherlands	0.80
Sweden	0.71
France	0.41
Belgium	0.35
Switzerland	0.33
Finland	0.32
Ireland	0.31
Canada	0.29
Australia	0.28
Japan	0.28
New Zealand	0.27
United Kingdom	0.27
Germany	0.26
Portugal	0.25
Spain	0.25
Austria	0.24
Italy	0.20
United States	0.10

UN target 0.7% GNP

World aid at a glance

ODA as a percentage of government expenditure

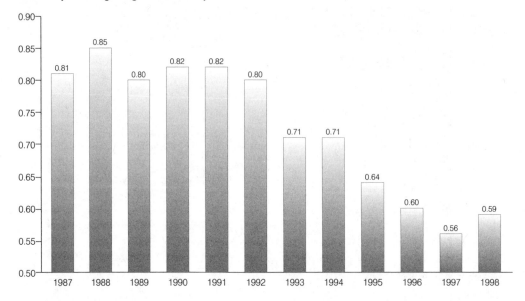

Table 1 Bilateral aid spent on emergencies, domestic priorities and technical cooperation (US$ millions)

	1994	1995	1996	1997
Bilateral aid spent on domestic priorities and emergencies				
Total bilteral ODA	41,300	40,628	39,091	32,343
Subsidy to exporters via tied aid*	1,907	1,051	1,591	1,516
ODA for emergency relief	3,469	3,062	2,692	2,150
of which aid spent on refugees in the donor country	964	8706	647	644
Total spending on domestic priorities and emergencies	5376	4113	4283	3666
Share of bilateral aid	13.02%	10.12%	10.96%	11.33%
Bilateral aid spent on technical cooperation				
Technical cooperation in US$ millions	12,848	14,249	14,120	12,875
Technical cooperation as a share of bilateral ODA	31.11%	35.07%	36.12%	39.81%

Note:
* Figure for tied aid in 1997 is estimated based on an average of the preceding three years
Sources: Tied Aid, DAC Report 1998 Table 24; DAC Report 1997, Table 31; Technical Cooperation: OECD, Geographical Distribution of Financial Flows to Aid Recipients, 1992–1997, pages 67 and 69

The context of international development cooperation

Humberto Campodónico, DESCO

Global changes bring local challenges

From 1990 to 1997, the international economic and financial context suffered a radical about-face, producing massive capital inflows to developing countries. Among developing countries as a whole, short- and long-term capital inflows increased 700%, creating an environment of high optimism about the potential for growth and business opportunities in these markets.[1]

On the plane of economic policy and ideas, the neo-liberal paradigm dominated emerging markets: economic freedom was the means and the end that would lead to sustained growth. In almost all these countries, structural adjustment programmes were applied, which involved liberalising and deregulating markets (financial, monetary, commercial, labour, land, pension systems and others). It also meant the State's withdrawal from all business activity and the process of privatising public companies.

Net aggregate private capital inflows rose spectacularly, from US$43.9 billion in 1990 to almost US$300 billion in 1997 (see Table 2). Rarely have we seen such enormous growth of private financing to developing countries.[2] Among the items that increased most were foreign direct investment (FDI), loans from private banks and bonds issued on the international capitals markets.

In contrast, the decline in net *official* financing for development has been equally spectacular, falling from US$63.5 billion in 1990 to US$52.2 billion in 1997.[3] The greatest decline occurred in bilateral (government-to-government) loans, which dropped from US$6.6 billion in 1991 to only US$1.1 billion in 1997.[4]

Grants also fell, from US$34.6 billion to US$31.1 billion. Nevertheless, loans from multilateral agencies (World Bank, IDB, African Development Bank, Asian Development Bank and others), rose during the period, from US$9.2 billion to US$13.7 billion.[5]

In the context of the application of the neo-liberal structural reforms, the inflows of capital allowed consumption and investment to grow again, inflation to remain low and macroeconomic equilibrium (particularly fiscal equilibrium) to be achieved without much turbulence.

In many 'emerging market' countries (Korea, Thailand, Indonesia, Philippines, Brazil, Argentina and Mexico), however, this growth was not built on stable foundations. Instead, it co-existed with a systematic trade and debt payment deficit. These deficits were covered by flows of foreign capital.

As long as incoming capital was not affected, the economic model allowed growth (and payment of the foreign debt) and functioned without many snags. In other words, while foreign capital was flooding into emerging markets – Latin America included – foreign debt payments more or less went unnoticed because we could not see the 'wood' (the weak, precarious reality of the countries of the region) for the 'trees' (incoming capital).

However, barely had the flows of capital (both long- and short-term) begun to diminish, as a result of the international financial crisis (which began in Thailand in July 1997, reached Russia in September 1998 and Brazil in early 1999), than we saw the precariousness and weakness of the foundations underlying the macroeconomic balance we had attained, as we shall discuss further on.

Erratic short-term capital flows (not shown in Table 2, which shows only net long-term resource flows) have led to volatility and precariousness in developing-country economies. According to the World Bank, short-term capital flows into developing countries as a whole fell from US$61.1 billion to US$4.9 billion between 1995 and 1998, with the most pronounced drop occurring in East Asia and the Pacific (from US$43.1 billion (positive) to US$–6.1 billion (negative) in the same period).[6]

The context

Table 2 Net long-term capital flows to developing countries 1990–98 (US$ billions)

	% 1990	1990	1991	1992	1993	1994	1995	1996	1997	1998
A Official Finance for Development	56.4%	56.9	62.6	54.0	58.3	45.5	53.4	32.2	39.1	47.9
A1 Concessional	44.8	51.0	44.0	41.5	45.8	44.6	40.0	33.3	32.7	
Grants	29.0%	29.2	35.3	30.5	28.3	32.4	32.3	28.9	25.7	23.0
Loans	15.5%	15.6	15.7	13.5	13.2	13.4	12.3	11.1	7.6	9.7
Bilateral	9.5%	9.6	9.3	7.0	6.7	5.6	5.1	2.9	0.2	2.8
Multilateral	6.0%	6.0	6.4	6.5	6.5	7.8	7.2	8.2	7.4	6.9
A2 Non-concessional		12.1	11.5	10.0	11.8	-0.2	8.7	-7.9	5.7	15.2
Bilateral		2.9	3.9	4.5	3.4	-2.5	5.0	-12.7	-8.0	0.8
Multilateral		9.2	7.6	5.5	8.4	2.3	3.7	4.8	13.7	14.4
Note:										
Use of IMF credit		0.1	3.2	1.2	1.7	1.6	16.8	1.0	14.7	21.0
Technical cooperation grants		14.3	15.9	18.0	18.6	17.3	20.6	19.4	17.0	16.1
B Total Private Flows	43.6%	43.9	60.6	98.3	167.0	178.1	201.5	275.9	298.9	227.1
B1 Private debt flows	15.6%	15.7	18.6	38.1	49.0	54.4	60.0	100.3	105.3	58.0
Commercial banks	3.2%	3.2	4.8	16.3	3.3	13.9	32.4	43.7	60.1	25.1
Bonds	1.2%	1.2	10.8	11.1	37.0	36.7	26.6	53.5	42.6	30.2
Others	11.3%	11.4	3.0	10.7	8.6	3.7	1.0	3.0	2.6	2.7
B2 Portfolio Investment	3.7%	3.7	7.6	14.1	51.0	35.2	36.1	49.2	30.2	14.1
B3 Foreign Direct Investment	24.3%	24.5	34.4	46.1	67.0	88.5	105.4	126.4	163.4	155.0
Total net flows	100%	100.8	123.2	152.3	225.3	223.6	254.9	308.1	338.0	275.0

Source: World Bank, Global Development Finance 1999, pp24 to 70.

Economic growth and improvement in social indicators

During this period 1990–97, characterised by strong capital inflows, economic growth in parts of the developing world was far superior to that in the industrialised nations, with China and the South-East Asian countries in the lead and sub-Saharan Africa providing the major exception.

With this state of affairs, it seemed that the policies of openness and liberalisation urged by the neo-liberal reforms were accomplishing the goals set by their mentors: they were attracting foreign capital and this, in turn, was producing economic growth.

Economic growth, according to theory, should have a direct effect in the alleviation of poverty. In the 1990s, poverty levels were seen to decrease in almost all emerging nations, especially in eastern Asia (see Table 4).[7] The countries in which poverty decreased most were Thailand, Malaysia, Indonesia and China.[8]

Poverty levels also declined in Latin America, but not as markedly as in South-East Asia and other regions. In effect, as the graph on page 10 shows, the decline in poverty was barely perceptible; the percentage of poor people dropped from 41% to 36% and the percentage of extremely poor, from 18% to 15%.

The benefits of economic growth, however, did not lead to much improvement in the unequal distribution of income in developing countries. For example, social inequality was seen to increase in Africa and remained unchanged in eastern Asia and Latin America, the region with the most unequal distribution of income in the world (see Table 5). In southern Asia, however, there was improvement in unequal distribution of income.

Economic growth, then, was not yielding the expected social results. Although overall poverty was reduced (more in South-East Asia than in Latin America and Africa), there was almost no improvement in the unequal distribution of income.

This led the multilateral agencies, such as the World Bank, to affirm that their central objective was to fight poverty. IADB president Enrique Iglesias stated that the extreme inequality in distribution of income in Latin America endangered the very continuity of the structural reforms.

The context

Box 2 Flows of capital into low income countries

It is important to note that the small, poor countries did not receive very significant flows of private capital during the 1990s. As seen in Table 3, although flows of capital into low income countries grew by 500% between 1990 and 1997, they had only reached US$17 billion by 1997, a little over 5% of the flows of capital to emerging markets as a whole.

Table 3 Net private capital flows to low income countries 1990–98 (US$ billions)

	1990	1991	1992	1993	1994	1995	1996	1997	1998
Total private flows	3.5	4.9	5.0	11.2	13.1	11.3	14.6	17.0	15.2
International capital markets	2.4	1.8	1.8	6.3	4.0	4.0	5.3	6.4	4.7
Debt	2.3	1.8	1.4	4.2	1.3	1.3	−0.4	4.0	4.3
Banks	2.2	0.4	1.6	3.7	1.0	1.0	−0.6	1.7	4.7
Bonds	0.1	1.4	−0.3	0.6	0.3	0.3	0.2	2.3	−0.4
Portfolio equity flows	0.1	0.0	0.4	2.1	2.7	2.7	5.7	2.4	0.4
Foreign direct investment	1.1	0.0	3.2	4.8	7.3	7.3	9.3	10.6	10.6

Source: World Bank, Global Development Finance 1999, Table 2.11, p37

For a small number of low income countries, mostly in sub-Saharan Africa or small states, international aid continued to be the main external source of income. For example, for the countries of sub-Saharan Africa, development aid accounted for 4.1% of GDP in 1997. For other regions, such as Latin America, South Asia and East Asia and the Pacific, official aid was only 0.2%, 0.5%, and 0.3% of the GDP, respectively.

Lastly, it must be noted that official development aid to low income countries declined sharply between 1990 and 1997, from US$32 billion to US$25 billion in 1997 (see graph, right).

Total net resource flows to low income countries

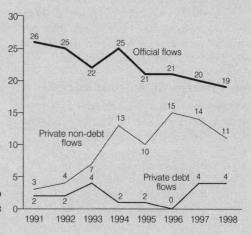

Asian crisis heralds a global crisis?

Many economic analysts affirm that the Asian crisis is only the beginning of a global crisis that has systemic characteristics, having not touched the 'important' centres: the economies of the United States and Europe (it reached Japan some time ago). In any event, a full discussion of this issue would be worthwhile, because the risks of underestimating it can be fatal; ie, whoever thinks there are no large obstacles in the road is simply not ready to face them.

One of the principal effects of the Asian crisis was the sudden reversal of the boom in capital inflows to the emerging markets, which had characterised the period 1990–97.[9] Private flows fell from US$298 billion in 1997 to US$227 billion in 1998 (see Table 3 and the graph in Box 2). Most of the decrease occurred in commercial bank loans, issuing of bonds and portfolio investments, while the decrease in foreign direct investment (FDI) was not as significant.

Official financing for development increased from US$48.3 billion to US$51.1 billion from 1997 to 1998, fundamentally due to rescue packages for economies in crisis in Asia, Russia and Brazil. This increase did little to counteract the massive private capital outflows during the period.

The context

Table 4 Percentage of poor people among the total population, East Asia 1975–95

	1975	1985	1995
Malaysia	17.4	10.8	4.3
Thailand	8.1	10.0	<1.0
Indonesia	64.3	32.2	11.4
China	59.5	37.9	22.2
Philippines	35.7	32.4	25.5
Papua New Guinea	NA	15.7	21.7
Laos	NA	61.1	41.4
Vietnam	NA	74.0	42.2
Mongolia	NA	74.0	42.2
TOTAL	57.7	37.3	21.2
TOTAL (exc China)	51.4	35.6	18.2

Source: World Bank, 1998

Furthermore, it is evident in Table 2 that grants and concessional loans have remained relatively stable from 1997–98 but very depressed as compared to their past levels.[10]

The sudden drop in private financing, just as the Asian crisis was beginning, helped to intensify the fall of the South-East Asian markets and, by extension, those of other emerging markets, in particular Russia and Brazil.

Aggravation of poverty and social inequality

The outbreak of the crisis had an immediate impact on the living conditions of the population in the affected countries. According to the President of the World Bank:

> 'In East Asia, estimates suggest that over 20 million people fell back into poverty last year (1997). In these countries, at best of cases, growth is likely to be halting and hesitant for several years to come. Today, while we talk about financial crisis, 17 million Indonesians have fallen back into poverty and across the region a million children will not return to school. Today, an estimated 40% of the Russian population now lives in poverty.
>
> 'Today, across the world, 1.3 billion people live on less than one dollar a day; 3 billion live on under two dollars a day; 1.3 billion have no access to clean water; 3 billion have no access to sanitation; 2 billion have no access to electricity. We talk of financial crises while in Jakarta, in Moscow, in sub-Saharan Africa, in the slums of India and in the barrios of Latin America, the human pain of poverty is all around us.'

> (World Bank, James D Wolfensohn, *The Other Crisis*, October 1998)

Latin America: trends in poverty and extreme poverty, 1980–97 (percentage of homes)

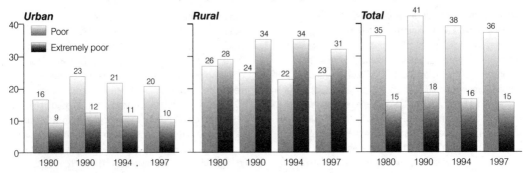

Source: Economic Commission for Latin America and the Caribbean, ECLAC

The context

Table 5 Global comparison of levels of inequality by region, 1980s–1990s

	1980s	1990s
Latin America and the Caribbean	49.8	49.3
Sub-Saharan Africa	43.7	47.0
Middle East and North Africa	40.5	38.0
East Asia and the Pacific	38.7	38.1
South Asia	35.0	28.9
Eastern Europe	25.0	28.9
High Income Countries	33.2	33.8

Note: This table shows levels of inequality using the Gini coefficient – a universally recognised indicator of distribution of income. The higher the coefficient, the more unequal the distribution of income in a given society.
Source: World Bank, 1998

What Wolfensohn is telling us is that the (highly relative) improvement in levels of poverty achieved during the 1990s is rapidly being lost to the financial crisis. Worse yet, the international agencies forecast that the recession or economic stagnation will last for several years.

Also, we cannot foresee that multilateral development banks will increase their loans in absolute terms. Worse, the loans that were being negotiated (many of them linked to social programmes), are at risk of being postponed due to the requests from developing countries for freely disposable credits for resolving the problems of insolvency brought on by the withdrawal of foreign capital.

In effect, structural adjustment loans (SALs) granted by the World Bank, which were growing rapidly until 1994 and came to constitute 33% of total World Bank credits, began to decline notably from that year. The World Bank consequently asserted that many countries had already graduated from a first phase of structural reforms by that time. However, in 1995, as a result of the Mexican crisis, these credits increased again for several countries of Latin America, principally Mexico and Argentina.

By 1996, those loans had again declined (see graph), representing only 2% of the total credits granted by the World Bank. However, as a consequence of the Asian crisis and of the rescue packages for those countries, these credits rose again rapidly to 39% in 1998, the highest figure granted by the bank in all its history. Preliminary reports indicated that this trend would hold in 1999.

Total net resource flows to Developing Countries

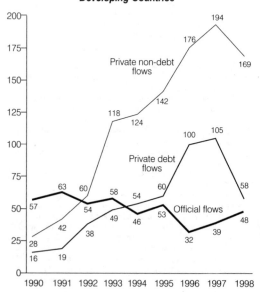

World Bank structural adjustment loans as a percentage of total loans

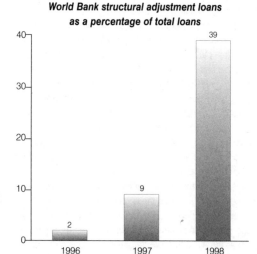

The context

Facing up to the fight against poverty and social inequality

Structural adjustment policies, even during periods of growth (such as 1990–97), have made little progress in the sustainable reduction of poverty or unequal distribution of income in developing countries.[11] We can only conclude, then, that while the economic growth of the 1990–97 period was not a sufficient condition for fighting poverty, the withdrawal of capital flows and the low economic growth foreseen will certainly aggravate poverty and social inequality.

Worse yet, when the international financial crisis broke out, with the consequent reduction in private capital flows to affected countries, it brought on huge economic crises that led to prolonged recessions, bankruptcies of financial systems, recession in production mechanisms, massive layoffs and reduction of fiscal spending for poverty allevia-tion programmes.

At present, the instability caused by the capital flows (both long- and short-term) has made the establishment of a new international financial framework the order of the day.[12] At the same time, the proposal of the Tobin Tax on short-term capitals, to decrease their negative effects, is gaining force.

As a result, we are entering a period that will see an increasing loss of credibility in the liberalisation, deregula-tion and privatisation policies urged by neo-liberal structural reforms, which have concentrated income worldwide (through mega-mergers of banks, oil companies, mining companies, etc), without resolving the problems of unequal distribution of income. The credibility of the statements of the G7 leaders, who always supported structural adjust-ment, is clearly called into question.

It is obviously necessary to explore alternatives for development that challenge the neo-liberal proposal based on the free play of market forces, in the different fields of economic and social policy. We can begin by stating that there are limits to the liberalisation of markets. One of the guiding principles for the discussion could be that: *there should be as much market as possible and as much State as necessary*. This is something that has not been done and would be difficult for today's governments to do, because they continue to believe in neo-liberalism and the arguments of the multilateral development banks.

Until now, the policies for fighting poverty and social inequality that have used the *targeting* approach. This is the reverse of the concept of universal benefits which underpins much rhetoric on poverty and international commitments such as the 20:20 Initiative. Targeting tries to ensure that benefits – such as lower electricity tariffs – are given only to selected groups.

One of the most important examples is provided by the Social Investment Funds, which have sought to identify the claimants' needs, financing their investments with funds from the State and multilateral development banks. In health and education reforms, the main objectives have centred on criticising the State's role in performing these functions and on promoting the influx of private capital to provide these essential services for the population. In Columbia for instance, public hospitals were privatised as part of a dogmatic adherence to a neo-liberal doctrine which treats health care as another good to be bought and sold in the market. The new private owners were unable to make them profitable – largely because patients could not pay for the services – so the hospitals went bankrupt. Currently, the hospitals are closed and have not been re-opened by the government. This policy approach is receiving strong criticism for its poor performance and the World Bank has recently been making changes to its origi-nal concepts.

The inability of such policies to reduce poverty indicates that we must explore further policies that stimulate the steady creation of sources of employment for the popula-tion. This is especially important in the sectors that generate added value, strengthen domestic savings and promote growth, such as industry, agro-industry and agriculture.

Notes

1   These countries were even renamed emerging markets, based on the international investors' interest in them. In Latin America, this brought a radical change from the 1980s (also called the 'lost decade') characterised by the foreign debt crisis and the conse-quent, massive flight of capital (more than US$235 billion left the region between 1982 and 1990), as well as by recession and infla-tion.
2   We must not forget, however, that more than 70% of these capital flows went to only ten countries (among them, China, South Korea, Brazil and Mexico).
3   These data are at 1996 prices and exchange rates. In current prices, ODA fell from US$52.9 billion in 1990 to US$48.3 billion in 1997.
4   OECD DAC Development Cooperation (DAC Report) 1998, OECD, Paris 1999 and previous years.
5   World Bank, 1999, *Global Development Finance 1999*, World Bank Publications, Washington DC, Table 1.
6   World Bank, 1999, *Global Development Finance 1999*, World Bank Publications, Washington DC, p31.
7   There are different methods for measuring poverty. In this paper, we are using the income method, which provides minimum bases for comparing countries. It should be made clear that many authors of *The Reality of Aid* consider the incomes approach too narrow. A broader understanding of poverty can be found, for example, in UNDP's *Human Development Report 1997*.
8   Nevertheless, in a publication subsequent to the outbreak of the crisis (September 1998), the World Bank wrote that 'Before the crisis there were three weak points, which were disguised: protracted

The context

poverty and growing inequality; concern for labor rights, growing demands for formal mechanisms to counteract domestic insecurity.' (World Bank, *Social Consequences of the East Asian Crisis*, p6).

9　'Much attention has been focused on the large number of structural weaknesses that exist in the affected countries, including: weaknesses in corporate governance arrangements, lack of transparency about the financial business situation and its relationship to government authorities; poor regulatory and supervising arrangements in the financial sector, and the tendency to high indebtedness and over-leveraging in business sectors, and to allowing financial institutions to continue operating with high levels of non-performing loans.

'While these structural deficiencies have played a major role in amplifying the crisis, and addressing them must be an important part of the solution, they have existed for many years without preventing the rapid growth and rise in living standards, that most of the region has enjoyed during the past 30 years or more. They cannot explain by themselves, the sudden collapse that the crisis countries have experienced' (OECD *Economic Outlook* No 63, June 1998, p9).

10　Financing under concessional conditions continued its descent of the last ten years, with aid flows falling from US$33.4 billion in 1997 to US$32.7 billion in 1998. At present, in real terms, these flows are one third lower than those of 1990 and they are likely to remain stationary or continue to decline (World Bank, *Global Development Finance 1999*). It should be noted that Official Development Finance

is not the same as Official Development Assistance – ODF includes both concessional and non-concessional finance for developing countries).

11　The countries of South-East Asia did not apply structural adjustment policies, but since the 1980s and early 1990s they liberalised their capital account and acceded to massive loans from international banks, as well as issuing bonds on world capital markets. The flight of private capital from Thailand in July 1997 (changing baht to dollars on leaving the country) was what triggered the crisis.

12　Lastly, the recent crisis has revealed a fundamental problem of the global economy: the huge discrepancy that exists between an international financial world that is increasingly sophisticated and dynamic (with a rapid globalisation of financial portfolios) and the absence of an institutional framework capable of regulating it. In short, today's institutions are inadequate for addressing financial globalisation. This can be said of international institutions, which have displayed significant deficiencies in terms of consistent macroeconomic policies, handling of liquidity and financial supervision and regulation. This can also be said of national institutions, even in industrialised nations, when it comes to dealing with globalisation. The systemic deficiency and the consequent threat of future crises, have highlighted the need for integral reform in the international financial system, with a view towards avoiding costly crises and managing them better when they do happen. This would improve economic and social prospects for the entire world. (United Nations, *Towards a New International Financial Architecture* 1999).

Trends towards the new millennium

Tony German and Judith Randel, Development Initiatives

The reality of aid on the threshold of a new millennium is that aid is not eliminating poverty. More than four million children born in the year 2000 will die before they reach the age of five.

During the past year, the gap between rich countries and poor countries, and between rich and poor people within even the richest countries has continued to grow.[1] That gap reflects not just extreme inequalities of income but structural, social and political inequalities that entrench people in poverty. The poverty gap is mirrored by the increasing wealth and shrinking generosity of donor countries, shown dramatically in the graph below.

It is clear that aid can only contribute effectively to the eradication of poverty where it is integrated into a comprehensive approach to development that addresses inequalities between and within countries. Central to this is the question of power relations. Giving political priority to reducing poverty is meaningful only where equal priority is given to overcoming the causes of poverty.

OECD countries choosing to ignore the rights of people in poverty: the widening gap between income and aid per capita of DAC members (at 1997 prices and exchange rates)

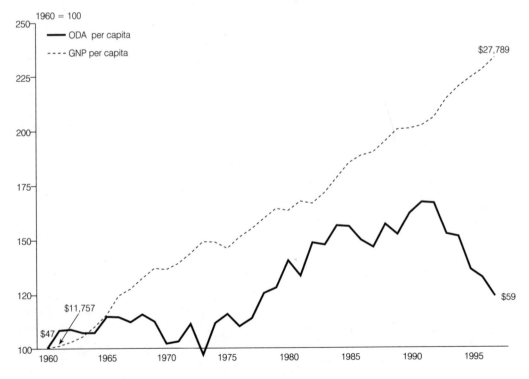

Trends towards the new millennium

Progress in policy ... the reality of aid

Three years ago, all donors who are members of the OECD's Development Assistance Committee (DAC) signed up to a new strategy called *Shaping the 21st Century: The Contribution of Development Cooperation*. This strategy had the eradication of poverty as its centre and stressed the need for developing country leadership.

In the last year, this poverty-centred development strategy has gained ground with almost every donor. These efforts are detailed in the At a Glance Chart on page 222.

The increased prominence of *Shaping the 21st Century* in the policy statements and annual reports of OECD donors ′ is a sign of progress. *Shaping the 21st Century* may be a foundation for improved donor coordination and a shared international effort to measure progress towards the goal of poverty eradication. The combination of lobbying by NGOs, the rooting of the targets in agreements from UN conferences, the focus on poverty, health and education and the partnership framework appear to have influenced donor thinking quite significantly.

But progress at policy level in OECD aid departments, is not translating into reduced poverty in developing countries. Nor is it resulting in serious attention by donor governments to the creation of an enabling environment within which developing countries have a realistic chance of ending absolute poverty.

Talk of partnership may have some meaning in the context of donors and developing countries working together on, for example, an education sector investment programme. But such aid partnerships – promising though some may be – cannot obscure the unequal relationship between developing countries on the one hand and OECD donors and the international financial institutions on the other. Modest improvements in aid policy do not obscure the fact that the wishes of OECD countries, and especially the G7, dominate international relationships. In practice, partnership with donors means following their recipe – which undercuts the idea of developing country leadership and ownership.

The reality of poverty ... an indictment of the global order

While aid can claim some successes in contributing to human well-being over recent decades,[2] the facts of global poverty in the year 2000 are an indictment of the global political, economic and social order. More than four households out of ten in the whole of South Asia remain in absolute poverty. About 1.3 billion people are living on less than a dollar a day – and the number is rising.

According to the World Bank:

- The financial crisis in Asia has led to significant increases in poverty in countries such as Indonesia, Malaysia and Thailand.
- The number of people living in poverty in India has increased from 300 million in the late 1980s to around 340 million in the late 1990s.
- Conflict, low commodity prices and adverse climate in sub-Saharan Africa seems to have reduced growth in 1998 to below population growth – implying a fall in per capita incomes.
- Financial crisis in Brazil, natural disasters such as El Niño and Hurricane Mitch and rising inequality in some areas are jeopardising the prospects for growth and reduced poverty in Latin America and the Caribbean.
- Conflict and financial crises in parts of Eastern Europe have caused a sharp worsening in poverty.

The overall picture suggests that absolute poverty is likely to have risen to 1.5 billion by the end of 1999.[3]

The world at the end of the 20th century not only overproduces food, but also a wide variety of luxuries and amusements. And yet around a billion and a half people are denied their basic human rights and needs. This illustrates not so much inertia and lack of imagination on the part of the comfortably off majority – the public in OECD countries are often generous in their response to NGO appeals. Rather it demonstrates the failure of political leadership on a grand scale.

Aid can only play a minor role in reducing poverty. It can achieve specific objectives and to some extent it is a proxy for the political commitment of the North to greater global justice. But it is after all only an instrument. The objective – the achievable goal of eliminating absolute poverty – must be the prime focus. So it is vital to look at some of the other major elements beyond aid that will determine whether poverty will be overcome.

Trends towards the new millennium

Globalisation, wealth and poverty

The globalisation of areas such as trade, finance, employ-ment and communications has become a reality during the 1990s. Every country is urged by the leaders of the world's richest nations to embrace globalisation. It is offered as the formula for rich and poor alike.

There is little doubt that globalisation has increased wealth and opened up opportunity and choice for many people in both rich and poor countries.

But there is also no doubt that globalisation is resulting in insecurity for many even in wealthy countries. And while for OECD countries, globalisation may have an overall impact that is positive, there is growing evidence that the side effects of some aspects of globalisation are taking a severe human toll in both developed and developing countries. UNDP notes the human impact of the Asian finan-cial crisis: 13 million people losing their jobs and real wages down 40–60% in Indonesia.[4]

Many of the poorest countries start off from such a position of disadvantage that it is unrealistic to talk about them competing effectively in a global economy. Winners and losers in the globalisation race are inevitable. But it is a fairly safe bet that the small élite and expanding middle class who set the rules of the race are going to be winners and that the vast majority of poor people, mostly living in developing countries, are going to be losers. At the moment, key questions, such as how to ensure that the process of globalisation enhances, rather than reduces, human security are barely being asked – let alone answered.

It took the advocates of structural adjustment a woefully long time to acknowledge that their programmes often made the most vulnerable people worse off. The globalisation prescription being offered to poor countries shares many characteristics with the adjustment model. Just as aid had to be used to mitigate the social costs of adjust-ment, it is now being used to mitigate the costs of rapid globalisation (Japanese aid for Asia being a case in point).

New Zealand NGOs make the point that social impact assessment, linked to restructuring tends to be an add-on to ameliorate the potential problems that arise. They argue that social impact should be assessed prior to decisions being made, to ensure that restructuring itself builds in positive measures to enhance the well-being of people in poverty .

However, there is little evidence that OECD countries are putting a human face on their global economic policies. The IMF may be smarting from the situation in Asia. But it has far from lost control of the global agenda, while the WTO, pressed by the industrialised countries, pursues its liberalised trade and investment agenda without any real assessment of the impact of the Uruguay Round on those living in poverty.

What about globalised rights and responsibilities?

Current orthodoxy suggests that globalisation of finance, communications, investment, employment, production and marketing are inevitable. But there is less talk of globalisa-tion of rights and responsibilities.

The Reality of Aid report has been positive about donors' adoption of the *Shaping the 21st Century* strategy and attempts to establish and monitor indicators of progress towards the 2015 International Development Targets (IDTs). But it has to be recognised that the strategy and the targets envisage just a halving of the *proportion* of people living in absolute poverty. This means that even if the strategy is successful, the best-case scenario is that in 15 years' time there will still be at least 900 million people living in absolute poverty.[5] At the 1995 World Summit for Social Development in Copenhagen, governments committed themselves to 'the goal of eradicating poverty in the world through decisive national actions and international coopera-tion'. If the best that donors can aim for is around a billion people still in poverty in 15 years time, it does not seem that they are fulfilling the commitment to decisive action.

Surely it is morally unacceptable for the rich world to enjoy the benefits of globalisation – increased affluence for many in the North – whilst refusing to take seriously the idea of globalised rights to have basic human needs met? Surely globalisation has to mean that the eradication of absolute poverty is a responsibility shared by governments in both the North and South.

OECD countries and particularly the G7 leaders, in practice shape much of the global order. Do they envisage a world with a permanent cadre of people in abject poverty? Is the price of globalisation that the most disadvantaged developing countries will be left in 2015 with millions of children dying prematurely, denied basic education and health, clean water and adequate nutrition – whilst the world's wealthy enjoy even higher standards of living?

The challenge is for political leaders, and especially those in the North, to go beyond aid and work now on a deeper and more comprehensive approach to intractable poverty.

The importance of equity

Both governments and the world's major financial institu-tions have stressed the need for growth to eliminate poverty.

Trends towards the new millennium

There has been plenty of rhetoric about pro-poor growth, but little done to achieve it. Few people dispute that growth is a necessary precondition for eliminating poverty. But a great deal of the growth that has occurred has not fed through into reduced poverty, because the issue of equity has been largely neglected.

As the evidence grows that income gaps are widening in both the North and the South, and that poorer income groups have seen few benefits from growth, it seems clear that more could have been done to ensure that the benefits of growth were spread more widely. Sweden's 1998 policy document, *The Right Support – Our Common Responsibility*, argues that a lack of rights is a key factor underlying poverty. An effective approach therefore needs to be based on growth with equity rather than basic social investments. A decade on from publication of the World Bank's 1990 Poverty Report, it is being recognised that profound inequality of income and social access is a cause, as well as a consequence of poverty. An increasing number of econo-mists suggest that income inequality in itself inhibits growth and poverty reduction – and that growth plus increased social spending may be an insufficient answer to poverty where social, political and economic systems channel power and resources inexorably to those who already enjoy them.

Questions of equity of course operate both within and between countries. Both the EU and UK chapters in this report show how a lack of attention to equity in the form of the legitimisation of EU protectionism, particularly in agricul-ture, has adverse consequences for food security and sustainable development in developing countries.

Failing to overcome poverty is a matter of political choice not necessity. The goal is neither economically nor technically beyond our current reach.

Undoubtedly, some steps have been taken towards it and these are highlighted below. The challenge to follow them through becomes ever more urgent.

Meeting basic needs moves slowly up the agenda

The *Reality of Aid* has always argued for a much greater proportion of aid to be spent on basic social services – basic health (including reproductive health), basic educa-tion, low-cost water supply, food and nutrition.

One outcome of the 1995 Social Summit was the 20:20 Initiative. This envisaged bilateral agreements between donor and recipient governments that 20% of donor's ODA and 20% of developing country government budgets should be allocated to Basic Social Services (BSS).

In late 1998 a number of donors and recipient countries reaffirmed their commitment to the universal provision of basic social services when they met to review the 20:20 Initiative in Hanoi.[6]

Following up the emphasis on basic health and educa-tion in the International Development Targets, in 1998, the DAC agreed to update its measurement of aid to BSS to enable a more realistic comparison of effort and to make the links with the IDTs as strong as possible.

To what extent are donors meeting these commit-ments? When *Reality of Aid* was first produced in 1993, this question was much harder to answer. Wildly different estimates were used to measure aid to basic needs or direct poverty reduction. This lack of credible data brought aid into disrepute, because it was difficult to compare donors' efforts or to have a serious discussion based on facts about how to improve the allocation of aid to poverty-focused sectors.

Since 1995, the DAC has been reporting on donor allocations to basic education and basic health. In the first year, only eight donors reported on basic education and seven on basic health. By 1999, 17 donors are reporting on basic education and basic health. Commitments as a percentage of bilateral ODA are now around 1.4% and 1.7% respectively. These are derisory sums in the face of both the stated commitment of donors to the goals and the enormous need. For example, Oxfam argue that an additional US$7 or 8 billion a year – of which US$4 billion would be aid from OECD countries – is needed to achieve universal primary education within a decade.[7]

As Table 7 shows only three countries – Sweden, Denmark and Luxembourg – met their fair share of the target for aid for BSS in 1997 and overall the DAC members have fallen short by over US$5 billion in 1997.

Gender equality no longer 'an optional extra'

NGOs in a number of countries have reported substantial developments in the treatment of gender equality issues in official approaches to poverty reduction.

In countries that have not prioritised this area in the past, there is evidence of some change. Portugal, for instance, has a new centre of expertise for gender equality; in Belgium a policy paper has been put before Parliament.

In Sweden, where gender issues have long been a major concern, there is no longer a separate division, but gender is treated as a key part of policy. Each department has its own resource person for gender equality, as do half of Swedish embassies, and together they form a Sida-wide

Trends towards the new millennium

network. As part of the process of mainstreaming, gender country profiles and gender-sensitive log frames have been developed.

While many countries report progress, this is still stronger at the level of policy than programming. In Canada, CIDA also has gender markers, handbooks and terms of reference, but many programmers and consultants do not take these seriously. As Canada reports, 'After 20 years of policies relating to gender issues, there is still significant misunderstanding of the implications of the policy and resistance to applying it to all development initiatives'. Implementation is said to depend more on individual initiatives than professional accountability. New Zealand's structured approach to mainstreaming gender makes it an integral part of policy, action plans, monitoring and reviews. Policy dialogue is common and a number of partner countries have agreed to a gender strategy. Progress on following this through into implementation is documented in the At a Glance Donor Approaches to Gender on page 261.

The world's largest donor, Japan, still pays little attention to gender as a policy issue; however, closing differentials in access to education and reducing maternal mortality are key goals of Japanese ODA.

How much does aid contribute to poverty reduction?

Aid needs to be spent both on interventions that benefit poor people directly and on supporting a wider policy environment for poverty elimination, in which poor people can voice their interests. In both cases, the chain of causation between the spending of each aid dollar and benefit to poor people needs to be evident and plausible.

NGOs and governments North and South agree on some aspects of the role of ODA in development strategies. Few would argue that all aid should be spent on direct services to poorer people or that investing only in the 'enabling environment' is enough. The World Bank Report of 1990, which argued in favour of pro-poor economic growth, plus investment in human priorities and provision for safety nets for people living in poverty, is still the basic text to which many donors refer.[8]

Most donor policies therefore favour a combination of actions focused on the rights and needs of poorer people, and development assistance that contributes to the overall environment for poverty eradication. This includes improving governance and accountability, enabling decentralisation, supporting the government budget in selected sectors, investing in economic infrastructure and enabling greater integration with the world economy.

Some positive steps on measurement and accountability

This two-pronged strategy demands two-pronged accountability. Donors must be able to show how much of their aid is directly targeted on improving the lives of poorer people. But they must also be able to demonstrate how their overall programme of development cooperation, inside and outside the confines of the aid ministry, is contributing to poverty eradication.

For some years, *The Reality of Aid* has been monitoring donor progress on mainstreaming and measuring aid for poverty reduction. In 1994 only seven donors had their own systems for assessing aid to poverty reduction. Substantial improvements have occurred since then. Germany, the country which in 1993 had the biggest divergence between its own and international estimates, now has a reliable and transparent system of reporting. Six countries are testing the proposed DAC poverty markers and poverty focused evaluation is on the increase.

Who is accountable for government-wide attention to poverty?

While poverty has clearly become more mainstream within official aid agencies, the accountability for aid spending designed to increase pro-poor economic growth often remains weak.

In a context of falling official aid, donors have referred to increased private investment as though this is an alternative. As contributions from Latin America to *The Reality of Aid* show, growth founded largely on the influx of foreign capital, without institutional reform or public policy designed to increase employment, is not reliable growth. Donor justification for their programme aid and other forms of investment in enabling pro-poor growth and employment tends to be very generalised. There is little recognition that pro-poor development is ultimately about politics. As Canada and Norway point out, to reduce poverty you need to address power relations, the cultural and social interests that sustain the unequal access to economic opportunity and social resources.

Aid spending that aims to support a broad pro-poor environment but fails to address these dimensions is unlikely to increase equity. At present, donor efforts to foster a pro-poor macroeconomic and political framework are hampered by a number of factors, which include:

- Country approaches that inadequately address the underlying causes of poverty;

Trends towards the new millennium

- Lack of concerted donor action on key obstacles to poverty reduction;
- Perceived mismatch between donor prescriptions for developing countries to increase equity and reduce poverty – and donors' own domestic and international action on the same issues.

Does improved policy mean reduced poverty?

Alongside the greater clarity at policy level, some aid agencies are taking steps to translate the poverty orientation of their policy into practice. This means attention to areas such as decentralisation, work with civil society, public participation and gender equality – important dimensions of a poverty-oriented approach to aid.

NGOs highlight the need for operational guidelines and also evaluation to follow up the implementation of poverty policies and their outcomes.

A key concern of Swedish NGOs, for instance, is how the new poverty policy will be translated into the practical work of Sida. Reports from the government focus on changes to policy on environment, gender and learning on poverty eradication. There is very little reporting about how the new policy is translated into concrete actions in the bilateral development programmes. A handbook is being produced by Sida and the ministry on how to translate policy into good country strategies, but that in itself does not answer the question of implementation.

If reducing poverty is truly the overriding aim of all aid interventions, evaluation must address specific impacts on poor people, on women and on all vulnerable groups and sectors. An approach to evaluation that is too focused on projects cannot assess the overall contribution to poverty reduction.

Below, we outline some of the improvements in aid management that NGOs have reported this year, including the new Sectoral Approaches, which many donors and governments are actively pursuing.

But first it is important to consider a fundamental uncertainty that underlies these improvements in aid management. That is the question of government ownership and the nature of partnership.

Ownership and partnership – who's at the helm?

The importance of national developing country ownership and leadership is frequently asserted as a principle for development cooperation and a condition for progress. One of the lessons that has been learned, at the level of rhetoric

at least, is that aid efforts are unlikely to succeed if recipients have programmes forced upon them, regardless of their own priorities. A government's commitment to a reform programme for instance is a much more important determinant of success than donor pressure imposed through conditionality.

In practice, ownership is too often nominal. Frequently so-called 'government plans' are likely to have been drawn up using (sometimes national) consultants working within largely donor-designed terms of reference. The country strategy agreed by Norway and Tanzania for instance is reported in *The Reality of Aid* this year to have been driven by the political agenda in Norway and more or less conveyed to Tanzania. There is a contradiction in such an approach, between donor insistence on 'developing country leadership' and even stronger insistence that recipient governments shall guarantee human rights, practise multi-party democracy, ensure good governance and adapt to globalisation on the terms of corporate capital.

The nominal nature of ownership is not surprising – lack of capacity makes it very difficult for southern governments to develop their own strategies in every area of development cooperation. Donors and governments need to be more honest about the contradictions and trade-offs.

A donor that focuses too heavily on its own priorities – however laudable in principle – without taking care to frame these within the local context, is not helping to promote ownership and the responsibility of the host government.

Since few donors are taking any steps to stand back and allow developing country governments the room to manage and 'own' their development programmes, ownership may be seen by southern governments as another donor 'hoop' held up for them to jump through.

The danger of ignoring the gap between rhetoric and reality on ownership is that government ownership will be cast as a failed development strategy when, in fact, it has never really been tried.

One way out of this dilemma is that donors can cooperate only with countries that share their own values – and leave them in the driving seat. The other option, as argued from Norway, is to transfer more resources through the United Nations system, where countries from the North and the South participate on a more equal basis and share responsibility for deciding which values to promote through international development cooperation.

In either case, donors need to look at the bigger picture, beyond their nationally defined development priorities to globally agreed commitments. As pointed out in the Netherlands chapter, governments in the South are party to

Trends towards the new millennium

the various UN agreements on development and poverty reduction, reached in the 1990s. Calling recipient countries to account for implementation of these agreements (for example, in the fields of gender equality and investment in basic social services) would be less patronising and more effective than imposing a conditionality of ownership.

As a starting point, donors might focus not on 'ownership' but simply on dialogue and engagement between donors, governments and civil society. Dialogue based upon inclusive, democratic principles should enable poor people, and organisations that genuinely represent poor people's interests, to make their voices heard.

Technical cooperation means ODA still in 'expert hands'

Funding for technical cooperation – the provision of experts to development programmes – is very largely spent in OECD donor countries. It is one indicator of the extent of donor – as opposed to developing country – management of ODA. In 1997, donors spent US$13 billion on technical cooperation. Over the past four years, as total aid has fallen, technical cooperation has increased its share from a fifth to a quarter of all aid disbursements.

Increased attention to sectoral approaches is encouraging

Many donors are giving increased priority to spending through sectoral approaches. These are long-term partnerships between a group of donors and government departments/local authorities, based on a government designed and led strategy for a particular sector. Health, education and roads are the most common. They are designed to increase government capacity to deliver services in the short- and the long-term.

A prerequisite of sectoral approaches is that donors work together, that procedures are streamlined to reduce pressure on government and that there are consistent and donor-wide systems for monitoring, financial accountability and tracking. This is proving difficult for several reasons:

- Government guidelines for international contracting and procurement for instance are notoriously resistant to change; donors need to 'fly their flag' and lose visibility when their efforts are merged with others; therefore, they continue to demand separate reporting that conforms to their own requirements.
- There is a tendency for aid agencies to be inflexible on timing in order to fit in with domestically driven approval and disbursement schedules.

Even apparently minor differences in donor requirements can multiply the burden of compliance when several donors are involved. Harmonised procedures need to be put in place.

More coherent development frameworks?

Several countries report greater coherence in the management of their development cooperation. Portugal is for the first time developing a coherent cooperation programme and an integrated development budget, covering all government departments that have a role in aid. Spain, like Portugal a new donor, is also making substantial efforts to move towards a coherent approach to development cooperation.

Almost the exact opposite is happening in the US, where the NGO InterAction reports that expenditures of traditionally domestic agencies – the Treasury, the Departments of Health and Human Services, Energy, Transportation, Housing, the Environmental Protection Agency and others – increasingly include an international component. A recent US government delegation to Nigeria to decide on a strategy for helping that country had representatives from ten different US agencies. Such fragmentation has long been a characteristic in other aid programmes – notably France and Austria – and in the US it is reported as likely to increase with the globalisation of US domestic policies and concerns.

This said, the need for institutions to keep pace with policy is widely felt. Spain, Belgium and other donors are recognising the need for deep institutional reforms to ensure that policies are made a reality. A widespread trend is the establishment of advisory centres with staff responsible for cross-cutting issues such as poverty reduction and gender equality.

Country strategies being used more

As noted above, aid policies can only be successful if they are put into practice in a way that recognises the capacities and priorities of developing country governments, and addresses the underlying causes of poverty. In this context it is encouraging that an increasing number of donors are making the development of coherent country strategies a priority. However, too few appear to be doing so in the context of a common (government-owned) country strategy. The negotiation of 21 separate and individual strategies with bilateral donors places an enormous and unnecessary burden on governments. If donors are, as they maintain, moving towards greater concentration on a limited number of countries and identifying their own comparative advantages, it cannot be justified.

Trends towards the new millennium

Table 6 Trends in technical cooperation (TC) 1994–97

Year	1994	1995	1996	1997
TC in US$ millions	12,848.3	14,249.5	14,120.9	12,875.8
TC as a share of ODA disbursements	20.9%	23.6%	24.1%	25.6%

Source: OECD, Geographical Distribution of Financial Flows to Aid Recipients, 1992–97, pp67, 69

However, having the strategy is only step one along the path. Norway notes that not enough is done to undertake a structural analysis of the conditions that cause poverty – and that too much emphasis is placed on specific interventions. Also critical is the degree to which civil society is able to participate in the development of country strategies.

Australia notes that AusAID has said little about how it intends to increase civil society participation in project design and implementation. In Canada, the NGO coalition CCIC has proposed a Civil Society Initiative for CIDA to develop an agency-wide strategic framework for strengthening interventions and impacts for civil society organisations in the development process.

Poverty focus not evident in country concentration

As part of the effort to increase aid effectiveness and to focus on countries that are likely to show results, a number of donors are reasserting their intention to concentrate ODA.

The Netherlands notes a major shift to concentration on a reduced number of countries (19) in order to make Dutch aid more effective and take account of limited Dutch executive capacity and budget availability. Spain aims to address what it regards as excessive geographical dispersal by focussing on 25 countries, which will receive the bulk of resources based on a country plan and budget.[9]

In the US, questions have been raised about whether decreases in staff will force the Agency to restrict further, or even abandon its country missions as it increasingly concentrates its organisation in Washington. However the US, like many countries, has simultaneously a concentration programme and a proliferation of smaller programmes in many countries.

Earlier *Reality of Aid* reports have noted the gulf between donor rhetoric on concentration and reality. Looking at recent data, we see *less* not more aid concentration.

In 1986/7, 30% of DAC aid was concentrated on the top 15 countries. In 1996/7, that had fallen to 25%. Only three countries have increased their concentration on the top 15 during the past ten years. *Two thirds of donors have reduced the concentration of their ODA on the top 15 recipients – some sharply.*[10]

In some cases a regional focus – for example, for Australia and New Zealand assisting small island states in the Pacific – can mean that a depth of understanding and expertise develops. This can be defended on the grounds of effective aid but not necessarily on the grounds of poverty eradication, since South Asia and Africa have the greatest concentrations of people living in poverty.

Where it is clear that donors are maintaining aid relationships essentially for diplomatic or trade purposes – at the cost of imposing a greater burden on host countries in terms of aid coordination and reporting – aid reviews should be robust in their comments. Donors, small or large, who want to bolster their geopolitical self-image by having an extensive list of client states should use export promotion or diplomatic budgets – not scarce aid resources. Of course, NGOs need to ensure that their own approaches fit in with the principle of aid concentration.

Aid spending not focused on the poorest countries

ODA to low income and least developed countries (LICs and LLDCs) fell by US$3.6 billion in 1997 – more than 12%.

While it is true that the share of total aid allocated to LICs and LLDCs increased by one percentage point in 1997, the world's poorest countries – with an average income of less than US$2 a day – are getting lamentably low percentages of reduced aid.

In 1997, the most recent year for which data is available, only half (50.7%) of ODA went to LICs and LLDCs.[11] The percentage to LLDCs – countries that are not only poor but especially vulnerable – increased slightly from 24.3% to 26.9%, but fell in volume from US$14.2 billion in 1996 to US$13.5 billion in 1997.

LICs got a smaller share of a smaller cake: falling from 25.3% to 23.8% of net disbursements and dropping by US$3 billion dollars from US$14.9 billion to US$11.9 billion

Allocation of aid to countries where poor people live may be a crude measure, but it is also a pretty fundamental first step on the road to poverty eradication. This decline indicates a complete lack of will to make the poorest people in the poorest countries a priority.

Trends towards the new millennium

Aid to sub-Saharan Africa – a region where per capita incomes have declined by one fifth since 1990 – has been falling steadily since 1994. In 1997 it dropped by US$1.9 billion, although its share increased slightly to 37.2% of total ODA compared with 35.3% in 1996. This was the first upturn in the share of ODA going to SSA since 1994. However, donor responses to the crisis in Kosovo in 1999 reflect what the UN describes as 'a dangerous trend'[12] of aid being diverted from development programmes in Africa to emergency relief in the North. By August 1999, donors had given less than half of the US$796 million the UN needed to assist people affected by conflict and famine in countries such as Angola and Somalia, while appeals for aid for Kosovo quickly realised the US$265 million target. According to the UN, major donors declared that their contributions to Kosovo were additional but Denmark at least was reported as cutting its funding to the UNDP by 23% as a direct result of donations to Kosovo. The UNDP feared that more donors would 'tax Africa to fund Kosovo'.[13]

In acknowledging that many donors are trying to increase their policy focus on poverty, it must also be said that unless some substantial changes occur in aid spending patterns very soon, then donor assertions of priority to poverty will begin to look rather hollow.

The focus on aid effectiveness

A very visible trend in aid during the 1990s has been the strong focus on the issue of aid effectiveness. From *Does Aid Work?* in 1994 to *Assessing Aid* in 1998, a whole series of books and studies have pondered whether aid makes a difference.[14]

Overall these studies have mostly concluded that aid can be effective in achieving specific objectives provided it is operating in conducive macroeconomic and political circumstances. But these studies make it clear that ambitions for aid must be modest – there is a major difference between aid achieving its proximate objectives and eliminating poverty. Aid can be a catalyst but its role is always going to be subsidiary to the major influences on poverty, which include government policy, economic and social stability, global trade and financial conditions as well as the efforts of poor people themselves.

In terms of eliminating poverty, two important points need to be drawn from this focus on aid. The first is that aid cannot be a substitute for other action. Richer countries cannot think that they are taking meaningful action on poverty if they give aid but fail to address some of the structural inequalities that consign one quarter of the world's people to live in absolute poverty. Equally, poor countries

should not focus only on the failure of OECD donors to meet their international commitments, when reform of domestic policy is also an area of unfulfilled obligations.

The second point is that aid must be seen by all governments as a scarce and precious resource – not to be wasted on projects that enhance the prestige or suit the convenience of donor or recipient but have little relevance to the poorest people. Where governments – donor and recipient – know that programmes are not working well even though they meet technical criteria for targeting basic needs, they should not continue to support them for the sake of exerting influence over constituents or clients.

Donors' work on aid effectiveness has had some important benefits. However there is also a potential danger that donors will now focus their efforts on countries where the political and economic environment is conducive to poverty elimination at the expense of people in poverty in countries where governance, human rights and economic and social conditions are still worse.

Recent history and predicted growth implies that many countries will halve their poverty rates by 2015. But many will not – including most of sub-Saharan Africa. An effective anti-poverty approach – as opposed to an effective aid approach – demands that poverty be addressed even in the most difficult situations. Other channels than government-to-government aid must be found and the slow process of supporting agents for change as they try to broaden the political space open to poor people must begin urgently.

Closer integration of aid and other government policy

Another major trend in aid visible in the 1990s – which can be both positive and negative in terms of poverty elimination – is the increasing integration of OECD government approaches to aid, development cooperation, foreign affairs, trade and security policy.

Dwindling aid resources are being asked to do more and more each year.

Japan's response to its own economic problems and the wider Asian financial crisis has included using aid spending to reflate its domestic economy and to assist other countries affected by financial crisis. Aid here can be seen as an instrument of mainstream economic policy.

Even looking beyond the Kosovo crisis, donors are finding the costs of caring for refugees and asylum seekers from their development budgets. The Netherlands has increased planned allocations for asylum seekers and Norway is now covering all the costs of the first-year reception of refugees in Norway within the aid budget contrary to

Trends towards the new millennium

its previous position. It seems that wherever they can, donors use aid money to meet international commitments and summit pledges.

Clearly development NGOs applaud when governments seem to be taking up a range of issues that are closely linked to poverty – environment, gender, human rights. In many cases the gender inequalities or the denial of human rights are root causes of poverty. But this does not mean that every action an OECD government pledges at the Beijing or Cairo Summits, at the Earth Summit in Rio or on human rights or habitat has to be paid for out of the very modest aid resources which are available. In fact, the inclusion of every possible activity under official aid shows the failure of so many donors to meet their commitment to the 0.7% GNP target in an even worse light.

Integration has not improved coherence

A potentially positive aspect of the mainstreaming of development cooperation policy into the wider business of government is the possibility of ensuring that agriculture, trade, economic and other policies at a minimum do not undermine efforts to eliminate poverty.

There are some specific instances of improvements in coherence. In Germany, the government-wide commitment to development has resulted in the Federal Ministry for Development Cooperation (BMZ) now having access to the Federal Security Council, which oversees all military exports. BMZ now articulates human rights and development concerns. To date it has always been overruled – but at least government priorities are more transparent. In New Zealand, the defence select committee has highlighted the need to look at the respective weight given to defence and ODA spending (the implication being that ODA should get a greater share of planned increases).

In the UK, while the development department has been separated from foreign affairs, an explicitly 'ethical' approach to foreign policy and Cabinet status for development has helped to mainstream development and human rights concerns in a way that is likely to improve transparency.

Despite examples of improved coherence, as long as the elimination of poverty remains low on the agendas of OECD governments, development priorities will take second place to other concerns.

Aid is not always *intended* to reduce poverty. A strikingly obvious illustration of how domestic priorities always tend to override any political interest in global poverty, is donor governments' failure to act decisively to reduce aid tying.

Previous *Reality of Aid* reports have explained how the tying of aid illustrates the precedence that domestic producer interests often take over the interests of developing countries. Tied aid is likely to be less effective, because reliance on external goods and services is built in; it adds about 15% in excess pricing to the overall aid bill and it does not build up local capacity.

Denmark's surprising defence of tied aid as important to maintain domestic support for aid rather lets down the country's overall positive record on most aspects of aid. In the case of Japan, the Ministry of Foreign Affairs has in the past eloquently explained why resisting pressure to tie aid was in the long-term interests of both Japan and recipients of Japanese aid. The arguments are just as strong now as when Japan deployed them to reduce tying several years ago – and also quite pertinent in the case of Denmark.

Huge aid decline in the 1990s marks lack of commitment on poverty

This chapter has stressed that aid alone is no answer to poverty. Aid at best can be a catalyst. But it can also be seen as a basic indicator of the commitment of richer countries to ending poverty.

The 1990s have seen a major decline in aid volume. With a few honourable exceptions – especially Denmark, Norway, Sweden and the Netherlands – donor countries have failed to live up to their commitments. And the world's richest and most powerful countries – the G7 – have been at the forefront only as far as reneging on their promises is concerned.

The choice by OECD governments to cut aid and to ignore pledges that they have given at a series of summit meetings to put human development higher up the political agenda effectively symbolises the attitude of so many governments to global poverty.

From 1992 to 1997, DAC members allowed their aid to suffer a disproportionate share of government spending cuts. Aid fell every year over this period, declining from 0.33% of GNP to 0.22%, from roughly a half to roughly a third of the UN 0.7% target. The real terms decline was more than 20%.

In 1998, the decline halted. Aid rose by US$3.2 billion, or 8.9% in real terms, but it remains at 0.23% GNP.[15] It is clear that this positive movement only represents a modest step to reverse the big cuts that have characterised the decade and is to some degree due to recovery packages for Indonesia and Thailand.

The overwhelming focus of OECD governments on the perceived need to reduce budget deficits was at the expense of people living in poverty. If aid had not been cut, more than 25 million fewer people could be living in

Trends towards the new millennium

Table 7 Annual fair shares of bilateral aid for basic social services: only three donors pay their fair share

Donors	Share of total OECD GNP 1997 (%)	Annual bilateral fair share of costs of basic education, basic health including reproductive health and low cost water and sanitation (US$ millions)	Total reported commitments to basic social services 1997	Gap between spending and fair share 1997	Gap between spending and fair share 1996
Sweden	1.01	112.91	153.23	40.32	89.40
Denmark	0.77	86.62	94.33	7.71	79.71
Luxembourg	0.08	8.76	16.44	7.68	−8.07
Norway	0.70	78.37	60.99	-17.38	-3.47
Finland	0.53	59.29	23.36	-35.93	-27.63
Portugal	0.46	52.07	3.27	-48.80	-43.44
Netherlands	1.68	188.19	135.57	-52.62	37.47
Austria	0.95	106.21	22.00	-84.21	-58.58
Belgium	1.13	126.83	41.90	−84.94	−89.83
Australia	1.74	195.41	109.08	-86.33	-70.52
Switzerland	1.22	136.63	43.39	-93.24	-87.68
Spain	2.44	273.77	62.50	-211.27	-203.70
Canada	2.75	308.32	35.53	-272.79	-226.07
Germany	9.59	1,073.96	739.01	-334.95	-255.06
Japan	19.55	2,189.16	1,765.15	-424.01	-103.88
France	6.44	721.82	216.47	-505.35	-367.10
Italy	5.28	590.86	55.31	-535.55	-529.86
United Kingdom	6.02	674.38	115.09	-559.29	-491.96
United States	37.10	4,155.60	679.11	−3,562.49	−3,218.50
Ireland	0.28	30.93	n/a	n/a	−23.80
New Zealand	0.27	29.90	n/a	n/a	n/a

Source: OECD DAC statistics for 1997 spending on basic social services. GNP data from *The DAC Report 1998*, OECD Paris, 1999

Annual Fair Shares of Bilateral Aid for Basic Social Services

At the time of the World Summit for Social Development in 1995, it was estimated that donors were contributing a total of around US$6 billion in ODA for Basic Social Services. On this basis, it was calculated that an additional US$40 billion was needed to ensure universal access to Basic Social Services. One quarter of this was to come from ODA, three quarters from developing country governments. DAC donors should therefore be finding a total of about US$16 billion in aid for Basic Social Services (the $6 billion a year that they were contributing in 1995 and $10 billion annually of the additional money needed).

The Fair share has been calculated as follows.

The fair share of aid to Basic Social Services is in proportion to the donor country's share of total DAC GNP. Data source: DAC Statistics.

If the overall amount needed from donors is $16 billion a year, then the bilateral share should be $11.2 billion – because 70% of ODA is bilateral.

The table above shows bilateral expenditure reported to the DAC in 1997 – the most recent year for which figures are available – for Basic Health, Basic Education, Population and Reproductive Health and total Water and Sanitation taken from OECD DAC Statistics. At the time of writing some donors had not reported their commitments so the data is partial. The data is also, almost certainly, an underestimate since it only captures activities that have BSS as their primary purpose and omits the BSS components of larger, sectoral programmes, multisector aid and, in some cases, aid through NGOs.

It is not possible to show multilateral contributions to BSS because as yet, complete data are not reported. It should also be noted that some fluctuation is inevitable from year to year as these data are commitments to multi year spending, not actual disbursements.

Trends towards the new millennium

absolute poverty.[16] The failure to translate sustained public humanitarian concern (documented in the At a Glance chart on page 269) into political support for aid, betrays a major lack of moral leadership within the OECD.

Inadequate action on debt also underlines lack of priority to poverty

The approach of donor countries to the burden of debt, discussed in previous reports, also illustrates the failure of political leaders to really engage with poverty as an issue and to take into account the human impact of their decisions.

In the case of Zambia, bilateral donor support has fluctuated substantially in line with donor assessments of governance. As the Zambia chapter notes, a fall of over 50% in donor flows from 1991 to 1997 particularly affected balance of payments support and debt relief. But the knock-on impact has been on children. Zambia is one of the most heavily indebted countries – and with a debt of more than $700 hanging over every person in the country – Zambia is spending 10% of its GDP on debt service but only 2% on primary education.

It is interesting to note that the US$10 billion a year which sub-Saharan Africa is spending on debt repayment is less than the annual amount donors would have to find if they were to restore aid to its 1990 level. As Oxfam and UNICEF point out, the annual cost of the reforms to the Heavily Indebted Poor Countries (HIPC) initiative, agreed in June 1999 at the G7 Cologne Summit, is only US$2 or 3 billion a year.[17] Again, the placing of short-term economic orthodoxies such as compliance with Enhanced Structural Adjustment Facility (ESAF) conditions, over long-term human concerns like educating children, only illustrates the inability of world leaders to prioritise poverty elimination.

Few NGOs would disagree with the proposition that debt relief must be clearly linked to investment in social sectors. And few NGOs are starry-eyed about the record of many developing country governments who have also failed to prioritise poverty. But the daily denial of education and health care to children in Africa, to pay debts for which they and their families have no responsibility, to people and countries who are at worst comfortably off, is seen as a fundamental injustice which cannot continue.

In 1994, *The Reality of Aid* quoted from USAID's draft strategy paper: 'The cost of not acting, or having to deal with the global impact of imploding societies and failed states, will be far greater than the cost of effective action'.

Several times since 1994, DAC donors have seen illustrations of the links between economic and political instability and human insecurity. But rich countries only seem moved to act when poverty and instability are very close to home or vital interests. Preparedness to intervene depends not so much on the scale of humanitarian problem as proximity to OECD donors: contrast the action on former Yugoslavia compared for instance to Rwanda.

The focus of European aid on middle-income countries such as Morocco, on the EU doorstep, tells the same story.

The world is not only entering the year 2000 with the majority of its people struggling needlessly on less than US$2 a day. It is also entering the new century prepared to accept that a billion will remain in poverty in 15 or 20 years' time.

If absolute poverty is to be overcome, it is likely that aid will play a modest part but that civil society, the private sector and the state will all need to be harnessed more effectively than they are today. But none of these things is likely to happen without political momentum that makes overcoming poverty not the purview of a middle-ranking government department, but one of the key priorities guiding overall government poverty in donor and developing countries alike.

At the moment, key questions on poverty, such as how to build enhanced human security in a globalised world economy are not being asked – let alone answered. The rhetoric of donors on *Shaping the 21st Century* is looking hollow when put alongside the reality of aid that has declined sharply over the 1990s while poverty has increased. A global human security agenda whose first priority is ensuring that people are able to enjoy economic, social and political stability is surely one around which an effective public and political consensus can be built. But this will happen only when political leaders replace platitudes on poverty and partnership with a willingness to take action.

Notes

1   *Human Development Report* 1999, United Nations Development Programme (UNDP),Oxford University Press, Oxford.
2   Living standards have risen dramatically in the last 25 years. Despite an increase in population from 2.9 billion in 1970 to 4.8 billion in 1996, per capita income growth in developing countries has averaged 1.3% a year. Life expectancy has risen by four months each year since 1970. Infant mortality rates have fallen from 104 per thousand live births to 59 in the same period. (see World Development Indicators 1998, World Bank Publications, Washington DC 1998.)
3   World Bank, www.worldbank.org/poverty/data/trends/2015.htm
4   The *Human Development Report* 1999, UNDP.
5   See p5 of World Development Indicators 1998, World Bank Publications, Washington DC 1998.
6   The fifth anniversary of the World Summit of Social Development 1995 (WSSD) where the Summit committed itself to the eradication of absolute poverty and to the 20:20 Initiative to provide universal access to basic social services – basic health including reproductive health, basic education, clean water and sanitation and nutrition.
7   Walkins, K et al, (1999) *Education Now: Break the Cycle of Poverty*, Oxfam International, Oxford.
8   The 1990 World Bank *World Development Report* (WDR) on Poverty set out a 'three-pronged' strategy of economic growth, investment

Trends towards the new millennium

in human resources and provision of safety nets. This strategy was further developed in the policy paper 'Assistance Strategies to Reduce Poverty' (1991), the Operational Directive 4.15 (1991, updated 1993) and the Poverty Reduction Handbook (1992).

90 Spain is one of the few countries that can point to increased concentration in the past year – rising from 37.6% of ODA going to its top 15 recipients in 1995/6 to 39.2% in 1996/7.

10 DAC Reports 1999 Table 34 and 1998 Table 42

11 Geographical distribution of Financial Flows 1992–1997 p67. Note that US$10,337.4 was unallocated by country in 1997. As a share of bilateral ODA reported in DAC Report 1999, Table 34, 53.8% went to LLDCs and LICs.

12 UN Under-Secretary General for Humanitarian Affairs Sergio Vieira de Mello, press statement August 1999.

13 Mark Malloch Brown, UNDP Administrator, quoted in *Independent on Sunday*, South Africa, 15 August 1999.

14 Cassen Robert, 1994, *Does Aid Work?*, Oxford: Clarendon. Dollar, David, 1998, *Assessing Aid: What Worls, What Doesn't, and Why*, Washington DC, World Bank.

15 Provisional figures issued by the OECD. PAC/COM/NEWS (99) 60, OECD, Paris 10 June 1999.

16 David Dollar makes the point in Assessing Aid that if aid were increased by an annual US$10 billion – which is less than the amount needed to restore aid cuts during the 1990s, an extra 25 million people in poor countries with sound economic management could be raised out of poverty.

17 For an assessment of the plans for HIPC Reform agreed at the G7 Cologne Summit see *Debt Relief and Poverty Reduction: Meeting the Challenge*, UNICEF and Oxfam, 1999.

Trends in basic education

Anne Jellema, ActionAid UK

Box 3 Basic education defined

Basic education was defined for the purposes of the 20:20 Initiative as follows:

- Primary schooling and alternative programmes: curriculum development, teacher education, provision of learning materials, evaluation of learning achievements, improved management at system and institutional levels.
- Early childhood development: child care, stimulation and initial learning through family and community-based programmes and pre-school institutions.
- Basic education for youth and adults: programmes in various sectors of activity that provide training in literacy and numeracy and other essential life skills. Basic education through traditional and modern media and social action to enable individuals and families to acquire knowledge and skills needed for better living.

Introduction

Basic education is a proven weapon in the fight against poverty, opening up access to knowledge and skills and helping to break down barriers that exclude poor and marginalised people from political and economic life. A universal system of public education is both equitable and politically sustainable: it benefits the poor and non-poor equally, and enjoys the support of both. And widespread access to quality education is necessary before the full poverty-reducing impact of other social services, such as improved health care, can be unlocked. But 40% of children in developing countries grow up without completing four years of primary school, the minimum needed to have a chance of acquiring basic literacy and numeracy.[1]

In a series of landmark declarations and summits during the 1990s, donors and governments recognised the crucial importance of increasing access to basic education. However, progress has been agonisingly slow. The target that the international community set itself for achieving universal primary education has already been shifted from 2000 (agreed in Jomtien in 1990) to 2015 (agreed in Copenhagen at mid-decade). And even if the meaning of 'education' is reduced to 'enrolment', the prognosis for 2015 is still uncertain. Oxfam argues that on current trends an estimated 75 million children will still be out of school in the year 2015 – most of them girls, and most of them in Africa.[2]

However, slow progress is not itself an indicator of failure – rather it should be taken as an impetus for rethinking and renewing the 'education for all' movement. There is no magic bullet, financial or otherwise, that donors could fire to reverse the crisis in education. Primary schools in many developing countries have suffered decades of political, financial and administrative neglect;[3] and the weak institutions that result are not only a main cause of failure in education systems, but also a formidable barrier to reform. Teachers and officials alike are badly trained and badly paid, planning is chaotic, political meddling is endemic, and there are seldom any mechanisms – formal or informal – for parents or voters to hold local or provincial authorities accountable for how well they manage schools. Moreover, many southern NGOs argue that the model of education being so badly implemented in these schools is itself bankrupt. Little changed in many respects from colonial days, it is too rigid to accommodate the complex realities of poor people's lives, too elitist, sexist and mono-cultural to empower them to take up active citizenship, too archaic to convey useful knowledge, too much based on learning by rote to unlock real skills of questioning and understanding.

Trends in basic education

In some cases, as the UN Special Rapporteur on the Right to Education recently pointed out, schooling actually violates children's rights, assaulting their dignity and their cultural identity.[4]

Common sense as well as bitter experience dictates that neither the fresh ideas nor the managerial capacity needed to overcome these institutional and imaginative failures can be injected overnight from outside. As this year's Denmark chapter points out, aid is at best 'a strategic intervention in societal development processes, power relations and capacity.' However, donors and governments could do more – much more – to improve the strategic effectiveness of development cooperation as a catalyst for education reform. Increasing the volume and improving the poverty targeting of aid is one part of what is needed to reinvigorate the 'education for all' movement, but even more important are changes in the modalities of development cooperation to better harness the energies and capacities of civil society organisations as actors in the process of change.

Trends: unpacking the crisis in demand

Discussions with parents in poor communities show that they are usually strong believers in the economic value and moral importance of education, and are willing to invest an enormous proportion of their meagre income in schooling. Indeed, 20 years ago the World Bank thought that poor people's demand for primary education was such a sure thing that it could safely ignore lending to this sector.[5] But this has changed.

In many of the world's poorest countries, both coverage and quality of basic education have deteriorated badly in the past quarter-century, and gains made over the 1960s and 1970s have been wiped out. Enrolments fell in sub-Saharan Africa between 1980 and 1995, with 16 African countries experiencing further declines in net enrolment over the first half of the 1990s. Other regions – notably South Asia – made substantial progress in expanding access (see Table 8).

Almost all developing countries, however, face growing gaps in completion and achievement between rich and poor and between men and women. This is manifest in high rates of early dropout among poor rural students and girls.[6] Latin America's universal primary enrolments, for example, are drastically undercut by the fact that four in nine pupils fail the first grade.

In the face of rising costs,[7] deteriorating quality, and restricted access to higher levels of education, parents, students, and even school officials, report scepticism about the relevance and value of the primary schooling actually available to them (Francis 1998, Khadka and Thapa 1998, Maclure 1994, Kelly 1999, Bennell and Segerstrom 1998, Ghana National Education Campaign Coalition 1999). 'In the past people saw education as their great hope and promise for the future. Many no longer do so,' concludes Kelly (1999). Though he is writing of poor communities in Zambia, villagers and slum-dwellers in many other places echo his words. In many countries, both poor and rich are choosing to abandon failing schools: the non-poor by putting their children into a rapidly growing number of private schools, the poorest by withdrawing their children (and particularly girls) from school altogether.[8]

The disintegration of public schools serving poor children, and the growth of private schools serving privileged ones, mean that the educational assets held by the poorest people in the poorest countries are falling further and further behind those of the wealthy and well-connected.

'In India and Pakistan, as well as in Benin and Mali (among other West African countries), the median grade completed among 15 to 19 year olds from the bottom 40 percent of households is *zero*', reports the World Bank, while Indian children from the richest 20% complete on average 10 years of schooling.[9] In Burkina Faso, the richest children are 12 times more likely than the poorest to complete secondary school. Brazil and Peru have much higher school enrolments overall, yet 50% of Brazilian women have not completed primary school, and the illiter-

Table 8 Trends in gross primary enrolment rates

Region	1970	1982	1993	1996
East Asia and Pacific	88	111	118	118
Latin America and Caribbean	99*	105*	109	114
South Asia	67	77	97	101
Middle East and North Africa	68	91	95	94
Sub-Saharan Africa	50	74	68	74 *

Note: * Nearest available year
Source: World Bank economic and social database

Trends in basic education

acy rate among indigenous Peruvians is nearly three times the national average. (This in turn is partly explained by Peru's failure to train enough bilingual teachers, and partly by the fact that effective hours of instruction are nearly twice as high in peri-urban schools, and five times as high in private schools, as in rural schools.) In Ghana, a nation-wide assessment in 1996 revealed that less than 2% of children in state primary schools could pass a basic maths exam, while nearly half of children in private primary schools passed the test.[10]

Perhaps the biggest failure of education policy during the 1990s has been the failure to overcome the growing trend towards two-tier education systems: one for the rich, another – underfunded, mismanaged and ineffective – for the poor. To some extent 'built in' to the models of schooling inherited from colonial days, these inequalities have been exaggerated both by deepening poverty in the wider society, and by specific policy failures which have undermined poor people's access to high-quality and affordable education.[11] When the state school system becomes a ghetto for the underprivileged, offering neither economic opportunity nor self-respect and social inclusion, poor parents reject it – while the non-poor lose any stake in maintaining it.[12] And when educational assets are unequally distributed, the potential of education to contribute to poverty eradication is much reduced.[13] Many NGOs have become increasingly sceptical that simply increasing enrolments is enough to achieve 'education for all' – unless the underlying failures of existing systems are simultaneously addressed. The massive expansion of primary schooling in the 1960s and 1970s accomplished universal primary enrolment, they argue, but not universal primary *education*.

Development cooperation and the challenges of reform

Development cooperation efforts in the education sector over the last few years yield both positive and negative examples to show that progress on the ground will be minimal unless governments have both the political will and the political capital to implement a coherent plan to make education serve poor and marginalised people better. This requires, on the one hand, an enabling macro-economic environment: debt repayment burdens alone can cripple government's ability to plan and sustain a coherent programme of investing in improved education. On the other hand, it also requires a participatory and transparent national process of reform.

As the previous section argues, education systems in developing countries are skewed in many ways towards the privileged and against women, the poor, indigenous peoples, and ethnic minorities. To quote this year's Canada chapter, overcoming educational exclusion is, like any other challenge in pro-poor development, 'ultimately about politics: affecting the power relations and cultural and social interests that sustain the inequitable distribution of society's economic opportunities and social resources'.

The test of development partnerships in education, then, must be whether they succeed in improving domestic priorities and strengthening the government's technical and political – as well as financial – ability to implement them. In the past, the record of external agency policy influence and capacity-building in the education sector has not been good.[14] Donor funds substituted for (or even reduced) government expenditure; donor conditions substituted for domestic political accountability; and expatriate consultants (or subcontracted NGOs) substituted for civil service capacity (see Box 5).

Many donors now accept that the traditional array of free-standing, donor-managed projects – 'islands of excellence in a sea of underprovision'[15] – were part of the problem rather than part of the solution. The 'sector approach', underway in only a handful of countries but heralded by influential donors as the only way forward for aid to education, represents a far more ambitious, co-ordinated and systematic attempt by donors to secure sweeping reforms across the education sector, even as they step away from hands-on implementation and management (see Box 4). 'The extension of policy-based lending into the education sector signifies a more concerted approach by the [World] Bank and the donor community to shape, or at least strongly influence, national educational policy as a whole,' argue Bennell and Furlong (1996).

Achieving this level of influence (as this year's Denmark chapter points out) involves donors in a difficult balancing act – a 'dialogue' as donors call it, using both incentives and conditions to bring about major changes in policy, but ensuring that government develops 'ownership' of the process. The European Union, among other donors, has recognised that success is more likely if the 'dialogue' is expanded beyond the top levels of government, bringing in the regional and local authorities and the civil society constituencies who ultimately have the power to push or to block the implementation of policies.[16] The politics of education reform demands democratic pressure from domestic constituencies outside the system itself, as well as champions within it.

Lack of participation in making education policies has contributed to the unimpressive record of actual implemen-

Trends in basic education

Box 4 Sector-wide approaches in education: the record so far

Though good evaluations of sector-wide programmes in education are in drastically short supply, many donors feel that the implementation and effectiveness of aid in countries has clearly improved in the handful of countries where sector or sub-sector-wide approaches (commonly called SWAPs) have been introduced.[17] They have spurred some donors to make (or at least propose) much-needed improvements in their own practices and systems:

* bringing their budgetary cycles into line with partner governments (as with UN agencies in Ethiopia);
* reducing the pressure on staff to produce visible results quickly (as Norway has recently accepted);
* streamlining and harmonising the reporting requirements they impose;
* increasing the transparency and consistency of their own reporting;
* reducing dependency on expatriate technical assistance;
* increasing the capacity and decision-making power of resident delegations.

Unfortunately, these good practices are still confined to a few donors who have put capacity-building at the top of their development agenda (Denmark, Sweden, and DFID stand out). Establishing common financial procedures and reporting mechanisms is a particularly important step, but one that some donors feel is risky. Risks should be minimised by careful work to improve accounting capacities and financial control mechanisms within ministries so that both donors and domestic stakeholders can be sure that expenditures will be tracked in a timely and transparent way.

More far-reaching changes are implied when donors say that sectoral approaches should enable governments to take the lead in development 'partnerships', that the modalities of external assistance should strengthen rather than undermine government 'capacity' to formulate and implement policy, and that donors and governments should be mutually accountable to one another for progress against coherent, jointly agreed targets. In some countries (Mozambique, Uganda and Nepal are frequently cited examples), sectoral approaches have indeed encouraged and enabled governments to take a more active role in driving donor priorities.

Even in these cases, however, 'policy dialogue' is often limited to a few top officials in the ministries of finance and education – creating difficulties of implementation and sustainability, as the Uganda chapter notes. 'Sectoral approaches are conceptualised by many as an engagement between bilateral donors and [central] governments', admits a recent report for UNICEF.[18] Though some argue that SWAPs are perfectly compatible with a decentralisation of education strategies, in practice they have often been centrally-driven and top-down. Lower levels of government are seldom consulted, and the expertise of the national education community is under-used; compliance with policies among broader constituencies is left to be dealt with at implementation phase.[19] Civil society organisations are sometimes invited in as service providers, or as 'participation entrepreneurs' brokering between officials and families at local level. They are seldom involved in setting priorities, formulating policies, monitoring implementation or evaluating impact.

---

tation. It makes it less likely that either the institutional capacity or the political consensus needed to sustain reform will be achieved, practically guaranteeing that ownership will remain vested in a small number of powerful officials and politicians at the centre.[20] It inhibits the development of strong democratic accountability of governments to citizens, needed to reduce the fungibility of public resources – whether aid or domestic revenue – committed to basic education. It makes it less likely that the educational needs of poor communities and the schools serving them will be effectively met, as donor staff and senior civil servants in the capital city are seldom well-placed to understand these frontline constraints. It impoverishes the search for effective

solutions adapted to local realities: in Ethiopia, for example, the recently designed education sector development programme focuses almost exclusively on the existing formal system, failing to learn any strategic lessons from the success of flexible, community-based alternatives.

Participation is not a panacea. As McClure(1994) argues, 'the dilemmas of a troubled system of primary schooling' are often closely related to the lack of democratic and equitable forms of governance in the wider society. Nevertheless, examples from Brazil and India suggest that building active participation and accountability on social priorities can make a real difference to access and quality. 'The commitment to programme objectives that emerges

Trends in basic education

from the process of consultation and consensus-building provides a powerful motivation for private stakeholders to hold government to its promises and to monitor progress towards achieving greater efficiency in the allocation of public resources,' writes Okidegbe.[21]

Civil society stakeholders should fully participate in defining sector-wide strategies, objectives, performance measures, and expenditures (which will require investment in the policy analysis capacities of local NGOs and other groups, such as teachers' unions).[22] Donor agencies should not bypass or undercut the democratic responsibility of governments to engage with and report to their own civil constituencies, but should support and encourage dialogue between governments and civil society organisations at every level. But such a 'democratisation' of the reform process will demand that donors and governments adopt and encourage a more flexible, creative and participatory approach to education strategies, instead of the techno-cratic reliance on (expatriate) 'expertise' that characterised the 1990s. An interesting example comes from Uganda, where donors (guided by the best education research) had for several years refused to fund school construction – but government surveys showed a strong political demand for new buildings, reflecting in part a shortage of classrooms, in part the wider role of the village school as an expression of the state's active responsibility towards its people. Democratically owned education strategies (and the social expenditure frameworks that shape them) will need to respond to the concerns of civil society and governments that education should promote empowerment, dignity, toler-ance, active citizenship, social cohesion, and national integration – not just individual economic opportunity.

At the same time (as sceptics might caution in the Uganda case), governments will need to be held account-able for husbanding resources towards improving education for the poorest, rather than simply for pursuing political popularity. Here again civil society organisations can work in concert with donors, not only to monitor the implementation and effectiveness of education policies and the trans-parency of education spending, but – as in Uganda – to build a popular consensus behind poverty eradication goals and increase political pressure for accountable and effective delivery of basic services.

Targeting aid better

It goes without saying that well-targeted investment in basic education is essential if donors want to improve poor people's access to learning. A few donors, but too few, have achieved a substantial increase in the proportion of aid that

they allocate to basic education; none meet the 8% target proposed by Oxfam International as the minimum donor contribution needed to achieve the 2015 UPE target. In fact, as a percentage of total commitments, most donors' contri-butions to education have been falling or stagnating since the second half of the 1980s.[23] Overall, basic education still accounts for only slightly more than 1% of total bilateral aid, and 5% of World Bank finance.

Despite significant increases in the share of education aid allocated to basic education, most donors are still doing a worse job of shifting towards poverty-focused spending in this sector than they are in the health sector. While aid to the health sector is heavily concentrated on basic care and on the countries with the worst health indicators, aid to educa-tion presents the reverse picture.[24] Only 12% of the bilateral aid committed to education goes to basic levels,[25] and only a third of all education aid is allocated to countries where less than half of children are in primary school.[26] World Bank lending to education in sub-Saharan Africa actually dropped precipitously in the 1990s, accounting for only 13% of total education finance over the past three years.[27] Further declines are predicted over the next three years due to the declining availability of concessional (IDA) loans for education. Similarly, the European Union (the second largest multilateral donor to education after the World Bank) makes much of its poverty focus, but its aid budgets show a notable shift to upper-middle income countries during the 1990s.[28]

The OECD data show that some donor countries (such as New Zealand, Australia, Austria, and Portugal), who give generously to education, could achieve a higher poverty impact by channelling more of what they spend to primary and basic levels. New Zealand and Australia could also improve poverty outcomes by allocating more of their aid to least developed and low income countries. Other countries, such as the US, have achieved effective targeting of their education spending on basic levels, but have plenty of room to increase the overall priority of education within their aid portfolio, and/or to improve their country targeting. A handful of countries, led by Sweden, Finland, the Netherlands, and Norway are performing well on all three counts.

In summary, donors are currently giving only a quarter of what would be needed, under the terms of the 20:20 Initiative, to reach the 2015 UPE target.[29] The limited ability (or willingness) of governments to 'absorb' more funding for basic education is often cited as a crucial constraint to increasing aid allocations. In response, Oxfam has proposed a 'Global Action Plan' (GAP) which would create an additional pool of money available as an incentive to

Trends in basic education

those governments which prepare convincing plans for achieving the 2015 UPE target – giving special priority to those African countries which are currently furthest off-track for 2015. Endorsed by the World Bank, UNICEF, and UNESCO, the GAP would help to overcome much-advertised problems of 'absorptive capacity' in recipient countries by providing an easy way for donors to assign additional (or unspent) money to basic education, without having to negotiate agreements with individual countries. It would also provide a mechanism for linking additional debt relief to education targets, as proposed by the G7 heads of state in June 1999. The GAP is compatible with the agenda for democratising education systems outlined above; it allows the possibility of an active role for civil society organisations in drawing up education plans and monitoring their implementation. Bilateral donors have so far been reluctant to accept the implied loss of control over (some of) their aid programming, but unless the donor community establishes a coordinated funding mechanism which gives substance to the notion that education is a global priority, the 2015 UPE target risks the same loss of credibility that afflicted the Jomtien Declaration.

Making structural adjustment programmes education-friendly

The financial contribution of aid is dwarfed by the continuing burdens of servicing debt and meeting IMF macro-financial conditionalities.

Many NGOs argue that structural adjustment programmes are often designed and sequenced in ways that undermine access and quality in public education and increase the exclusion of poor and marginalised children from schooling. This needs to change, and bilateral donors need to put more pressure on the IMF to reform its practices.

Education sector budgets typically account for a very large share of total public spending, so they are natural targets when the IMF demands that governments reduce budget deficits and cap public spending. In theory, a sustainable and coherent medium-term framework for overall government expenditure should improve the chances of a sustainable and coherent education strategy, and there are cases where allocations to primary education have increased under SAPs. On average, however, evidence suggests that SAPs have failed to improve – and in some cases have worsened – either the volume or the composition of spending on education. Relatively few governments have responded to budget cuts by reallocating the remain-

ing resources towards basic services: according to the Bank, 'with a few exceptions, most countries have made little effort to shift resources into primary education and basic health care'. The resulting problems of persistent under-funding have, it admits, 'all but crippled public social services in many countries'.[30]

Efforts to make up the shortfall by introducing user fees or other forms of cost recovery have hit poor households hard, particularly in countries already suffering declining per capita income. Girls (who already make up 60% of the 145 million children around the world who never go to school) have been particularly disadvantaged, since even a small increase in fees may raise the 'opportunity cost' of girls' education beyond what parents are willing to pay. At the same time, the plummeting real value of teachers' salaries has eroded commitment and morale, encouraged covert forms of privatisation and even bribery (such as demanding extra payments for supplementary exam coaching), and helped to create a growing 'informal sector' of untrained, underpaid teachers. Negative effects such as these need to be anticipated and avoided through strategies which are tailored to local constraints, and which include explicit protection for education budgets among the 'triggers' (binding conditions) for release of loans.

IMF ceilings on government borrowing often force the ad-hoc diversion of social expenditure, including funds committed to education, to debt servicing. These deficit management policies, Alexander suggests, should be redesigned to achieve a better balance between the need for fiscal discipline and the need for public investment. Alternatives should be piloted in several countries, she adds, to determine impact on education and health spending.

Finally, a recent evaluation of IMF programmes highlighted the role that top-down policy prescriptions have played in undermining government capacity to implement reforms. In developing strategic options and assessing their social impact, the IMF and World Bank should work with teams of government officials drawn from an array of ministries – not just the finance ministry – together with representatives of civil society organisations. For consultation to be effective, both institutions need to disclose more information to domestic constituencies at all stages of the negotiation and design of assistance packages. In addition, they should work with civil society organisations and the UN agencies to monitor carefully the impact of SAPs on education and other social indicators, with particular attention paid to poor and vulnerable groups.

Trends in basic education

Avoiding policies that increase inequity

Some commentators express concern that sectoral co-ordination of donor support to education may consolidate rather than counteract what they see as a strong trend towards neo-liberal 'demand-side' solutions inappropriately exported from the US and Northern Europe (see Box 5). A review of more than 100 education sector studies initiated by donors to African countries from 1985 through the early 1990s showed a remarkable similarity of recommendations, focused on reducing the central government role in providing education and increasing efficiency and choice at school level. A set of preferred donor options can be seen in a growing number of policy frameworks supposedly designed and owned by national governments:[31]

* Shift public resources to lower secondary and primary levels, where human capital theory says that returns will be greatest, by increasing fees at higher levels;
* Concentrate on the existing formal system as the main vehicle for delivering basic education; but
* Decentralise the management of schools and share both costs and decision-making with parents;
* Use market incentives to increase demand among excluded groups, such as bursaries for girls;
* Expand the role of private education providers, whether profit-making private schools or not-for-profit NGO projects;
* Improve efficiency through multi-grade classrooms, investment in instructional materials, double-shifting; recover costs, squeeze salary budgets and other recurrent expenditure.

These universal prescriptions rest heavily on an economic analysis of education which the World Bank and other donors sometimes credit with far more scientific power than it actually possesses. Far-reaching conclusions have been drawn on the basis of a small and often unrepresentative selection of country studies, and policy options that have proven unwieldy and expensive to administer in the developed North have been cut-and-pasted into the drastically different realities of diverse Southern countries.

The jury is still out on the actual impact of many of these supposedly efficiency-promoting measures. But it is clear that in some cases they have spurred the growth of educational inequalities between rich and poor, centre and periphery, men and women. In these cases, their long-term effects on access and quality are also likely to be negative and their contribution to efficiency is suspect (particularly if efficiency is defined in terms of poverty impact). Cost-sharing through levies on parents, for example, not only tends to exclude poor children and girls, as argued above, but is also costly to administer, prone to corruption, and can further undermine government responsibility for guaranteeing quality education for all. In most cases, argues a recent study commissioned by DFID, the use of cost-sharing as a public financing mechanism has not only contributed to 'stagnation in enrolment ratios and failure to improve the quality of educational provision', but 'has enabled governments to avoid difficult reforms'.[32]

Decentralisation and school choice are other policies which have had a debatable impact on poor people's educational chances. In many cases, they have been designed with scant attention to institutional and political realities on the ground. DFID's recent education policy paper lists 13 broad conditions which must be met for decentralised school systems to be effective, accountable and equitable. Some of these, such as strong, democratic and highly-skilled local government structures and the 'willingness ... to countenance a shift in power between communities and education professionals', are wishes for the future rather than descriptions of reality. Even when cost-sharing, school choice and decentralised management are working as intended, they will still tend to widen the gaps between relatively prosperous, well-informed and well-connected communities or parents and those who lack the skills and resources to work the system effectively. This demands that central and/or provincial levels of government are able to play an equalising, cross-subsidising role to ensure that minimum standards are met. But making such measures work is complex and expensive even in countries with strong institutions and a skilled civil service.

Sustaining progress

The International Development Targets focused on increasing primary enrolments provide extremely useful quantitative benchmarks for monitoring donor performance, and (together with the 20:20 Initiative) have helped to focus public scrutiny on the need for both donors and governments to make more and better allocation of resources to basic education and other basic social services. Novib, for example, has argued that the Dutch government has a responsibility to hold partner governments specifically accountable for progress towards the IDTs. But the targets are not ends in themselves.

The point of targets is to simplify, but this in turn may encourage a simplified, top-down approach to setting priorities and implementing policies, undermining local ownership and sustainability. The drive to reach these targets may

Trends in basic education

Box 5 Making better use of technical assistance

In a review of more than 100 studies produced by consultants on behalf of donors, Samoff found that a national researcher had led none of them. Moreover, 'few ... seemed to have been the product of a sustained dialogue between the external agency and the education community ... both official and unofficial, within the country studied' (Samoff 1997: 19–21).

Such practices are a major barrier to capacity development, ownership, and sustainable reform. There is an urgent need to reconceive technical assistance – which accounts for a large part of the 60–80% of all aid to education which is spent in donor countries[33] – so that skills in research, policy design and programme evaluation are built up at national level, and so that consultancy work better serves the practical needs of governments. More active efforts to use local experts, reducing the disparity in pay rates between foreign and national consultants, and more transparency over recruitment and contracts would be positive steps for many donors and governments.

However, hiring national rather than expatriate consultants to carry out the same work is not enough. Given that good information, creative ideas, and policy expertise are crucial to the successful reform and effective functioning of education systems, knowledge production itself needs to be reconceived as a major development output, not just an enabling mechanism. This means that the use of technical assistance should be subject to the same careful planning and rigorous evaluation as other parts of sector development programmes. Given their overriding concern for poverty eradication, donors need to look more imaginatively at the role of knowledge production in building capacity and consensus for pro-poor reforms. How can the educational needs and interests of poor people, women and excluded groups best be understood and promoted within government ministries and among other stakeholders. Through research reports? Through participatory assessments? Through conferences and the media? How can the design and monitoring of policies intended to benefit poor people best be improved? What kind of training do officials and others need to implement such policies effectively? How can dialogue and transparency between the government and civil society be strengthened?

---

tempt governments and donors to embark on school expansion programmes which make the country look good in international statistics, and make the ruling party look good to voters, but do little to ensure that children will continue to come to school, stay in school, or learn what they need to know when they are there. Initiatives such as this bring questionable benefit to the poor. Increasing enrolments at the expense of quality, for example, may lead to high dropout rates, which actually penalise the poor (who drop out earlier and in greater numbers).[34] Likewise, simply getting more girls into classrooms is no magic bullet for gender equity: much depends on whether they gain confidence, status, and useful knowledge from being there.

Communities in Soroti, Uganda, saw the recent introduction of free primary education as something dictated from on high: 'The government spoke as in the book of Genesis: "Let there be light, and there was light"; but there were no teachers or books or furniture for so many children.' The resulting deterioration in quality has had the unintended consequence of fuelling the growth of a fee-paying private sector – while many of the poorest children, and girls, are still excluded from public schools because other costs are still prohibitive.[35] To reduce poverty and overcome gender

inequity through basic education, 'quality and sustainability of provision are as important as quantitative achievement.'

The pursuit of IDTs should open up, rather than crowd out, the space for national governments and civil society constituencies to define and renew their own vision of the role and purpose of education. Poor people themselves point out that schooling is little use unless it enables them to live as integrated, dignified and fulfilled members of their society. Even while using the IDTs to keep broad spending on track, donors also need to work with governments and NGOs to find creative, practical ways of implementing a locally-owned vision of education. In many countries, this will mean finding equitable ways of increasing access to, and quality of, secondary and tertiary education as well as primary education. In some countries, it will mean ensuring that education validates and respects indigenous cultures and languages, even if this increases 'unit costs'. In others, it will demand paying attention to needs for citizenship education, leadership training, and other forms of adult learning, and drawing on the best of NGO programmes as a basis for 'deformalising' an overly rigid and academic formal system.

Trends in basic education

Conclusion

Children whose schooling consists at best of doomed attempts to memorise the contents of a few tattered textbooks, quite probably in a language not their own and in a setting that constantly reinforces passivity, subordination and 'backwardness', are not only condemned to grow up illiterate. They are also denied the incomparably powerful experience of *learning*, of developing skills and confidence to engage more fully and more effectively in the life of a community, a culture and a nation. That this is the reality for the vast majority of children growing up today in the 'global South' is a cause for public outrage not merely because it is unjust, but because there exist enough counterexamples to show that education *can* be empowering and emancipating.

Changing the educational chances of these children demands more resources and better coordinated and more equitable use of those resources, including external assistance (aid and IMF/World Bank loans) as well as domestic revenue. It also demands political change to support institutional reform and technical innovation. The governments whose education systems are most in need of fundamental change have weak institutions, a fragile political base, and little will or power to override entrenched élites in pursuit of more equitable social policies.[36] Donors wish to use their funding and expertise to leverage improvements in policy, but are wary of further eroding the State's financial and political responsibility for basic education. The active and informed participation of civil society in setting priorities, monitoring impact and ensuring accountability could go a long way towards overcoming these dilemmas.

Notes

1   UNICEF and World Bank, 1998. Universal access to basic social services: a key ingredient for human development, paper prepared for the Hanoi Meeting on the 20:20 Initiative, Hanoi, Vietnam 27–29 October 1998.
2   Other commentators are more optimistic. In research undertaken for the OECD's Development Assistance Committee, Hanmer argues that the 2015 targets for enrolment are likely to be met 'by default' as a byproduct of predicted economic growth. She adds, however, that learning outcomes are likely to remain extremely poor without concerted intervention. Lucia Hamner, 'The feasibility of the 21st century development targets for education'; speech delivered to the ActionAid-Oxfam conference on 'Facing the Global Education Crisis', London, 8 September 1999.
3   Between 1980 and 1987, real per capita spending on education plummeted, falling by about 40% in Latin America and the Caribbean, and 65% in sub-Saharan Africa. Colclough, C with Lewin, K M *Educating All the Children: Strategies for primary schooling in the South* (Oxford, 1993), p20.
4   Katarina Tomasevski, 'Facing the Global Education Crisis', speech delivered to the ActionAid-Oxfam conference of the same title, London, 8 September 1999.
5   Jones 1997.
6   World Bank, 'Investing in Education', *Poverty Lines* no 2, April 1996.

7   For evidence of rising costs to parents as governments shift the burden of education finance to 'communities', see Mehrotra, S and Vandemoortele, J, Cost and Financing of Primary Education: Options for reform in sub-Saharan Africa, UNICEF Staff Working Papers, EVL-97–006, 1997; Bray, M., *Counting the Full Cost: Parental and Community Financing of Education in East Asia* (World Bank and UNICEF, 1996); Mehrotra, S. and Delamonica, E., 'Household costs and public expenditure on primary education in five low-income countries: A comparative analysis', *International Journal of Educational Development* 18(1) 1998: 41–61.
8   In some countries, the picture is reversed, with high unofficial and official fees driving the poorest into makeshift 'community' schools or fly-by-night private academies, which charge less than government schools. In other countries, overwhelming reliance on 'voluntary' contributions from parents has created massive inequities between poor and rich communities within a nominally public system. In all cases the net effect is to destroy any possibility of a unitary education system within which all have the right to an education that meets minimum quality standards.
9   Filmer, D and Pritchett, L 1999. The effect of household wealth on educational attainment: Evidence from 35 countries. *Population and Development Review* (March 1999).
10 Alexander 1998: 20.
11 NGOs need to critically examine their own role in this process. In many cases they have been unwitting partners in the creation of a fragmented system of multiple providers, which (whatever the benefits in terms of diversity and innovation) has ultimately weakened political commitment to universal coverage and minimum quality standards and has undermined the State's responsibilities as guarantor and chief financier. UNICEF and World Bank, Universal access to basic social services, p14.
12 UNICEF and World Bank, Universal access, p14.
13 Dollar, D, Glewwe, P and Litvack, J, eds., *Household welfare and Vietnam's transition to a market economy*; World Bank (1998).
14 In a recent survey of bilateral aid, Cox and Healey found little evidence that donor influence was promoting re-orientation of domestic public spending towards basic social services. According to an internal World Bank review, only a third of education loans completed between 1993 and 1998 achieved 'substantial institutional development'. Cox, A and Healey, J *Promises to the Poor* (ODI, 1998), p1. World Bank, *Education Sector Strategy* (Washington, May 1998), p6.
15 Department for International Development, 'Learning opportunities for all: A policy framework for education' (London, 1999), p38.
16 EU Education Experts Group, report of meeting, October 1996.
17 For a useful overview, see Development Initiatives/UNICEF, 'Challenges to Promoting Basic Education through Sectoral Approaches in Education' (draft, April 1999).
18 Development Initiatives/UNICEF, op cit, note 17; see also UNICEF, 'An information note on SIPs and SWAps', December 1997.
19 Lene Buchert in ADEA Newsletter, vol 10 no 2.
20 Lene Buchert, op cit, note 19.
21 Okidegbe, N (1997), Fostering sustainable development - the sector investment program. World Bank Discussion Paper #363. World Bank, Washington
22 Harrold, P et al (1995), The broad sector approach to investment lending: sector investment programs. World Bank Discussion Paper #302. World Bank, Washington.
23 P Bennell and D Furlong, 'Has Jomtien Made any Difference? Trends in donor funding for education and basic education since the late 1980s', IDS Working Paper no 51 (Sussex University, 1996), p5.
24 See DAC 1998: 69–70. It can be argued that education presents more complex problems of poverty targeting than health, where there are widely accepted, inexpensive and simple measures for reaching the poor. Even so, current aid to education looks embarrassingly off-target for poverty impact.
25 Some under-reporting occurs because education activities can be integrated into non-education projects and programmes. Research

Trends in basic education

on aid spending in 1994/95 suggested that these activities were taken into account, the share of basic education rose to about 19% of bilateral education spending. Bennell and Furlong, op cit, note 23, 55. This is still far less than the share of health sector aid that goes to basic care.

26 'Due to incomplete donor reporting, the geographical distribution of aid to basic education is not known' (DAC 1998: 72). World Bank reports show large regional variations in targeting. In South Asia, basic education programmes comprised about 80% of World Bank education lending in the period 1991–96; in sub-Saharan Africa the ratio was 'barely one-half' (Bennell and Furlong, op cit, note 23, p13).

27 World Bank Annual Review 1998.

28 Caddell, M and King, K 1999. European Commission Aid to Education: Ten Points for Consideration and Action. ActionAid report (draft, 28 June 1999).

29 DAC 1998, Table IV–I, p68.

30 World Bank, Social Dimensions of Adjustment, p. 22. See also IMF 1999.

31 Reviewing World Bank loans approved in 1990 with loans approved in 1980s, Jones found that all projects approved in 1990 involved increased privatisation and cost-sharing, as compared to only 1/3 of loans in 1980; and projects to expand secondary and tertiary education declined from 1 in 2 to 1 in 10. Jones, P W, World Bank Financing of Education: lending, learning and development (London and New York, 1992).

32 Penrose, P, Cost sharing in education: Public finance, school and household perspectives. DFID Research Papers, serial no 27 (London, 1997).

33 Bennell and Furlong, op cit, note 23, p50. The World Bank found that technical assistance absorbed more than 5% of the budget in 14 of the 19 sector-wide programmes for which information was available; in three cases, the figure was more than 20%. World Bank, Sector Investment Programmes: an update, Knowledge Information and Technology Center, Africa Region, 1997.

34 In response to these shortcomings in donor finance, Oxfam has proposed a 'Global Action Plan' which would create an additional pool of money available as an incentive to those governments which prepare convincing plans for achieving the 2015 UPE target – giving special priority to those African countries which are currently furthest off-track for 2015. Endorsed by the World Bank, UNICEF, and UNESCO, the GAP would help to overcome much-advertised problems of 'absorptive capacity' in recipient countries by providing an easy way for donors to assign additional (or unspent) money to basic education, without having to negotiate agreements with individual countries. It would also provide a mechanism for linking additional debt relief to education targets, as proposed by the G7

Heads of State in June. The GAP is compatible with the agenda for democratising education systems outlined above; it allows the possibility of an active role for civil society organisations in drawing up education plans and monitoring their implementation. Bilateral donors have so far been reluctant to accept the implied loss of control over (some of) their aid programming, but unless the donor community establishes a coordinated funding mechanism which gives substance to the notion that education is a global priority, the 2015 UPE target risks the same loss of credibility that afflicted the Jomtien Declaration.

35 Christian Aid, Distant Targets? Making the 21st century development targets work (London, 1998).

36 DAC 1998: 4, op cit, note 24.

References

Alexander, N 1998. 'Paying for education: the influence of the World Bank and IMF on education in developing countries'. Draft report for Oxfam USA.

Bennell, P and Furlong, D 1996. 'Has Jomtien Made any Difference? Trends in donor funding for education and basic education since the late 1980s'. IDS Working Paper no 51. University of Sussex, p5.

Bennell, P and Segerstrom, J 1998. 'Vocational education and training in developing countries: Has the World Bank got it right?' Int J Educational Dev 18(4): 271–287.

Francis, P et al 1998. 'Hard lessons: Primary schools, community and social capital in Nigeria'. World Bank Technical Paper no 420.

Ghana National Education Campaign Coalition 1999. 'The state of Primary Education in Ghana: A literature review'. Draft report, November.

IMF 1999. Review of social issues and policies in IMF-supported programmes. Fiscal Affairs and Policy Development and Review Departments, August 27.

Jones, P 1997. 'On World Bank education financing'. Comparative Education 33(1): 117–219.

Kelly, M J 1998. 'Primary education in a Heavily-Indebted Poor Country: The case of Zambia in the 1990s'. A report for Oxfam and UNICEF.

Khadka, R and Thapa, H 1998. 'Primary education in a shambles: Investigative report on the status of basic, primary and non-formal education in Nepal'. Report for ActionAid Nepal.

Maclure, R 1994. 'Misplaced assumptions of decentralisation and participation in rural communities: Primary school reform in Burkina Faso'. Comparative Education 30(3):239–254.

Samoff, J 1997. 'Cooperation, but limited control and little ownership'. Paper presented at the 1997 Biennial of ADEA. Dakar, Senegal, 15–18 October.

Part II
A Review of
Aid Donors

Australia

Garth Luke, ACFOA

Policy shifts focus to poverty reduction but still no increase in aid volume

Australia's generosity as a country has continued to wane and its ODA/GNP ratio has now fallen to its lowest level ever. Later in this chapter we look in some detail at this key failure of the Australian Government.

On a more positive note, the new anti-poverty focus of Australia's aid policy, which emphasises five priority sectors – education, health, governance, rural development and infrastructure – has brought about several improvements. This policy was developed by the conservative coalition Government, after a review committee it had appointed (the Simons Review) had criticised the long-standing three-fold – strategic, commercial and humanitarian – objectives of Australia's aid programme.

The new approach was generally welcomed by Australian development NGOs, despite some concerns that the government aid agency, AusAID, would focus too strongly on general economic growth as the main mechanism to achieve poverty reduction.

The improvements in Australia's aid programme as a result of the new policy are:

- *Increased funding to the five priority areas and to the subset of basic social services*. There is a 9% real increase in funding to the priority areas between 1998/9 and 1999/2000; basic social services have increased slightly from 13% to 14% of total aid in this period and have grown by 22% in real terms since 1995/96. This indicates that AusAID is putting less emphasis on general economic growth strategies.
- *Better measurement and reporting on the sectoral allocation of funds* – AusAID now reports in the budget papers on the five priority sectors and is providing detailed figures on total expenditure for basic social services.

- *Greater openness by AusAID* – in providing information on its programmes and on consultation with the Australian public and key civil society players.
- *Increased funding for public information and education on aid* – funds will increase from A$1.3m in 1998/9 to A$1.8m in 1999/2000; AusAID is also working more closely with NGOs on gauging public opinion and promoting aid.
- *The development of three-year country strategy papers* for all major recipients of Australian bilateral aid. The new strategies have a stronger emphasis on poverty reduction and on the five priority sectors, and also focus more on poorer areas and groups within countries.
- *A greater emphasis on sectoral approaches, aid coordination and capacity building*, which has the potential to provide more sustained improvements and more efficient use of funds.
- *An attempt to more thoroughly measure the effect of aid interventions and learn from this experience* – using results-based budgeting and more thorough evaluation and monitoring processes.
- *Greater funding and emphasis on human rights and civil society issues* – 34% of governance funding and 4.4% of sector identified funding is going to human rights projects.
- *Increased gender awareness* – gender and development training is provided for all new staff and there is an increase in expenditure on projects with a direct gender component from A$34.5m in 1998/9 to A$43.3m in 1999/2000.
- *A broadening of the range of commercial groups gaining contracts with AusAID and an increased weight put on quality in tender decisions.*
- *Efforts have been made to provide a cohesive and OECD-leading foreign policy response to the situations in Indonesia/East Timor and to the East Asian financial crisis* – extra aid funds have been pledged for East

Australia

Percentage of national income spent on aid: a 30-year picture

How much aid does Australia give?

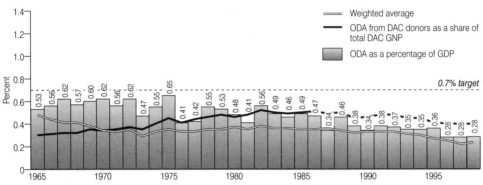

Legend:
- Weighted average
- ODA from DAC donors as a share of total DAC GNP
- ODA as a percentage of GDP

0.7% target

Where is Australian aid spent?

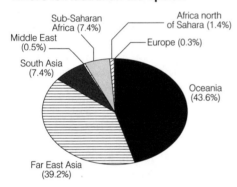

- Sub-Saharan Africa (7.4%)
- Africa north of Sahara (1.4%)
- Middle East (0.5%)
- Europe (0.3%)
- South Asia (7.4%)
- Oceania (43.6%)
- Far East Asia (39.2%)

How much Australian aid is spent through multilateral organisations?

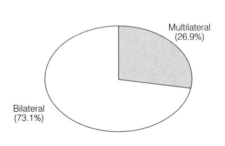

- Multilateral (26.9%)
- Bilateral (73.1%)

What is Australian aid spent on?

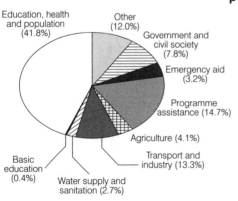

- Education, health and population (41.8%)
- Other (12.0%)
- Government and civil society (7.8%)
- Emergency aid (3.2%)
- Programme assistance (14.7%)
- Agriculture (4.1%)
- Transport and industry (13.3%)
- Water supply and sanitation (2.7%)
- Basic education (0.4%)

For notes on data and sources see page 286

How much Australian aid goes to the poorest countries?

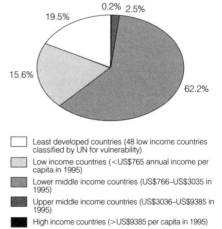

0.2% 2.5%
19.5%
15.6%
62.2%

- Least developed countries (48 low income countries classified by UN for vulnerability)
- Low income countries (<US$765 annual income per capita in 1995)
- Lower middle income countries (US$766–US$3035 in 1995)
- Upper middle income countries (US$3036–US$9385 in 1995)
- High income countries (>US$9385 per capita in 1995)

Box 6 Australian aid at a glance

How much aid does Australia give?

Australia gave	US$998m (A$1,589m) in 1998
that was	0.28% of GNP
and	0.84% of total government expenditure
which meant	US$54 or A$86 per capita for 1998

Is it going up or down?

In 1998 Australian aid	fell by US$63m in cash terms. Because of inflation and exchange rate changes, the value of aid rose by 10.4% in real terms over 1997
Australia was	equally generous in 1998, remaining at 0.28% of GNP
The outlook is	that there is little likelihood of an increase over the next three years.

How does Australia compare with the other 20 donors?

Australia ranks	13 out of 21 for its volume of aid
It is	13 out of 21 in the generosity league
It gives	35.1% of its aid to low income countries, the lowest in the DAC
Private flows	amounted to US$151m, 14% of ODA*
Total flows	to developing countries were 0.35% of GNP and rank 18 out of 21 in the DAC

What proportion of bilateral aid goes to basic education and basic health?

Australia committed	5.6% of bilateral ODA to basic education, 4.7% to basic health and 0.8% to population and reproductive health

How important are commercial interests in aid?

Australia reported that	21.9% of its bilateral aid commitments were tied to the purchase of goods and services from Australia

* Only NGO flows are noted here, as Australia has not reported its private flows at market terms since 1995

Timor and Australia has played a major role in negotiations with Indonesia and the UN; in response to the East Asian financial crisis, Australia has provided extra aid funds as well as taking the lead in providing IMF credits. The Government has also played an active policy role in reforms to the international financial system and in assisting East Asian economies to regain stability.

This is a time of considerable change for Australia's aid programme and the staff of AusAID and the Minister should be congratulated for the many improvements that they have made to the programme.

Holistic approach to poverty reduction still some way off

However there are a number of areas that still require change. The needs include:

Further improvements in consultation and feedback

While AusAID's information provision and consultation with Australian civil society has improved considerably, it could be argued that it has still not reached the levels of 'openness to innovation and contestibility of ideas' identified in its corporate goals.[1]

There is currently very good consultation with Australian NGOs on NGO funding issues but the depth of

Australia

discussion on broader aid issues is patchy and appears to be dependent on the attitudes of individual AusAID officers. For example, in the development of a number of the new country strategy papers involvement of NGOs was hampered, as very little time was allowed to provide feedback. We still appear to be a long way from the levels of consultation that exist in some other country agencies, such as CIDA in Canada where regular joint NGO and CIDA sectoral forums are organised.

Reduced turnover of staff

Levels of staff turnover appear to be very high, due to both people leaving the organisation and very high levels of movement within AusAID. This is a problem experienced by a number of Australian Government departments. While better documentation and structures can improve organisational memory and skill levels, very rapid staff turnover impairs communication and external participation, and reduces team effectiveness and knowledge.

Greater cohesiveness in policies and a more active approach with multilateral institutions

There is considerable room for improvement in Australia's policy coherence and a more holistic approach to poverty reduction is needed. For example, there appears to be little consideration of the effects of Asia Pacific Economic Cooperation Forum (APEC) policies and other trade and economic reforms on poor communities in the region. There is little coordinated strategy between Treasury, AusAID and the Department of Foreign Affairs on debt issues and how Australia could play a more active role in resolving these problems. As a major contributor to the Asian Development Bank, Australia is also in a strong position to improve the public accountability and poverty focus of the ADB. Perhaps the interdepartmental communication approaches used in both the UK and Canada could be useful models for Australia.

Projected AusAID spending on basic social services using current rates of growth

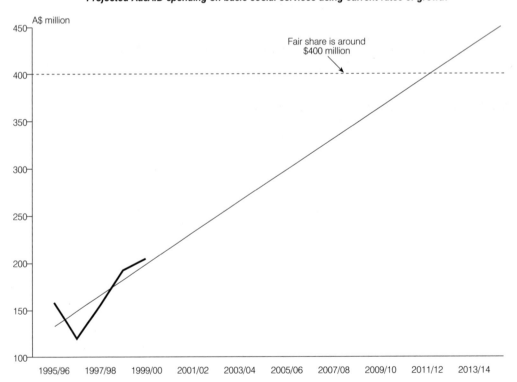

Note: the figures used in this graph are total BSS spending extrapolated from sector allocated counts provided by AusAID
Source: AusAID budget papers

Greater emphasis on civil society support and involvement in developing countries

This is of course one of the most difficult tasks but also one of the most important. To date AusAID has said little about how it intends to increase civil society participation in project design and implementation.

Greater levels of financial support to NGOs

Despite a recognition of the skills that NGOs offer in terms of community-based programmes, government funding for NGOs has dropped by 13% in real terms since the present Government came to office in 1996.

Increased funding to basic social services

While there has been enhanced funding to these areas, the rate of growth needs to increase if we are to contribute our share towards the DAC 21st century goals. ACFOA has argued that Australia's fair share of basic social service funding is approximately A$400m per year.[2] At the present rate of growth in BSS funding, about 5% per annum over the last four years, Australia will not reach this level until around 2012 – far too late to ensure the 2015 goals are met.

A fairer geographic distribution of funds

Australia continues to target the bulk of its aid funds to East Asia and the Pacific, despite the fact that about 60% of the world's poorest people live in South Asia and Africa. Australia does have a special relationship with the Asia-Pacific and this needs to be recognised. However, there is a fundamental contradiction between Australia's new 'needs-based' aid policy and the continued focus on this region. In light of this, Australian NGOs have suggested to the Government a funding model[3] that would achieve a more humane balance, by maintaining real support to the Asia-Pacific and allocating growth funds over the next several years to South Asia and Africa.

Increased quality standards for AusAID commercial contractors

In the last few years more stringent accreditation standards have been set for NGOs seeking AusAID funding. A strengthening of the standards required for commercial contractors is likely to improve further the quality and accountability of Australia's aid programme.

Further improvements in gender emphasis

It is important that the significant improvements in this area as a result of the greater focus on gender issues and staff training are supported by an adequate number of gender advisory positions.

A stronger focus on poverty reduction in project planning, implementation and evaluation

Even though poverty reduction is a central goal of Australia's aid programme there has been limited debate and clarification about what a poverty reduction focus implies.

There has been a greater emphasis on poorer groups and regions, and on sectoral areas which impact most on poor people, but it would be an exaggeration to say that AusAID has a comprehensive and thoroughly executed approach to poverty reduction. In particular, issues surrounding power and poverty need more attention and poverty needs to be seen as much more than a simple lack of financial resources or services. AusAID could benefit from the Scandinavian aid agencies and their more thorough work in this area.

There is a growing emphasis in AusAID on the need to consider explicitly a project's effects on the poor and on disadvantaged groups, such as women and indigenous people. However, these effects are not evaluated unless that is a specific objective of the project.

In the coming year, AusAID plans to carry out an evaluation of the effectiveness of the aid programme in alleviating poverty. It is to be hoped that this study will help to increase the poverty reduction focus of the programme.

Not imposing a narrow economic model on countries in the Pacific

While improvements in economic governance are necessary for a number of Pacific economies it is important that the strategies applied are owned by local people, are appropriate to each culture and economy and seek to ameliorate negative transitional effects. There is concern among some NGOs that AusAID has paid insufficient attention to these issues.

Canberra faces the ultimate test of concern

Within this generally improved approach, the most significant unresolved issue is that of overall aid volume. This is a problem that cannot be solved by AusAID but is squarely the responsibility of Australia's federal politicians.

In 1999/2000 Australia's aid to GNP ratio will be 0.25% – the lowest level ever. The Australian Government likes to say that our aid to GNP ratio is higher than the weighted

Australia

Box 7 Basic education benefits from priority status

Basic education is one of the areas of greatest recent growth for AusAID. Since 1995–96 funding has risen from about A$20m per annum to about A$50m in 1999/2000. This is 4.5% of sector identified funds and may increase as funds are allocated this year.

In 1996, AusAID introduced a new education policy which gives a greater focus to basic and vocational education, and which emphasises greater equity in access to education and capacity building for basic education. This was reinforced in 1997 when the Government identified education as one of the five priority sectors for aid.

The impressive rate of increase in funding has been possible because of the movement from general budget support to project and programme funding for Papua New Guinea,[4] the low base levels of basic education funding and the historically high levels of funding for tertiary scholarships in Australia. Part of the growth has been achieved by a move away from tertiary funding.

AusAID is actively implementing the new policy through its education policy group and through the development of country strategies which highlight education as one of the agency's new priority sectors.

The DAC 21st century goals, which Australia supports, include two goals related directly to education:

- the achievement of universal primary education in all countries by 2015; and
- the elimination of gender disparity in primary and secondary education by 2005.

Recent work by Oxfam and UNICEF has made clear that these goals will not be reached without significant increases in basic education funding. To this end, Oxfam has calculated that donors need to allocate an additional US$4 billion per annum to basic education.[5] Australia's fair share of this cost would be about A$125m per year, or 2.5 times AusAID's present expenditure on basic education. Discussions with AusAID staff indicate that this sort of level will be achieved; however the timetable is not clear. AusAID may need to increase substantially the number of basic education advisers to ensure that quality is improved along with volume.

The vast bulk of Australian basic education funding in 1998/9 went to primary school projects, with very little to pre-schools and non-formal education.

AusAID is involved in sectoral approaches in countries where it is a relatively significant donor, such as PNG and the Pacific. For example, AusAID has assisted the PNG Government in a major review and redevelopment of its primary education system, which has been characterised by poor access and low retention rates. This has resulted in the development of a new school model. This provides education up to year two in village-based elementary schools using community languages and then years three to eight in larger primary schools.

Table 9 Spending on basic education 1998/99 (A$)

Country	Expenditure
Papua New Guinea	28,622,170
Philippines	8,005,007
India	4,700,000
Indonesia	2,809,010
Bangladesh	2,691,573
China	1,828,000
Fiji	1,140,815
Sudan	872,000
Samoa	837,274
Laos	544,885
Pakistan	462,038
Vietnam	414,150
Regional – South Pacific	133,333
South Africa	100,000
Total	53,160,255

Source: AusAID Gender and Education Group, March 1999

While Australia has been a key player throughout this redevelopment, AusAID's emphasis has been on support rather than direction. The radical model proposed is a good indication that the programme is truly locally controlled and there are strong indications that both girls and boys are benefiting from the programme. Grade six to seven transition rates have risen from 40.1% to 58.4% for boys and from 34.2% to 54.6% for girls over the last ten years.[6]

Australia

Index of Australia's ODA and GNP per capita 1966/67 to 1999/2000

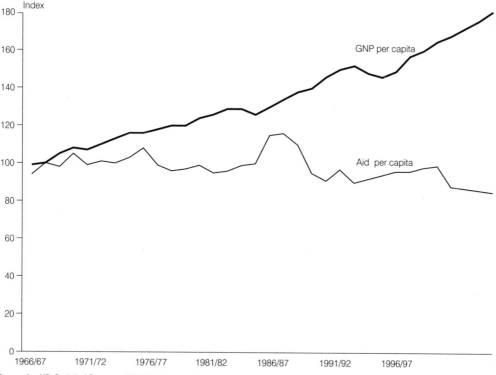

Source: AusAID, Statistical Summary 1995/96 p34 extrapolated with Australian Bureau of Statistics data

average for all OECD countries. However the latter figure is reduced by the very low levels of aid given by the two largest economies – the US and Japan. The simple unweighted average for OECD countries gives a much clearer position of our Government's concern for poor people in other countries. The unweighted OECD average is 0.40% of GNP, that is 60% more than Australia gives.

The Australian Government has reiterated its support for the international goal of 0.7% of GNP to aid but it refuses to identify interim goals or a path to reach that target. While the Australian people continue to give more to overseas aid in private donations, increasing 8% in real terms in just the last year, the level of government aid has plummeted in comparison with our wealth.

Australian aid NGOs have put forward a practical and achievable plan to increase aid by using a small proportion of the annual growth in government revenues. This plan calls for an increase of 0.02% of GNP each year to reach an interim target of 0.4% by 2007/08.

If The Netherlands, Denmark, Norway and Sweden can all give more than 0.7% of their GNP to aid, and if the UK

can significantly increase its aid programme, then why can Australia only afford to give 0.25%?

The graph above is a very sad testimony to the lack of concern shown by our federal politicians. The divergence between what is received and what is given is not the result of the decisions of the Australian people but the direct result of the decisions of the small number of people elected to sit in Canberra. It is time they showed sufficient courage and compassion to do something about it.

Notes
1   AusAID *Corporate Plan 1998–2000*
2   See ACFOA *Pre-budget Submission* 1998–99
3   See ACFOA *Pre-budget Submission* 1998–99
4   PNG is Australia's largest aid receiver and because of our special historical relationship used to receive most of its aid funding as general budget support. This is gradually being phased over to
'   programme funding.
5   See UNICEF *State of the Worlds Children 1999* and Watkins, K 1999 *Education Now: Break the Cycle of Poverty* (Oxfam)
6   Thomsom, G and Josephs, J 1999 *The State of Education in Papua New Guinea* (paper presented at the PNG High School Principals' Conference, Port Moresby March 1999)

Canada

Brian Tomlinson, Canadian Council for International Cooperation (CCIC)

Government called upon to 'end global poverty'

In March 1999, CCIC and more than 30 prominent Canadians released an Open Letter to the Prime Minister and Cabinet calling for government leadership to ensure that poverty reduction is the real, as opposed to simply the rhetorical, central purpose of Canada's aid programme.

The letter was supported by detailed recommendations in a longer, policy background paper, *A Call to End Global Poverty: Renewing Canadian Aid Policy and Practice*.[1] Canadian aid budgets have dropped dramatically – by 37% – since 1991, while CIDA, along with other donors, has had to assume an ever-expanding set of objectives – constructing peace in countries emerging from civil conflict, improving systems of governance, supporting the private sector, servicing infrastructure. In comparison with 21 OECD donors, only Belgium, Italy, Finland and the United States cut deeper than Canada into their ODA commitments in the 1990s. Dramatic reductions in funding have compounded the problem of a diffuse aid programme spread over many competing objectives.

While well-articulated policies are now in place, Canada's aid programme lacks an overarching strategic framework to implement its commitments to reduce poverty globally. In its Open Letter, CCIC argues that Canadian contributions to improving human development and human security require an unambiguous and strategic focus on poverty eradication for the aid programme. The *quality* of Canadian aid relationships, complemented by sufficient resources, is the fundamental issue for achieving a sustainable impact on poverty reduction.

The cuts in aid have been so deep and the changes in the international context so dramatic that there is an urgent need to rethink the priorities and practices of aid. The challenge is to integrate the goals of the aid programme strategically with other government initiatives in trade, finance, and environmental policy, both domestically and internationally. The CCIC policy paper suggests that the future role of aid needs to be measured as much by the standards and values its brings to the totality of policies as by volume. It says that those policies must work coherently to end global poverty.

The intent of CCIC's policy initiative on aid has been to stimulate discussion among a wide variety of development actors, to increase our understanding of poverty-sensitive aid and to strengthen its implementation by CIDA, NGOs and all partners. In responding to the Open Letter, Jean Chretien, the Prime Minister of Canada, expressed the view that the aid programme *does* take poverty reduction as its overarching goal, but also noted that much more needs to be done.[2]

In a major foreign policy speech at the end of March, the Prime Minister indicated an interest in rebuilding the aid budget, and working with G7 colleagues to promote fuller debt cancellation for the poorest countries. The Minister for Foreign Affairs, Lloyd Axworthy, and the Prime Minister have been promoting the foreign policy framework of 'human security', as Canada assumes a seat on the UN Security Council. While to date this agenda seems narrowly focused on intra-state conflict and peace-building, Diane Marleau, the Minister for International Cooperation, has suggested 'that all development assistance is an investment in human security'. Both the Prime Minister and Diane Marleau underlined the importance of working together with CIDA partners to draw lessons from our aid experience to help better position Canada's aid programme for the 21st century.

CCIC intends to work with senior government ministers and officials responsible for Canada's international policies, including CIDA, to explore and shape the recommendations of a *Call to End Global Poverty* to contribute to this process for renewing the role of aid within Canadian foreign policy.

Plan of action for renewing aid to reduce poverty

The Letter and Policy Paper make specific proposals for renewing and reforming the practice of Canadian aid for poverty reduction in four major areas:

- Focus on those living in poverty;
- New ways of working to promote 'ownership' in the aid relationship;
- Educate and engage Canadians;
- Rebuild aid resources and pursue deep debt cancellation.

Focusing on those living in poverty

In order to focus on the needs and interests of those living in poverty, CCIC proposes that at least 60% of Canadian aid directly improve the conditions and rights of people living in poverty.[3] The remaining 40% of aid would support activities that indirectly enable poverty reduction. Among the recommendations made, this implies:

- Increased targeting of aid to low-income countries and least developed countries, taking account of the importance of improved institutional capacities and positive pro-poor policies in recipient countries, to assure sustainability of efforts;
- Meeting sustainable basic human needs with at least 30% of (non-emergency) aid targeted to these purposes;
- Improved targeting of aid to the sectors and places where poor people are concentrated (including systematic gender analysis), with, for example, increased attention to poor communities in rural economies and to the needs of sub-Saharan Africa;
- Removing Canadian commercial interests in the allocation of Canadian aid, while recognising the important role of the private sector in aid through partnerships based on private sector experience with, and expected contributions to, the goal of poverty reduction. This orientation implies maximising employment and training for poor people and those vulnerable to falling into poverty, respect for workers' rights, assuring balanced, positive sustainable impacts on communities, and introducing appropriate technologies and building local private sector capacities.

New ways of working

Poverty is a complex phenomenon that requires nuanced understanding of poverty conditions in distinct local realities, including local power relations, culture, and global economic and political inequalities. For donors, it suggests foremost that humility, long-term engagement and a learning culture are critical ingredients to effective development cooperation.

For the most part people have escaped from poverty through their own efforts. ODA in this light is most effective as a catalyst for poverty reduction. The most effective and sustained results are achieved when strategies and programmes are developed and implemented with significant citizen engagement and participation, particularly on the part of those living in poverty.

The quality of partnership in the aid relationship is, therefore, crucial. If aid is not to become marginalised in North-South relations, a great deal hinges on improving CIDA's practice of policy dialogue and programme implementation in working relationships with southern partners and other donors. Fundamental to CCIC proposals are partnerships guided by locally-generated development strategies and concomitant attention to the capacities and skills required for both recipient and donor institutions. Given an emerging donor consensus on the importance of 'ownership', Canada may need to be more available for in-country policy dialogue and CIDA may, therefore, need to address creatively the appropriate locale and authority in allocating its human resources.

Promoting local ownership for poverty reduction implies the following:

Promoting the rights of poor people within civil society as key to sustainable strategies for poverty reduction.

Pro-poor development is ultimately about politics: affecting the power relations and cultural and social interests that sustain the inequitable distribution of society's economic opportunities and social resources. This is a complex and sensitive undertaking.

Evidence suggests that most CIDA spending for human rights and good governance in the 1990s has often only indirectly strengthened peoples' rights and supported organisations that represent those who are living in poverty and/or excluded from the political process. In this regard, CCIC has proposed a Civil Society Initiative for CIDA to develop an Agency-wide strategic framework for strengthening interventions and impacts for civil society organisations in the development process. This would include, for example, a commitment to assess development interven-

Canada

Percentage of national income spent on aid: a 30-year picture

How much aid does Canada give?

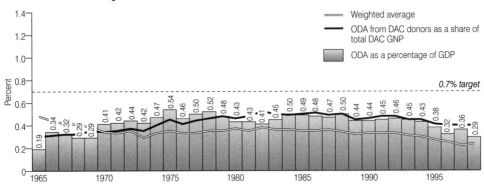

Legend:
- ═══ Weighted average
- ━━━ ODA from DAC donors as a share of total DAC GNP
- ▨ ODA as a percentage of GDP

0.7% target

Values along bars: 0.19, 0.34, 0.32, 0.29, 0.29, 0.41, 0.42, 0.44, 0.42, 0.47, 0.54, 0.46, 0.50, 0.52, 0.48, 0.43, 0.43, 0.41, 0.45, 0.50, 0.49, 0.48, 0.47, 0.50, 0.44, 0.44, 0.45, 0.46, 0.45, 0.43, 0.38, 0.32, 0.36, 0.29

Where is Canadian aid spent?

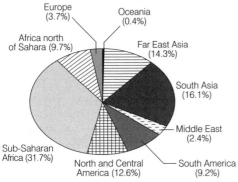

- Europe (3.7%)
- Oceania (0.4%)
- Africa north of Sahara (9.7%)
- Far East Asia (14.3%)
- South Asia (16.1%)
- Middle East (2.4%)
- South America (9.2%)
- North and Central America (12.6%)
- Sub-Saharan Africa (31.7%)

How much Canadian aid is spent through multilateral organisations?

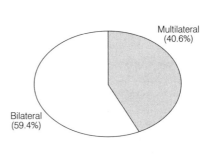

- Multilateral (40.6%)
- Bilateral (59.4%)

What is Canadian aid spent on?

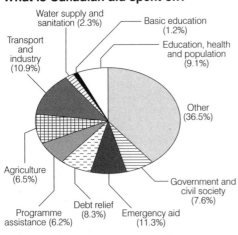

- Water supply and sanitation (2.3%)
- Basic education (1.2%)
- Transport and industry (10.9%)
- Education, health and population (9.1%)
- Other (36.5%)
- Agriculture (6.5%)
- Government and civil society (7.6%)
- Programme assistance (6.2%)
- Debt relief (8.3%)
- Emergency aid (11.3%)

For notes on data and sources see page 286

How much Canadian aid goes to the poorest countries?

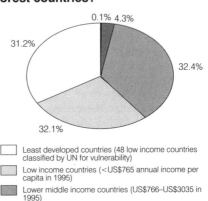

- 0.1%
- 4.3%
- 31.2%
- 32.4%
- 32.1%

Legend:
- ☐ Least developed countries (48 low income countries classified by UN for vulnerability)
- Low income countries (<US$765 annual income per capita in 1995)
- Lower middle income countries (US$766–US$3035 in 1995)
- Upper middle income countries (US$3036–US$9385 in 1995)
- ■ High income countries (>US$9385 per capita in 1995)

Box 8 Canadian aid at a glance

How much aid does Canada give?

Canada gave	US$1,684m, 2,498 million Canadian dollars in 1998
that was	0.29% of GNP
and	0.67% of total government expenditure
which meant	US$56 or C$82 per capita for 1998

Is it going up or down?

In 1998 Canadian aid	fell by $361m, a drop of 11.4% in real terms over 1997
Canada was	less generous in 1998, dropping from 0.34% of GNP to 0.29%
The outlook is that	that despite some small increases in the volume of aid, the proportion of GNP is still falling and this trend is likely to continue for the next two years

How does Canada compare with the other 20 donors?

Canada ranks	9 out of 21 for its volume of aid
It is	11 out of 21 in the generosity league
It gives	63.3% of its aid to low income countries, a higher proportion than 11 other donors
Private flows in 1995	amounted to $6,907m, 3.4 times ODA
Total flows	to developing countries were 1.67% of GNP and rank 2 out of 21 in the DAC

What proportion of bilateral aid goes to basic education and basic health?

Canada committed	0.4% of ODA to basic education, 0.8% to basic health and 0.9% to population and reproductive health. CCIC's estimate for 1997/98 is that 2.9% of ODA was spent on basic education.

How important are commercial interests in aid?

Canada reported that	68.5% of its bilateral aid commitments were tied to the purchase of goods and services from Canada

tions against core labour rights, as advocated by members of the trade union movement.

Strengthening CIDA-recipient capacities for policy dialogue

This relates both to the enabling conditions for effective poverty-focused intervention and to coordinating and determining appropriate roles for donors. Suggestions include:

- More systematic use of CIDA's Regional and Country Policy Frameworks, with explicit accountability to the overarching poverty reduction policy.
- Reducing the relatively high proportion of Canadian aid tied to the purchase of Canadian goods and

services, while practising (and promoting among other donors) pro-poor procurement strategies; and

- Exploring with Canadian and southern organisations options for Canadian government promotion and financing of fair trade partnerships, including support for strategies to increase market access for fairly traded goods.

Engagement of Canadians

While Canadians live in a country of relative prosperity, there are no Canadian-only solutions that isolate Canadians from the turbulence of changes around the world. Core values that opinion polls demonstrate are shared by many Canadians – justice, fairness and respect for individual and collective

Canada

human rights – suggest that Canadians should be open to assuming creative roles and activities as global citizens. But in recent years, this has not been evident on such specific issues of environmental degradation or global poverty.

Canadians are insufficiently challenged to understand how global issues impinge on their lives. In a world facing increasingly complex humanitarian crises, the challenge is to transform immediate charitable impulses into public understanding and action. This must focus on the urgent need to make hard choices for poverty reduction, in our own society and globally.

Global citizenship is made practical when there are opportunities for Canadians – farmers, fisherfolk, or students – to learn about and exchange with counterparts in developing countries innovative means to achieve local and global development. CCIC is proposing that government assume a leading role in stimulating public understanding and debate on global issues, and on the imperative to end poverty. NGO members of CCIC have made public engagement a high priority with the *In Common* campaign, whose goal is to put global poverty eradication more firmly on the Canadian public policy agenda.[4] CIDA has invested increased resources in development information and education, and in 1999 will be setting out a multi-faceted strategy for public engagement, including partnerships with schools, NGOs and community organisations, and the media. CCIC's Policy Paper sets out some elements that are critical for new initiatives in this area:

- An emphasis on making global citizenship meaningful in people's lives;
- Exchange and learning between Canadians and citizens of developing countries (particularly youth) on issues of common concern;
- Pilot opportunities and new methodologies for Canadians to participate in community 'public deliberation' work on policy choices on global issues; and
- Provide funding commensurate with these goals, building towards 2.5% of CIDA programming resources to public engagement by 2005/06.

Rebuilding ODA resources for development cooperation

After more than seven years of cuts in the 1990s, there is little scope to fund new innovative programming without the infusion of a predictable increased allocation of resources. CCIC has suggested that the government commit itself publicly to a timetable to rebuild Canadian ODA to at least 0.35% of Canadian GNP by 2005/06 –

reaching half of Canada's stated target of 0.7% over the next five years.

Making one-off and retroactive infusions of funding for ODA, as has been the practice in the past two federal budgets, does not create conditions for long-term planning and renewal. Aid allocations for 1999/2000 are budgeted to be less than actual expenditures for 1998/99.[5] Reallocations from many government departments, including CIDA, to cover the costs of Canada's participation in NATO's intervention in Kosovo and Serbia, as well as expected contributions to post-war reconstruction, may well keep Canadian aid for this year at 0.26% of GNP (compared to 0.29% for 1998/99).

Basic education: a case in point for aid renewal

Some of the overall trends for CIDA allocations to *sustainable* Basic Human Needs (ie excluding humanitarian assistance and emergency food aid) show modest improvement in the 1990s, growing from 13% of ODA in the early 1990s to 17% in 1997/98.

While no data is available to deduce similar trends in basic education, CCIC (with support from CIDA) has made some detailed calculations for 1997/98. In that year, approximately Cdn $74 million was allocated to basic education.[6] These disbursements represent 2.9% of ODA (excluding an unknown portion of the World Bank's IDA loans for basic education that can be attributed to Canada for that year) and 4.8% of CIDA programming resources.

OXFAM International's *Education Now* campaign has set a target of 8% of donor ODA for basic education to meet international commitments to achieve universal basic education for all by 2015. This target would have implied increased disbursements of Cdn $193.5 million in relation to total ODA or Cdn $123.1 million in relation to CIDA programming resources in 1997/98.

Donors and NGOs alike have stressed the fundamental importance of basic education for achieving goals for poverty eradication. In 1999 CIDA launched a long-overdue process to elaborate an agency strategy for basic education, which will be completed in 2000. Last year's *Reality of Aid* chapter drew attention to the relatively small number of bilateral projects focused on basic education from which to draw lessons to inform this strategy. Key institutional challenges remain if basic education (and poverty-focused ODA in general) is to achieve greater priority. Nevertheless, the highly inclusive and participatory process underway for the development of the strategy will certainly provide scope to increase understanding and (it is hoped) expand CIDA commitments to basic education. A review of selected CIDA's basic education programme experience suggests some important considerations and directions for the strategy.[7]

1 Equality and Quality in Education Opportunities

Throughout the world, education systems are in crisis. In many countries, the most important causes of this crisis lie outside the education system itself. They include widening social and economic inequalities, debt-induced resource constraints on the state, corruption at all levels of government, cultural barriers and systematic discrimination affecting the participation of girls and women, and the absence of democratic recourse for poor citizens to affect change.

Donors, governments and NGOs are working to expand education opportunities for poor and marginalised groups. But as societies become increasingly polarised and unequal, there may also be an emerging trend in education towards universal enrolment in low-quality, dysfunctional, basic education for the poor majority, and high quality, opportunity-creating, private education available to an élite. Donor basic education strategies must take account of the broader policies and opportunities for poor people if their interventions are not to reinforce these inequalities.

2 Ownership

Given the responsibility of government in meeting the educational needs of its citizens, CIDA achieves significant impact with limited resources where interventions are clearly coordinated by the recipient government. An illustration of this approach is current programming in the education sector in South Africa. This experience suggests the importance of several factors:

- Clear vision and policies on the part of the recipient government;
- Strong political leadership in the coordination process;
- Strengthened technical capacity in the line ministries;
- Clear divisions of labour allocated by the recipient government;
- Transparency by both donors and recipient governments.

A significant goal of national governments in coordinating donor interventions should be to assure a relative balance and devolution of resources for all provinces/districts based on their level of development.

While civil society organisations were understood to play important roles in establishing local ownership in basic education, CIDA programmers involved in different projects in Africa view their contributions to broader policy and priority-setting processes with some ambiguity. Advocacy roles are clearly important, particularly for national umbrella groups such as teachers' federations. Yet the experience to date suggests that there are few civil society organisations with broad knowledge, skills and capacity to effectively participate in national institutional policy dialogue. One role for donors might be to strengthen this capacity for key organisations.

3 Role of technical assistance

External technical assistance for basic education must be carefully managed by recipient governments and institutions. In South Africa, for example, the ministry insists that all technical expertise be fully integrated into the national education programme and that they be active practitioners, not consultants, working with South African counterparts to resolve specific problems or issues. Canadian technical collaborations in the education sector in South Africa take the form of CIDA-initiated Canadian teams drawn from universities, colleges, provincial ministries of education, and NGOs, who work on short-term missions with selected South African counterpart teams. Often, however, recipient governments are guided into accepting large numbers of inappropriate technical experts as a result of Canadian and other donors' emphasis on tied aid.

CIDA's current heavy reliance on consultants in basic education programming results in the loss of CIDA's capacity to capture lessons and experience for itself. CIDA has little internal expertise in basic education, with only three to five persons who have specialised knowledge out of approximately 1100 permanent person years in staffing. With no central locus for learning (programming consultants have no formal relationship to the basic education specialist in Policy Branch), it is not surprising that basic education has been a low priority for programming and is often interpreted very differently by individual programmers.

4 Ways of working in sectoral strategies

For Africa in particular there is the perception that a sectoral approach is the only option. On the whole, stand-alone projects have had limited success and are often not sustainable. A sectoral approach for CIDA will require new ways of working that point to the need for skilled personnel to be present in ongoing policy dialogue, and to bring Canadian niche programming to the table. Some key conditions identified for successful sectoral strategies include:

- Open democratic governmental processes;
- Donor/recipient trust (highly dependent on individuals);

Canada

- Donor trust of each other (highly dependent on individuals);
- Willingness to go at the pace of recipient country capacities;
- Donor willingness to untie aid to developing countries, including high-cost donor-driven technical assistance.

Sectoral strategies for education and other basic social programming make sense for efficient donor/recipient government management of the aid relationship. A recent DAC consultation, however, raised important questions about the implications of a sector approach for broader issues of legitimacy and governance. Do they bypass country-specific political processes that are more inclusive of local/regional political actors? Do they thereby displace important decisions on priorities in favour of a dialogue between government aid specialists on both sides of the table? CIDA needs to enter sectoral strategies carefully and as a staged process, with due attention to government capacities and consultative mechanisms that include civil society actors.

What are potential niche programmes for CIDA in basic education? Among others, current experience suggests:

- Targeted interventions to strengthen institutional capacities of the public education system and organisations that promote good policy and practice (for example, in mainstreaming gender analysis and programming);
- Flexibility to pilot particular initiatives identifying success factors and lessons in key high-risk areas (for example, basic education and child labour in India);
- Increased CIDA and recipient capacity for effective policy dialogue, including engagement with civil society, support and dissemination of key policy documents to influence government priorities;
- Collaboration with other donors/governments in subsectoral programmes (for example, building on CIDA's African girl-child programme and its support to BRAC in Bangladesh to integrate girls in formal and informal basic education).

Overall, CIDA's strategy should encourage conformity with recipient government policy frameworks. Where these do not exist or are weak, interventions should encourage 'champions' within government and/or pilot initiatives with civil society actors to create space and will to develop an official policy framework supportive of basic education priorities.

Conclusion

Over the past year, important efforts have emerged from key policy and programme quarters in CIDA, spurred on by DAC commitments and NGO activism, to translate poverty reduction and other recent related policies (such as basic human needs) into stronger programming directives. These voices in CIDA have strong, if at times, challenging allies in parliament, among NGOs and other actors. The process for a basic education strategy demonstrates an effort to achieve synergy among these allies. CCIC's *Call to End Global Poverty* is a foundation upon which CIDA and its allies might work together to clarify changes required to meet the stated poverty-focused policy goals of the agency.

But it must also be said that history demonstrates that positive trends and voices will not on their own be enough to reorient Canadian aid to a firm commitment to end poverty in the long term. Sustained advocacy and dialogue are essential to induce shifts in understanding of aid and poverty on the part Canada's political leadership and other decision-makers inside and outside government. In the short-term, strong Cabinet commitment is required to make poverty reduction a real priority – creating the scope for aid to be part of a more coherent Canadian foreign policy strategy on the eve of the 21st century.

Notes

1   Both the Open Letter and the Background Policy Paper are available on CCIC's web site (www.web.net/ccic-ccci). This chapter has been written with the support of Betty Plewes, Gauri Sreenivasan, Tim Draimin and Esperanza Moreno, all colleagues at CCIC. The background policy paper benefited from CCIC's ongoing collaboration with the North South Institute on Canadian aid policy. Information on CIDA's experience in basic education would not have been possible without the generous sharing of views in a number of interviews and in forums with CIDA staff working in basic education. However, CCIC is solely responsible for the analysis and conclusions reached.

2   The Open Letter received widespread media coverage in major newspapers and radio reports across the country. This coverage emphasised both the importance of aid, and how currently, conflicting aid objectives undermine aid's ostensible purpose of meeting the needs of the poorest people.

3   There is no available measure of the current amount of aid that directly improves the conditions and rights of people living in poverty. For more information, see the At A Glance table on page 234 for the current status of CIDA poverty reduction commitments. CCIC's recommendation means that 60% of programmes within CIDA's six priority areas should be directed towards activities that directly touch the lives of people living in poverty as direct beneficiaries. While CIDA does not measure its programmes in these terms, CCIC's understanding of current programmes leads us to believe that implementing this proposal would require significant adjustment of programme content over the next five years.

4   Information on CCIC's In Common campaign is available on the In Common web site, www.incommon.web.net.

5   See CCIC, 'Canadian ODA Update: Analysis of CIDA 1999/2000 Estimates, Part III Report on Plans and Priorities' on CCIC's web page (www.web.net/ccic-ccci).

6   This disbursement of $74 million represents a more accurate indica-
    tor of CIDA commitment to basic education than the amount
    reported each year to the Development Assistance Committee of
    the OECD. Averaged over three years (1995 to 1997) new project
    commitments amounted to $32 million in Canada's report to the
    DAC.
7   The following section is CCIC's summary of issues and observation
    based on a series of CIDA forums on basic education and personal

interviews with selected CIDA staff with experience in basic education. The interviews were based on a sample of CIDA bilateral
projects; time did not permit a comprehensive review of all CIDA
programming. In particular, a more complete picture would have
included interviews with NGO and other implementing partners. The
author is grateful for the thoughtful comments of those who made
time available to discuss these issues.

Japan

Akio Takayanagi, Japanese NGO Center for International Cooperation (JANIC)

Outlook gloomy despite support for Asia

Because of the prolonged recession, the outlook for Japan's aid programme is pessimistic. Although the anticipated cut in the aid budget in 1999[1] was avoided, the net disbursement of aid has been in decline since 1996. There is increased pressure from the business community to 'retie' aid.

Following the Japanese Government's decision to cut the aid budget for 1998–2000, aid was reduced by more than 10% in 1998. Despite this decision, the aid budget for 1999 showed a very slight increase – of 0.2%. Behind this increase was the Government's idea that for Japan to get out of prolonged stagnation, it is necessary to revitalise the Asian economies through aid.

At the ASEAN summit, held in Hanoi in December 1998, Prime Minister Keizo Obuchi announced that Japan would provide special loans to Asian countries in economic crisis. The Government decided to freeze its plan to eliminate the budget deficit, because the budget cut had been one of the causes of stagnation of the Japanese economy.

If we look at the details of the 1999 aid budget, grants will be kept at the level of 1998, while loans will be cut by 3.5%. Multilateral aid is to be increased by 11.1%.

The net disbursement of Japan's ODA in 1997 was US$9.43 billion, a 1.8% decrease compared to 1996, but in 1998, because of increase of aid to Asian countries which have suffered from economic crisis, the net disbursement recovered to US$10.7 billion, a 14.2% increase compared to 1997. The amount has still not recovered to the level in 1995, which was US$14.5 billion. The ODA/GNP ratio has gone down and up again rapidly, from 0.28% in 1995 to 0.20% in 1996 and 0.22% in 1997, and then to 0.28% in 1998.

Despite this increase, the outlook for aid remains rather gloomy since reducing the budget deficit is still high on the agenda for Japan. Also, much of the recent discussion on aid has been focused on how it could contribute to revitalisation of the Asian economies, whose economic crisis is connected with recession in Japan. While poverty reduction has increasingly been discussed among the aid community, government aid agencies and NGOs, it is of less concern to the public and other parts of the government.

If we look at the figures for 1997 (as the details of aid allocation for 1998 are not available at the time of writing), while multilateral aid was increased by 25.5%, bilateral aid was cut by 20.9%. Bilateral loans were particularly hard hit, with a cut of 43.4%; grants suffered less, decreasing by 9.6%.

There has been little change in terms of allocation of aid; in 1997, geographically, 46.5% went to Asia and, sectorally, economic infrastructure remains the largest target of Japan's ODA.

Public support declines

A survey carried out in December 1997 by the Association for Promotion of International Cooperation (APIC), a parastatal under the Ministry of Foreign Affairs (MoFA), found the following:

- 15.6% of the Japanese public said aid should be increased;
- 46.0% considered that aid should be kept at the current level;
- 14.8% favoured reduction of aid;
- 1.8% thought the aid programme should be closed.

This means the number of people who support an increase in aid has halved, compared to the survey quoted in last year's *Reality of Aid* (in which 31.2% favoured increasing aid). The responses to a question on the 10% cut in the aid budget in 1998 were as follows;

- ODA is an important means for international contribution and, despite the budget deficit, should be kept at the current level: 14.9%.
- Since other budget items are also cut, aid should be cut to some extent, but a 10% cut is too big: 16.8%.

- Aid budget had been too big. 10% cut is appropriate: 33.9%.
- Don't know: 34.5%.

We can see that the recession and the budget deficit have brought decline in public support for aid. Although people support the current level in principle, they also think that, considering the budget deficit, a cut in the short-term is inevitable.

Self-interest drives response to crisis

The special Yen loans announced in December for Asian economies suffering from economic crisis total 600 billion Japanese Yen (US$5 billion) over the next three years. While the interest rate, at 1.0%, is lower than the ordinary Yen loan (2.7%), it will all be tied aid.

The objective of this programme is twofold: to revitalise the economy in Asia and to increase business opportunities for Japanese industry. This could be considered, to greater or lesser extent, a response to the pressure from the business community to 're-tie' Japan's ODA. Loans will be provided to projects in transportation, economic infrastructure and disaster prevention.

Other initiatives regarding aid for Asian countries include measures for supporting poor people hit by the crisis. For example, emergency aid of 4 billion Yen was provided to Indonesia for purchasing medicine and dried milk.

Restructuring raises concern

As part of the restructuring plan of the Japanese bureaucracy, the Overseas Economic Cooperation Fund (OECF), the agency in charge of ODA loans, was due to merge with the Japan Export Import Bank (EXIM Bank) in late 1999. The new organisation is to be named Japan International Cooperation Bank. Because the EXIM Bank has been in charge of financing investment and trade of Japanese businesses, as well as other official flows to developing countries, there is a concern that this merger will prompt commercialisation of aid.

What is needed instead of this merger is the establishment of a single governmental agency that deals with all types of ODA – grants, technical aid and loans, as well as multilateral aid, and whose major mission is poverty elimination.

Poverty elimination – a big Yes but little Yen

The Japanese government has repeatedly reconfirmed its commitment to achieving the goals in the DAC's *Shaping the 21st Century* (S21C). The government sponsored the Tokyo Conference on the DAC's New Strategy, in June 1998, and S21C was considered the basic framework for the second Tokyo Conference on African Development (TICAD II) in October 1998.

Despite all the rhetoric and statements, it must be questioned to what extent S21C is reflected in the actual allocation of Japan's aid. The Japanese Government maintains too broad a definition of basic human needs (BHN); it includes under BHN the total of all aid for social infrastructure, education, health, population, water, agriculture, food aid and emergency aid.

Using this broad definition, although aid to BHN increased relatively until 1995, it started to decline slowly after 1996. From Table 10, we can see that Japan is far below the DAC average in most of the sectors possibly related to BHN. For Japan, building economic infrastructure, rather than poverty elimination, is the mainstream of its aid

Table 10 Allocation of Japan's ODA to BHN sectors (%)

	1991	1995	1996	1997	DAC 1996
Social infrastructure	12.3	26.7	20.9	22.8	30.0
Education	6.3	8.9	5.5	7.4	10.8
Basic education	n/a	0.5	0.2	n/a	1.3
Health	1.5	1.8	2.7	2.7	2.7
Basic health	n/a	0.6	1.6	n/a	1.3
Agriculture	9.4	9.4	14.3	11.4	9.5
Food aid	0.3	0.4	0.2	0.3	2.8
Emergency aid	0.0	0.3	0.4	0.5	5.1
Total BHN	22.0	36.7	35.7	35.0	47.4
Economic infrastructure	40.6	44.5	41.0	44.7	23.1

Source: DAC Annual Report and Japan's ODA (annual)

Japan

Percentage of national income spent on aid: a 30-year picture

How much aid does Japan give?

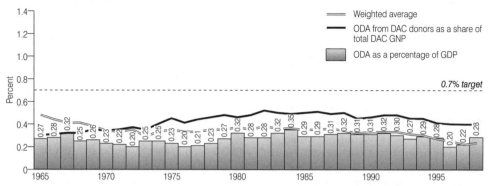

Legend:
- ═══ Weighted average
- ▬▬▬ ODA from DAC donors as a share of total DAC GNP
- ▨ ODA as a percentage of GDP

0.7% target

Values along bars: 0.27, 0.28, 0.32, 0.25, 0.26, 0.23, 0.22, 0.20, 0.25, 0.25, 0.23, 0.20, 0.21, 0.23, 0.27, 0.32, 0.28, 0.32, 0.35, 0.29, 0.29, 0.31, 0.32, 0.31, 0.31, 0.32, 0.30, 0.27, 0.29, 0.28, 0.20, 0.22, 0.28

Where is Japan's aid spent?

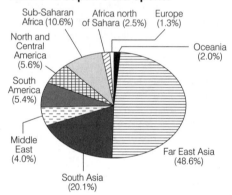

- Sub-Saharan Africa (10.6%)
- Africa north of Sahara (2.5%)
- Europe (1.3%)
- North and Central America (5.6%)
- Oceania (2.0%)
- South America (5.4%)
- Middle East (4.0%)
- Far East Asia (48.6%)
- South Asia (20.1%)

How much of Japan's aid is spent through multilateral organisations?

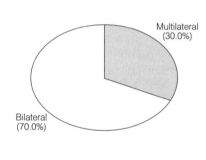

- Multilateral (30.0%)
- Bilateral (70.0%)

What is Japan's aid spent on?

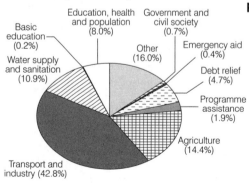

- Education, health and population (8.0%)
- Government and civil society (0.7%)
- Basic education (0.2%)
- Water supply and sanitation (10.9%)
- Other (16.0%)
- Emergency aid (0.4%)
- Debt relief (4.7%)
- Programme assistance (1.9%)
- Agriculture (14.4%)
- Transport and industry (42.8%)

How much of Japan's aid goes to the poorest countries?

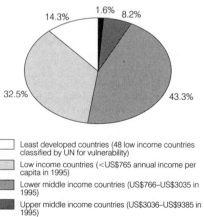

Values: 1.6%, 8.2%, 14.3%, 32.5%, 43.3%

- ☐ Least developed countries (48 low income countries classified by UN for vulnerability)
- ▨ Low income countries (<US$765 annual income per capita in 1995)
- ▨ Lower middle income countries (US$766–US$3035 in 1995)
- ▨ Upper middle income countries (US$3036–US$9385 in 1995)
- ■ High income countries (>US$9385 per capita in 1995)

For notes on data and sources see page 286

Box 9 Japanese aid at a glance

How much aid does Japan give?

Japan gave	US$10,683m, 1,398 billion Yen in 1998
that was	0.28% of GNP
and	0.77% of total government expenditure
which meant	US$85 or 11,083 Yen per capita for 1998

Is it going up or down?

In 1998 Japanese aid	rose by $1325m, a rise of 23.1% in real terms over 1997
Japan was	more generous in 1998, rising from 0.22% of GNP to 0.28%
The outlook is that	Japan had scheduled cuts in ODA of around 10% up to the year 2000; however, there will be a small increase in the 1999 budget to assist the Asian economies

How does Japan compare with the other 20 donors?

Japan ranks	First out of 21 for its volume of aid
It is	12 out of 21 in the generosity league
It gives	46.8% of its aid to low income countries, a lower proportion than 16 other donors
Private flows in 1995	amounted to $16,176m, 1.73 times ODA
Total flows	to developing countries were 0.7% of GNP and rank 14 out of 21 in the DAC

What proportion of bilateral aid goes to basic education and basic health?

Japan committed	1% of bilateral ODA to basic education, 0.5% to basic health and 0.1% to population and reproductive health

How important are commercial interests in aid?

Japan reported that	none of its bilateral aid commitments were tied to the purchase of goods and services from Japan

---

allocation. Despite the Government's recent emphasis on poverty reduction, officials have also continuously mentioned that there should be a 'balance' between aid for direct poverty elimination and promoting growth.

As mentioned earlier, bilateral grants in 1999 will remain at the level of the previous year while loans will be slightly cut. Budget for the Grant Assistance to Grassroots Projects (a programme handled by local Japanese embassies and available to NGOs –southern, international or Japanese – and local governments) will be increased from 5.7 billion Yen in 1998 to 7.0 billion Yen in 1999. Grants for children's health projects will be more than doubled: from 2.5 billion Yen to 5.2 billion Yen, which may be intended to indicate commitment to the S21C.

A new scheme introduced by Japan International Cooperation Agency (JICA)[2] in 1999 is tentatively named

a 'development partner programme'. JICA will contract out eight technical assistance projects in social development and enhancement of market economy to its partners. Organisations eligible as JICA's partners include NGOs, local governments, universities and other non-profit organisations.

JICA expects to contract out projects in social development to NGOs and projects related to enhancement of market economies to universities and research institutes. One aim of this new scheme is to make use of knowledge that is available in NGOs and other institutions, and not in JICA. In this scheme, expenses for overheads and administration could be included in the contracts. The objective of contracting out social development projects to NGOs is to increase effectiveness in poverty elimination.[3]

Japan

Box 10 Enhanced NGO-government policy dialogue

Mutual evaluation and learning

This aims to improve the quality of both NGO and ODA interventions in BHN sectors, through joint evaluation and mutual learning of strengths and weaknesses of the projects and programmes. In October and November 1997, a joint team of three NGO personnel, an officer from the Evaluation Division of MoFA's Economic Cooperation Bureau, one private think-tank staff member and a consultant carried out evaluations of a community-organising project run by Shapla Neer (a Japanese NGO that works in Bangladesh and Nepal), and two rural development projects of JICA. The team examined effectiveness, sustainability, efficiency, impact and replicability of the three projects. The report of this team was published in January 1999. Another mission, of four NGO personnel, two government officers and one consultant, was sent to Cambodia in March 1999 to evaluate Sotoshu Volunteer Association's project in basic education and a government project in rural development (whose beneficiaries are returned refugees).

Joint Workshop by NGOs and JICA

In early March 1999, a workshop jointly sponsored by the NGO community and JICA was held in Okinawa. Its objective was to enhance mutual understanding and collaboration between NGOs in Asia and Japan, and the Japanese government including JICA. Five speakers were invited from NGOs in South-East and South Asia. Issues covered in the workshop included roles of southern NGOs in community development, NGO-government relations in Japan, partnership between Asian and Japanese NGOs, and future prospects for collaboration among Asian NGOs, Japanese NGOs and the Japanese government.

NGO–Government dialogue enhanced

The relationship between NGOs and the Government has developed rapidly, both in terms of increased government funding to NGOs and through policy dialogue. One product of the seasonal dialogue meeting between NGOs and MoFA is mutual evaluation and learning. Another series of dialogue meetings (five to six times a year) is scheduled to start between NGOs and JICA. It is expected that the enhanced policy dialogue will improve government's views, methods and capacity in aid projects and programmes related to poverty elimination and meeting BHN.

Country Policies developed

Japan has made country aid policy for 24 countries (listed in Table 11). The government's idea to 'balance' aid for meeting BHN and promoting growth is reflected in policies for countries in Asia. Similar ideas could be found in the policies for countries such as Egypt and Brazil. There is more focus on BHN-related sectors in country policies for African countries.

Economic infrastructure as a whole, or a few sectors of economic infrastructure (such as transportation and electricity), are named as priority areas in country policies for Indonesia, Vietnam, Thailand, China, The Philippines, Laos, India, Sri Lanka, Nepal, Pakistan, and also for Egypt and Brazil.

For The Philippines, Malaysia, Laos, India, Nepal, Pakistan, Bangladesh, Ghana, Senegal, El Salvador, Nicaragua, Brazil and Peru, poverty elimination – or meeting BHN in general – is considered the priority area.

For Indonesia, Thailand, The Philippines, Malaysia and Brazil, there is some mention of addressing the widening income gap.

Education is named as a priority area in Indonesia, Vietnam, Thailand, Philippines, Mongolia, Laos, Pakistan, Bangladesh, Egypt, Jordan, Ghana, Senegal, Tanzania, El Salvador, Nicaragua and Peru.

Health is a priority issue in most of the 24 countries.

At TICAD II, Foreign Minister Masahiko Komura said that Japan would provide grants of 90 billion Yen during the next five years to support African countries in achieving the goals of universal education and reduction of maternal and infant mortality. Capacity building and human resource development were also named as priority agenda items for African countries.

Minimal share to basic education

Despite the government's emphasis on achieving the goals of S21C, there is little evidence that allocation to basic education has increased. As we saw in Table 100, the share of aid to basic education went down from 0.5% in 1995 to 0.2% in 1996. It was decided that Japan would support

Table 11 Countries with aid policy

Asia	Middle East	Africa	Latin America
Indonesia	Egypt	Ghana	El Salvador
Vietnam	Jordan	Kenya	Nicaragua
Thailand		Zimbabwe	Brazil
China		Senegal	Peru
Philippines		Tanzania	
Malaysia			
Mongolia			
Laos			
India			
Sri Lanka			
Nepal			
Pakistan			
Bangladesh			

Source: Japan's ODA 1998

construction of school buildings and provision of necessary facilities in 16,000 schools from 1993–97.

The bulk of Japan's aid in the education sector has gone to higher education and training. For example, in 1996, only 16.1% of JICA's technical cooperation budget in the education sector was allocated to basic education (preschool, primary and secondary education), while 26.7% was spent on higher education and 32.1% on vocational training.[4]

Lack of knowledge and human resources on the Japanese side, and the recipients' preference for receiving Japanese aid for higher education, technology and training are obstacles to the expansion of Japan's aid for basic education. Also, some countries hesitate over receiving outside support for basic education, as it is connected with language and culture policies that have a lot to do with national integration and sovereignty.

Major channels for aid for basic education include JOCV (Japan Overseas Cooperation Volunteers) and the Grant Assistance to Grassroots Projects. 28.5% of JOCV volunteers in the education sector were involved in pre-school, primary and secondary education. 23.5% of the Grant Assistance to Grassroots Projects was allocated to basic education.[5]

It has been mentioned repeatedly in government publications that Japan should increase aid for basic education to achieve the goals in S21C. As mentioned earlier, in many of the country policies, basic education is named as a priority sector. If aid for basic education is really to be enhanced, increased collaboration with the academic and education communities, and NGOs is indispensable.

Conclusion

It is certain that the Japanese Government has put more emphasis recently on poverty elimination and meeting BHN than it did in the past, as we can see from its repeated commitment to achieving the S21C goals. But if we look at how aid has been allocated, whether the rhetoric has been put into practice is still a question.

On one hand, there have been positive developments, such as increases in the Grant Assistance to Grassroots Projects and grants for children's health, and enhanced dialogue between NGOs and government aid agencies. But the prolonged recession has brought about a reduction of aid volume, declining public support for aid and increased pressure for commercialisation of aid, all of which would impact negatively on poverty elimination.

Poverty elimination and meeting BHN has still not been mainstreamed in Japan's aid policy and practice; most aid is still allocated to growth-oriented economic infrastructure.

The agenda for the NGO community regarding ODA includes:

- Dialogue with the government and public campaign, advocating mainstreaming of poverty elimination and meeting BHN.
- Public campaigning to maintain and enhance public support for Japanese commitment to poverty elimination.

Japan

Notes

1 All dates refer to the financial year unless otherwise stated.
2 JICA is in charge of technical aid and part of grants.
3 This is not the first government-aid agencies contract with NGOs. For example, Shapla Neer was contracted for evaluation of an OECF loan to the Grameen Bank.

4 *Report of the JICA Study on DAC's New Aid Strategy* (Japanese), JICA, 1998.
5 Author's calculation from the data of JICA and the Ministry of Foreign Affairs.

New Zealand

Pat Webster, Council for International Development (Kaunihera mõ te Whakapakari Ao Whãnui)

Research finds poverty focus lacking

During 1998, the Council for International Development (CID) conducted research into NZODA performance on poverty issues. Its report emphasised:

- The government's lack of any timetable for reaching the 0.7% GNP target for NZODA;
- The lack of a clear poverty-focused programme;
- A strong imbalance between senior secondary/tertiary education and basic education;

and the need for:

- More aid to the poorest countries of Asia and Africa, with an acceptance that the Pacific will continue to remain the key focus of NZODA;
- A poverty focus in the Pacific;
- A stronger focus on basic education and health, particularly in the Pacific;
- More coherence between macro-economic activity and social policy programmes;
- More involvement of civil society in implementation of the aid programme.

Balancing commitment with other priorities

New Zealand's aid budget continued to increase in 1998/99. The increase was expected to maintain it at 0.25% GNP. NGOs are concerned that the momentum for progress apparent during the last few years has slowed. While it may be significant that a government that is committed to cutting public spending has managed to maintain increases in NZODA, it is noteworthy that greater commitments to spending on defence have been a feature of the last year. An interim Select Committee report on New Zealand's Defence Beyond 2000 has highlighted the need to look at the respective weight given to defence and NZODA spending.[1] However, there does not appear to be sufficient interest in the issue among Government MPs and no significant action has resulted.

New Zealand will have an election this year and present indications are that there will be a change of government. Although the major opposition party is committed to improving New Zealand's performance on aid levels and is looking to strengthen the poverty focus of the programme, it is also emphasising the lack of money for new spending and NZODA will have strong competition for any extra money from the domestic social sector. There is likely to be strong support for increased ODA spending from the likely Coalition Partner.

Proximity outweighs poverty

New Zealand concentrates on the Pacific Islands countries. While there are very few LLDCs in the Pacific, NGOs support the growing recognition that vulnerability to environmental, economic and social problems is a marked feature of small island states, and they support the continued major focus on New Zealand's closest neighbours. However, in recognition of the greater need that exists in the poorest regions of the world, NGOs also wish to see improvements in programme funding for South Asia and Africa. These areas receive about 2% of NZODA and NGOs want this increased to 10%.

Poverty linked to poor participation

The NZODA Policy Framework outlines the government's view that a major factor inhibiting poverty eradication for some countries, and for some groups within countries, is the level of constraint on their participation in the global economy. They identify country size, geography, social and political history, and natural resource endowment as potential constraints. Some countries are particularly vulnerable to natural disasters and raw material price fluctuation, while some are undergoing institutional restructuring and are not yet able to participate in the world economy.

The Policy Framework points to countries and groups identified as likely to be more vulnerable and therefore in

New Zealand

Percentage of national income spent on aid: a 30-year picture

How much aid does New Zealand give?

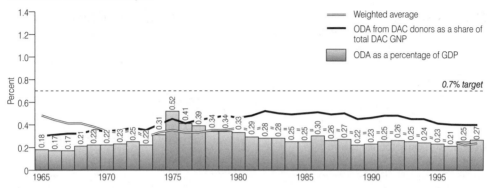

Where is New Zealand's aid spent?

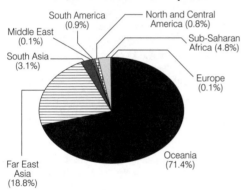

South America (0.9%)
Middle East (0.1%)
South Asia (3.1%)
North and Central America (0.8%)
Sub-Saharan Africa (4.8%)
Europe (0.1%)
Oceania (71.4%)
Far East Asia (18.8%)

How much of New Zealand's aid is spent through multilateral organisations?

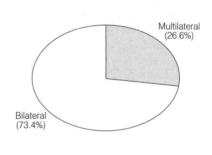

Multilateral (26.6%)
Bilateral (73.4%)

What is New Zealand's aid spent on?

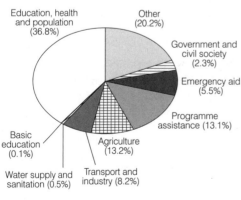

Education, health and population (36.8%)
Other (20.2%)
Government and civil society (2.3%)
Emergency aid (5.5%)
Programme assistance (13.1%)
Agriculture (13.2%)
Transport and industry (8.2%)
Water supply and sanitation (0.5%)
Basic education (0.1%)

How much of New Zealand's aid goes to the poorest countries?

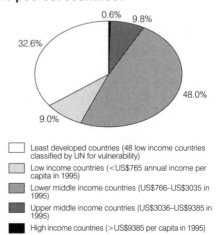

0.6% 9.8%
32.6%
48.0%
9.0%

Least developed countries (48 low income countries classified by UN for vulnerability)
Low income countries (<US$765 annual income per capita in 1995)
Lower middle income countries (US$766–US$3035 in 1995)
Upper middle income countries (US$3036–US$9385 in 1995)
High income countries (>US$9385 per capita in 1995)

For notes on data and sources see page 286

New Zealand

Box 11 New Zealand aid at a glance

How much aid does New Zealand give?

New Zealand gave	US$130m, 243 million New Zealand dollars in 1998
that was	0.27% of GNP
and	0.62% of total government expenditure
which meant	US$35 or 65 New Zealand dollars per capita for 1998

Is it going up or down?

In 1998 New Zealand aid	fell by US$24m in cash terms. Because of inflation and exchange-rate changes, the value of aid rose by 2.6% in real terms over 1997
New Zealand was	more generous in 1998, rising from 0.26% of GNP to 0.27%.
The outlook is	that aid will increase at approximately 0.01% per annum despite continued cutbacks in government spending

How does New Zealand compare with the other 20 donors?

New Zealand ranks	bottom out of 21 for its volume of aid
It is	15 out of 21 in the generosity league
It gives	41.6% of its aid to low income countries, a lower proportion than 19 other donors
Private flows	amounted to $28m, 18% of ODA
Total flows	to developing countries were 0.31% of GNP and rank 19 out of 21 in the DAC

How much does New Zealand spend on basic health and basic education?

New Zealand has not reported	but the most recent data for 1994 show that 0.7% of bilateral ODA was committed to basic health and 0.1% to basic education

---

need of specific assistance to enhance participation in the globalisation process.

NGOs can identify this policy approach with the Government's domestic economic agenda. While there are differing views in the NGO sector about the approach to globalisation, there is general agreement that any adaptation to external forces must be people-centred and address the complex inter-relationship between social, environmental and economic spheres. There is widespread recognition that the current model is, in fact, causing damage to delivery of important social services within New Zealand. As a result NGOs are concerned about the use of this model in the ODA programme.

'In Papua New Guinea, for example, budget constraints, war and structural adjustment have interacted and "resulted in serious decline in rural health services, the introduction of a user pays system in some cases, few supplies, poor support and low staff morale.'"[2]

While social impact assessment is part of the restructuring programmes funded by NZODA, this work appears to be added on as a means of ameliorating the potential problems that arise from the restructuring, rather than being conducted prior to decisions on the nature of the restructuring process itself.

For NGOs the major problem with the Government's approach to poverty eradication is the lack of any clear underpinning poverty strategy in the NZODA programme. NZODA is administered within the framework of the Ministry of Foreign Affairs and Trade, and is part of a diplomatic and strategic package of policies. Aid, therefore, has a variety of purposes, of which poverty reduction is but one. Other relevant strategies include gender and equality.

'The principal purpose of NZODA is to achieve lasting improvements in the living conditions of present and future generations of men, women and children in developing countries, especially the poor.'[3]

New Zealand

For some years NGOs have been seeking more information on poverty eradication programmes in NZODA. There have been signs of significant effort to tackle key issues. Specialists were appointed to work on health and education issues in the Pacific regional programmes. The Social Impact Specialist was tasked to develop a policy paper on poverty for NZODA but this work was accorded a low priority. The specialist left in 1999 having produced a 'Review of literature and selected donor policies'. However work continues in this area and a major policy paper on NZODA and poverty is expected before the end of 1999.

In a recent dialogue between NGOs and the Development Cooperation Division (DEV) of the Ministry of Foreign Affairs and Trade (MFAT) it was stated that the following activities contributed to the poverty focus in NZODA, even thought these were not made explicit in key policy statements:

- Checklists and questions focusing on the poverty aspects (including participation of beneficiaries and gender issues) as part of all project and programme development. A poverty indicator will soon be used in the approval process.
- Improved relationship between DEV and NGOs over the last 12 years and increasing amounts of money delivered through New Zealand-based and in-country NGOs.
- Increasing emphasis on gender equality, particularly in the area of poverty eradication.
- Outer island development and rural development in Asia, as well as micro-credit and basic education programmes.
- Attempts to integrate social and gender components into assistance for public sector reform in the Pacific, as it is seen to be important to take account of the social impact of the reforms.
- Efforts have been made to reorient the whole Fiji bilateral aid programme towards poverty reduction. The proposed programme will include capacity building for NGOs, micro-credit, institutional strengthening of the Department of Social Welfare, labour issues for female garment workers and casual seasonal workers, and an NGO fund for women.

The NGO Aid Works campaign, for which *Partners in a Common Future* was produced, is promoting a clear poverty focus in NZODA. NGOs argue that publicly available country strategy documents are needed in which poverty is the overriding issue to be addressed. NGOs would like to see the NZ Government adopt the 20:20 Initiative as a basis for these discussions. New Zealand did not sign up to this agreement in Copenhagen. Government argues that this arrangement does not necessarily fit well with its particular focus on small island states in the Pacific and may not always be appropriate in a programme driven by partner priorities.

NGOs have argued for an increase in social development expertise in DEV. Diplomats continue to work in DEV on a rotational basis, which means that there is a high turnover of key staff and potential for a lack of consistency in some areas of the programme. As well as a stronger core of permanent specialist staff, NGOs want to see more training in aid and development for diplomatic staff. Information from NZODA indicates that a number of New Zealand diplomatic posts in the Pacific have up to a third of their activity focussed on aid and development issues.

One area that is receiving a great deal more support, and which can contribute to a more poverty-focused programme is the NGO sector. NZODA has strengthened this area in recent years. Particularly significant activities in the past year include:

- Appointment of an NGO Programme Manager. The person appointed has a strong background in NGO activity and has been given a key role in promoting better coordination of NGO activity throughout NZODA.
- An evaluation of the Voluntary Agency Support Scheme (VASS) which showed that it compared very favourably with similar schemes in other countries.[4] This is the major NZODA fund for NGOs. It is a participatory scheme in which funding is allocated by a panel of NGOs, elected from registered NGO users of the fund.

The evaluation has produced recommendations for further improvements in the scheme which include:

- A New Partnerships Scheme which will be grant-based and will encourage partnership development between a variety of NGOs in New Zealand and overseas.
- A shift to Gender and Development away from earlier Women in Development schemes.
- A Capacity Building Fund to help strengthen NGOs both in New Zealand and in partner countries.
- Increased use of self-evaluation techniques among NGOs.
- A stronger focus on learning from experience.
- A report on development of linkages between Maori and Pacific Island initiatives for women in New Zealand

and women in the Pacific region.[5] The report says that the programmes and initiatives selected fell primarily into the categories of health, education, employment, business development, economic development and tourism.

- A survey of NGOs in the Solomon Islands to identify ways in which NZODA could support the development of NGOs. Support for capacity building of environmental NGOs in Papua New Guinea.
- Increased availability of funding for NZNGO activity in bilateral programmes, such as in the post-conflict reconstruction process in Bougainville.
- Increased direct funding of NGO activity within partner countries.

Gender policy adopted

A Gender Policy is now included in the NZODA Policy Framework. Its goal covers participation of men and women in contributing to and benefiting from NZODA. Its objectives include:

- Strengthening of institutional capability to address gender equality;
- Consistency with the Beijing Platform for Action;
- Mainstreaming of gender perspective in NZODA policies;
- Specific activities aimed at closing the gender gap.

Education: a shift away from scholarships?

In the NZODA Policy Framework, basic education is recognised as a key underpinning element of economic development. Education plays a major part in NZODA. It is, however, substantially and for historical reasons focused on scholarship programmes. (For further background information see *The Reality of Aid* 1998).

In recent years, following Parliamentary delegations to the Pacific, a Special Education Initiative was established to overview the whole education programme and to improve the focus on basic education. So far this programme has largely involved increased teacher in-service training and resource and curriculum development.

NGOs are making a strong case for change in the education emphasis of NZODA. Partners in a Common Future calls for at least 5% of NZODA to be spent on primary education. NGOs want to see at least 50% of the education spending in NZODA contribute to programmes at primary and lower secondary school, and to adult literacy.

Oxfam NZ, as part of its recent launch of the Oxfam basic education campaign, also supports this stance.

Last year the Minister's Advisory Committee on External Aid and Development also recommended that NZODA adopt an even balance between basic and higher level education.[6] The Associate Minister, in his response, indicated that he is not yet convinced by the arguments in this area and has asked his Advisory Committee to do further research on the approach to education.

At the same time, DEV has begun in-depth research into the education and training component of NZODA, a move greatly welcomed by NGOs. Outcomes from scholarship and award schemes will be analysed and, where possible, tracer studies will be undertaken to identify work and study histories. There will also be an analysis of NZODA programmes to identify trends over time and the current extent of support for basic education and literacy. NGOs expect the study to provide important information for guiding future scholarship programme development.

DEV has been strengthening the development focus of the scholarship programmes in line with recommendations from past reviews. There is now more emphasis on study within the region. There is also more emphasis on data collection to assess the progress of students in the programmes.

Support for a change in emphasis is not without problems. Politicians, in particular, tend to support retention of scholarships because they are a highly visible means of reminding people of New Zealand's presence. NGOs are also concerned about strong anecdotal evidence that people in positions of influence are able to put pressure on scholarship selection processes in some countries to benefit colleagues and extended family members.

Shift to in-country education support

In recent years there has been a move away from supply of teachers from New Zealand because this does not enable a country to develop a sustainable education system. There has been a shift to teacher training and in-service training, and to curriculum and resource planning. Even so difficulties have been identified in addressing cultural and perceptual differences. Attempts to overcome this will be made through building stronger understanding of the strategy and analysis required to develop curricula in-country.

One interesting model, which may provide a pointer to the future is the development of a partnership between institutions in New Zealand and those in-country to build the capacity of the in-country institution. Dunedin Teachers College and Solomon Islands College of Higher Education (SICHE) have developed a training programme for early childhood teachers, which provides pre-service training at

New Zealand

the SICHE and access to Early Childhood Education qualifications for untrained early childhood teachers working in kindergartens. Field workers provide training locally.

NZODA reports increased support for the use of local languages in the early years of literacy development. However, production of local language resources, especially for small, scattered populations, is expensive. This is a particular problem in Melanesia, where there are many languages in any one country.

Increased localisation of teaching positions has resulted in a significant drop in numbers of native English-speaking teachers. Many local teachers, particularly untrained teachers are not sufficiently fluent in English. Regional Senior Secondary examinations, which cover ten Pacific countries, are in English. Children who wish to advance academically must, at some stage, learn English. This is now happening at a later stage and as a result different resources must be produced at additional cost. Increased use of indigenous language in the early years of school also has an impact on support requirements of NZODA programmes, particularly in the area of material development.

Doubts about donor coordination in education

New Zealand has been involved in education cooperation with donors in Samoa. Donors have divided responsibility for funding programmes by education levels. Canada funds pre-school programmes, Australia funds primary and New Zealand secondary level. Support focuses on resource development and curriculum planning but there is concern that the process may produce a disjuncture between the different levels because of differences of methodology between donor countries.

Policy coherence questioned

Basic education has been adversely affected by structural adjustment in the Pacific. Public spending cuts have affected teacher numbers, class sizes and salaries. There has been anecdotal evidence about demoralisation among teachers, which is having an impact on the quality of education, particularly in the outlying areas. There has been growing pressure on Volunteer Service Abroad to reverse previous decisions to withdraw from teacher supply.

Conclusion

While there have been no radical changes in NZODA's approach to poverty eradication, there are signs that the issue is beginning to be addressed more seriously. The Minister of Foreign Affairs hosted the launch of the NGO campaign on aid and formally acknowledged the role of the research as a foundation for discussion and debate on policy. The steps that the Ministry and the Associate Minister have taken to research the education programme are much overdue and very welcome. More reviews of country programmes that focus on poverty eradication, such as that done in Fiji, will be a step in the right direction.

Notes

1   *NZ Defence Beyond 2000* – Interim Report of Select Committee, Wellington, 1998
2   Low and Davenport, *Partners in a Common Future*, Council for International Development, Wellington page 76
3   Ministry of Foreign Affairs and Trade (MFAT), *Investing in a Common Future*, May 1998, MFAT, Wellington, page 4
4   Clark, K, Clark, D, Nowland-Foreman, G and Quinn, M *Evaluation of the Voluntary Agency Support Scheme*, MFAT, Wellington, 1998
5   Opportunities for Developing Closer Linkages Between Maori and Pacific Island Initiatives for Women in New Zealand and Women in the Pacific Region, August 1998
6   NZODA and Human Rights, ACEAD, 1998

Norway

Gunnar Garbo, Norwegian People's Aid

The market and the majority combine forces

Through its declining aid shares in the mid-1990s, Norway seemed bent on becoming the first member state ever to reach the UN 0.7% aid target *in a downward movement from the top*. But in 1997 the Norwegian aid volume was stabilised at 0.88% of GNP. That year, the new centre coalition government declared that it intended to increase aid anew, restoring the 1% level by the year 2001. However, in 1998 'the market' punished expansive Norwegian financial and income policies by pressing the local currency down and forcing interest rates up. Backed by an overwhelming parliamentary majority, the minority government felt forced to introduce more contractive policies. In its budget proposition for 1999 it stated that the aid escalation plan had to be postponed by one year.

The aid budget for 1999 still comprises 0.88% of GNP, but this level is only being achieved by counting *all* the costs of the first-year reception of refugees in Norway – contrary to previous positions by the governing parties. It is an open question whether Norway will really be able to restore the 1% target by the year 2001.

Last year the Labour Party refused any budgetary cooperation with the Government because of a heated controversy about a particular social policy reform. The party made it a precondition for budgetary deals that the Government changed its favoured system of cash compensation to families who are *not* sending their young children to publicly supported kindergartens. This the Government refused to do. Instead it sought support from the rightist parties, a choice which had a definite impact on the adopted budget. The future aid budgets will very much depend on whether a new alliance can be established between the Government coalition and the parties of the traditional Left.

Poverty reduction through the World Bank?

In its latest budget proposition the Government declares that it puts the fight against poverty at the centre of its development policies. However, during the last 10 to 15 years support to the economic restructuring programmes of the World Bank has been an overriding aim of Norwegian cooperation agreements with its poor partners in the South. Within the Bank, Norway has fairly consistently sought to promote poverty reduction, partly through interventions in the Bank's governing bodies and partly by providing the Bank with earmarked contributions to priority areas. But an evaluation of the World Bank and poverty in Africa by the Michelsen Institute in Bergen, in July 1998, stated that the adjustment operations, which still dominate the Bank's lending portfolio, have at best had a limited impact and at worst contributed to an increase in poverty.

The evaluation report also suggested that the main beneficiaries of the World Bank's poverty-focused projects in Africa may be the 'better-off' among the poor, rather than those living in extreme poverty, who may in some cases be worse off in the short- to medium-term. Neither is there much evidence to show that gender inequalities are addressed, despite the negative implications of these inequalities on agricultural productivity, household nutrition and women's health and well-being.

The report stated that until recently the Bank had paid scant attention to key determinants of growth and poverty reduction: the distribution of assets, both physical (eg land) and human capital, the distribution of political power and the ability of poor groups to influence public policies. Economic liberalisation remains the main World Bank policy prescription. Income distortions and social inequities as possible causes rather than consequences of poverty have simply not been an issue for the Bank.

In a close review of World Bank policies in Malawi, Zambia and Zimbabwe, the report also noted that the

Norway

Percentage of national income spent on aid: a 30-year picture

How much aid does Norway give?

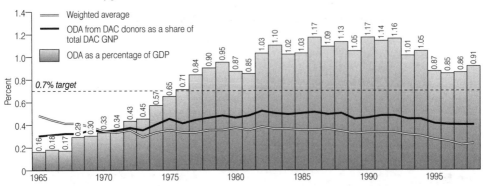

Where is Norway's aid spent?

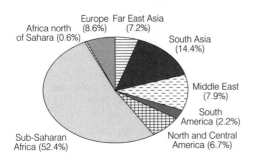

Europe (8.6%)
Far East Asia (7.2%)
Africa north of Sahara (0.6%)
South Asia (14.4%)
Middle East (7.9%)
South America (2.2%)
North and Central America (6.7%)
Sub-Saharan Africa (52.4%)

How much of Norway's aid is spent through multilateral organisations?

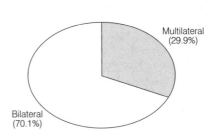

Multilateral (29.9%)
Bilateral (70.1%)

What is Norway's aid spent on?

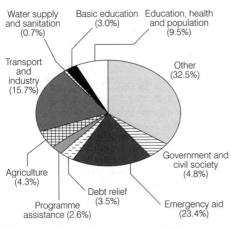

Water supply and sanitation (0.7%)
Basic education (3.0%)
Education, health and population (9.5%)
Transport and industry (15.7%)
Other (32.5%)
Agriculture (4.3%)
Debt relief (3.5%)
Programme assistance (2.6%)
Government and civil society (4.8%)
Emergency aid (23.4%)

For notes on data and sources see page 286

How much of Norway's aid goes to the poorest countries?

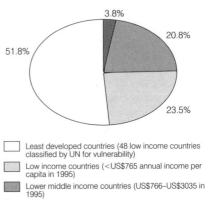

3.8%
20.8%
51.8%
23.5%

☐ Least developed countries (48 low income countries classified by UN for vulnerability)

Low income countries (<US$765 annual income per capita in 1995)

Lower middle income countries (US$766–US$3035 in 1995)

Upper middle income countries (US$3036–US$9385 in 1995)

■ High income countries (>US$9385 per capita in 1995)

Norway

Box 12 Norwegian aid at a glance

How much aid does Norway give?

Norway gave	US$1,321m, 9,967 Norwegian Krone in 1998
that was	0.91% of GNP
and	1.92% of total government expenditure
which meant	US$301 or 2,270 Norwegian Krone per capita for 1998

Is it going up or down?

In 1998 Norwegian aid	rose by $15m, a rise of 8.4% in real terms over 1997
Norway was	more generous in 1998, rising from 0.86% GNP to 0.91%
The outlook is	that the 1% of GNP target by 2001 has been postponed by one year because of the economic situation

How does Norway compare with the other 20 donors?

Norway ranks	12 out of 21 for its volume of aid
It is	2 out of 21 in the generosity league
It gives	75.3% of its aid to low income countries, a higher proportion than 16 other donors
Private flows	amounted to $342m, 26% of ODA
Total flows	to developing countries were 1.08% of GNP and rank 7 out of 21 in the DAC

What proportion of bilateral aid goes to basic education and basic health?

Norway committed	3.7% of bilateral ODA to basic education, 2.2% to basic health and 1.2% to population and reproductive health

How important are commercial interests in aid?

Norway reported that	11.5% of its bilateral aid commitments were tied to the purchase of goods and services from Norway

---

impact of debt issues, world prices and trade regimes is hardly touched upon in the country assistance strategies, though these factors have important implications for poverty trends. As far as the evaluation group was able to establish, Norway has not made any substantial criticism of the main pillar of the Bank approach: macroeconomic liberalisation policies which are expected to lead to broad-based growth. The group did not find this surprising, as it cannot see that Norway has itself developed any clear poverty reduction strategy.

The centre coalition Government has declared that it will seek to combine development aid with an effort to improve external conditions for developing countries in the fields of debt, trade and environment. It remains to be seen how this pledge will be carried out.

No clear Norwegian strategy against poverty

In 1996 the Norwegian foreign ministry published a review of aid evaluation studies completed between 1986 and 1992. This included the experiences and lessons from interventions to reduce poverty and improve living conditions for very poor people. The study concluded that even when the evaluations found positive impacts, such as in some rural development programmes, some health and child-related projects, and the Norwegian volunteer service, hardly any of these reports demonstrated that poverty was reduced as a result of the aid effort. Often it was found that the development activities had rather loose links to the poorest population groups, who were seldom accurately identified during the planning of projects and programmes.

In March 1999 the Michelsen Institute submitted a report to the foreign ministry about policies and strategies

Norway

for poverty reduction in Norwegian development aid. Poverty reduction has remained an overarching goal for Norwegian aid. Though the report found no specific and articulate strategy for achieving this goal, it saw what it termed an underlying model or approach. There is a fairly broad consensus that multi-pronged interventions are required, that the role of the State and public policy is crucial, and that framework conditions are critical for poverty reduction. Support to the poorest countries, social sectors and rural development in a few prioritised countries have remained fairly constant features. In the latter half of the 1990s there has been an increased emphasis on the provision of basic social services, in line with the 20:20 Initiative.

But in spite of the general understanding that poverty is a phenomenon that is caused by a number of economic, political and social factors, internal as well as external, even this report found that the emphasis was on internal political and economic aspects.

This seems strange in view of the fact that Norway's own historical experience shows how poverty reduction can be achieved through a broad set of policy reforms, focusing as much on general conditions as on specific interventions. The report identified several issues that must be addressed if poverty reduction is to be further mainstreamed in Norway's development aid. The recommendations included:

* Operational guidelines;
* Better monitoring;
* Efforts to strengthen poverty analysis and policy making, both at country level and in the headquarters in Oslo.

Africa focus in aid to basic education

Norway has embarked upon a programme to radically increase aid to the education sector, in line with the world declaration on Education For All. Education is not seen simply as a means to increase production, but as a human right. But during most of the 1990s only 4–6% of Norwegian development aid went to the education sector. Support to primary schooling comprised a minimal share compared to higher and vocational education. Basic education should, however, be seen as more than primary schooling; it is also a question of adult and non-formal education. But only from 1999 does the statistical reporting system allow for an identification of the type and level of education projects funded by Norway. Though basic education is now the growth area in Norwegian aid to the education sector, Norway still applies a sector-wide approach, seeing support to basic education in connection with the development of higher education and research.

Total aid to the sector may have surpassed 10% in 1999, and the Government's target of 15% seems to be in sight. During the last few years, a wide range of new initiatives has been adopted in pursuit of basic education for all children. In general, all support to education benefits women as well as men but, until now, only 12% of Norwegian-funded educational projects have been directed specifically towards women. Such issues as increased access for girls and rural populations have now been approached with new vigour.

The intention of the Government is to contribute half of Norway's total aid to sub-Saharan Africa. Per capita income in this huge region has declined by one fifth since 1980. Available data suggest that scarcely more than half of the primary school-aged population were attending school in 1992, and the decline in both gross and net enrolment continued after that time. Uniquely among developing regions, a majority of countries in sub-Saharan Africa now has a smaller proportion of children in school than was the case in 1980. On average, but with countrywide variations, 20% fewer girls are enrolled than boys. Policies that do not neutralise the special pressures reducing the enrolment and performance of girls would be unlikely to permit education for all.

Fifteen years ago the World Bank found that the public investment programmes in Africa had become little more than the aggregation of projects that donors wished to finance. Evidently aid coordination is necessary in order to improve the efficiency of development programming. However, backed by the conditionalities attached to its massive loans, the World Bank has acquired a hegemony of coordination in Africa. But government commitment to a reform programme is a much more important determinant of successful implementation than donor pressure imposed through conditionalities.

An evaluation report to the Norwegian foreign ministry about aid to basic education in Africa concluded that recipient countries must take a much firmer grip on the process of foreign aid to the development of education. The role of donors should be to help the developing countries to acquire the capacity to do so.

Steps towards unilateral debt cancellation

Last year Parliament approved the Government's plan to initiate a campaign for easing the debt burden of the poorest and most highly indebted countries. According to this plan Norway will strengthen its efforts within bodies such as the World Bank, the IMF and the Paris Club, in order to increase multilateral debt cancellations and improve initiatives such as the HIPC. The most important new element of the plan is an arrangement for unilateral Norwegian debt cancellation for the benefit of countries which have carried out an HIPC debt operation. This cancellation will be additional to the Paris Club alleviations. Another important point is that the debt cancellation will *not* be debited from Norway's aid budget.

Norway has claims amounting to 1400 million Norwegian kroner, based on previous commercial credits to 22 highly indebted countries, which are eligible for unilateral cancellation. However, this will not be an automatic process. Cancellation will only be accorded if Norway is satisfied that the action will benefit the poorest section of the country's population.

Local ownership of northern dictates?

There is a contradiction between Norway's definition of the aims that should be promoted through its development cooperation and its equally strong insistence on recipient responsibility. Recipients are not responsible if they have to follow a path that others have chosen for them. This dilemma is of course common for most of the present international development cooperation. According the developing countries freedom to use the international aid to the best of their abilities may lead to less heed being paid to northern preferences. Using a more dictatorial approach may, on the other hand, reduce the impact of the programmes.

Even the World Bank discovered long ago that its efforts were inefficient if recipients felt that the programmes were forced upon them by others, regardless of their own priorities. The Bank called, therefore, for local ownership and participation. But the dominant expectation of both the Bank and the bilateral donors is still that recipients internalise the prescriptions of the North, that they meekly accept the 'ownership' of other people's ideas.

Even the practice of a country as strongly committed to recipient responsibility as Norway is still marked by donor domination. A good example was given by the present country strategy agreed by Norway and Tanzania, though the Tanzanian partner had only seen a short English summary of the Norwegian text. According to an evaluation study, the whole process was driven by the political agenda in Norway and more or less conveyed to Tanzania.

There are two ways out of this dilemma. One is that the donors choose cooperation partners who by and large share their own values – and leave them in the driving seat. The other option is to transfer more of the development resources through the United Nations system, where countries from the North and the South participate on a par and where they have a joint responsibility in deciding which values to promote through international development cooperation.

Switzerland

Richard Gerster, Swiss Coalition of Development Organisations

Deficits and diversions shrink aid share

In 1998, the *volume* of Swiss ODA increased slightly, by 57 million Swiss Francs (CHF), to CHF1,287 million. Therefore, the share of 0.32% of GNP was maintained.

This modest upward move is due rather to technical reasons than to a change in the long-term downward trend. ODA fell from 0.34% of GNP in 1994 to 0.32% in 1998 and will reach 0.28% in 2002, according to the financial perspectives of the Government. This contradicts the Government's declared goal of 0.4%.

Among the *reasons* for this decline budget deficits figure most prominently. The year 2001 is constitutionally scheduled for a balanced budget. In years to come, there may be better opportunities for an ODA increase. The budget deficits are, however, not the whole story. The ODA share of federal government budgets has been shrinking steadily, from 3.2% in 1990 to 2.6% in 1998, indicating higher than average cuts and lower political priority.

In the 1990s, Switzerland witnessed the deepest recession since the great economic crisis of the 1930s. These difficulties made employment and social welfare – beyond the challenge of European integration – top priorities in politics. Moreover, migration and refugees generated a lot of political interest and public expenditure.

Going back to 1980, expenditure for refugees was less than 10% of ODA. By 1990, it had reached 40%. In 1999, the revised budget for refugees in Switzerland (CHF1,500 million) for the first time *exceeded* the ODA budget by 20% – and due to the crisis in Kosovo a further increase cannot be excluded. However, refugee expenditure is not included in ODA. Although the DAC permits some refugee costs to be counted as ODA, it is the conviction of the Swiss authorities that refugee activities in Switzerland are not comparable to development efforts.

In party politics during this decade, development cooperation has not been a theme of great controversy. The right-wing Swiss People's Party (SPP) has been broadening its popular appear, militating against foreigners and membership of the European Union. As the SPP also believes in the humanitarian tradition of Switzerland, it has not radically opposed development cooperation, but it has asked for limited additional cuts.

In 1998/99, the framework credit – projecting the volume of new obligations in the coming four years – for technical cooperation and financial assistance of CHF4 billion was due to be renewed. In the People's Chamber, a Swiss Social Democratic Party (SSDP) MP proposed an increase to CHF4.5 billion – the amount the Swiss Coalition had been proposing. As a counterbalance, an MP of the SPP asked for a cut to CHF3.6 billion. While the cut was refused and a majority of MPs voted in favour of the increase, the hurdle of a quorum could not be cleared Finally, the framework credit as proposed by Government was approved by 126 :1. In the plenary session of the Senate, the votes cast were 32:0 in favour.

Bilateral budget bears the brunt

A major concern of Swiss NGOs is the allocation between bilateral and multilateral aid. They support, of course, both forms of cooperation, while lobbying for changes in selected multilateral organisations. Being confronted with ODA cuts, experience shows that bilateral programmes are often seen as negotiable, whereas multilateral obligations are considered sacrosanct. The share of multilateral cooperation in the budget of the Swiss Agency for Development and Cooperation (SDC) stood at 30% in 1991, rose to 34% in 1994, 35% in 1997 and will be above 37% from the year 2000. Putting a ceiling on the share of multilateral cooperation at one third of total ODA is a matter of policy for Swiss NGOs.

Poverty impact hard to measure

Until 1999, there was no *formal* poverty reduction policy. Operational activities were based on provisions scattered through various policy papers, in government reports to parliament, and in country programme planning.

An independent assessment by the British Overseas Development Institute (ODI), on behalf of DAC, came to the conclusion that: 'Whilst in principle there was a great deal of commitment towards the principle of poverty reduction, in practice, programmes and projects were relatively weak in incorporating explicit poverty reduction goals'.[1]

As an overall assessment, the ODI/DAC study concluded that: 'There are no explicit methodologies for measuring poverty reduction impacts or efforts. As a result, it is difficult for SDC to say anything meaningful about the poverty impact of their activities'.[2]

Even the 1996 and 1998 messages[3] of the Government to Parliament, asking for framework credits of Swiss Francs 0.96 billion and 4 billion respectively, for the next four years, hardly treat poverty reduction in an explicit way. In the 1999 revised guiding principles (*Leitbild*), poverty reduction is just one out of eight priority areas. This is quite a surprise and in contrast to the many efforts outlined below.

Stimulated by the Social Summit in 1995, SDC formulated a Policy for Social Development,[4] focusing on poverty, which was approved in 1999. It declared: 'SDC will focus in all country analysis, all country programmes, project planning, and when contributing to multilateral organisations, more strongly on social issues (disparities in the access to production factors, consumption goods, decision processes and power)'.[5] To implement the policy, SDC has constituted a working group. Key elements of the poverty reduction policy are:

- Contributing to the provision of *basic social services*, such as basic education, basic health – including drinking water and sanitation – food security and humanitarian emergency assistance;
- Promoting economic growth in view of a *pro-poor-path*, by employment generation, promotion of small businesses, improving access of poor people to means of production such as land and capital;
- Promotion of *empowerment* of disadvantaged individuals, groups and organisations, to improve access of poor people to credit, land and skills, thereby changing the structural causes of poverty;
- *Gender-balanced development*, which is seen as a concern of social justice but also of effectiveness, efficiency and sustainability of poverty reduction efforts;

- Adding *long-term social assistance* in special cases, such as street children and refugees, is seriously considered by SDC.

The Federal Office of Foreign Economic Affairs (FOFEA) relates the main causes of persistent poverty to deficient or inadequate policies, poor governance, weak management, deficient accountability, etc, but has no formal poverty reduction policy. Budget aid allows for prioritisation of public expenditure for poverty reduction. While not targeting specific poor groups, the partner countries are selected according to criteria such as per capita income, good governance and synergies with SDC. FOFEA believes that economic growth is a crucial condition for poverty reduction. Private sector development and trade promotion are considered effective engines for growth and, as such, are FOFEA priorities.

SDC and FOFEA follow a policy of 'country concentration'. Important criteria for selection for SDC are:

1. Affiliation of a country to the category of low-income countries according to the DAC list;
2. Development policy efforts and priorities – in particular poverty reduction – favouring sustainable development.[6]

But, in 1998, only 44% of the allocated bilateral ODA was channelled into SDC's 16 key countries, ten of them LLDCs and a further four low-income countries. In contrast to the declared concentration policy, Switzerland provides ODA to 110 countries (1998). This widespread geographic pattern is due to the fact that FOFEA does not follow the same concentration policy as SDC and neither scholarships nor NGO co-financing are subject to the concentration policy. Obviously, in practice the poverty reduction orientation is not as significant as one might expect given the policy.

For each of SDC's 16 key countries, a 'country programme' with a time horizon of five years is drawn up. The country planning is done in a participatory way. At the outset, there is consultation with partners and other relevant institutions, including local governments, NGOs and business, in the recipient country. This effort is seen as a very useful chance for dialogue and coordination. Further steps include consultation of SDC Swiss partners (NGOs, universities, business) operating in the country on their own behalf or contracted by SDC.

SDC has taken steps to mainstream poverty reduction in sector programmes and project planning. Teaching aid and training modules are in preparation to assist programme staff. To increase coherence for Bolivia, a joint

Switzerland

Percentage of national income spent on aid: a 30-year picture

How much aid does Switzerland give?

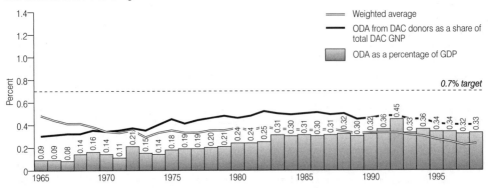

Legend:
- Weighted average
- ODA from DAC donors as a share of total DAC GNP
- ODA as a percentage of GDP
- 0.7% target

Bar values: 0.09, 0.09, 0.08, 0.14, 0.16, 0.14, 0.11, 0.21, 0.15, 0.14, 0.18, 0.19, 0.19, 0.20, 0.21, 0.24, 0.24, 0.25, 0.31, 0.30, 0.31, 0.30, 0.31, 0.32, 0.30, 0.32, 0.36, 0.45, 0.33, 0.36, 0.34, 0.34, 0.32, 0.33

Where is Swiss aid spent?

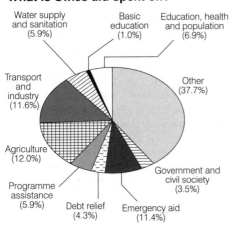

- Africa north of Sahara (2.5%)
- Europe (8.1%)
- Far East Asia (9.2%)
- South Asia (18.2%)
- Middle East (2.8%)
- South America (11.3%)
- North and Central America (6.9%)
- Sub-Saharan Africa (40.8%)

How much Swiss aid is spent through multilateral organisations?

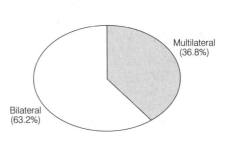

- Multilateral (36.8%)
- Bilateral (63.2%)

What is Swiss aid spent on?

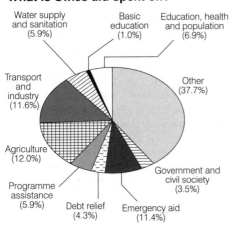

- Water supply and sanitation (5.9%)
- Basic education (1.0%)
- Education, health and population (6.9%)
- Transport and industry (11.6%)
- Other (37.7%)
- Agriculture (12.0%)
- Programme assistance (5.9%)
- Debt relief (4.3%)
- Emergency aid (11.4%)
- Government and civil society (3.5%)

For notes on data and sources see page 286

How much Swiss aid goes to the poorest countries?

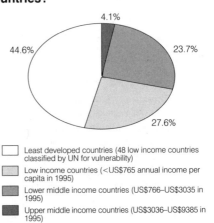

- 4.1%
- 44.6%
- 23.7%
- 27.6%

Legend:
- Least developed countries (48 low income countries classified by UN for vulnerability)
- Low income countries (<US$766 annual income per capita in 1995)
- Lower middle income countries (US$766–US$3035 in 1995)
- Upper middle income countries (US$3036–US$9385 in 1995)
- High income countries (>US$9385 per capita in 1995)

Switzerland

Box 13 Swiss aid at a glance

How much aid does Switzerland give?

Switzerland gave	US$888m, 1,287 million Swiss Francs in 1998
that was	0.33% of GNP*
and	0.68% of total government expenditure
which meant	US$125 or 182 Swiss Francs per capita for 1998

Is it going up or down?

In 1998 Swiss aid	measured in Swiss francs increased slightly. Measured in US dollars it fell by $23m, a drop of 3.6% in real terms over 1997.**
Switzerland was	less generous in 1998, dropping from 0.34% GNP to 0.33%
The outlook is	that if the current trend continues, Swiss ODA will drop to 0.29% of GNP by 2001

How does Switzerland compare with the other 20 donors?

Switzerland ranks	14 out of 21 for its volume of aid
It is	8 out of 21 in the generosity league
It gives	72.2% of its aid to low income countries, a higher proportion than 14 other donors
Private flows	are estimated at Sfr 2,255 m , US$1,555m for 1997, 1.75 times ODA***
Total flows:	are estimated at US$2,443m, 0.92% of GNP

What proportion of bilateral aid goes to basic education and basic health?

Switzerland committed	1% of its bilateral ODA to basic education and 1% to population and reproductive health in 1996. It has not reported on its basic health spending.

How important are commercial interests in aid?

Switzerland reported that	7.1% of its bilateral aid commitments were tied to the purchase of goods and services from Switzerland

* The Swiss Government has reported 0.32% of GNP as ODA in 1998 because of slight differences in the method of calculation.
** The difference is a result of exchange rate fluctuations
*** Data comes from the Swiss Government Statistical Services

---

country programme (SDC/FOFEA) has been elaborated for the first time and will be followed by further joint exercises for other key countries.

A cross-cutting analysis of SDC project proposals approved during 1992–97 was undertaken to explore how poverty alleviation was tackled in practice. This report[7] contains interesting results and recommendations:

- None of the approved proposals referred to a poverty assessment before the start of a project. Only 3% of the project proposals described the poverty situation explicitly; another 42% made implicit reference to poverty.

- Targeting for poverty reduction is weak in SDC. Three quarters of the project proposals examined did not mention a target group at all or in very general terms only. The geographic and sectoral approaches to poverty reduction are no substitute for operational targeting.

- In most of the analysed projects SDC practised an *indirect* approach to poverty reduction. 19% of SDC's bilateral measures are targeted at modifying the macro context, 73% aim at improving income generation, 42% at the satisfaction of basic needs. SDC intervenes rather at the micro and meso levels, focusing on

Switzerland

sectors such as agriculture, education, finance, health, urban development, water and sanitation.

- Key indicators to *monitor* and *evaluate* the poverty reduction activities are lacking. Monitoring of poverty reduction and documentation of the experience gained are therefore weak, most of the information being assembled at the country coordination offices in an inaccessible manner. An assessment of the trickle-down effect on poor people proved difficult.

- A comprehensive promotion of poverty reduction and empowerment requires strengthened links between projects and policies. Only 15% of the project proposals mentioned a relationship between the local project, its progress and the need to influence the overall framework.

As far as poverty monitoring indicators are concerned, SDC made a major effort in attaching a poverty code to its bilateral and multilateral programmes and projects. The latest figures for 1998 show 18% of SDC aid had a direct impact on poverty, 46% had an indirect impact, 24% had no immediate impact, and 12% remained uncoded.

The effort mirrors the increased attention of SDC to poverty issues; however, the reliability of these data remains doubtful as there is a high degree of subjectivity and arbitrariness. For example, the Swiss contribution to the reconstitution of IDA alone makes a difference of 13% and its classification as having a 'direct impact' is not indisputable. The problem that: 'our statistical service is confronted with the difficulty of adding up pears, apples, kiwis and mangoes', as an SDC staff member puts it, remains unsolved. SDC is aware of these shortcomings and plans to rectify them. It is following with particular interest the development of indicators in the DAC, UNDP and the World Bank. FOFEA does not apply such a coding system. FOFEA underlines the possibilities of dialogue with partner governments focusing on poverty reduction strategies. Comprehensive data on these dialogues and their impact do not exist or are not accessible.

Considerations of the gender dimension form part of the new SDC Policy for Social Development. The Gender Unit actively participates in the working group for the implementation of the policy. The teaching aid in preparation for mainstreaming poverty reduction will include a gender perspective. In country strategies, gender as a cross-cutting issue is often included. If and how gender is included in policy dialogue with partner governments varies from one concentration country to another. A new statistical code was introduced in 1999, including markers for a gender focus. The information gathered will be of a rather general nature.

Restructuring: a step towards coherence

Major changes in personnel and structure have taken place. Both Ministers responsible for ODA retired in 1998/99. Since early 1998, the Federal Department of Public Economy, in charge of FOFEA, has had a new head. In May 1999, the Foreign Minister, in charge of SDC, changed. Also the director of the FOFEA retired. FOFEA is responsible for economic measures in development cooperation. The significance of this reshuffle cannot yet be assessed but it may be an opportunity for fewer tensions and more coherence between SDC and FOFEA.

In the course of restructuring the administration, international cooperation with the South and the East has been integrated into SDC (technical cooperation) and FOFEA (financial cooperation). This is a welcome step towards improved coherence and efficiency.

In 1999, after three years of preparations, the FOFEA launched the Swiss Development Finance Corporation (SDFC). 51% of its capital of CHF55 million is held by the private sector, 49% by the Confederation. The SDFC shall co-finance joint ventures of mainly Swiss small and medium enterprises, and partner enterprises in developing countries as well as transition economies. NGOs criticised the mission statement for focusing on economic growth instead of sustainable development, for the neglect of poor developing countries as potential partners, for giving management incentives biased to economic returns instead of poverty reduction and for the lack of transparency and absence of NGO participation in the board.

The nuclear tests in India and Pakistan led the Swiss Government to end cooperation with the central governments, to stop some planned projects and to review thoroughly SDC's cooperation programme with these two concentration countries – the mandate did not cover FOFEA. A major evaluative focus was the poverty orientation of the Swiss support both at the project as well the policy level. The results were mostly positive. The choice of regions and sectors mainly relied on poverty considerations. However, most interventions targeted poor people indirectly only and the participation of the beneficiaries needs to be improved. The cooperation programme is continued with some exceptions and modifications.

Basic education emphasis strengthened

Switzerland follows three approaches in basic education: support for literacy and adult education, support for community-based education programmes for children not attending school, and support to official primary education. Educational efforts are usually integrated into an overall country cooperation strategy and as such oriented towards poverty reduction. Informal education as a central focus of Swiss support is targeted at groups marginalised by formal education systems and aims at their empowerment by strengthening negotiating and organisational capacities.

Switzerland increased spending on basic education from CHF11 million in 1995 (as reported in *The Reality of Aid* 1998) to CHF15 million in 1997 and 1998, despite the stagnating ODA level. In reality, emphasis on basic education is stronger than these figures suggest. Due to the informal and integrated approach, several programmes are not indicated as such but are earmarked, for example, as support to women's groups.

Switzerland has actively participated in Jomtien and initially also in the follow-up process. Due to other priorities, this participation was given up. Formal education being the focus of Education for All, it often does not correspond to the needs of marginalised people. After some years in school, many drop back into illiteracy, meaning that such investments are largely ineffective. Education is a basic right but formal education is not necessarily the most appropriate channel to follow it up. Literacy programmes can easily be linked to an empowerment process, which matters more for the people than formal education as stipulated in Jomtien. The applicability of this approach depends, of course, on country and local circumstances, and may be more appropriate in sub-Saharan Africa than in Latin America.

One of the priorities in SDC's sector policy on basic education is to 'support initiatives intended to increase and improve the access of women and girls to education and training programmes'. This implies a targeted support for women's organisations and NGOs working in this field. SDC support is demand driven and depends on the needs expressed by the partner groups. The Swiss priorities in basic education include access for girls, particularly based on private initiatives. Teacher training is considered more important than infrastructure. Secondary and tertiary education hardly enter the Swiss focus, except occasionally through exchanges between Swiss and developing country universities. Cooperating with governments in basic education, Switzerland concentrates on teaching aids and teacher training. Sustainability of Swiss interventions is secured by partner initiative and participation. Switzerland refrains from financing entire programme costs.

Notes

1   Goodwin P (1999) DAC Informal Network on Poverty Reduction: Switzerland Case Study, forthcoming from Overseas Development Institute (ODI) p19
2   Goodwin 1999, op cit pp29-30
3   Bundesrat (1998) Botschaft über die Weiterführung der technischen Zusammenarbeit und Finanzhilfe zugunsten von Entwicklungsländern, Berne 7 December 1998
    Bundesrat (1996) Botschaft über die Weiterführung der Finanzierung und über die Neuausrichtung von wirtschafts- und handelspolitischen Massnahmen im Rahmen der Entwicklungszusammenarbeit, Berne 29 May 1996
4   DEZA (1999) DEZA: Politik für soziale Entwicklung, vervielfältigt, Berne
5   DEZA 1999, op cit p14
6   Bundesrat 1998, op cit p83
7   Egger Monika/Egger Jean-Pierre (1998) Armutsbekämpfung und Empowerment. Querschnittsanalyse im Auftrag der DEZA, Bern

United States

Carol Lancaster, InterAction

Budget surpluses fail to bring increases

United States bilateral aid is in a period of transition. The federal budget deficits, which contributed to declining aid levels for several years, have turned into large and growing surpluses. Yet, these surpluses have not led to significant increases in US foreign aid.

The US Administration has recently emerged from a war in the Balkans and it is clear that the costs of that war, including the claims on US aid (for relief and eventually for reconstruction) are certain to be large and prolonged. US engagement in peacemaking in the Middle East and relief operations in Central America in the wake of the devastating hurricane there also promise to be expensive and in the case of the Middle East, prolonged.

Budgetary uncertainties in this time of transition are heightened by two other important changes. A new President will be elected in 2000 and the campaign has already begun. It may be too soon to suggest who the two major candidates will be, or which party is likely to win, but the first administration in the new millennium is likely to take a new look at foreign aid (given the organisational and budgetary controversies associated with it over the past several years). It may decide to make some significant changes in the light of developments in the world during the past decade. These include the tendency for the US to assume leadership on issues of peacemaking, especially in Europe, the rise in prominence of global issues, such as health and environment, and the turbulence of globalisation, represented by the Asian financial crisis, which for a time was seen as a potential threat to the US economy. All of these trends create demands on US foreign assistance resources and raise questions about the future purposes of those resources, as well as how US foreign aid should be organised. These are questions the next US President, whether Democrat or Republican, is likely to want to address.

Another significant transition is more immediate: the Administrator of USAID for the past six years, Brian Atwood, has departed and his replacement assumed the position in July 1999. While it is extremely difficult for a new administrator to initiate any significant changes in the last year of an administration, the moment of transition always brings a measure of uncertainty and the possibility of unexpected shifts of policy or programmes.

Congress contributes constraints and uncertainties

Over the period 1998–2000, the level of US foreign aid has stabilised and even increased by a small amount. The following chart shows the various kinds of US aid. Aid in the Economic Support Fund flows primarily to Israel and Egypt. Funds for the 'NIS' are to Russia, the Ukraine and other countries of the former Soviet Union. (These categories include a number of countries that are not included in foreign aid data compiled by the Development Assistance Committee because of their relatively high per capita income levels.) The column under the year 1999 will rise considerably due to emergency supplements for reconstruction in Central America which appear to be at a level of US$687 million and for relief for Kosovar refugees which may run over US$1 billion.

Within the Development Assistance account, a rising amount (US$595 million in 1999) has been earmarked by Congress to promote 'child survival'. Activities funded within this category include childhood inoculations, oral rehydration therapy, maternal child health and nutrition services, lowering HIV transmission and impact, mitigating the impact of infectious diseases and providing basic education for children.

These earmarked funds have been appropriated at levels above the administration's requests because key members of Congress feel that activities aimed at improving

United States

the lives of children are popular with their constituents. USAID officials, however, feel that while these activities are worthy and important, the increase in these and other areas earmarked by Congress constrains the Agency's flexibility to undertake a wide range of development activities at the levels it would prefer and to shape those activities to fit local priorities.

The US government does not calculate ODA and the following are provided as estimates and are subject and likely to change: US$8.1 billion in 1998; US$9.74 billion in 1999; and US$9.97 billion in 2000.

The prospects for future aid levels rest on a number of uncertainties. The levels agreed to by the Clinton administration and Congress several years ago in multi-annual budget plans showed a continuing decline in foreign aid. However, those plans were agreed to when there was a budget deficit. Now that there is a surplus, what are the likely aid levels? It does not appear that foreign aid will increase significantly despite the increasing budget surplus. Except in situations of humanitarian crisis, there is not a compelling rationale that would garner the support in Congress or among the public for such increases. However, the budget surplus also appears to have made continuing cuts unlikely, along with the overall budget plans agreed to in the past.

Three further uncertainties are the implications for foreign aid of the crisis in the Balkans, the agreement with Israel signed at the Wye Plantation and the impact on USAID staffing and operations of continuing decreases in its operating expenses. The first two are likely to make significant demands on foreign aid and it is possible that some of those demands may be met by reductions in assistance for development in the future. The third raises the more fundamental organisational question of whether USAID will have to decrease its staff further and whether, at some point, decreases in staff will force the Agency to restrict greatly, or abandon its field-based configuration and concentrate more of its organisation in Washington. Having closed its missions in nearly 30 countries already (but maintaining and even increasing smaller programmes in many countries), USAID is already de facto moving in this direction. This will surely be one of the major issues for the incoming Administrator and those who follow.

Organisational reform a likely priority

The issue of the relationship of USAID with the State Department (responsible for foreign affairs) appears destined to continue into the foreseeable future. In recent weeks, a new State Department-led study on the organisational location of US emergency response capabilities has been initiated. At present, programmes to support refugees are located primarily in the Department of State and Programmes supporting responses to humanitarian disasters are located in USAID. One option to be considered is to combine them in USAID or the Department of State. The recently departed USAID Administrator strongly opposed the latter option as programmatically flawed and politically unwise. However, it seems unlikely that any changes in the organisation of these programmes will be made before the next administration takes office.

There is one other, little-recognised, organisational issue involving US foreign aid that is likely to take on considerable importance in the new millennium: the increasing role that nearly all US government agencies are playing abroad, including dispensing aid. The expenditures of what have long been thought of as primarily domestic agencies – the Treasury, the Departments of Health and Human Services, Energy, Transportation, Housing, the Environmental Protection Agency and others – increasingly include a foreign component. These agencies have also established their own international affairs bureaux and offices. When cabinet officers travel abroad (which they do with increasing frequency), they often like to leave behind joint projects or assistance for the governments and countries they visit. Some of this assistance has been funded in the past by USAID. Increasingly it appears that it is funded by the individual agencies themselves. A recent US government delegation to Nigeria to decide on a strategy for helping that country had representatives from ten different US agencies. This fragmentation in US aid is likely to increase in the future with the globalisation of US domestic policies and concerns. It presents a challenge of coherence and coordination to the administration as a whole and perhaps, eventually, to the organisation and funding of USAID. It also raises questions about the evolving purposes of foreign aid. Domestic agency aid is rarely aimed at promoting growth or reducing poverty but at resolving global issues and problems. And this aid tends to be government-to-government, seldom involving civil society organisations or grassroots activities. These trends are likely to be a harbinger of future differences over the purposes and modes of implementation of foreign aid.

Planning undermined by lack of control over resources

USAID has been a leader in adopting strategic planning and 'managing for results' in the way it does business. While these programming processes have their advantages, they can also create problems for the efficient and effective implementation of aid-funded activities. USAID's experience

United States

Percentage of national income spent on aid: a 30-year picture

How much aid does the US give?

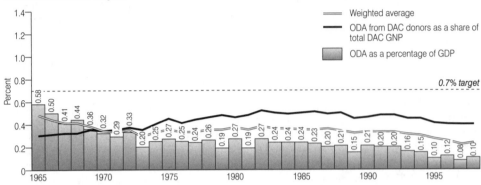

Legend:
- Weighted average
- ODA from DAC donors as a share of total DAC GNP
- ODA as a percentage of GDP

0.7% target

Where is the US's aid spent?

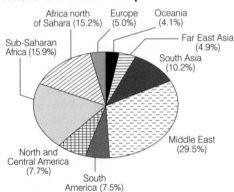

- Africa north of Sahara (15.2%)
- Europe (5.0%)
- Oceania (4.1%)
- Sub-Saharan Africa (15.9%)
- Far East Asia (4.9%)
- South Asia (10.2%)
- Middle East (29.5%)
- North and Central America (7.7%)
- South America (7.5%)

How much of US aid is spent through multilateral organisations?

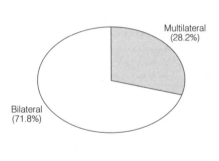

- Multilateral (28.2%)
- Bilateral (71.8%)

What is the US's aid spent on?

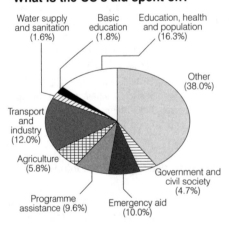

- Water supply and sanitation (1.6%)
- Basic education (1.8%)
- Education, health and population (16.3%)
- Other (38.0%)
- Transport and industry (12.0%)
- Agriculture (5.8%)
- Government and civil society (4.7%)
- Programme assistance (9.6%)
- Emergency aid (10.0%)

For notes on data and sources see page 286

How much of US aid goes to the poorest countries?

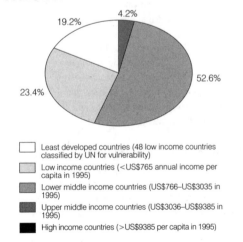

- 4.2%
- 19.2%
- 52.6%
- 23.4%

- Least developed countries (48 low income countries classified by UN for vulnerability)
- Low income countries (<US$765 annual income per capita in 1995)
- Lower middle income countries (US$766–US$3035 in 1995)
- Upper middle income countries (US$3036–US$9385 in 1995)
- High income countries (>US$9385 per capita in 1995)

United States

Box 14 US aid at a glance

How much aid does the US give?

The US gave	US$8,130m in 1998
that was	0.1% of GNP
and	0.29% of total government expenditure
which meant	US$30 per capita for 1998

Is it going up or down?

In 1998 US aid	rose by $1,252m, up 17% in real terms over 1997
The US was	more generous in 1998, rising from 0.09% to 0.1% of GNP
The outlook is	that aid is unlikely to increase significantly over the next two years due to budget constraints, increases in military spending, domestic issues and a continued lack of emphasis and marginalisation of foreign aid

How does the US compare with the other 20 donors?

The US ranks	second out of 21 for its volume of aid
It is	bottom in the generosity league
It gives	43.2% of its aid to low income countries, a lower proportion than 17 other donors
Private flows	amounted to $67,826m, nearly 10 times ODA
Total flows	to developing countries were 0.93% of GNP and rank 11 out of 21 in the DAC

What proportion of bilateral aid goes to basic education and basic health?

The US committed	1.1% of bilateral ODA to basic education, 3.3% to basic health and 4.4 % to population and reproductive health

How important are commercial interests in aid?

The US reports	that 71.6% of its bilateral aid commitments were tied to the purchase of goods and services from the US

---

in this regard may well prove useful for other aid agencies contemplating the adoption of similar approaches to programming.

The principal problems now evident are two. One is the assumption inherent in any strategic planning process that the agency has significant control over the allocation and use of its resources. USAID does not have such control. As noted earlier, the US Congress earmarks or directs the administration to spend its funds for specific uses or in specific countries, whether these are the priorities of USAID or not. Further, USAID often finds itself having to change its plans for funding to meet unanticipated foreign policy contingencies (Hurricane Mitch, Kosovo, Bosnia). At times, USAID also feels compelled to respond to pressures for funding from powerful groups or individuals within the

Administration or in the public sector. The mismatch between the assumptions of control over resources and the way USAID really functions comes close to making a strategic planning process unrealistic and inoperable.

The second problem with USAID's programming processes also involves control, specifically, how the funds are actually managed in the field. 'Managing for results' requires that the agency dispensing the funds set broad goals for those organisations actually implementing activities in the field, and then hold those organisations accountable for results. What has apparently happened is that a number of USAID officers, fearful of failure or mistakes in the way aid is spent, have tended to 'micro-manage' many of these activities, claiming more rather than less control over how the funds are actually spent.

United States

Table 12 US foreign aid (US$ millions)

Bilateral aid	1998	1999	2000
Development assistance	1,725	1,789	1,848
Economic Support Fund	2,420	2,433	2,389
NIS	771	847	1,032
Eastern Europe	485	430	393
Sub-total	5,40l	5,499	5,662
Multilateral Development Banks	1,459	1,476	1,394
Total	6,860	6,975	7,056

Source: US Department of State, FY 2000 International Affairs Budget, www.state.gov/www/budget/2000

Further, the indicators of success or failure have themselves become something of a problem. USAID officers and implementing organisations have spent an inordinate amount of time gathering data and preparing documents on indicators that have a weak or non-existent causal relationship to aid expenditures, or which are of little relevance to the impact of those expenditures. USAID is trying to reform this process to make it more efficient and realistic. It remains to be seen if that can be achieved in ways that improve the effectiveness of what are, in essence, often experimental activities funded with foreign assistance and whose benefits are often intangible (and difficult to quantify) or appear only after years, or even decades.

Basic education a priority for poverty reduction

Despite the challenges facing USAID in managing its resources, the Agency remains committed to addressing issues of poverty and underdevelopment abroad. It helped to formulate the DAC goals for the 21st century and many of its programmes are consistent with reducing poverty. In terms of education, USAID elevated human capacity development to the status of one of the Agency's seven major goals. Within human capacity development,[1] emphasis is placed on basic and higher education, with 85% of the strategic objectives in this area associated with basic education.

The Agency estimates that in 1997 it spent US$128 million on basic education in 23 countries in Latin America, Africa and Asia. Within basic education, a priority is placed on expanding access to education for girls. One success USAID has reported from its activities involving basic education is supporting, through seed grants, the creation of community schools in Ethiopia, Ghana, Guinea, Mali and Malawi. These schools have engaged parents, community leaders and teachers in managing and assuming 'ownership' of the schools and in some cases, creating schools where none have been. In regard to girls' education, USAID has published an evaluation of its past activities in this

area.[2] It has found that more and better primary schools for girls (with female teachers and administrators) are needed in societies where separate educational facilities for girls and boys are maintained, and more primary schools are required overall in societies where boys and girls are educated together. Also important is the perceived quality of primary education. Where parents perceive that quality to be low, they are less likely to send their girls to school.

Conclusion

USAID, and US foreign aid in general, is in a state of flux: that flux involves purposes, organisation, budget and personnel. It does not appear likely that any major changes will occur in the last year of the Clinton Administration. But these issues will surely be on the agenda of the Administration that follows it.

There seems little doubt that the US will continue to provide assistance in some form to address issues of development and poverty abroad. The more humanitarian aspects of those activities, including those involving children, remain relatively popular with the American public.

The US will continue to spend concessional resources abroad to promote its diplomatic goals, in particular those involving peacemaking. It will also surely allocate funds to address critical global issues such as health, environment and other issues of importance to a government and public who are beginning to realise that problems abroad can quickly become problems at home. But the size, organisation and modalities of these activities in the coming century remain to be decided.

Notes

1   Much of the material in this section is taken from USAID, Agency Performance Report 1998, Washington DC, April 1999.
2   Center for Development Information and Evaluation 'More but not yet better': USAID's Program and Policies to improve girls' education in Developing Countries, USAID, Washington DC 1998.

European Union

Mirjam van Reisen, Eurostep[1]

Defining the development programme

Treaty on European Union

The 1992 Treaty on European Union (TEU) stipulated that the European Community (EC) shares competence in development cooperation with the Member States. Neither the Maastricht Treaty, ratified in 1993, nor the Amsterdam Treaty, ratified in 1998, defined the division of competencies between the EC and the Member States. Consequently, the division of responsibilities between the EC as a whole, the European Commission as the executive body of the EC, and the Member States is a political matter rather than a legal one.[2]

Horizon 2000

Following the agreement on the TEU in 1992, the EC began to define the objectives that had been agreed and to clarify principles for implementation at Community level. This was called the 'Horizon 2000' process. It had been preceded by the 1991 Council resolution on human rights, democracy and good governance. The resolutions that followed related both to objectives of policy and to mechanisms for implementation. They apply both to the European Commission and to the Member States.

While most of the resolutions request that the Commission reports to the Council on progress made, such reports have not been made, with the exception of gender. In this area also, the implementation of the resolutions by the Member States is reported.[3] The Commission also prepared a document on the implementation of gender policies in the field of education.[4] On human rights, a progress report is also in preparation. A communication on complementarity was presented to the Council but this did not identify any new perspectives to define further the boundaries of activities between the Member States and the European Commission.[5] The Commission failed to report as promised during a specific debate on coherence in the Council and began preparing a progress report on this issue for the Meeting of the Development Council in

---

Box 15 Treaty on European Union amended by the Treaty of Amsterdam (Title XX, Articles 177–181)

The objectives of the EC development programme are:

1   The campaign against poverty;
2   Social and sustainable development of the developing countries;
3   The integration of the developing countries into the world economy.

The principles for implementation of the EC development programme were agreed as:

1   Complementarity of programmes implemented by the Member States and by the European Commission;
2   Coordination between Member States and the European Commission on development;
3   Coherence between EU policies with development objectives;
4   Consistency of Common foreign and security policy with development policy.

European Union

Table 13 Resolutions of Council

Year	Resolution	Topic
1992	Development cooperation in the run-up to 2000	Coordination
1993	Coordination of development policies	Coordination
	Fight against poverty	Poverty
	Procedures for coordination between the EC and Member States	Coordination
1994	Cooperation with developing countries in the field of health	Health
	Food security policies and practices	Food aid
	Education and training	Education
	Fight against HIV/AIDS in the developing countries	Health
1995	Complementarity between the development policies and actions of the Union and the Member States	Complementarity
	Integrating gender issues in development cooperation	Gender
	Structural Adjustment	SAPs
1996	Gender and crisis prevention, emergency operations and rehabilitation	Gender
	Human and social development and European Union development	Social policy
1997	Coherence of the EC's development cooperation with its other policies	Coherence
1998	Guidelines for operational coordination	Coordination
	Integrating gender issues in development cooperation	Gender

November 1999.[6] This report is supposed to be presented annually to the Council – as others are – but has not been presented since the Resolution in 1997.

Financial Perspective

The Council agreed in April 1999 the financial perspective for the seven-year period 2000–2006. The perspective establishes the ceilings for the annual budget under different budget headings.

Table 14 shows that the heading for agriculture continues to absorb half of the EU budget and is not decreasing. The heading on external actions has decreased by one third compared to the previous perspective. This is because pre-accession aid has been moved to a separate heading.[7] This includes the PHARE programme for Central and Eastern Europe.

(In)coherence between development and trade

Coherence between development policies and other policies affecting developing countries is of crucial importance for the effectiveness of aid. Without an enabling environment it is not possible for social development to take place. The issue of coherence relates to a number of thorny issues, particularly in the area of trade.

Mexico-EU Free Trade Agreement

In December 1997, the European Council and the Mexican government signed an Economic Partnership, Political Coordination and Cooperation Agreement.[8] This agreement is in the process of ratification by European Member States, with some (Germany, Belgium) expressing concerns about the mechanisms for monitoring violations of human rights and democracy.[9]

The extraordinary aspect of the Agreement between the EU and Mexico is that it is the first of a generation of 'agreements', in which parliaments are basically sidelined. The agreement includes only general headings and an overall direction. It is merely a very broad framework for negotiating a Free Trade Agreement (FTA) but does not define the content, substance or conclusions.

Remarkably, however, it gives the power of approving the substance of the FTA on the EU side to the EU Council of Ministers. Even though the European Parliament initially had great reservations about this procedure, it eventually assented. MEPs were reportedly being put under pressure from Spain, and with deals cut in relation to the South Africa Free Trade Agreement being finalised at the same time, the European Parliament gave away the right to assent to the Treaty not knowing its content or the results of the negotiations on the substance of the agreement.[10] In other words:

Table 14 Financial perspective 2000–2006, appropriations for commitments, 1999 prices (billion Euro[7])

Budget	2000	2001	2002	2003	2004	2005	2006
1 Agriculture	41.0	43.0	44.0	44.0	43.0	42.0	42.0
2 Structural operations	32.0	32.0	31.0	31.0	30.0	30.0	30.0
3 Internal policies	5.9	6.0	6.0	6.0	6.0	6.0	6.0
4 External action	4.5	4.6	4.6	4.6	4.6	4.6	4.6
5 Administration	4.5	4.6	4.7	4.8	4.9	5.0	5.1
7 Pre-accession aid	3.1	3.1	3.1	3.1	3.1	3.1	3.1
Total appropriations for commitments	92.0	93.0	93.8	93.0	91.5	90.8	90.3
Ceiling on appropriations for payments	89.6	91.0	98.3	101.5	100.6	101.3	103.5

Note: Budget heading 6 is not included. It includes reserves, among which the reserve for humanitarian aid is set at 200 million Euro for each year

'By ratifying the Global Agreement, the European Parliament gave the European Commission a "blank check"'.[11]

Rather, a blank cheque was given to the EU Council, also by the EU national parliaments. These are also in the process of ratifying the agreement, and are equally giving their assent to an empty shell, without taking responsibility for the substance with which the shell will be eventually filled. This is an unacceptable form of abstinence from exercising control, which is the primary responsibility of parliament.[12]

The actual content of the FTA between the EU and Mexico is of great importance to sustainable social development in Mexico. Liberalisation in the context of the North American FTA between Mexico, the US and Canada (NAFTA) has demonstrated a variety of grave negative consequences, that started most clearly with the collapse of the financial markets – later followed by financial crises in South-East Asia, Russia and Brazil. The consequences of these are most apparent in the export processing zones, the *macquilladores* in North Mexico. This is the final refuge for those without a future in other parts of Mexico and people in these areas are in desperate situations, with no labour or environmental protection, huge unemployment and terribly low wages.

Further liberalisation of Mexico, with greater competition from European products in the agricultural sector – produced not only with export subsidies, but also direct subsidies to European farmers – is likely only to further aggravate the situation of people living in poverty in Mexico.

The Mexico-EU agreement will be a model for the negotiations with the Southern 'Cone' countries of Latin America (under MERCOSUR), and other countries and regions.

South Africa–EU Free Trade Agreement

After four years of negotiations marked by substantial hurdles, the EU and South Africa finally agreed on a FTA. Although the agreement was concluded with South Africa alone, it will have a tremendous impact on the region as a whole.

Since South Africa is a member of the Southern African Customs Union (SACU), the FTA means a direct loss of customs revenue for Botswana, Namibia, Lesotho and Swaziland (BNLS). This loss is substantial: for Swaziland it represents about 50% of the entire government revenue[13] and for Namibia around 24% of government revenue.[14] The FTA will also require high adjustment costs in the region. Products that enter the South African market freely from the EU can then – without any custom duties – enter the BNLS markets. At the same time, the EU market is still well-protected against BNLS imports through tariff and non-tariff barriers.

It is also expected that investment will divert to South Africa, because the current comparative advantage of BNLS under the Lomé Convention will be eroded by the establishment of the FTA. It can be expected that industries will move to more efficient locations in South Africa where higher profits can be made. This reality makes the safeguard clause important in order to protect BNLS markets from detrimental effects in sensitive sectors. The EU and South Africa agreed to a safeguard clause but BNLS need the cooperation of South Africa in using it.[15] Since the interests of South Africa may differ from BNLS, the

European Union

safeguard clause will at best increase their political dependency on South Africa. In the worst case, the clause will fail to guarantee protection. In that situation, BNLS will effectively be in a FTA with the EU without being party to the agreement and without any increased access to the EU.

The agreement with South Africa was concluded under great pressure. Spain and Portugal demanded that there be a quick phasing out of South African labelling using the names port and sherry. With further concessions from South Africa on this issue, the Council approved the agreement in Berlin, in March 1999. The statement of Commissioner Pinheiro to the Development Committee of the European Parliament,[16] in defence of the Pinheiro-Erwin compromise[17] graphically illustrates his view of the gains and losses of both parties to the agreement:

> 'We have squeezed the orange to the last drop, we can not squeeze it further. We are bullying South Africa. After 12 years the use of the names port and sherry will disappear, so what is the problem? South Africa has produced under these names for more than 100 years. Are we trying to humiliate Mandela?'

Whether South Africa, and indeed the southern African region as a whole, will benefit from this agreement remains to be seen. The agreement between the EU and South Africa will have complex implications for the wider region, and also for the African, Caribbean and Pacific States (ACP) as a whole. The potential consequences in relation to the trade negotiations in the context of the ACP-EU negotiations are discussed below.

Regional Economic Partnership Agreements
In the context of the negotiations on the future agreement between the EU and the ACP, the EU has proposed the introduction of Regional Economic Partnership Agreements (REPAs). REPAs are essentially negotiations on regional free trade areas, though the proposals are somewhat confused.

Firstly, the REPAs are intended to be regional agreements, but the LLDCs could also choose to keep the Lomé preferences. Since REPAs will give less rather than more access to the EU market, the LLDCs have little interest in engaging in them. At the same time, the options to non-LLDCs are reduced, and, consequently, REPAs may seem attractive to them. However, non-LLDCs are located in regions with LLDCs. When some countries within the regions engage in REPAs, this will affect the LLDCs, unless effective barriers between the countries of the regions are

set up. It is, in practice, however, very unlikely that LLDCs can defend themselves against EU exports entering the markets through one EU-REPA partner. The REPAs, therefore, do not encourage regionalisation but, on the contrary, are likely to undermine regionalisation in the ACP.[18]

Secondly, the REPAs assume that there are existing 'regions' with which the EU can negotiate. Even though this may seem to be true for some regions, such as the Southern African Development Community (SADC), the West African Economic and Monetary Union (UEMOA), and the Caribbean Community (CARICOM), it is not evident even for these that a REPA can be negotiated or that conclusion of an agreement would be in their interest.[19]

Additionally, these regions are not clear-cut; for example, Tanzania is a member of both SADC and the East Africa Community (EAC), while Ghana has not joined UEMOA, and would only consider doing so if Nigeria did as well. Meanwhile, a large number of ACP countries are not fitting into any meaningful regional arrangement, with a few regions, such as the Horn of Africa, being at war. The interest of supporting regionalisation should, therefore, predominate over the negotiations of reciprocal trade agreements between the EU and the ACP.

As a consequence of the problems identified above, the timing of entering into negotiations is rather crucial. Firstly, what REPAs would entail should be further defined to allow more precise assessments. Secondly, there must be thorough examinations of the expected contributions of REPAs to achieving development objectives, particularly the eradication of poverty. Thirdly, the parameters within which REPAs would be negotiated should be clarified. They should include the reform of the European Common Agricultural Policy (CAP) – on which multilateral negotiations have not even started. This is of crucial importance because the CAP, in its current form, protects European farmers and creates obstacles for those outside Europe.[20] Finally, and most importantly, the outcome of a potential new round of multilateral trade negotiations, which the EU supports, will need to be taken into account by future negotiations towards REPAs.

This proposed new round of negotiations raises some additional issues. Firstly, the little, and already overstretched, capacity in ACP countries should be available for participating in the WTO negotiations, rather than for parallel, complex negotiations with only one of the economic blocs. Secondly, efforts should be focused on ensuring that this round will serve the interests of developing countries. The EU has identified this as one objective of the new round.[21] However, this stated intention should be regarded with some caution given that:

European Union

- The EU has not implemented measures agreed for compensating LLDCs for losses related to the Uruguay trade agreement;
- The extent to which the EU will agree to regulations in the interest of the developing countries will depend fully on the willingness of the US and Japan to support this;
- The EU has not succeeded in implementing fundamental reforms of the CAP, related to the Uruguay Round and there are no plans for far-reaching reforms yet on which agreement could be reached in the next round. For the developing countries this is the key issue, because it is in the agricultural sector where they could most easily have a comparative advantage if they had access to the EU market.

The integration of the developing countries is, therefore, rather a problem of protectionism (by the largest economic blocs) than a problem of liberalisation. As has been admitted by the European Commission, further liberalisation of the ACP countries will give the EU greater access to the ACP markets, but the ACP producers will not gain more access to the EU market.[22] Additionally, the ACP will lose in some cases substantial amounts of tariff revenues. While the EU promises compensation for these losses, this is by no means guaranteed – as the financial perspectives on resources for assistance are declining, particularly in the light of announcements by European development ministers that the available development budgets will be used for rehabilitation in Kosovo.

Coherence with other policy areas

Policies on Debt
Despite initiatives of the Commission and prompting from the Parliament and the ACP-EU Joint Assembly, the Member States have absolutely refused to discuss the issue of debt in terms of a comprehensive EU solution. ACP countries have raised the question of debt relief and debt resulting from EC loans granted in early Yaoundé and Lomé Conventions with European Member States. Their attempts have remained largely unsuccessful, apart from a 1998 initiative for exceptional assistance under the HIPC for ACP countries, funded with a reservation of ECU 40 million. This was financed from interest accrued on the funds deposited with paying agents handling some parts of the European Development Fund (EDF).[23] In June 1999, the G7 agreed a package of US$70 billion for faster, broader and deeper debt relief. Unfortunately, there is no clarity as to how this

decision will be implemented in view of the resources set aside for the Balkans.[24]

Review of the World Summit on Social Development
The Copenhagen Declaration of the Social Summit clearly established a link between enabling economic and political environments as an indispensable foundation for social development. The review process of the Social Summit (UNGASS), to be held in Geneva in April 2000, will identify further actions and initiatives to implement the commitments made in Copenhagen. The EU has, as one of the major players, disabled the process by arguing that macro-economic issues, including a discussion of the consequences of the financial crisis for social development, should not be part of the agenda of the Summit.[25] This is clearly in contradiction with EU Council resolutions that have established the link between macro-economic conditions and social development.

Implementation

The aid programmes managed by the Commission are, on the one hand, budget lines of the EU budget (Asia and Latin America (ALA), Mediterranean Basin (Med), PHARE, TACIS,[26] European Community Humanitarian Office (ECHO) and special budget lines). On the other hand, these are the EDFs that relate to the intergovernmental agreement between the EU and the ACP. The EDFs do not come into the EC budget and are voluntary contributions by the Member States.

Restructuring of the Commission
Proposals for the shape of the next Commission have been made against the collective resignation of the whole Commission in March 1999, following the report by a Committee of Independent Experts set up to investigate allegations of serious fraud and mismanagement within the Commission.[27]

Under the proposed new structure, there will be four Commissioners with external relations responsibilities. Chris Patten, as Commissioner for External Relations, will have a broad portfolio, including a coordinating role for the Commission's external relations as a whole and development policies towards Asia, Latin America and the Mediterranean countries. He will also be in charge of the Common Service (SCE), which deals with implementation of development programmes, including those for the ACP countries. Poul Nielson will be responsible for development of policies towards ACP countries and humanitarian assis-

European Union

Table 15 Commitment appropriations by geographic area, including ACP (1997/98) (million ECU[29])

	ALA	MED	CEEC/NIS	South Africa	Other[30]	ACP
1997	655	1,078	1,774	123	1,811	616
1998	657	1,101	1,729	145	1,919	2,219

Table 16 Payment appropriations by geographic area, including ACP (1997/98) (million ECU[31])

	ALA	MED	CEEC/NIS	South Africa	Other32	ACP
1997	433	628	1,490	73	1,951	na
1998	408	533	1,646	65	1,863	na

tance. Pascal Lamy will cover trade and Günter Verheugen will be responsible for the EU's enlargement and its pre-accession strategy. Chris Patten and Poul Nielson will jointly assume responsibility for all of the EC's official development assistance.[28]

The main problems associated with this division of portfolios are:

1   The ACP countries are separated from the other development regions in a separate Directorate General (DG) for development and are in danger of being ghettoised;
2   Policy towards the ACP countries and implementation of policy are the political responsibility of two different Commissioners and it is unclear how consistency between policy and implementation can be assured;
3   Moving all trade issues relating to developing countries to the DG for Trade is liable to weaken the relationship between trade arrangements and development. The interests of developing countries will be further undermined in the EU's approach to trade negotiations.

Budget implementation

The establishment of the Common Service in 1998 appears to have created further chaos in the already understaffed external relations DG. The responsibilities for compiling figures for external relations budgets and the EDF have not been clearly defined. It has been extremely difficult to identify the implementation rate of commitments and payments to different regions in 1998, since comparative figures for development assistance by region, or by sector are not easily available.

Comparative figures on real commitments and payments by region under the different budget lines and the EDF were not available by July 1999. An estimation of

comparative figures by region can only be achieved on the basis of the real commitments and payments by regional budget line. This excludes budget lines that do not have a regional focus, which are brought together under the heading 'other'.

The table shows that real payments continue to be much lower than real commitments. In particular, the implementation of the Med programme is totally inadequate.

Unspent funding a double blow to developing countries
The sixth EDF (covering the Lomé Convention of 1985–89) still had 1 billion ECU outstanding for payments at the end of 1998. According to the Commission, most of this was realised in the first half of 1999. In the seventh EDF (covering the period 1990–94), 4 billion ECU was still outstanding for payments. As a result, no calls have yet been made on the Member States to release part of their contributions to the eighth EDF (1995–99), even though 465 million ECU have been committed from this fund. In fact, the Commission is unlikely to begin calling down contributions from the Member States before 2002/03 – a few years after the Lomé Convention to which the fund is connected has ended. This demonstrates the prevailing problem of the unspent funding of Member States' contributions to the Commission. If these funds were collected in an interest accruing account, all the funds and interests accrued could benefit the ACP.

Health and Education
There is no formal information available on the budget implementation in health and education. It is estimated by the Commission that the commitments for the health and education sectors in the National Indicative Programmes (NIPs) for the eighth EDF have increased dramatically, to 30% of all the programmable funds. Approximately 80% of

European Union

the funds for education committed in the eighth EDF would be destined for primary education.[33] Education has been identified by 19 ACP countries as a concentration area in the National Indicative Programmes (NIPs) and in three Regional Indicative Programmes (RIPs). In each of the health and education sectors, financial decisions worth approximately 100 million ECU were approved in 1998 for the eighth EDF.[34]

Rolling programming

With regard to the successor agreement between the EU and the ACP, the Commission has proposed introducing 'rolling programming'. This would involve a more continuous process of planning and programming, implementation and monitoring with two-year cycles of resource disbursements. Previously, an EDF was programmed for the whole period that it would take to exhaust the funding. This could be up to 12 or 13 years. Clearly, what would have been relevant at the time of approval of the programme, would not necessarily be a priority ten years later. Rolling programming will provide more flexible mechanisms for planning and adaptation of plans to suit changing priorities.

The new approach will also allow for a more policy-oriented approach, rather than project-based activities. The financial support would come increasingly in the form of budget support to the government of the recipient country, earmarked for specific sectors.[35] The Commission has introduced annual review processes as a mechanism to monitor implementation against the agreed NIPs.

Rolling over

In the context of Rolling Programming, the EDFs would not be implemented separately but managed as part of the more flexible approach with biannual releases of resources for the implementation of overall agreed policies. In order to integrate the remaining funds of the seventh and eighth EDFs for this purpose, the Commission has sought the approval of the Member States. Some have replied that this will only be possible if such a decision is ratified by the national parliament.[36]

The role of the EDF Committee

The EDF Committee, which administers EDF resources, consists of representatives of the governments of the EU Member States, working under the auspices of the European Commission. The Committee is set up as part of an internal agreement between the Member States, under the specific financial protocols of each EDF. The rules of procedure of the EDF Committee are adopted by the

Council, acting unanimously. Within the EDF Committee, the votes of the Member States are weighed. The Committee acts on a qualified majority vote.[37] It decides, among other things, on all projects and programmes with a value greater than two million Euro.

Even though the EDF Committee is set up as a mechanism 'in the interest of consistency and complementarity', it creates severe implementation problems. Firstly, the EDF Committee, which meets in Brussels, takes decision-making power and authority away from the Heads of EC Delegations in the ACP countries. The Heads of Delegations are charged with the preparation, implementation and monitoring of the Lomé Convention in close cooperation with the National Authorising Officers (NAOs), charged with implementation by the ACP countries. However, their decision-making power is severely circumscribed by the powers of the EDF Committee.

The EC, including the Member States, attaches great value to increasing 'ownership' over aid programmes by beneficiary countries. Unfortunately, the EDF Committee does not contribute to strengthening ownership by the ACP countries. Last year, the Committee cancelled its project visits because of 'a lack of capacity both in terms of time and money.[38] Being in Brussels, without any direct relationship with those involved in the planning and implementation of the programmes – and worse, with no direct contact with those in whose interests they are intended to be taking decisions – the Committee members serve as national representatives preserving the interests and policies of the individual Member States. This gives the EDF Committee a purely political nature that clouds the transparency of implementation of the Lomé Convention.

The low rate of implementation of the EDFs has reached unacceptable levels and has worsened in recent years. It is caused by the nature of the programme and the capacity it demands in the ACP states to manage it, by the insufficient administrative capacity in the Commission and by the ever-tightening procedures of financial control.

When a project proposal is sent to the Committee, it takes at least two months for it to be translated into 11 languages, so that it can be considered. There is also a question related to the motivation of some of the members of the Committee to accelerate the implementation process, as members have expressed the view that 'if things were really speeded up it would be even more difficult for ACP countries to absorb aid.'[39] Such attitudes cast doubt on the legitimacy of the EDF Committee – and add force to the argument that the EDF needs to become an ordinary part of the EC budget.

European Union

Inefficiency diminishes public support

The Chapter on the European Union in *The Reality of Aid* 1997/98 analysed how unspent monies from Member States for the EDF return to the national treasuries and never leave the Member States' countries. These unspent monies never reach the developing countries. While Member States increasingly state that they can not afford to make sufficient funds available for assistance to developing countries, including for debt relief, the inefficient spending under the Lomé Convention is unacceptable. Moreover, It should be noted that 76% of the people in the European Union consider aid to developing countries as important or very important.[40] Of those who believe that development aid should be decreased, 45.2% said it was because 'the money will be misused and will not reach those who need it'.[41] This demonstrates the public importance attached to efficient implementation.

Notes

1 Eurostep is a European coordination of 23 non-denominational non-governmental development organisations. Guggi Laryea assisted in the research for this chapter. I would like to thank Paul Wheeler, from CIFCA, for his help and comments on the draft.

2 The question is further examined in: Reisen, van M., *EU Global Player. The North-South Policy of the European Union*, International Books, Utrecht, September 1999. It has been published in an earlier version in German: Reisen, van M., *Global Player EU. Die Nord-Süd-Politik der Europäischen Union. Analyse-Kritik-Reformansätze*, WEED, terre des hommes, Bonn, April 1999.

3 Commission of the European Communities, *Progress Reports on Gender 1997/1998*, Brussels, 1998/1999.

4 Commission of the European Communities, Document sur les questions 'Genre et Education', Internal Document, Brussels, 1999.

5 Commission des Communautés Européennes, *Communication de la Commission au Conseil et au Parlement Européen sur La Complémentarité des politiques de la Communauté et des états membres dans le Domaine de la Coopération au Développment*, Bruxelles, Com(1999)218 final, 6/5/1999.

6 Eurostep, *Eurostep Dossier on CAP & Coherence. Coherence in EU Policies towards Developing Countries*, Brussels, The Hague, April 1999. Letter from the European Commission to the author, 30/7/1999 JDPD(99).

7 Council of the European Union, Presidency Conclusions, Berlin European Council , 24 and 25 March 1999.

8 The interim agreement and the global agreement are essentially the same. The global agreement will replace the 'interim agreement' when it has been ratified. See: Council of European Union, Council Decision concerning the conclusion of the Interim Agreement on trade and trade-related matters between the European Community, of the one part, and the United Mexican States, of the other part, *Official Journal of the European Communities*, No C 356/97; Council of European Union, Council Decision concerning the conclusion of the Economic Partnership, Political Coordination and Cooperation Agreement between the European Community, of the one part, and the United Mexican States, of the other part, *Official Journal of the European Communities*, No C 350/97. See also: Declaracion Conjunta, Position Paper from the Mexican NGOs; CIFCA, The Mexico-EU Trade Agreement, Background Information, May 1999.

9 Germany expressed this with the ratification, Belgium has not yet ratified the agreement.

10 European Parliament, *Recommendation on the proposal for a council Decision concerning the conclusion of the Economic Partnership, Political Co-ordination and Co-operation Agreement between the European Community and its Member States, on the one part, and the United Mexican States, on the other part*, Committee on external Economic Relations (Rapporteur: Ana Miranda de Lage), DOC_EN\RR\377\377118 PE 230.532/fin.

11 Ciudadan@s de Mexico frente a la union europea, May 1999 *Declaration*, The Free Trade Agreement between Mexico and the European Union: For Transnationals, Everything. For the People, Rhetoric.

12 Under pressure of Mexican NGOs, it was negotiated that in Mexico the results of the negotiations of the trade agreement must be submitted by the President to the Senate of the Republic.

13 In fiscal year 1993/94 customs revenue accounted for 46% of the entire government revenue. In: European Parliament, 1997, ibid, p4.

14 In fiscal year 1994/95. National Assembly of the Republic of Namibia, 1996, ibid, p12.

15 Department of Trade and Industry, Trade, Development and Cooperation Agreement. *A briefing document by the Department of Trade and Industry on the conclusions of the agreement*, Cape Town, 25 March 1999.

16 Brussels, 16/3/99.

17 The compromise was signed by previous EU Commissioner of Development Mr. Pinheiro and SA Minister of Trade, Mr. Erwin.

18 Keet, D, The implications of a reciprocal free trade agreement with the EU in relation to regional integration and development in Southern Africa. *Presentation* to the International Hearing and Workshop on the Implications of the EU's Proposed Alternatives to the Lomé Convention – Königswinter, 23–25 April 1999. Greenidge, What trade agreements between the EU and the ACP would be most desirable in view of the conclusion of the SA-EU Free-Trade Agreement, Paper for a Seminar on the conclusion of the EU-SA Free Trade Agreement organised by Eurostep, Hotel Dorint, Brussels, 5 May, 1999.

19 The European Commission commissioned impact studies to identify the possible consequences of REPAs for ACP regions, which all came to this conclusion. IDS, *Study of the Economic Impact of Introducing Reciprocity into the Trade Relations between the EU and CARICOM/Dominican Republic*, Final Report, Sussex, September 1998; Imani Development, *Study on the Impact of Introducing Reciprocity into the Trade Relations between the EU and the SADC Region*, Final Report, Mauritius, September 1998; Groupe Planistat, *Etude de l'Impact Economique sur l'UDEAC-CEMAC de l'Introduction de la Réciprocité dans les Relations Commerciales UE-ACP*, Final Report, Bruxelles, 1998; ECDPM, The EC's Impact Studies on Regional Economic Partnership Agreements, *Lomé Negotiating Brief*, Maastricht, February 1999; McQueen, M, *The Impact Studies on the Effects of REPAs between the ACP and the EU*, University of Reading, March 1999; Laryea, G., Comparison of REPA Impact Studies, Eurostep, January 1999.

20 Stevens, et al, *Levelling the field. Will CAP reform provide a fair deal for developing countries?* Discussion Paper, CIIR, 1998.

21 Commission of the European Communities, Trade and Development in the new Round: Proposals for an EU comprehensive policy approach, non-paper, 4 May 1999. See also: Commission of the European Communities, *Discussion Paper on Trade and Development in the new WTO Round*, DG1, Brussels, 26 May 1999, I.G.1/(99). Clearly, these Commission proposals have not been approved by the member states. The European Council reaffirmed the importance it attaches to a new WTO Round of trade negotiations which would, among others, include sectors and issues of '*particular interest to developing countries*'. General Affairs Council, 2192nd Council meeting, Luxembourg 21–22 June 1999, 9008/99 (presse 198), Provisional version.

22 Letter Philip Lowe, Director General of DG 8, to Eurostep. June 1999.

23 Council of the European Union, Council Decision of 6 July 1998 concerning exceptional assistance for the heavily indebted ACP countries, *Official Journal of the European Communities*, L198, 15/07/1998, p40–41.

24 For instance, in Germany cuts of 500 million ECU have been announced, and in the Netherlands the Balkans has been incorporated into the list of principal aid beneficiaries.

25 German Presidency of the European Union, First Substantive Session of the Preparatory Committee for the Special Session of the General Assembly on the Implementation of the Outcome of the World Summit for Social Development and Further Initiatives. Agenda item 4: Further Action and Initiatives to Implement the Commitments made at the World Summit on Social Development. *Suggestions for Further actions and Initiatives by the European Union*, New York, May 19, 1999.

26 Programme for the Countries of the former-USSR.

27 Under the Amsterdam Treaty the Commission President has responsibility for determining the political direction of the Commission as a whole. He has greater powers than his predecessors to allocate portfolios to members of the Commission and to reassign their duties during their term of office.

28 Both are new Commissioners and have headed the bilateral aid departments of their respective countries.

29 Commission Européenne, Compte de Gestion et Bilan Financier, Afférents aux Opérations du budget de l'exercice 1997, Volume 1 (section III, Commission), SEC (98) 519, Bruxelles, 1998; Commission Européenne, Compte de Gestion et Bilan Financier, Afférents aux Opérations du budget de l'exercice 1998, Volume 1 (Section III – Commission), SEC (99) 412, Bruxelles, 1999. European Commission, *InfoFinance* 1998. This table does not include destination of other budget lines, some of which are relatively large, such as food aid, humanitarian assistance, NGOs, Southern Africa, etc.

30 These are budget lines which do not have a specific regional designation, for instance, food aid or humanitarian assistance.

31 European Communities, *InfoFinance*, This table does not include destination of other budget lines, some of which are relatively large, such as food aid, humanitarian assistance, NGOs, Southern Africa, etc.

32 These are budget lines which do not have a specific regional designation, for instance, food aid or humanitarian assistance.

33 Letter from the European Commission to the author, 30/7/1999 JDPD(99).

34 European Commission, Rapport annual 1998, dans la domaine de la Santé, du SIDA et de la Population, internal document, 1999.

35 European Commission, Slide Show Presentation of the EU Proposals on Rationalisation of the Instruments and Rolling Programming, DG 8, Task Force ACP-EU Negotiations, Negotiating Group 4 (Financial Cooperation), 11 January 1999, CE/TFN/GCF4/09-OR.

36 Interviews.

37 Expressing a vote in favour by at least eight Member States. Council of European Union, Internal Agreement between the Representatives of Governments of the Member States, meeting within the Council, on the financing and administration of the Community aid under the Second Financial Protocol at the fourth ACP-EC Convention, *Official Journal of the European Communities*, L 156, 29/05/1998, pp0108–0124.

38 Interview.

39 Interview.

40 INRA, *Eurobarometer 50.1, European and Development Aid*. Report written by INRA (Europe) for Directorate General VIII 'Development', managed and organised by Directorate-General X 'Information, Communication, Culture and Audiovisual Media', 8 February 1999.

41 Ibid.

Austria

Karin Küblböck and Michael Obrovsky, Austrian Foundation for Development Research (ÖFSE) in cooperation with ArbeitsGemeinschaft EntwicklungsZusammenarbeit (AGEZ)

Decline halted but policy still piecemeal

After a decline of more than 20%, from 7.7 billion Austrian Shillings (ATS) in 1995 to ATS 5.9 billion in 1996, Austrian total ODA rose slightly to ATS 6.4 billion, or 0.26% of GNP in 1997.

This increase is exclusively due to a rise in contributions to multilateral institutions, namely to the International Development Association (IDA), which is not taking place on a regular yearly basis. Other main ODA components, such as the budget for development programmes and projects, the reported amount of export credits and imputed students costs did not change significantly. In 1997, export credits amounted to ATS 560 million, or 8.7% of total ODA, while imputed student costs, calculated on the basis of university costs for 7774 developing country students, were ATS 590 million (9.2% of ODA). Costs for 'de-facto' refugees from former Yugoslavia coming to Austria were reduced by half and amounted to 7% of total ODA in 1997, compared to 15% the year before. Austria continues to report flows such as the whole amount of export credits, imputed student costs and costs for refugees as ODA, despite repeated criticism by the DAC and other institutions.

Policy coherence needed

The overall coordination of Austrian Development Policy lies with the Department for Development Cooperation (DDC) of the Ministry for Foreign Affairs. However, the only component which the Department is able to influence is the budget for Programme and Project Aid, and – to a certain degree – contributions to multilateral institutions. The budget for Programme and Project Aid, out of which Austria is funding its development projects, accounts for about 15% of total ODA. It has – in nominal terms – remained the same in the last six years, which means a reduction of about 20% in real terms. In 1997, the DDC budget accounted for 0.11% of the total national budget.

DDC has been developing policy guidelines for the Programme and Project Aid. Due to the strict division of powers between Austrian ministries, it is very difficult to achieve a common Austrian development policy that covers other ODA components or other policies related to developing countries, such as trade or investment policy.

A call for greater political importance

The political importance and broad support accorded to development policy deserves improvement in Austria. Parliament is involved only marginally in decision-making concerning the process of designing a development cooperation policy. The only formal parliamentary discussion takes place once in three years, when a report on development cooperation is presented by the Minister for Foreign Affairs. A sub-committee of the Committee for Foreign Affairs deals with development issues. By definition, it cannot take formal decisions, but only make recommendations to the committee.

However, some activities have taken place since 1997 which give reason for hope that Parliament will become more involved in the future:

- Members of the sub-committee report that development-related issues are discussed on a more structured basis.
- Since the end of 1997, the Austrian position in the international financial institutions is presented and discussed on a bi-annual basis.
- A conference on EU-Southern African cooperation was organised in October 1998 in Parliament.
- A one-day meeting was held in Parliament in January 1998 on relations between NGOs and the DDC. The issues and questions raised resulted in a parliamentary request to the responsible minister.

Parliamentarians and NGOs claim that more involvement of Parliament in the design and control of development policy should be formalised in the new development law (to be adopted after the elections in October 1999).

NGOs need capacity for advocacy

Compared to other donor countries, Austrian NGDOs are relatively small. Besides concrete project implementation work, they have to cover many different issues. In order to improve concrete and effective policy and advocacy work (eg concerning WTO, financial flows etc) they need more capacity in those areas.

The Austrian campaign against the Multilateral Agreement on Investment (MAI) at the beginning of 1998 can be seen as a positive example for advocacy work. The campaign was linked to the international anti-MAI movement. In the first half of 1998, advocacy work of NGDOs and other civil society organisations focused on campaigning against this agreement. Events took place all over Austria. NGDOs, environmental and human rights organisations formed a broad and very active platform, calling for an immediate interruption of the negotiations, which contributed to the fact that, in June 1998, the Chancellor declared a 'break for reflection' in the negotiations.

EU Presidency has positive impact

After becoming a member of the European Union, Austria has linked its development policy more to the international mainstream. The Austrian presidency of the EU in the second half of 1998 resulted in a deeper involvement in European development policy and cooperation. For the first time, Austrian officials had to act from a European point of view.

Due to the fact that some EU budget lines concerning social, humanitarian and development issues were not suffi-ciently backed by legislation, a conflict arose between the EU Parliament and the Commission. As a result, those budget lines were frozen. The international network of NGOs helped ensure the release of those funds during the Austrian presidency.

The Austrian EU-platform of NGOs took the opportu-nity of the presidency to organise several international events, including a conference on enlargement of the EU and the role of NGDOs and a conference dealing with the future of the Lomé conventions.

Development cooperation policy more focused

Until some years ago, development cooperation policy of the DDC was mainly influenced by NGOs and their selection of cooperation countries and projects. The selection of official priority countries, the ongoing design of official country and sector programmes, and the establishment of regional offices has introduced a significant change and has led to a more focused cooperation policy. Priority countries have received around 60% of the total DDC budget since 1995.

During the EU presidency, the Austrian regional offices were also in charge of the coordination of the EU policy in the respective countries. Officials report that this has improved cooperation with other donors.

The existence of regional offices has also enhanced official bilateral relations. Improved contacts with the local authorities in recipient countries means that aid can be channelled directly with more efficiency and this has led to an increase in direct flows from the DDC budget to public institutions in developing countries. The percentage of direct flows in the DDC budget rose tenfold, from 1.4% in 1994 to 14% in 1997. It is a declared aim of DDC to further increase direct flows to 25% of its budget. Since joining the EU, Austria has been adapting its aid policy to the international mainstream. Increasing the proportion of direct aid is a response to DAC recommendations but it also reduces the administrative burden on Austria, because it enables larger amounts of money to be disbursed more quickly..

In this context, DDC has stated its intention to increase contributions to national sector development programmes. Up to now, contributions have only been made for programmes in Uganda; other priority countries will follow.

Role of civil society unclear

Austrian NGOs are concerned that the increase of direct flows will reduce the involvement of local civil society in the design and implementation of development projects. NGOs are further concerned that the role and competencies of the regional offices are not clearly defined, and that existing Terms of Reference tend to be too broad, which leaves much space for individual interpretation. Moreover, some NGOs deplore that their role and involvement in this process is not clear – even if officials stress the importance of their know-how in the process of designing country programmes.

The strength of NGO reaction reflects the fact that they see themselves both as partners of civil society in the South and representatives of southern civil society in the North. They argue that they can work with civil society organisa-tions in cases where the Austrian government might not be willing to cooperate with a southern government, and that they are well placed to work with disadvantaged or excluded groups (for example in Guatemala). Of course, NGOs are

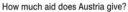

Austria

Percentage of national income spent on aid: a 30-year picture

How much aid does Austria give?

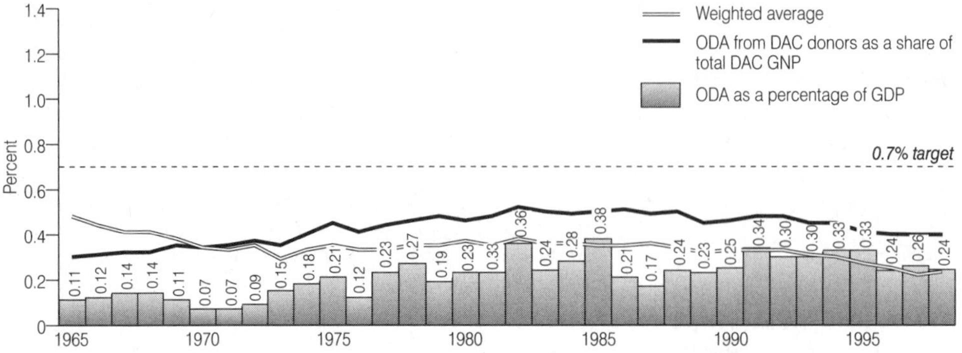

Weighted average
ODA from DAC donors as a share of total DAC GNP
ODA as a percentage of GDP
0.7% target
Percent
1.4
1.2
1.0
0.8
0.6
0.4
0.2
0
1965
1970
1975
1980
1985
1990
1995
0.11 0.12 0.14 0.14 0.11 0.07 0.07 0.09 0.15 0.18 0.21 0.12 0.23 0.27 0.19 0.23 0.33 0.36 0.24 0.28 0.38 0.21 0.17 0.24 0.23 0.25 0.34 0.30 0.30 0.33 0.33 0.24 0.26 0.24

Where is Austrian aid spent?

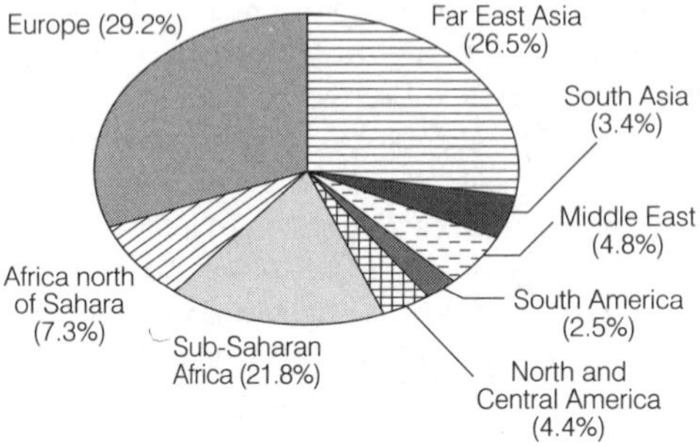

Europe (29.2%)
Far East Asia (26.5%)
South Asia (3.4%)
Middle East (4.8%)
South America (2.5%)
North and Central America (4.4%)
Sub-Saharan Africa (21.8%)
Africa north of Sahara (7.3%)

How much Austrian aid is spent through multilateral organisations?

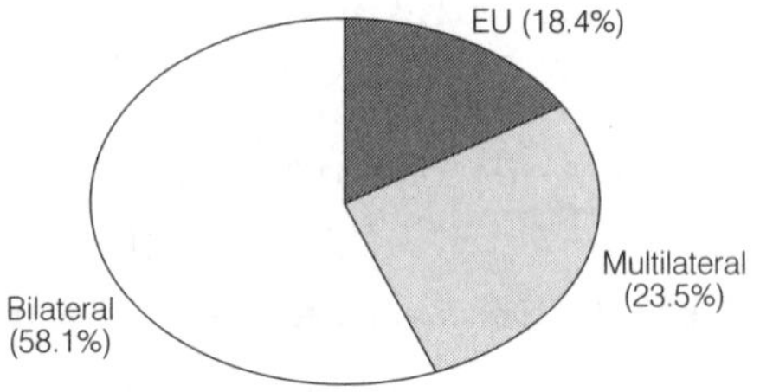

EU (18.4%)
Multilateral (23.5%)
Bilateral (58.1%)

What is Austrian aid spent on?

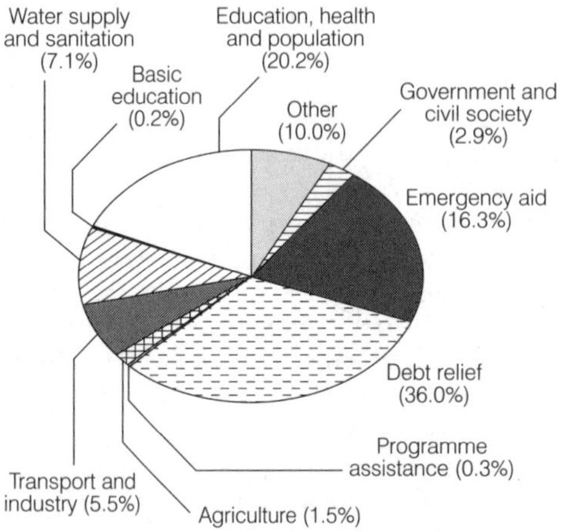

Water supply and sanitation (7.1%)
Basic education (0.2%)
Education, health and population (20.2%)
Other (10.0%)
Government and civil society (2.9%)
Emergency aid (16.3%)
Debt relief (36.0%)
Programme assistance (0.3%)
Agriculture (1.5%)
Transport and industry (5.5%)

For notes on data and sources see page 286

How much Austrian aid goes to the poorest countries?

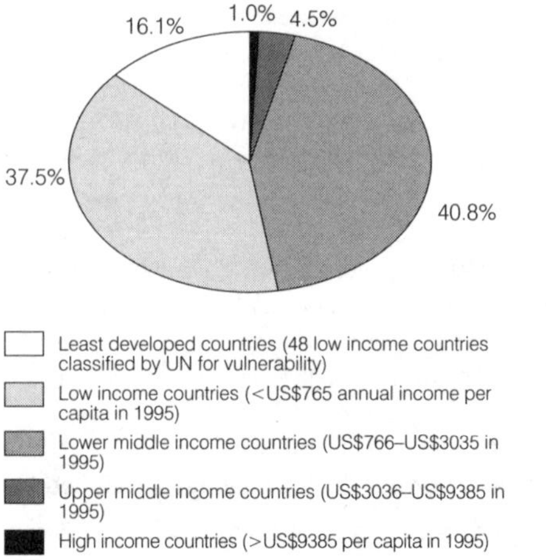

16.1%
1.0%
4.5%
37.5%
40.8%
Least developed countries (48 low income countries classified by UN for vulnerability)
Low income countries (<US$765 annual income per capita in 1995)
Lower middle income countries (US$766–US$3035 in 1995)
Upper middle income countries (US$3036–US$9385 in 1995)
High income countries (>US$9385 per capita in 1995)

Austria

Box 16 Austrian aid at a glance

How much aid does Austria give?

Austria gave	US$506m, 6,262 million Austrian Schillings in 1998
that was	0.24% of GNP
and	0.48% of total government expenditure
which meant	US$63 or 776 Austrian Schillings per capita for 1998

Is it going up or down?

In 1998 Austrian aid	fell by $21m, a drop of 3.7% in real terms over 1997
Austria was	less generous in 1998, dropping from 0.26% of GNP to 0.24%
The outlook is	poor. There have been few mentions of the 0.7% target and aid continues to fall but there is some speculation that the situation will change for the better.

How does Austria compare with the other 20 donors?

Austria ranks	16 out of 21 for its volume of aid
It is	19 out of 21 in the generosity league
It gives	53.6% of its aid to low income countries, a lower proportion than 13 other donors
Private flows	amounted to $985m, 1.87 times ODA
Total flows	to developing countries were 0.8% of GNP and rank 12 out of 21 in the DAC

What proportion of bilateral aid goes to basic education and basic health?

Austria committed	0.7% of bilateral ODA to basic education, 0.9% to basic health and 0% to population and reproductive health

How important are commercial interests in aid?

Austria reported that	39.4% of its bilateral aid commitments were tied to the purchase of goods and services from Austria

---

also anxious to defend their role in development policy because of their reliance (apart from church-linked organisations) on government funding.

Legal framework under review

The legal basis for Austrian development cooperation is a law from the year 1974 that needs urgent revision. Discussions about a new development cooperation law have been going on for years. An initiative has now been taken by the government that experts hope will lead to a reformulation of the law.

At present, neither income tax deductions nor fiscal incentives for the private sector are provided for charitable donations. Recently, the discussion about introducing a provision for such deductions has been launched again and is taking place among different public and private institutions.

Overview of policy commitments

Poverty guidelines awaited

A study was presented to serve as a basis for guidelines for policy decisions concerning poverty eradication. Official criteria and policy guidelines are still to be developed on this basis.

These criteria will apply only to the DDC budget. NGOs are not yet in a position to comment on whether this initiative might improve the quality of poverty alleviation programmes as the study has not be published.

Gender equality criteria set

Since 1997, the gender equality dimension is more systematically included in the design of programmes and projects. There is an explicit recognition of the need for a gender-

Austria

oriented development policy that will help overcome structural, gender-specific discrimination. A series of criteria has been developed for assigning gender markers in the DAC statistics.

Local capacity building enhanced

Concerning the objective of local capacity building, statistics show an increase of flows and commitments to the sector 'Government and civil society' – especially to the subsectors 'legal and judicial development' and 'government administration', which leads to the assumption that enhanced efforts are undertaken in these sectors.

Environment funds dry up

After the UNCED conference in Rio in 1992, a budget of ATS 200 million was assigned for environmental projects. These funds have been spent, largely on tropical rainforest projects, and no replenishment of this budget is planned.

Every project that is considered to have a potential impact on the environment is supposed to be submitted to an environmental impact assessment, including socio-ecological aspects by a consultant company in Austria. Experts consider the quality of those assessments as satisfactory

Aid still tightly tied

A closer look at flows reported as ODA shows that only a very small part could be untied in practice. Flows such as export credits, imputed student costs, or costs for refugees in Austria are tied by definition. The only significant component which could be partly untied would be the DDC budget. This is favoured neither by the Austrian government nor by the NGOs.

The development administration believes that the low status of development cooperation, both in terms of the national policy environment and public support, would be further diminished if projects funded by Austrian public money were implemented by foreign companies.

Austrian NGOs often help southern partner organisations to prepare project proposals for government funding. They are concerned that untying of funds would require a greater capacity for project formulation by local institutions and that this would exclude many grassroots groups from receiving funds.

Little movement on debt reduction

Austria supports the HIPC initiative and underlines the importance of a concerted effort of all multilateral creditors to help reduce indebtedness. So far, Austria has not

contributed to the HIPC trust fund but intends to do so in the foreseeable future.

Austria also acknowledges the need for bilateral debt reduction, but holds that sufficient reduction is already offered through the Paris Club.

Importance of basic education recognised

In the past, DDC's emphasis has been on vocational training, academic vocationally-oriented education (Foreign Study Promotion Programmes) and training in science and technology. The recently adopted Education Sector Policy now includes basic education – apart from the earlier mentioned educational levels – as one of the main areas of work, thus recognising its importance.

Within the measures undertaken, priority is given to institutional and capacity building activities in the different levels of education, with the aim of supporting the restructuring and reform of education systems. To increase the sustainability of educational cooperation activities, guidelines have been included in the Education Sector Policy. Projects and programmes have to:

- Contribute to the development and strengthening of a partner's problem-solving capacity;
- Have a model character for other activities or measures and;
- Contain multiplier effects for other development processes.

In priority countries, DDC supports basic education in cooperation with local government institutions, as well as with NGOs, in the framework of integrated sector programmes which have been developed in collaboration with local partners (eg in Cape Verde).

So far, assistance in the field of basic education is targeted at primary education and on out-of-school activities, including basic vocational training, literacy and skills development projects. Activities range from the support of education sector programmes, new teaching methods, curriculum development, training of teachers and educational planners to the development of educational statistic systems and institutional structures. The gender equality aspect is included in most of the basic education activities.

In order to get a full quantitative and qualitative recording and description of all educational activities and especially of basic education activities, DDC has started to work on the improvement of the collection of data of Austrian educational projects and programmes. This will improve the monitoring and evaluation of those activities.

Belgium

Melanie Schellens, Nationaal Centrum voor Ontwikkelingssamenwerking (NCOS)

Prospects for spending and performance improve

The continuing decrease in development aid from Belgium is likely to have been arrested since 1998. New structures should enable the administration to perform better. This in itself improves the quality of development spending – within the existing budget – but it also takes the wind out of the sails of everyone opposing budget increases on the grounds that 'the administration is not able to disburse the committed resources properly'.

The Reality of Aid 1998/1999 mentioned these new structures for Belgian development cooperation. One element is the construction of a more or less autonomous agency (Belgian Technical Cooperation or BTC), responsible for the execution of bilateral direct programmes and projects. The second is the redesign of the administration. In future it will be responsible only for policy preparation and evaluation, and will be integrated within the Department of Foreign Affairs, as 'Directorate-General for International Cooperation' (DGIS). Last but not least, the conversion of the general policy paper into a law on international cooperation has been approved by Parliament, giving more continuity and juridical backing to at least that part of development cooperation managed by DGIS (about 70% of total ODA). Implementation of these new structures started in the spring of 1999 and should reach 'cruising speed' by the end of the year.

The combination of a restructured and better performing aid administration, increased budgetary space and increased ODA expenditure by other departments (particulary on debt cancellation) will increase the *quantity* of aid, although it remains to be seen to what extent the increase in volume will lead to a substantial increase in the proportion of GNP. The new government programme, introduced following the elections in June 1999, promises a substantial increase of the budget from 2000 and states that the government will strive again for the 0.7% target.

The growing share, included in the ODA figure, of non-ODA debt cancellation remains a concern. This amounted to more than 11% (3.7 billion Belgian Francs (BeF)) of total ODA in 1998. This (relative) loss of income does not represent a real expenditure of new money; its effects are just added to the DAC statistics. It is counted as part of ODA at its nominal value. But the *actual* value of the debts (and thus the real loss) is considerably lower (on secondary markets, claims value on average about 25% of their nominal value), because the international financial markets do not expect (full) repayment. The debt cancellation is, of course, relevant for the countries concerned, but it artificially inflates ODA figure, at no cost to the donor.

From statements to practice

In the 1997 general policy paper for development cooperation('Kleur Bekennen', 'Showing our Colours', described in *The Reality of Aid* 1997/98)), poverty eradication was conceived as the struggle against the growing gap between rich and poor in society – worldwide as well as within countries. Belgian development cooperation is, therefore, described as cooperation for human development through the eradication of 'physical' poverty. This will be pursued with respect for principles of sustainable development, human rights and genuine partnership.

Elaborating strategies for change

These general principles are being elaborated by the aid administration (BADC[1]) in strategy papers for each sector (education, health, agriculture and food security, basic infrastructure, 'societal consolidation' and conflict prevention), for each cross-cutting theme (gender equality, social economy, ecological sustainability) and for each of the 25 'concentration countries'. Some of these strategy papers have been published, some are waiting for approval by the Minister of Development Cooperation and others are still in preparation.

Belgium

Percentage of national income spent on aid: a 30-year picture

How much aid does Belgium give?

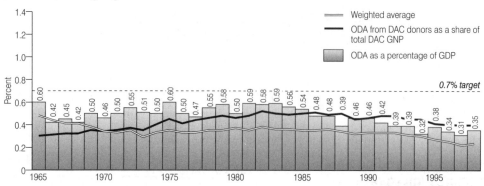

Legend:
- Weighted average
- ODA from DAC donors as a share of total DAC GNP
- ODA as a percentage of GDP

0.7% target

Bar values (1965–): 0.60, 0.42, 0.45, 0.42, 0.50, 0.46, 0.50, 0.55, 0.51, 0.50, 0.60, 0.50, 0.47, 0.55, 0.58, 0.50, 0.59, 0.58, 0.59, 0.56, 0.54, 0.48, 0.48, 0.39, 0.46, 0.46, 0.42, 0.39, 0.39, 0.32, 0.38, 0.34, 0.31, 0.35

Where is Belgian aid spent?

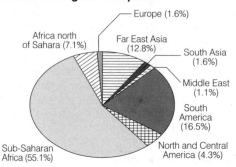

- Europe (1.6%)
- Africa north of Sahara (7.1%)
- Far East Asia (12.8%)
- South Asia (1.6%)
- Middle East (1.1%)
- South America (16.5%)
- North and Central America (4.3%)
- Sub-Saharan Africa (55.1%)

How much Belgian aid is spent through multilateral organisations?

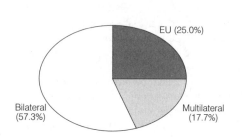

- EU (25.0%)
- Bilateral (57.3%)
- Multilateral (17.7%)

What is Belgian aid spent on?

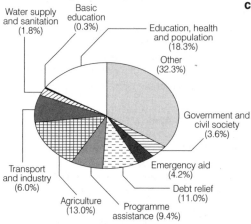

- Water supply and sanitation (1.8%)
- Basic education (0.3%)
- Education, health and population (18.3%)
- Other (32.3%)
- Government and civil society (3.6%)
- Emergency aid (4.2%)
- Debt relief (11.0%)
- Programme assistance (9.4%)
- Agriculture (13.0%)
- Transport and industry (6.0%)

For notes on data and sources see page 286

How much Belgian aid goes to the poorest countries?

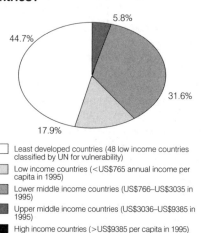

- 5.8%
- 44.7%
- 31.6%
- 17.9%

- ☐ Least developed countries (48 low income countries classified by UN for vulnerability)
- Low income countries (<US$765 annual income per capita in 1995)
- Lower middle income countries (US$766–US$3035 in 1995)
- Upper middle income countries (US$3036–US$9385 in 1995)
- ■ High income countries (>US$9385 per capita in 1995)

Belgium

Box 17 Belgian aid at a glance

How much aid does Belgium give?

Belgium gave	US$878m, 31,869 million Belgian Francs in 1998
that was	0.35% of GNP
and	0.69% of total government expenditure
which meant	US$86 or 3,134 Belgian Francs per capita for 1998

Is it going up or down?

In 1998 Belgian aid	rose by US$114m, a rise of 14.6% in real terms over 1997
Belgium was	more generous in 1998, rising from 0.31% GNP to 0.35%
The outlook is	improving, with 1998 appearing to be a turning point for Belgian aid. Restructuring of the aid administration and increased budgets indicate an overall increase in the quantity of ODA

How does Belgium compare with the other 20 donors?

Belgium ranks	15 out of 21 for its volume of aid
It is	7 out of 21 in the generosity league
It gives	62.6% of its aid to low income countries, a lower proportion than 11 other donors
Private flows	were negative. A net $12 237 million came into Belgium from developing countries.
Total flows	More money came to Belgium from developing countries than Belgium gave in aid and private investment. Flows from developing countries amounted to 4.66% of GNP, more than any other DAC country

What proportion of bilateral aid goes to basic education and basic health?

Belgium committed	0.5% of bilateral ODA to basic education, 5.5% to basic health and 0.2% to population and reproductive health

How important are commercial interests in aid?

Belgium reported that	29.7% of its bilateral aid commitments were tied to the purchase of goods and services from Belgium

This process, although in an 'experimental' phase, is an important element for a new development cooperation policy, for it forces people to think strategically, clearly and, ideally, more operationally. The administration provided for rigorous consultation within the administration and its field representatives. A problem, however, is that until now there has been little external communication on the papers. Only after final review and endorsement by the Minister, is there some possibility for debate on the sectoral papers – in Parliament as well as in the Commisson on Women and Development, and in the Federal Council for Sustainable Development (where a delegation of development NGOs has a seat). Strategic *country* notes are being sent to Parliament but are not conceived as public documents. The degree of external consultation during the drafting of the papers seems to depend mainly on the individual goodwill and 'openheartedness' of the writers.

Relevant people within the receiving country are supposed to be consulted in the process of writing the country strategy paper, which is a task for the Belgian representative for development cooperation ('attaché') in the concerned country. The paper does not require approval by the authorities of the country concerned but, as it is one of the basic elements of the 'indicative programme' for the country, there should be at least some informal agreement on the basic options. The indicative programme itself is

Belgium

based not only on the strategy paper, but also on national plans and project proposals from the governments of the country concerned. This is a more formal description, to be negotiated with the authorities of the country concerned. The new law on international cooperation foresees an evaluation and adjustment of the strategy papers after four years.

Evaluation improving despite constraints

Another promising element for the improvement of Belgian development cooperation is the expansion of evaluation activities. To quote a BADC employee: 'in the last two years we have made more evaluations than in the past ten years together'. This valuable work is impeded by severe financial control procedures which question the very importance of evaluations, but nevertheless, enormous progress is being made.

There are no overall poverty assessment studies undertaken for the whole or for broader parts of Belgian development cooperation. But within specific projects and programmes, a logical framework ('Process Integrated Management') includes the evaluation of the results in relation to a whole range of parameters, including poverty reduction. The yearly report of the evaluation service[2] brings most of these evaluations together in an interesting overview. The evaluation and policy department of BADC furthermore produced a handbook to make clear what is expected of employees involved in evaluation studies.

There are still difficulties on the level of executing the evaluations, but – in line with the observations made in the DAC peer review[3] – the concerns are even stronger on the level of feedback. To quote officials at the evaluation unit again, it is a question of creating a 'culture of evaluation'. This means breaking walls between units, breaking with traditionally rigid control mechanisms and fear of being sanctioned, getting people to think of evaluation as a learning process and opening issues for debate. On the other hand, several NGOs mention still (very) rigid administrative control mechanisms countering this 'new culture'.

The evaluation unit in the recent past was an 'empty box'. It now employs four people – some of them with temporary contracts. It is part of a group of about ten staff members of the evaluation and policy department. The unit is also involved in DAC working groups elaborating further criteria and specific targets on issues like gender equality and environment. Under the new Directorate-General, the size of the evaluation unit would be doubled.

Commitment to concentration

The concentration policy, announced in the general policy

paper, is backed by a legal guarantee that the administation can continue its concentration efforts. A new minister cannot change this policy as easily as has happened in the past.

Several previous ministers of development cooperation announced a stronger concentration policy but were unable to realise it – and in fact added other countries to the lists of their predecessors. The new law describes the criteria for the geographical concentration on 25 countries and regions – a separate Royal Decree specifies those countries. The concentration policy is threefold: it focuses on a smaller number of countries, a limited number of sectors and a limited number of multilateral institutions.

The countries are:

- In sub-Sahara Africa: Burkina Faso, Burundi, Congo (Kinshasa), Rwanda, Benin, Ivory Coast, Mali, Niger, Uganda, Kenya, Ethiopia, Tanzania, South Africa, Angola and, separately, the South African Development Coordination (SADC) region.
- In Northern Africa and the Middle East: Morocco, Tunisia and Palestine.
- In Asia: Philippines, Cambodia, Laos and Vietnam.
- In Latin America: Bolivia, Ecuador and Peru.

Given the modest quantity of Belgian development cooperation, this is still a long list. Several of these 'partner countries' still receive less than BeF 200 million (approximately US$5.5 million) a year. And in 1998, the group of 'partner countries' only received roughly 55% of total BADC bilateral expenditure (note that the concentration policy applies only for bilateral direct relations and to some of the indirect actors, like universities. It does not apply explicitly to NGOs). This means that the administration still has a long way to go to realise the concentration policy.

Effective implementation a long way off

On the level of conceptualisation, strategic thinking and elaborating evaluation efforts, Belgian development cooperaton is making serious efforts to catch up with international standards. On the level of implementation, however, there remains a long way to go.

By way of illustration, NCOS is making a country study of the Belgian support for the Philippines Land Reform Programme. Summarising the preliminary conclusions (at the risk of doing injustice to the much richer and more balanced study) we can state that Belgian cooperation in the programme still relies heavily on expensive Belgian expertise and has difficulties in involving local beneficiaries in planning and decision making. This remains centralised in

Brussels offices and not in the field. Procedures formulated in Brussels headquarters are judged too complicated and too rigid to apply in a flexible way in the field. With regard to evaluations, base line studies have been designed, but progress is only measured at quite general levels, not at household level.

The 1998 report on the evaluation service is keen on the principles of local participation and capacity building, especially for women. The report points to problems regarding these aspects in various projects and programmes – governmental as well as non-governmental – but it also reports on positive developments, for instance in the projects of the Belgian Survival Fund – an initiative specifically aimed at poverty reduction.

The report also comments on the lack of coordination between the executing partners. Although the technical execution of projects is in general well done, the report mentions a lack of integration of individual projects within the policy and within the dynamics of the regional and national authorities. Within the process of each evaluation, specific recommendations are made to remedy these problems. The report mentions improvements regarding the follow-up of the evaluation process, but states that this still remains a weak point. Recommendations to improve this feedback and follow-up process include: simplified administrative procedures; a systematic application of the project methodology (process-integrated management (PRIMA)); and structures for better communication.

30–40% of ODA escapes legislation

It should be clear that several improvements and promising evolutions are on their way for the Ministry of Development Cooperation. But a main concern for development organisations remains the limited scope of this ministry, which handles only 60 to 70% of total ODA expenditure, and which has very little influence on other measures which are likely to have an impact on developing countries.

A few examples illustrate this.

The new law on international cooperation only covers the ODA part of the Ministry of Development Cooperation. This means, for example, that the geographical and sectoral concentration policy does not apply to the system of ODA loans and export credits, nor to the relief of non-ODA debts.

Neither does the untying of aid, proclaimed by the Minister of Development Cooperation, apply to the other parts of ODA. It was not possible, in fact, to formulate the principle of untying of aid as an article in the new law, so the practice of untying will be limited to the part of ODA administered by the development administration. The new

government programme (July 1999) however, makes a strong statement in favour of the untying of aid.

The Interdepartmental Working Group on Development Cooperation, bringing together several relevant ministries, in order to bring more coherence in all aspects of international cooperation, has not shown much initiative. It has been activated and challenged on various occasions by joint NGO campaigns but it has not had any independent momentum.

Until now, the evaluation efforts have covered only BADC programmes. In the new structures, however, evaluations can be expanded to other parts of ODA such as concessional loans.

Basic Education

Priorities well established...

Since 1996, the officially stated main priorities of the educational sector in Belgian governmental development cooperation are:

- Primary education and literacy (basic education in its strict sense).
- Vocational and technical education.
- Teacher training and institution building, including explicit attention to access for women and girls in these fields.

In the past five years, the sector has been shifting from a strong emphasis on secondary and higher education to basic education and vocational and technical education. This shift has been made already on the conceptual level, in general policy papers and statements. In general terms and concepts, the education sector relies on Jomtien definitions of basic learning, pre-school education, primary school, literacy, basic knowledge and skills for better living, without age limits.

Education programmes are linked to the broader poverty alleviation programme, at least at the conceptual level. As an illustration, the Belgian educational programme in the Philippines endorses the Philippine Plan of Action: 'basic education as an anti-poverty instrument can provide the skills, attitudes, knowledge and values that people can use to organise themselves for common access to useful information, and a united approach to greater productivity. It can also empower the marginalised and prevent their exploitation and alienation from the development process.'

Belgium

...but practice still shaky

This shift in thinking has now to be disseminated and applied in concrete strategies, programmes and projects.

By mid-1998, specific basic education activities were spread as follows:[4]

- *In Africa*

  Basic education support goes mainly indirectly, via financing of NGO interventions (about 50) and multilateral programmes. Only in Burkina Faso is there a bilateral direct basic education project. Several proposals for Rwanda are still to be put in practice due to the Rwandan government giving priority to other education levels. Primary education support in Burundi is limited to school building and rehabilitation, as an element of an integrated rural development programme.

- Central and South America:

  Support for basic education runs exclusively through the subvention of indirect actors. There is only one governmental vocational education project in the whole region.

- Asia

  Educational support applies mainly through the financing of indirect actors (eg NGOs in India, with programmes that specifically fit within poverty alleviation programmes, with a strong emphasis on women and girls).

  The only governmental support for basic education is in the Philippines and in Vietnam (primary school teacher training). Governmental programmes for vocational and technical education run in Indonesia, Philippines and Thailand.

  Basic education aspects of larger integrated programmes, for example in the Survival Fund, are not reported here, although they can be substantial. The official codification of BADC does not foresee a code for non-formal education; other education acitivies are hidden in multi-sectoral programmes such as integrated rural development, or in 'trans-sectoral themes' such as gender equality or environment.

  Clearly, there are not many explicit cases yet to analyse concrete implementation. Where basic education is a stated priority for the receiving country, it seems easier to organise a larger consultation of people concerned, in order to elaborate a programme. In the

case of the Philippines, the identification mission consisted in conversations with external experts as well as meetings at grassroots level. The more concrete project preparation was mainly done by Belgian consultancy services and Belgian experts, but for the final implementation the programme will rely on local personnel. Belgian input includes organisational support and the provision of materials (books, rehabilitation of buildings, etc). One can ask why the option was for aid in kind, instead of budget support. Was it due to a lack of understanding the system of budget support, or a lack of trust in the receiving partners, or both?

Belgium is not (yet) involved in any sectoral approach to education, but this step is being prepared with, among other things, an informative paper on 'Sectorial Education Support', published for the people concerned within the administration.

Capacity still a constraint

Education and basic education activities should be integrated where possible in national education programmes and – at best – in overall social or poverty reduction programmes of the receiving country. Here and there, this option is becoming visible in practice: eg the education activities within the Belgian support programme for Philippines Land Reform, or the educational support in Vietnam. Nevertheless, the 'state of affairs paper' already mentioned, points to the risks (citing former Dutch minister of development cooperation Jan Pronk) of NGOs (and by extension also donor governments) taking on too many responsibilities and competences in a domain that fundamentally belongs to the national government.

As far as bilateral direct aid is concerned, an agreement from government to government is needed. And in some cases (Rwanda was cited as just one of the examples), the receiving country's authorities do not endorse the basic education emphasis. This is to some degree due to the higher 'prestige' of higher education, but there are strong lobbies for higher education in donor countries as well as receiving countries.

Education programmes in Belgian development cooperation still face capacity problems. In the policy preparation service in 1998, there was only one person with responsibility for education. He was not officially mandated and was working only on a temporary contract. Some larger geographical desks in Brussels and some larger overseas sections can count on education specialists (totalling about seven), but an overall structure is lacking. This makes it diffi-

cult to disseminate the new priorities and strategies to the various geographical desks as well as in relations with the counterparts in receiving countries.On this issue, too, the new structure should be able to bring some improvements as the policy preparation unit, among others will be extended, with at least one education specialist.

Notes

1   BADC: Belgian Administration for Development Cooperation, responsible for about 60 to 70% of total Belgian ODA. The remaining 30 to 40% are being disbursed by the Ministry of Finance and other departments, and cover multilateral aid and debt relief.
2   1998 Annual Report of the evaluation service of BADC (February 1999, in Dutch).
3   OECD/DAC Development cooperation review series no 23, Belgium (1997).
4   BADC, priorities in education policy; a state of affairs paper (August 1998).

Denmark

Bibi Linder, Mellemfolkeligt Samvirke

Sustained support for 1% target

Denmark has donated 1% of its Gross National Income (GNI) to development aid for many years, and it is still the Government's policy to do so. The new EU system of measuring GNI requires an increase in aid volume in absolute terms (of around 10%) from the year 2001, in order to keep to the 1% goal, and it is most likely that the political support for this exists.[1]

Furthermore, Denmark continues giving aid through a special appropriation called the Environment, Peace, and Stability Facility (formerly the Environment and Disaster Relief Facility), which is intended to reach 0.5% of GNI in the year 2002. At the same time, a tendency of diverting aid away from poor countries and towards disaster relief in areas of conflict, such as Kosovo, can be seen.[2]

In 1999, it is planned to divert 590 million Danish Krone (DKK) from development aid to disaster relief in Kosovo. This is around 5% of total aid volume. Out of this, more than half has been diverted from multilateral aid, and one third from bilateral aid.[3] This is part of a Danish practice of using part of the aid budget for humanitarian assistance. In times of specific need for humanitarian aid, development aid is adjusted accordingly. In future, aid for reconstruction of Kosovo is most likely to be taken from the Environment, Peace and Stability Facility.

On the right path to poverty reduction?

Poverty eradication is the major goal of Danish aid. But Danida's approach to reaching the goal is not very specific. This makes it difficult to monitor progress and to ensure that the goal is reached. Both human resource development and activities leading more directly to economic growth are seen as part and parcel of a poverty reduction strategy. There is debate among practitioners and researchers about the best means to attain the goal.

All activities should be related to poverty reduction. Danida seems to believe that as long as it is working in poor regions in a poor country then poor people will benefit, regardless of whether it is supporting human resource development or economic growth.[4] Often, there is no specific analysis to find out whether poor people are actually benefiting as a result of projects. For example, in an infrastructure project, roads may benefit poorer people by enabling them to sell their crops in town. On the other hand roads can enable middlemen to take a larger share of rural incomes.

Researchers find[5] that the starting point for a poverty reduction strategy should be a thorough analysis of poverty in a given area, identifying poor groups, the causes of poverty and the mechanisms sustaining poverty. Such analyses are not required by the Danida Guidelines for Sectoral Programme Support. Furthermore, Danida has developed an indicator system[6] which, according to researchers, is focused on physical outputs and lacks a measurement of changes in poverty.[7]

Sectoral Programme support – where are the poor?

The targeting of aid towards poor people can prove difficult when working at a more general policy level. The intention is to keep a good dialogue with the recipient government, leaving 'ownership' of the process to that government, and at the same time trying to induce major changes in policy.

For example, in the agricultural sector, a real poverty eradication strategy would quite often require land reform. Danida at times seems not to have taken up this challenge, rather aiming to increase agricultural output. Danida argues that this focus on production should be followed up by social policies but there is a great danger that this will not happen and that production-focused interventions will not, therefore, really benefit poor people.[8] However, where change is really initiated by the national government, such as the land reform in Bolivia, following a recognition of the rights of indigenous people, Danida is ready to assist with institutional support, support for people's participation and support to bilingual, inter-cultural education programmes.[9] The programme for the agricultural sector in Zimbabwe is also a good example of sectoral aid targeting poor people and small-scale producers.[10]

...and where are the women?

Not surprisingly, efforts towards women's empowerment and gender equality in aid meet problems in the Sectoral Programme approach, similar to those encountered in targeting poor people as a group. Working at the sectoral level means working with institutions. While this brings opportunities for introducing changes that will influence the development process, Danida quite often works with institutions that are not gender-sensitive, and there is reason to fear that policies on gender equality will not move beyond rhetoric to any major changes.

Promoting the empowerment of women means challenging existing power structures in society. Work needs to be done not only within government institutions, but also with strong links to civil society and women's movements. After all, these are the most important actors in working for political changes towards empowerment of women.[11]

There is no hard evidence that Danida is working in a radical way to empower women, nor that this is its aim. But gender analysis has been recognised as integral to aid and poverty reduction, and there is an ongoing process of development of tools and training for this work. Gender equality is said to be a cross-cutting issue in Danish aid, which should always be addressed.[12]

National ownership – a compromise between aim and practice

The inherent conflict in Sectoral Programme aid is between creating national ownership of the process within the recipient government and, at the same time, assuring that certain donor aims, such as good governance, are met. Danida consistently sends out a large number of Danish experts to work with recipient governments. Their brief is to build capacity and to guarantee that money is spent as planned, that time schedules are met, and targets groups reached. This is done in spite of an intention to send out fewer Danish experts.[13]

Conflicts between Danida as donor and a national government cannot always be solved by compromises. This was seen in Kenya around New Year 1999. The health

sector was the last sector in Kenya where Danida supported the national government directly. After a long period of total dissatisfaction with the national handling of the aid money, Danida decided to almost halve its assistance to the sector and to completely bypass the national level, and deal directly with local level government and NGOs instead.[14]

Given the focus on local ownership, the impact of aid is measured not so much by its quantity, as by its quality, as a strategic intervention in societal development processes, power relations and capacity. The fact that Sector Programme aid is conducted in close cooperation with the government – the ruling élite – can be a major obstacle to ensuring quality. Specific approaches are often required to involve the political opposition in the process and to increase access to power and resources by the target group.[15] In several instances Danida has engaged in a fruitful dialogue with Danish NGOs and has been able to agree upon a strategic division of labour in-country.[16]

Danida has also attempted to strengthen dialogue with recipient countries on its priorities and policies. In 1998, Danida held a meeting in Harare for governments and other players in southern Africa to discuss development issues and regional integration. This is a promising step towards more genuine partnership.

Basic education – an inclusive approach

Danida bases its support for basic education on the Jomtien Education for All Declaration and has not yet published any specific policy papers on the Danida approach to the educational sector. It generally prioritises support to basic education for children in the formal sector but recognises the need for both child and adult education in both formal and informal institutions. In 1998, 10.2% of bilateral aid went to the educational sector and, out of this, 36% went to formal primary education.[17]

Danida believes that basic education cannot be seen in isolation from the rest of the educational system, for instance there has to be access to secondary education after primary or basic education. Danida pays specific attention to the involvement of poor children, girls and children with disabilities in schools, and where Danida cannot reach with official aid through the national government, it sometimes supports the educational work of NGOs.[18]

The educational sector has been chosen as a sector for programme cooperation in only five out of 20 countries and in two of these – Nepal and Eritrea – a Sector Programme Plan has been concluded with the national government. Nepal is a good example of how Sector Programme aid, donor coordination, national capacity build-

Denmark

Percentage of national income spent on aid: a 30-year picture

How much aid does Denmark give?

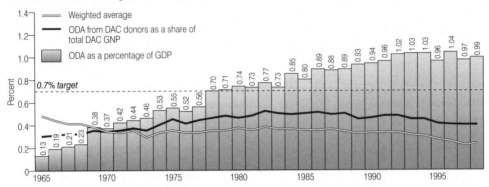

Where is Danish aid spent?

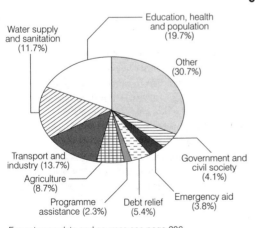

Africa north of Sahara (4.1%)

Europe (0.5%)

Far East Asia (14.2%)

South Asia (15.6%)

Middle East (0.6%)

South America (3.5%)

North and Central America (6.4%)

Sub-Saharan Africa (55.1%)

How much Danish aid is spent through multilateral organisations?

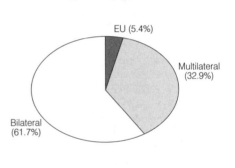

EU (5.4%)

Multilateral (32.9%)

Bilateral (61.7%)

What is Danish aid spent on?

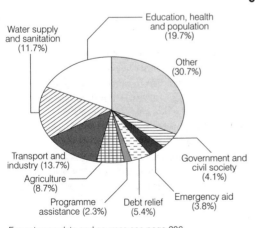

Water supply and sanitation (11.7%)

Education, health and population (19.7%)

Other (30.7%)

Transport and industry (13.7%)

Agriculture (8.7%)

Programme assistance (2.3%)

Debt relief (5.4%)

Emergency aid (3.8%)

Government and civil society (4.1%)

For notes on data and sources see page 286

How much Danish aid goes to the poorest countries?

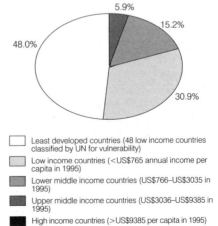

5.9%

15.2%

48.0%

30.9%

☐ Least developed countries (48 low income countries classified by UN for vulnerability)

Low income countries (<US$765 annual income per capita in 1995)

Lower middle income countries (US$766–US$3035 in 1995)

Upper middle income countries (US$3036–US$9385 in 1995)

■ High income countries (>US$9385 per capita in 1995)

Denmark

Box 18 Danish aid at a glance

How much aid does Denmark give?

Denmark gave	US$1,704m, 11,410 million Krone in 1998*
that was	0.99% of GNP*
and	1.78% of total government expenditure
which meant	US$323 or 2,161 Danish Krone per capita for 1998

Is it going up or down?

In 1998 Danish aid	rose by $67m or 265 million Krone in cash terms, a rise of 4.1% in real terms over 1997
Denmark was	more generous in 1998, rising from 0.97% GNP to 0.99%.
The outlook is	good with ODA remaining at around 1% of GNP

How does Denmark compare with the other 20 donors?

Denmark ranks	8 out of 21 for its volume of aid
It is	first out of 21 in the generosity league
It gives	78.9% of its aid to low income countries, a higher proportion than 18 other donors
Private flows	amounted to $147m, 9% of ODA
Total flows	to developing countries were 1.15% of GNP and rank 6 out of 21 in the DAC

What proportion of bilateral aid goes to basic education and basic health?

Denmark committed	0.2% of bilateral ODA to basic education, 1.4% to basic health and 0.3% to population and reproductive health

How important are commercial interests in aid?

Denmark reported that	38.7% of its bilateral aid commitments were tied to the purchase of goods and services from Denmark

* The Danish government reports total ODA as 10,720 million Krone and 1% of GNP

---

ing and national ownership of the process can work together.[19] Danida emphasises quality in education and, therefore, quite often supports development of educational material, teacher training, and educational research.

Moreover, Danida promotes a child-centred education approach, creating skills for life and enabling learners to identify problems and find solutions to them. Methods used in teaching and taught to educators are very focused on this, and on how to teach with reference to well-known daily life situations.

In Zambia, Danida has two experts posted in the Ministry of Education, working on new curricula in education and on teacher training. The approach used is very far from mere literacy and numeracy, and much more in line with efforts to empower and enable learners. Adding to the principles just mentioned, teaching is planned to include dialogue in the classroom and out-of-class sessions. Teacher training is planned and piloted at low-cost rates, with on-the-job training, and with the involvement of parents and communities.

At the multilateral level, Danida supports and gets inspiration from UNESCO in educational efforts. While Danida is pleased to support the broad scope of UNESCO's work, it does emphasise its own priorities, namely inclusive schooling/special needs education and the development of teaching materials.[20] UNESCO received DKK 34.6 million in 1998 – 0.73% of Danish multilateral aid.[21]

Active Multilateralism

Around 44% of Danish aid in 1998 went to multilateral insti-

Denmark

tutions and around half of this to the UN system. It has been decided to use these donations to gain more influence in the multilateral institutions, through a policy called 'Active Multilateralism'. Under this policy, there have been cuts in aid channelled through WHO and FAO, because these organisations did not meet Danish demands. However, according to a leading Danish development researcher, Poul Engberg-Pedersen,[22] Denmark has not gained the influence it hoped for. Engberg-Pedersen suggests that Danida should set aside more human resources for the pursuit of Active Multilateralism and that, pending changes in the UN agencies to meet Danish demands, it should channel a larger proportion of aid funds as bilateral aid.

Self-interest stands in the way of poverty policy

Generally, the Danish government likes to project itself as very development friendly, hosting the World Summit on Social Development in 1995 and being very active in the follow-up to the 1992 UN Conference on Environment and Development (the Rio Earth Summit). There is no doubt that Denmark takes a leading position in terms of development

assistance and environmental protection. Furthermore, a number of major decision-makers in parliament and government do have a vision of a world with a more equal distribution of wealth and a more even development structure, and they see this as important from both a humanitarian and a self-interest point of view.

However, when it comes to international relations on trade, debt and investment, a more coherent policy is needed. Developing countries are still largely neglected in the reform process of the EU Common Agricultural Policy. And Denmark could go further on the issue of debt cancellation for Least Developed Countries. In the preparations for the coming round of the negotiations in the World Trade Organisation (WTO), however, the interests of developing countries and issues such as workers rights and environmental protection have been given considerable attention.

Good facility, bad coordination

The specific Danish appropriation Environment, Peace, and Stability Facility was evaluated in 1998. The facility supports initiatives that foster improvements in environment and

---

Box 19 Danish NGO assistance to the educational sector

Education plays an important role in the activities of Danish development NGOs. Generally, though, the organisations have not developed particular policies on education. Educational activities are integrated into and based on the principles of the various aid programmes as a whole. Generally, the principles include people's participation in development, cooperation with local partners and a focus on poor and suppressed people. However, a more careful look at the educational activities shows that even if a specific policy on education has not been formulated, thought has been given to the role of education in the development process. In addition, ways of using education for empowerment of people have been developed at the concrete level.

The approaches vary. One NGO states directly that 'education and training are central tools in the fight by poor and suppressed groups to gain more influence over their own lives… It is not a goal in itself to offer education. It must be a kind of education that will be able to equip poor and suppressed groups with the language and skills relevant for building up and participating in democratic processes…'[23]

NGOs cooperate with local governments in various ways. One NGO supports local partners in building up bilingual and intercultural education for indigenous people, and in lobbying in order to make the central government take over this responsibility.

Another NGO works with non-formal education, but aims to integrate the learners (adult or child) into the formal school system. One NGO has taken the process a bit further, stating that 'literacy is more than the ability to read and write and practise numeracy. It includes the ability to interpret and understand the environment around oneself and seek alternatives for transforming it'.[24] It has been decided, therefore, that literacy should be integrated in all aspects of the development work undertaken in cooperation with partners. Finally, some NGOs work directly with governments – developing their educational policies, developing new methods, reaching new target groups, or supplementing the existing educational system.

Dealing with education as an issue raises a question central to all kinds of development work undertaken. 'Where, and how, does learning actually take place? What happens in the mind of the pupil when he or she receives information and how is this used afterwards?' All kinds of capacity building and sensitisation work stand and fall on this.[25]

---

stability, and was created as a follow-up to the Rio Conference. It is planned that the amount spent through this facility should reach the level of 0.5% of GNI by the year 2002.

The evaluation is generally positive but highlights a lack of coordination between the two implementing agencies, Danida and Danced (an office in the Ministry of Environment created for this purpose).

The facility has been criticised for mostly supporting middle-income countries and not poor countries. But politically one can hope that cooperating in the environmental sphere with politically strong development countries like Malaysia and India promotes the understanding of environmental concerns among developing countries.

Notes

1 Information, 17 May 1999. The final decision on this will be made when the Finance Act is passed.
2 Information, 2 June, 1999.
3 Information, 30 July, 1999.
4 For example in Uganda Danida supports construction of roads in a number of poor regions, with the emphasis on construction of main (tarred) roads and feeder (dirt) roads (which are expected to reach the rural poor) *and* to use local entrepreneurs in construction of the feeder roads. (Personal communication to the Danish Embassy, Kampala. Refer also to Danish Sector Policies: Transport).
5 For a thorough analysis of problems in the Danida poverty reduction strategy, refer to Engberg-Pedersen, Lars: Danida og de fattige (Danida and the poor) in *Den Ny Verden (The New World)* 1998:4:61-76, Center for Development Research, Denmark.
6 Impact and outcome indicators refers to long-term or medium-term development change, p8. First Guidelines for an Output and Outcome Indicator System, Danida, September 1998.
7 Personal communication to Engberg-Pedersen, Poul.
8 Vilby, Knud: Danida's dilemma – nedsivningsteori eller fattigdomsorientering (The Dilemma of Danida – theory of trickle down or

focus on poverty) in *Den Ny Verden (The New World)* 1998:4:77-90, Center for Development Research, Denmark.
9 *Development Today*, 1998:VIII:12-13:6.
10 Danida Annual Report 1998.
11 Refer to Susanne Wendt (researcher and former WID expert in Danida): Er fattigdom feminin – køn og bistand (Is poverty feminine – gender and aid) in *Den Ny Verden (The New World)* 1998:4:48-60, Center for Development Research, Denmark.
12 Strategy for Danish Development Policy Towards the Year 2000 'A World in Development', 1994.
13 Degnbol-Martinussen, John and Engberg-Pedersen, Poul: Bistand, udvikling eller afvikling. En analyse af internationalt bistandssamarbejde (Aid, Development or De-involvement. An Analysis of International Development Cooperation), Mellemfolkeligt Samvirke, 1999, p322.
14 *Development Today*, 1999:IX:1:1.
15 Ibid.
16 For example on the issues of corruption, Danida works with the Government pushing for good governance and accountability, while a Danish NGO works with NGOs trying to create popular mechanisms for holding Government accountable.
17 Danida Annual Report 1998, p215.
18 Personal communication to the two educational experts in Danida, Poul Erik Rasmussen and Knud Mortensen.
19 All donors involved in the educational sector in Nepal co-operate jointly with the Ministry of Education; they have supported capacity building in the Ministry by urging the Ministry to do research on the educational sector and use this for the production of a national plan for the sector. The donors then fit into this plan. The donors were also able to establish a joint evaluation team for the sector, thereby relieving the Nepal Government from the burden of receiving many different evaluation teams.
20 Personal communication to Knud Mortensen.
21 Danida Annual Report 1998 p220f.
22 Interviewed in *Information*, 17 May 1999.
23 Vision 2012, U-landsorganisationen Ibis 1999 (the Development Organisation Ibis).
24 Policy Paper MS-Zambia, 1996.
25 Personal communication to Johnny Balterzen, Centre for Development Programme of Education.

Finland

Folke Sundman and Mark Waller, Service Centre for Development Cooperation (KePa)

Major developments brighten prospects for aid

Some significant events and decisions have influenced Finnish development cooperation since mid-1998. These are, most notably:

- The Finnish Government issued the statement 'Finland's Policy on Relations with Developing Countries' in October 1998;
- The DAC peer review on Finnish development cooperation was issued in November 1998;
- Parliamentary elections in March 1999 resulted in a new government and a new programme for the next four-year electoral period.

Positive response to policy

The new policy statement (see below on poverty reduction) was generally quite well-received by the NGOs. At the same time, KePa criticised the approach to trade and investment issues for remaining too close to neo-liberal ideas on how the international economy should be developed, and for not recognising the change in attitudes that had already emerged during the second half of 1998.

The critique of the trends of liberalisation and deregulation of the international economy became stronger, partly due to events in (South-East) Asia and Russia, and gradually the debate engaged around ideas for building a counterweight to the free market and new means of steering development to meet social needs. Later in the year, this new trend influenced the political scene, particularly in three areas:

- A growing criticism of economic concepts of the IMF, particularly in connection with the proposal to increase the capital stock of the IMF (requiring substantial commitments from members), but also in terms of the role of the Bretton Woods institutions in general;
- The dead end in the Multilateral Agreement on Investments (MAI) negotiations, a result partly of NGO lobbying and public pressure, but also because of changes in positions of several governments, including the Finnish, which moved from a fairly unreserved positive position towards MAI to a much more critical one (close to the new German position);
- The success of the Jubilee 2000 campaign, making debt a real issue on the political agenda of the big industrialised states as well as developing countries.

In the light of these changes, the policy statement was to some extent outdated by the time it was formally adopted. In it, the structural adjustment programmes of the Bretton Woods institutions are given credit, but no opinion is given on the need to reform these institutions and their policies. Support is given to the proposed MAI, disregarding the shift in the Government's position on this. There is no reference to the need for new forms of regulation of the international economy, which has become a key issue in the debate as has the Tobin tax. The Tobin tax did not make a breakthough in the same sense as the other above issues but in some industrialised countries (Canada, France, Germany – and Finland) it returned to the political debate as one serious example of how the international economy could be regulated in a new way.

The new policy statement also fails to reverse the neglect of gender equality issues in the work of the Department for International Development Cooperation (DIDC), not least in its internal organisation. Mainstreaming these issues remains generally misunderstood and resisted, and by mid-1999 the DIDC still had no one responsible for gender and the situation of women.

Finland

Peer review criticises 'flexibility'

The DAC peer review on Finnish aid emphasised the positive changes and trends in Finnish development cooperation since the previous report in the mid-1990s. The Decision-in-Principle on Finnish aid from 1996 implied an enhancement of the quality and practices of Finnish aid, and the Government has managed to turn the trend in the aid volume from the drastic cuts of the first half of the decade to an absolute, if modest, increase.

Some of the critical findings in the review were in line with what the Advisory Board of the Foreign Ministry on Relations with Developing Countries and KePa have expressed. This is true particularly regarding the new so-called flexibility approach incorporated into the new Finnish strategy.

According to the DAC review: 'The policy challenge with *flexibility* is that it carries the risk of generating a dispersed range of ad hoc activities which cannot be adequately appraised and monitored by the relatively small corps of Finnish aid managers. There may also be a predilection for opportunistic 'visible' projects that carry the Finnish flag, rather than for the kind of joint long-term aid partnerships and programmes that are seen by the international aid community, including the DAC, as the way in which aid-giving can most effectively contribute to development goals and build up capacities in the partner countries. In other words, the long-term development quality of the Finnish programme could be compromised.'

The flexibility approach, and its potential consequences, has remained the key subject in the dialogue between the administration and the NGO community on the content of Finnish bilateral aid.

Development issues on election agenda

From 1995 to 1999, Finland was governed by a so-called 'rainbow coalition', a politically strange animal comprising five parties, led by the Social Democrats and including the conservatives, the centre-right Swedish People's Party, the Greens and the Left Alliance (former communists). The only Green minister in the cabinet had a combined portfolio on environment and development cooperation, a first in Finnish politics.

The Social Democrats lost many seats in the latest elections but remained the biggest group in Parliament. The conservatives were among the main winners, but the new government was formed by the same rainbow coalition. The Greens kept the combined environment and development portfolio, and their chairperson, Ms Satu Hassi, has taken the Green seat in the government.

KePa made a serious effort to get some development and global issues into the public debate before the elections. Three issues were selected: the quality and quantity of Finnish aid; debt and the Tobin tax. These were – obviously – not the major topics of the debate, but they were real issues. The Tobin tax especially became a serious political issue in the debate and the media, as a result of KePa's campaign. NGO sector lobbying and campaigning on Finnish ODA is nowadays coordinated directly by and through KePa. Taking the three examples that KePa put forward for public debate before the elections, one can say that ODA did not become a real issue but remained in the margin. While there is no serious political or public opposition to increased aid, there is widespread indifference. The debt issue and the Tobin tax got much more political attention, clearly moving from the margins to the political centre.

The programme of the new rainbow coalition includes just a few sentences on global and development issues. However, it is worth noting that the only issues covered in these few sentences are the three that KePa focused on during the electoral campaign, namely the quality and quantity of aid, debt and the Tobin tax.

The positions of the Government on the debt problem and the Tobin tax are vaguely formulated but at least we have influenced the setting of the agenda. Regarding debt, the NGOs will focus on demanding the cancellation of what is left of bilateral ODA credits to the poorest indebted countries. For the Tobin tax, the short-term focus will be to get the Government to produce an official report on the issue and to get it on the EU agenda for joint political consideration and action.

The short passage on development cooperation states: 'The aim of the development cooperation policy of the Government is to strengthen the capacity of the developing countries in improving their welfare and security, and in preventing conflicts. The Government pursues a comprehensive policy aiming at the reduction of poverty, preventing environmental threats, and promoting equality, democracy and human rights in the developing countries. The Government increases the development aid resources through additional funding and aims at reaching the recommendation of the UN when the economic situation so allows.'

Besides this, the Government has decided to monitor the development of the aid budget to ensure it will not go below the present GNP rate of 0.34%. In the tentative budgetary planning frames for the next four years, the increase is estimated to be about 450 million Finnish

Finland

Percentage of national income spent on aid: a 30-year picture

How much aid does Finland give?

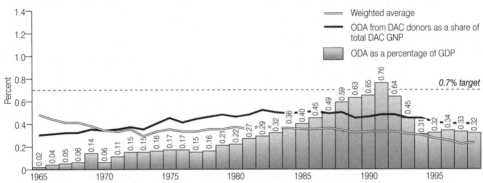

Legend:
- Weighted average
- ODA from DAC donors as a share of total DAC GNP
- ODA as a percentage of GDP

0.7% target

Bar values: 0.02, 0.04, 0.05, 0.06, 0.14, 0.06, 0.11, 0.15, 0.15, 0.16, 0.17, 0.17, 0.15, 0.16, 0.21, 0.22, 0.27, 0.29, 0.32, 0.36, 0.40, 0.45, 0.49, 0.59, 0.63, 0.65, 0.76, 0.64, 0.45, 0.31, 0.32, 0.34, 0.33, 0.32

Where is Finnish aid spent?

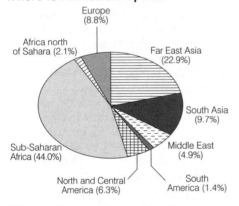

- Europe (8.8%)
- Africa north of Sahara (2.1%)
- Far East Asia (22.9%)
- South Asia (9.7%)
- Middle East (4.9%)
- South America (1.4%)
- North and Central America (6.3%)
- Sub-Saharan Africa (44.0%)

How much Finnish aid is spent through multilateral organisations?

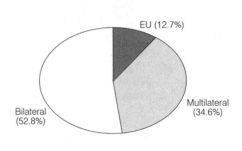

- EU (12.7%)
- Multilateral (34.6%)
- Bilateral (52.8%)

What is Finnish aid spent on?

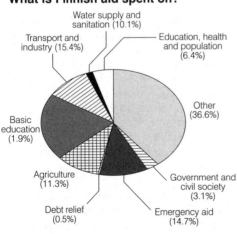

- Water supply and sanitation (10.1%)
- Transport and industry (15.4%)
- Education, health and population (6.4%)
- Basic education (1.9%)
- Other (36.6%)
- Agriculture (11.3%)
- Government and civil society (3.1%)
- Debt relief (0.5%)
- Emergency aid (14.7%)

How much Finnish aid goes to the poorest countries?

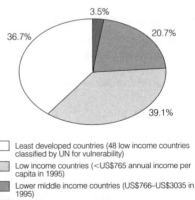

- 3.5%
- 20.7%
- 36.7%
- 39.1%

Legend:
- Least developed countries (48 low income countries classified by UN for vulnerability)
- Low income countries (<US$765 annual income per capita in 1995)
- Lower middle income countries (US$766–US$3035 in 1995)
- Upper middle income countries (US$3036–US$9385 in 1995)
- High income countries (>US$9385 per capita in 1995)

For notes on data and sources see page 286

Box 20 Finnish aid at a glance

How much aid does Finland give?

Finland gave	US$396m, 2,117 million Finnish Markka in 1998
that was	0.32% of GNP
and	0.64% of total government expenditure
which meant	US$77 or 412 Finnish Markka per capita for 1998

Is it going up or down?

In 1998 Finnish aid	rose by $17m, a rise of 5.2% in real terms over 1997
Finland was	less generous in 1998, falling from 0.33% of GNP to 0.32%
The outlook is	Very poor. The Government initially stated that the 0.4% target was an interim one, and now says that even this will not be reached in time.

How does Finland compare with the other 20 donors?

Finland ranks	17 out of 21 for its volume of aid
It is	9 out of 21 in the generosity league
It gives	75.8% of its aid to low income countries, a higher proportion than 17 other donors
Private flows	amounted to –$13m, –3%times ODA
Total flows	to developing countries were 0.37% of GNP and rank 17 out of 21 in the DAC

What proportion of bilateral aid goes to basic education and basic health?

Finland committed	3% of bilateral ODA to basic education, 0.2% to basic health and 0.7% to population and reproductive health

How important are commercial interests in aid?

Finland reported that	26.2% of its bilateral aid commitments were tied to the purchase of goods and services from Finland

Markka (FIM). Ministry officials have admitted informally that if economic growth materialises as estimated, that is 3% on average during the next three years, FIM 450 million will not be enough to keep the GNP rate at 0.34%.

The new minister and others have defended this decision by saying that ODA is one of the only three items that will have a real increase during the electoral period. This explains how difficult the debate has been inside the Government, but it is not good enough. The Government has deviated from its principle commitment to the 0.7% target, and there is a need for an open political debate about this fact. The only valid conclusion that can be made so far is that the conservatives –personified by the Party chairman, alias the Finance Minister – have been steering the decision-making.

Who pays for rebuilding the Balkans?

In June 1999, the first article on the potential threat the reconstruction of the Balkans poses to funding of development cooperation in the South appeared in the leading Finnish daily *Helsingin Sanomat*. It included very worried comments from high-level officials from the DIDC. This was the first public sign in Finland that Eurostep's appeal (at its Annual General Meeting in Berlin on 4 June) for the reconstruction of the Balkans to be funded through additional and not reallocated ODA budget, hit the heart of the matter.

This will be a key political issue in the Finnish development aid debate for the next few years. It was expected to be the most difficult issue at the internal budgetary negotiations of the Government in early August. There is an open dispute (partly traditional) between the Finance and the Foreign ministries. Finance wants most of the Finnish contribution to

Finland

humanitarian aid and reconstruction of Kosovo to be made through a reallocation of present ODA. The expected growth from about FIM 2.3 billion this year to FIM2.5 billion next year, will mostly go to Kosovo if Finance gets its way.

EU Presidency boosts lobby for coherence

Finland took over the rotating EU Presidency in the second half of 1999, which means that it is overseeing the work of the EU's Development Council and negotiations for a follow-up to the Lomé Convention. The Finnish Platform of the EU-NGDO Liaison Committee, which comprises some 60 Finnish groups and organisations, is lobbying for greater coherence, fairness and cogency in the EU's relations with developing countries. Under the Finnish Presidency, the Development Council will assess the evaluation made of all EU aid methods. Finland is keen that this process eventually leads to the formulation of a clear development policy statement by the Union.

The Presidency is also putting special emphasis on environment in relation to development – focusing on the integration of environmental concerns in development practices, sustainable development and climate change. While the Finnish Platform welcomes this emphasis on environment, it argues that coherent trade policies that tackle poverty are also needed.

In addition, the Finnish Platform is working for a positive input by Finland to the EU's approach to the post-Lomé process. It stresses several priorities here. It wants to ensure that poverty reduction is the goal of EU-ACP cooperation and trade. It wants commitments to the 20:20 Initiative realised by devoting a significant portion of development cooperation funds towards social development. It believes that gender perspectives should be explicit and should pervade all areas of cooperation. The participation of civil society in EU-ACP political dialogue and in the planning and realisation of programmes is also seen as essential

Poverty reduction gets top priority

The Ministry for Foreign Affairs' document 'Finland's Policy on Relations with Developing Countries', released in October 1998, adds much substance to the comparatively brief 1996 Decision-in-Principle (DIP) on development cooperation. While tackling poverty reduction is seen as a central task of development in the DIP, the new approach places poverty reduction more emphatically in the forefront of development policy and gives a more coherent view of what this means.

The primary goal of development cooperation is to promote broad security, which, in going beyond military concerns, addresses human and ecological security. The 'reduction of widespread poverty' is given top priority in the effort to guarantee this broad security, followed by action on human rights and democracy, global environmental problems, and economic integration. These last three issues are seen as integral to reducing poverty, as the problems they embrace are basic to the causes and increase of poverty.

Although the document takes a positive view of economic globalisation, its negative impact of weakening 'the ability of countries to control their economic or social development' is also raised, in terms of the 'marginalisation of many countries or population groups who lack the prerequisites to participate in increasingly global economic competition'. Economic growth, though, is not seen by the government as the sole remedy.

The lack of democracy in many poor countries – and implicitly also in global-level decision-making – is seen as maintaining poverty by excluding people, and whole nations, from decision-making and preventing socio-economic equality.

The debt burden on poorer countries is also seen as an obstacle to reducing poverty. Finland supports the Jubilee 2000 debt cancellation campaign but it also takes the line that the final responsibility for the debt lies with the indebted countries. Their way out of the debt trap, it believes, depends on their readiness to adhere to a market economy, together with social policies that give priority to cutting poverty and advancing social justice and democracy. Finland has cancelled the repayment of most – but not yet all – of its bilateral development loans, or made agreements exchanging debts for commitments to social and environmental spending.

In practical terms, the bulk of Finnish ODA has long been directed at cooperation with Low Income Countries, particularly in sub-Saharan Africa. Finland's poverty reduction goals, outlined in the DIP and reiterated in the new policy lines, focus on four main social areas: basic education and health, food security, the participation of women and the status of people with disabilities.

The proportion of LLDCs and LICs in Finland's total ODA is still relatively high compared to other DAC member states. However, these proportions (especially for the poorest countries) have dropped considerably over the years. The whole donor community, including Finland, now faces enormous pressure to start channelling huge amounts of support to Kosovo and Serbia (to repair the damage caused by NATO bombings). It is extremely important for NGOs (and others) to play the role of active moral watch-

Finland

dogs so that the costs of this will not fall on the LLDCs (and LICs).

The share of Finnish bilateral aid to LLDCs and LICs has hovered around the 80% mark since 1996, when the government stopped cutting overall ODA. The general direction of programme and project support with certain of Finland's southern partners, such as Tanzania, Nepal and Vietnam, is towards more grassroots-oriented assistance for people's needs. Such assistance would be decentralised, channelled towards building local capacity and away from superstructure or production-focused schemes. Other partnerships, such as in Ethiopia and Tanzania (in the Rural Integrated Project Support programme conducted in the Mtwara and Lindi regions) have been consistently poverty-focused. This is true, too, for the majority of Finland's bilateral programmes. Some examples are:

- Ethiopia: education sector, rural water supply and environment, democracy fund.
- Kenya: livestock, democracy fund.
- Mozambique: basic education, local government reform, health sector, mine-clearing.
- Namibia: health and social sector, rural water, anti-desertification, forestry, local government reform.
- Zambia: rural integrated (Luapula), education sector, forestry action plan, democracy fund.
- Tanzania: RIPS, education sector, rural roads, forest protection, local government reform, tax reform, democracy fund.
- Egypt: rural water supply and sanitation.
- Vietnam: rural integrated development (including credit), forestry, urban water.
- Nepal: rural water and sanitation, local government reform, basic education.
- Nicaragua: local social sector (FADES), people with disabilities (SIRES), reproductive health and rights, livestock and rural development (PRODEGA).

Despite this general direction, there is a perceived need, as has been pointed out in studies for the Overseas Development Institute, to hone the work of the DIDC in ways that will direct planning methods, implementation approaches and administrative procedures more palpably towards poverty reduction. Though perhaps generally appreciated within the DIDC, poverty reduction tends to lack methodological rigour in the way programmes are conceived and executed. The Central Evaluation Unit of the DIDC has for some time planned to launch a thematic evaluation of the poverty orientation of the DIDC's work, but at the time of writing this remains undone.

Clarity needed on gender and inequality
Lack of conceptual clarity and practical information characterise the treatment of gender in the context of poverty reduction. Although the policy lines emphasise that the situation of women and girls is a priority concern in tackling poverty and in promoting democracy and human rights, clear approaches to gender and equality are rarely explicit in partnership programmes. Mainstreaming, implying that attention to equality between women and men should pervade all development policies, strategies and interventions, is not consistently applied in the programme work done in the DIDC, nor in that carried out with the partners.

A study published by the DIDC this year on Gender Equality in Finnish Development Cooperation Projects in Africa finds that there has been positive overall change in how gender issues are approached. However, it pinpoints shortcomings in the form of a persistence of gender blindness on the one hand, and the lack of evaluations of the gender impact of programmes and projects on the other. By June 1999 there was still no gender adviser at the DIDC; appointing one is the key to progress on improving work on gender equality, let alone its interrelationship with poverty reduction.

Basic education – the poorest have to pay

Basic education is regarded as a key aspect of Finnish development cooperation, and of particular importance to poverty reduction. The substantive goals of the DIDC's work on basic education remain the same as those outlined in the last edition of *The Reality of Aid*. The priorities of these goals are:

1   To reduce widespread poverty;
2   To combat environmental threats and;
3   Promote social equality, democracy and human rights.

Activities carried out under the first of these priorities focus on access, quality, efficiency and equity-related goals. In being coupled with approaches that emphasise community involvement in decision-making, as well as support to disadvantaged groups, these clearly aim to increase the involvement of poor people in basic education, especially in rural areas.

The rationale for sustainability in basic education recognises the high social rates of return that it brings to society and to tackling poverty and inequality. The DIDC sees that, economically, basic education contributes to earnings and productivity, while in social development it

Finland

Table 17 Percentage share of all Finnish bilateral ODA commitments in 1997 and 1998 to education (total) and basic education

	1997	1998 (provisional data)
Education (total)	8.0%	6.0%
Basic education	3.0%	4.2%

contributes to reduced fertility and better child health and nutrition.

The goal should be free basic education for all. In reality, the objective of free education has been dropped in some of the poorest partner countries, where education support tends to be moving towards the principle of 'matching grants'. In these cases, donor/government support is directed only to those communities who can raise local contributions (for example 50%) which will then be matched with another 50% from the donor/government. The equalisation of opportunities between the more and less wealthy communities is still an unresolved dilemma in most of the education projects. This should be a matter of concern for DIDC, whose policies commit it to equalising the distribution of benefits within poor societies. The DIDC also notes that the higher a person goes in education, the higher is the private rate of return, and that this justifies the use of cost-sharing and user fees in secondary, technical and higher education.

Particular stress is put on support to girls' education, to reduce the gender gap in basic education, through such things as targeted programmes and scholarships, and supply-related questions. These include meeting needs such as the location of schools near to home, the provision of girls' toilets, having female teachers and principals,

and having gender-sensitive education materials and curricula.

Being a partner in the sector development programmes, Finland addresses the stipulations of Education for All. It does this by increasing activity focused on access and on the reconstruction and rehabilitation of school facilities, and by focusing on quality-related features of work on basic education.

Though Finnish ODA has not increased significantly in recent years, more money is being spent on basic education. There are plans also to increase work in higher or tertiary education, but not to compete with work on basic education. Agreements have been signed recently with Tanzania and Nepal focusing wholly on basic education. Similarly, more emphasis on basic education is being given in cooperation with Nicaragua. In Ethiopia and in Zambia, Finland has long been involved in basic education and is now preparing the next phase of cooperation. In Mozambique, additional funding is being made available for basic education and for technical and vocational education.

(For more information on official Finnish development cooperation policy, go to the Department for International Development Cooperation (DIDC) website at http://global.finland and for more on Finnish NGO activity on development issues go to KePa's website at www.kepa.fi)

France

Olivier Blamangin, Centre de Recherche et d'Information pour le Developpement (CRID)

Falling short on quantity and strategy

French ODA reached 37 billion francs[1] (US$6.35 billion) in 1997. This commitment amounted to 0.45% of GNP, which places France in sixth place behind Denmark, Norway, the Netherlands, Sweden and Luxembourg, and at the top of G7 donors.

While Paris seems to want to keep its position as leading donor of the G7 and to maintain 'a high level of public aid',[2] the French Government continues its policy of budgetary restriction. Between 1996 and 1997, French ODA fell by nearly 3% and there is little doubt today that its steady decline since 1994 (when it reached Ff47 billion and 0.64% of the GNP) is not accidental but a strong tendency that will continue. Thus, in 1998, the French aid was not expected to exceed Ff35 billion (0.41% of GNP and –a drop of 5.5% compared to 1997) whereas 14 of the 21 Member States of OECD displayed an increase in their ODA, seeming to break away from the trend of the early 1990s.

These amounts of ODA include the aid to the French Overseas Territories (TOM), which once again has not been affected by budgetary constraints. French Polynesia and New Caledonia accounted for 7.6% and 7% respectively of bilateral aid in 1997, coming first and second among the recipients of French aid, with an even greater share than the previous year. If the Overseas Territories are excluded, French ODA that year amounted to just over Ff32.4 billion, or approximately 0.39% of GNP.

Thus, French ODA has lost more than one quarter of its volume since 1994. Expressed as a percentage of GNP, the figures of 1997 and 1998 are the worst since 1981. The Government does not formulate quantitative targets any more and the Foreign Minister, Hubert Védrine, admitted in the National Assembly that these budgetary constraints were 'durable'.[3] Indeed, the 1999 budget does not look more auspicious. This is worrying, more especially as a reform of French cooperation was carried out in 1999 (see below) and a political signal was awaited in this context.

Public opinion rallies behind aid

The French public, however, have remained supportive of overseas development aid, according to the annual survey commissioned by the Catholic Committee against Hunger and for Development (CCFD) and *La Croix* newspaper. The 1999 survey[4] shows that 64% of those interviewed are in favour of an increase in ODA (the highest level since 1993 and two points up on 1998). Most people remain concerned about how aid is used; more than half of those interviewed said aid should only be increased if it was better used. 30% of those interviewed believed that assistance should not be increased but simply used better and 3% said that it should be reduced (slightly up on last year). These results reinforce last year's finding that support for international cooperation and the eradication of global poverty has been reestablished.

Slow rise of multilateral aid

Within the context of budgetary restriction, multilateral aid has held up better than bilateral aid. While increasing from Ff8.7billion in 1996 to Ff8.9 billion in 1997 (+2.3%) and from 22.8% to 24.1% of ODA (the estimated level for 1998 is 25.5%), the multilateral component is held up as a real priority of French cooperation, which is traditionally very reticent about delegating control over resources to multilateral institutions.

In 1997, the European Union got the lion's share, as every year, with Ff5.2 billion (57.6% of global multilateral aid),[5] a 20% increase on 1996 (Ff4.3 billion). International financial institutions, with the World Bank group and regional funds and banks ranking first, were in second position, with Ff3.1 billion or nearly 35% of multilateral ODA. The United Nations agencies seem neglected as, with Ff667 million,

France

Percentage of national income spent on aid: a 30-year picture

How much aid does France give?

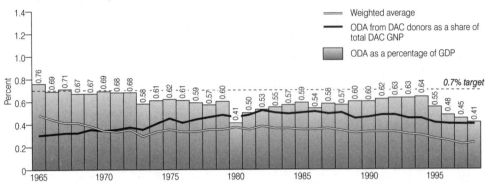

- Weighted average
- ODA from DAC donors as a share of total DAC GNP
- ODA as a percentage of GDP

0.7% target

Where is French aid spent?

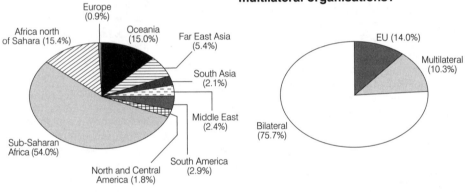

Europe (0.9%)
Africa north of Sahara (15.4%)
Oceania (15.0%)
Far East Asia (5.4%)
South Asia (2.1%)
Middle East (2.4%)
South America (2.9%)
North and Central America (1.8%)
Sub-Saharan Africa (54.0%)

How much French aid is spent through multilateral organisations?

EU (14.0%)
Multilateral (10.3%)
Bilateral (75.7%)

What is French aid spent on?

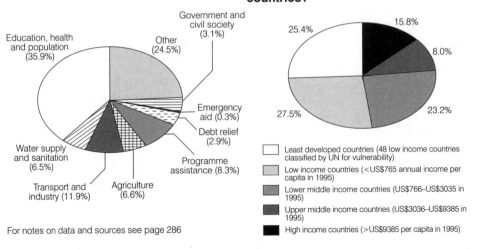

Government and civil society (3.1%)
Education, health and population (35.9%)
Other (24.5%)
Emergency aid (0.3%)
Debt relief (2.9%)
Programme assistance (8.3%)
Water supply and sanitation (6.5%)
Transport and industry (11.9%)
Agriculture (6.6%)

How much French aid goes to the poorest countries?

25.4%
15.8%
8.0%
27.5%
23.2%

- Least developed countries (48 low income countries classified by UN for vulnerability)
- Low income countries (<US$765 annual income per capita in 1995)
- Lower middle income countries (US$766–US$3035 in 1995)
- Upper middle income countries (US$3036–US$9385 in 1995)
- High income countries (>US$9385 per capita in 1995)

For notes on data and sources see page 286

France

Box 21 French aid at a glance

How much aid does France give?

France gave	US$5,899m or 34,801 million French Francs in 1998
that was	0.41% of GNP
and	0.76% of total government expenditure
which meant	US$101 or FF 594 per capita for 1998

Is it going up or down?

In 1998 French aid	fell by $408m, a drop of 6.2% in real terms over 1997
France was	less generous in 1998, dropping from 0.45% to 0.41% of GNP
The outlook is	not hopeful, with the current decrease continuing in both percentage and volume terms. The Government is, however, still committed to maintain what it calls a 'high level of public aid'.

How does France compare with the other 20 donors?

France ranks	3 out of 21 for its volume of aid
It is	6 out of 21 in the generosity league
It gives	52.9% of its aid to low income countries, a lower proportion than 15 other donors
Private flows	amounted to $7,623m, 1.2 times ODA
Total flows	to developing countries were 1% of GNP and rank 8 out of 21 in the DAC

What proportion of bilateral aid goes to basic education and basic health?

France	has not yet reported to the DAC on its basic health and basic education spending

How important are commercial interests in aid?

France reported that	34.5% of its bilateral aid commitments were tied to the purchase of goods and services from France

---

they hardly amount to 7.5% of multilateral aid and still do not reach the contribution level of the beginning of the 1990s. During the budgetary debate in parliament, the Foreign Minister claimed, however, that the second French priority for 1999 would be 'to give to our country the means to get back its influence in the UN multilateral system, with the restoration of our contribution level'. One can thus expect a significant increase of the French voluntary contributions in the coming years.

While multilateral aid may be, *a priori*, a smaller stake than French bilateral aid, which is, due to political, economic or strategic interests, stuck in the traditional mud of the management of its African 'pré carré' (countries in the French sphere of influence), questions occurred nevertheless concerning its increasing share in French ODA. Some personalities, such as the MP Yves Tavernier, have remarked on the will 'to profit from a leverage effect'[6] for French firms

and to increase French influence. In fact, French firms managed to rank second among all the countries profiting from World Bank markets.[7] But this slow rise of multilateral aid should be analysed as a simple *withdrawal* as there is a lack of alternative strategy for French cooperation, always in search of a project.

Geographical priorities unchanged

The ten major recipients of French ODA[8] are, with one exception (Mayotte, retrogressing to the twelfth place to be replaced by Madagascar), the same as in 1997. As every year, the order within this top-ten list has changed according to circumstances, but the following countries are always indispensable: New Caledonia and Polynesia for TOM, Egypt, Morocco and Algeria for North Africa, Cameroon, Senegal, Ivory Coast for sub-Saharan Africa.

France

French bilateral aid remains concentrated, given that the top ten shared 48% of allocations in 1997; but it is also very scattered, as the other 52% was sprinkled across more than 130 countries. As we underlined in *The Reality of Aid* 1998/99, for the moment the budgetary restrictions do not have significant consequences on the number of countries aided by France;[9] they simply share a less significant cake.

The distribution of French aid underwent some changes in 1997, considering the balance between the major geographic regions, and this will have to be confirmed in future to be interpreted. North Africa seems to stop its progression, attracting 13.3% of bilateral aid, compared to 1996 (15.6%) and 1995 (14.5%). It is too early yet to say that this is not just an interruption in the growth trend beginning in 1990.

Sub-Saharan Africa naturally remains French main cooperation priority with 45% of bilateral aid. This region, traditionally privileged by France, has undergone slow but quite real erosion of its share in bilateral ODA since the beginning of the 1990s. This downward trend seems to have stopped given that sub-Saharan Africa gained nearly three percentage points compared with 1995 and 1996, and even managed to consolidate the volume of bilateral ODA, despite budgetary restriction, at around Ff12.7 billion, against 12.4 billion in 1996. The significant support for sub-Saharan Africa was mainly profitable to middle-income countries and, generally speaking, France devoted only 21.8% of its global aid (multilateral ODA included)[10] to LDCs.

Which strategy for poverty eradication?

The totality of French ODA contributes officially, directly or indirectly, to the eradication of poverty, which is regarded as one of the four major objectives of French cooperation, the others being (1) the great macroeconomic equilibriums, (2) the reinforcement of the state of law and democracy, (3) sustainable development. But the small share of French aid devoted to the LDCs and the scatter of aid on more than 140 countries are symptomatic of the lack of strategy concerning the eradication of poverty. Generally speaking, this geographical dispersion is guided by economic or political interests, since the overriding goal is to maintain the French presence and its potential for influence.

There is no clearly displayed will, nor quantitative targets, to concentrate French aid on particular sectors, such as meeting basic needs, health or primary education. In 1997, a broad share of French bilateral aid was devoted to economic and financial support, ie to initiatives for cancellation or alleviation of debt (Ff6.4 billion, or 23%) and

programme assistance such as aid connected to structural adjustment and budgetary aid (amounting to Ff1.2 billion, or 4.3%). The efficiency of such contributions in terms of eradication of poverty is limited. The share of economic support, and particularly of programme assistance, has been reduced, however, in favour of technical and cultural cooperation (Ff9.9 billion, or 35.4%) and 'project assistance' (Ff3.8 billion, or 13.7%), including projects in the education, primary health, water and sanitation and basic needs sectors. The greater part of this technical cooperation and project aid is devoted to productive projects (rural development, energy, transport), and to institutional development or to support for French language speaking in foreign countries.

Basic education gets 'priority' but not investment

The approach to basic education is also illustrative of the lack of a strategy for the reduction of poverty. France devotes about 20% of its annual sectoral expenditure to education, considering all instruments of aid, including the technical aid. The expressed priority is naturally to basic education, which seems to have been the object of renewed attention, compared to secondary and university education, in recent years. So far, however, this commitment is not reflected in the allocations. The 'education' component of French aid covers several sectors, with primary education receiving between 15% and 20%, technical or professional education nearly 30%, secondary education between 30% and 40%, and the remainder going to university education, the teaching of French, scholarships for more than 4500 students or trainees, a significant level of institutional aid, research aid, etc.

Reform of the cooperation system – too little, too late?

In last year's *The Reality of Aid*, we presented the broad outline for the reform of the cooperation system announced at the beginning of 1998.[11] While everybody thought that the implementation of this reform project would take a long time, one is forced to note that excuses and delays followed one another so that the Interministerial Committee of International Cooperation and Development (ICICD), in charge of the coherence of the French cooperation policy, did not even meet until 28 January 1999, nearly a year after the operational launching of the reform. Consequently, even though the project specifications are known, it is too early this year for an assessment of the reform.

In any case, if change is eagerly awaited by all the international solidarity actors, it is advisable to underline the

France

limits to this reform. It is primarily an administrative effort targeting the rationalisation of the cooperation structures. It will not have great meaning without the definition of a coherent and mobilising strategy for French cooperation. At the moment, the NGOs can only subscribe to the displayed will to simplify the system, seek greater coherence, greater efficiency and transparency. NGOs hope that this reform will not be limited to a rationalisation of cooperation structures that will only lead to a further squeeze on public expenditure.

The reorganisation concerns only a little more than a quarter of the French ODA (the budget of the Cooperation Minister, the Foreign Affairs Minister and the French Development Agency) and does not answer the fundamental question of the shared responsibilities in the definition and the implementation of the policies of ODA. In the new system, the Ministry of Economy and Finance, traditionally more worried about the figures for French foreign trade, the level of the budget deficit and the liberalisation of southern economies than by the reduction of poverty or sustainable development, maintains its domination, controlling, directly or indirectly, more than half of the French aid.

Ultimately, one can only wonder about the direction of a reform of the cooperation system which happens in the context of significant erosion of the resources devoted to ODA.

The organisation chart of the new services for cooperation channelled through the Ministry for Foreign Affairs is known today. Its orientation appears to be in favour of French cultural influence. Not surprisingly, the priority zone of solidarity as defined by the Interministerial Committee for International Cooperation and Development includes essentially sub-Saharan Africa, the Maghreb, the countries of the Indo-Chinese Peninsula and the Caribbean, ie an area a little bit larger than the traditional French sphere of influence. All observers agree, however, that there cannot be a reform of French cooperation policy without normalisation of relations between France and the African countries. Moreover, the High Council for International Cooperation, announced last year to give to representatives of the civil society (associations, NGOs, local collectives, trade unions,

experts, etc) the means to express their opinions on French cooperation, but this is still not set up. After long delays, its chairman was finally appointed but the constitution has not been published and, apparently, this is not a priority matter.

To summarise the concerns but also the expectations of the NGOs, these attempted reforms lack the true political will to redefinine a coherent strategy of cooperation which is not reduced, as it is today, to simple objectives of cultural, technological, political or economic influence.

Notes

1   Sources: unless otherwise specified, all figures are extracted from the DAC questionnaires dated 1996 and 1997, from the website of the Ministry of Foreign Affairs (http://www.diplomatie.gouv.fr) and from the memorandums from France to DAC for the 1990–96 period.
2   'Overseas development aid', press report distributed during the press conference given by the French Prime Minister, M. Lionel Jospin, *The cooperation reform*, Paris, 4 February 1998.
3   Preliminary 1999 Budget, oral communication of the French Ministry of Foreign Affairs, M. Hubert Védrine, National Assembly, 2 November 1998.
4   Sources: 10th French international solidarity barometer, CCFD/*La Croix*, survey carried out in February 1999 among a sample of 1000 people representative of the French population. Survey published in *La Croix*, 13, 14 March 1999.
5   In 1997 France gave Ff1.9 billion to the European Development Fund and Ff3.2 billion to the European Community budget.
6   Yves Tavernier, French cooperation for bilateral and multilateral development. Evaluation, analysis, prospects. Report to the Prime Minister, December 1998, p23.
7   In 1998, French firms received 9.1% of the World Bank contracts, ranking second after US firms. Source: Report to the parliament on IMF and World Bank activities, 30 June 1999.
8   The top ten recipients of French ODA in 1997 were in numerical order: French Polynesia (7.6% of bilateral ODA), New Caledonia (7%), Madagascar (6.5%), Egypt (5.9%), Congo (5%), Cameroon (4.2%), Morocco (3.2%), Senegal (3%), Algeria (2.8%), and Ivory Coast (2.8%).
9   144 countries received French ODA in 1997 (152 in 1996); this figure includes Swaziland, Zimbabwe, Jamaica and Pakistan, for whom the ODA balance was negative (they paid back more than they received in 1997).
10 Source: http://oecd.org/
11 Incorporation within the Ministry of Foreign Affairs of the Secretariat of State for Cooperation, with a progressive amalgamation of their budgets from 1999. Creation of an Interministerial Committee for International Cooperation and Development (ICICD), definition of a priority solidarity area, creation of a High Council for International Cooperation particularly including representatives of civil society, etc.

Germany

Birgit Dederichs-Bain and Thomas Fues, Deutsche Welthungerhilfe and terre des hommes

New words, new deeds?

The political framework for development cooperation in Germany has been transformed since the change of government in October 1998. The new majority, of social democrats and Greens, has announced a major overhaul of the aid programme. They have committed themselves to an enhanced role for development – in quality as well as in quantity.

German policies towards the South are to be guided by the principles of human rights, gender equality, ecology, conflict prevention, coherence and cooperation with civil society. These words will be put to the test.

Taking a global view

In their coalition agreement, the ruling parties have replaced the traditional concept of aid to poor countries with the innovative idea of global structural policies. Based on a synthesis of ethical concerns and long-term, enlightened self-interest, the Ministry for Development Cooperation's (BMZ) new mission is to focus on global issues. From this perspective, national interests are best served by effectively solving global problems. The coalition agreement defines this as follows:

> 'Development policy today means global struc-
> tural policies that aim at improving the economic,
> social, environmental and political conditions in
> developing countries. Such policies follow, inter
> alia, the paradigm of global sustainable develop-
> ment.'

The rich countries of the North cannot hope to survive as islands of prosperity and peace in an ocean of human misery, collapsing ecosystems and violent conflict. The accelerating trends of economic, political and cultural globalisation call for a regulatory framework that can harness the positive effects and contain the negative impact of deepening but asymmetric interdependencies within the international system.

In order to facilitate the reorientation of aid policies towards global issues, the position of the BMZ at the cabinet table has been strengthened: it is now responsible for Habitat and the follow-up process of the World Social Summit. Under the new Government, the BMZ has gained access to the Federal Security Council, which oversees all military exports. The role of the BMZ in European aid to ACP countries has been upgraded, though the Foreign Office maintains a strong presence in this field. The BMZ has also been assigned as lead agency for support programmes to the transitional countries of Central and Eastern Europe.

Other fields, as well as international institutions relevant to development, such as humanitarian and democ-ratisation aid, and UNICEF, were not transferred to the BMZ but remain under the authority of the Foreign Office and other ministries.

Deutsche Welthungerhilfe (DWHH) and terre des hommes (tdh) welcome the fact that the status of develop-ment cooperation as an autonomous Ministry has been confirmed by the Government, despite proposals to integrate it into other departments. DWHH and tdh support the enhanced role of the Aid Ministry at the cabinet table and its new mission of global structural policies. As far back as 1996, the two organisations had begun to articulate the need for a paradigm shift in this direction.[1] However, in order to fulfil its new role, BMZ's staff and its financial resources need to be expanded considerably.

There is some concern that the Government has not yet come up with a consistent plan for institutional reform in foreign policies. As more and more ministries see their inter-national responsibilities grow in geographic reach and policy scope, the role of the Foreign Office has become blurred. The new mandate of the BMZ on global structural

Germany

policies has added to the seeming rivalry between this Ministry and the Foreign Office. Parallel and obviously competing efforts have been launched in important areas such as dialogue with civil society and conflict prevention.

DWHH and tdh urge a comprehensive institutional reform that will ensure overall coherence and a clear division of labour among all ministries charged with international tasks. Without this, the BMZ's new mission of global structural policies could be frustrated at an early stage. Global structural policies that follow the principles of sustainable development will, if taken seriously, require certain changes in Germany's society and economy. The BMZ should, therefore, play an active role in promoting policies at home that reflect the need for environmental conservation and social equity on a global scale.

Pledges hide decline in spending

No specific targets have been set for future aid volumes. The coalition agreement says: 'In order to approach the internationally agreed 0.7% target, the coalition will reverse the downward trend of the aid budget and, in particular, continuously increase commitments in a moderate way.'

In presenting the Government programme for this legislative period, the new Chancellor committed himself to stop the decline of the German ODA/GNP quota, which fell to an unprecedented low of 0.26% in 1998.

According to the original draft of the 1999 budget, cash disbursements of the BMZ were to be raised to 7,800 billion Deutschmarks (DM). This would have been a definite increase compared to the old administration's figure of DM7,676 billion for the same year. The BMZ handles more than two thirds of total German ODA, which amounted to DM9,832 billion in 1998.

Due to general financial pressures, Parliament later approved an across-the-board cut of 0.5% for all parts of the federal budget. The BMZ was not spared from the austerity programme, although the coalition agreement explicitly aims at increasing aid resources. The final 1999 budget figure for BMZ thus stands at DM7,763 billion, which is still higher than the target set by the old administration. In addition, DM76 million, generated by selling off development loans, will be channelled into financial cooperation. Another DM20 million provided by the Finance Ministry for the transitional economies will also be handled by the aid administration. This brings total authorisation of BMZ disbursements in 1999 up to DM7,859 billion. Possibly, the BMZ will receive further money for 1999 out of the general fund set up for emergency aid to Kosovo, although it is not yet known how the money will be distributed among differ-

ent ministries. This fund, standing at DM300 million in 1999, is additional to the aid budget. It also covers increased costs of the military and other expenditure items.

The apparent increase of the BMZ budget figures has to be put into perspective. In recent years, the old administration introduced an innovative mechanism to raise additional resources for development. It began to sell off outstanding loans generated by the widely-used instrument of financial assistance.[2] New revenues of this kind came into the Ministry's hands as additional income from debt service. As a consequence, in 1998 cash disbursements of DM7,925 billion surpassed the budget plan of DM7,666 billion. The old administration had intended to raise DM200 million over and above the official budget line through this mechanism in 1999. If the actual BMZ disbursements of DM7,925 billion in 1998, (the last year of the old administration), are compared with expected resources of DM7,859 billion for 1999, it is clear that the new government did not reverse the decline of German ODA. On the contrary, it allowed it to fall even further in its first year in office.[3]

The government's budget plan for 2000, which still has to be passed by Parliament, includes drastic cuts in the aid programme. BMZ allocations are fixed at DM7,089 billion – that is 8.7%, or DM674.3 million less than in 1999. This means that the BMZ is contributing much more than other ministries to the austerity programme, since the overall reduction rate of the federal budget is planned to be only 1.5%. Worse, BMZ funds will continue to shrink in the years after 2000, although the total budget is expected to increase slightly.

The 1999 budget marks a further push for composite financing.[4] The Government has raised the maximum volume of export credit guarantees by DM100 million, to a total of DM265 billion. Correspondingly, commitments for financial assistance were increased by DM95 million. The target group of countries for composite financing has been expanded considerably as the risk requirement for debt service capacity was lowered from 'very good' to 'good'. Now recipients such as Chile, Brazil and Malaysia qualify for financial assistance.

Support for projects of German NGOs has been raised by DM2 million for 1999, compared to the old draft. In addition, funding of public information and educational efforts of NGOs has been increased to DM6 million for 1999, compared to DM4.75 million scheduled by the old administration.

DWHH and tdh are not at all satisfied with this volume of aid, although they realise the need for austerity measures. By cutting subsidies for old industries and closing tax

Germany

Percentage of national income spent on aid: a 30-year picture

How much aid does Germany give?

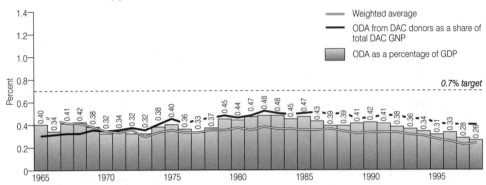

Legend:
- Weighted average
- ODA from DAC donors as a share of total DAC GNP
- ODA as a percentage of GDP

0.7% target

Where is German aid spent?

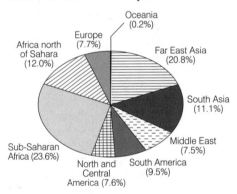

- Oceania (0.2%)
- Europe (7.7%)
- Africa north of Sahara (12.0%)
- Far East Asia (20.8%)
- South Asia (11.1%)
- Middle East (7.5%)
- South America (9.5%)
- North and Central America (7.6%)
- Sub-Saharan Africa (23.6%)

How much German aid is spent through multilateral organisations?

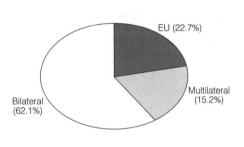

- EU (22.7%)
- Multilateral (15.2%)
- Bilateral (62.1%)

What is German aid spent on?

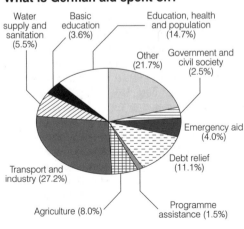

- Water supply and sanitation (5.5%)
- Basic education (3.6%)
- Education, health and population (14.7%)
- Other (21.7%)
- Government and civil society (2.5%)
- Emergency aid (4.0%)
- Debt relief (11.1%)
- Programme assistance (1.5%)
- Agriculture (8.0%)
- Transport and industry (27.2%)

How much German aid goes to the poorest countries?

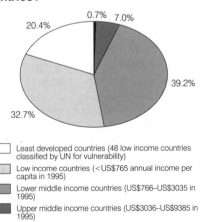

- 0.7%
- 7.0%
- 20.4%
- 39.2%
- 32.7%

- Least developed countries (48 low income countries classified by UN for vulnerability)
- Low income countries (<US$765 annual income per capita in 1995)
- Lower middle income countries (US$766–US$3035 in 1995)
- Upper middle income countries (US$3036–US$9385 in 1995)
- High income countries (>US$9385 per capita in 1995)

For notes on data and sources see page 286

Germany

Box 22 German aid at a glance

How much aid does Germany give?

Germany gave	US$5,589m, DM 9,832 m in 1998
that was	0.56% of total government expenditure
and	1.44% of public administration
which meant	US$68 or 120 Deutsch Marks per capita for 1998

Is it going up or down?

In 1998 German aid	fell by US$268m, a drop of 4.1% in real terms over 1997
Germany was	less generous in 1998, falling from 0.28% of GNP to 0.26%
The outlook is	that despite a firm commitment from the new Government towards an increase in quality and quantity of German aid, the financial resources are currently not forthcoming. A major cut, estimated at minus 8.7%, is planned for the aid budget in 2000

How does Germany compare with the other 20 donors?

Germany ranks	4 out of 21 for its volume of aid
It is	16 out of 21 in the generosity league
It gives	53.1% of its aid to low income countries, a lower proportion than 14 other donors
Private flows	amounted to $14,365m, 2.45 times ODA
Total flows	to developing countries were 0.95% of GNP and rank 10 out of 21 in the DAC

What proportion of bilateral aid goes to basic education and basic health?

Germany committed	2.1% of bilateral ODA to basic education, 1.8% to basic health and 1.8% to population and reproductive health

How important are commercial interests in aid?

Germany reported that	40% of its bilateral aid commitments were tied to the purchase of goods and services from Germany

---

loopholes, the Government could mobilise additional resources for a more effective aid programme. The BMZ can only address global issues successfully if it has adequate financial resources.

Since the Government expects a 2% growth rate of real GNP in 2000 and an inflation rate of 1 or 2%, the BMZ budget as a major part of ODA would need to climb by 3–4% just to arrest the decline of the ODA/GNP quota as the Chancellor promised. To be on the safe side, a 5% increase in the BMZ budget would be necessary to reverse the negative trend of the German aid programme.

As in previous editions of *The Reality of Aid*, DWHH and tdh urge that the instrument of composite financing be treated with scepticism. One concern is that financial assistance associated with composite financing might be increasingly channelled to relatively well-off countries that, for good reasons, were graduated from this instrument. Due to declining allocations to financial assistance, this will certainly be a pressing issue soon. A possible consequence may be that countries at a lower level of income will begin to suffer from a shortage of resources in the German aid programme.

Poverty focus/basic social services

The dominant German approach to poverty alleviation is not limited to social sectors but operates from a cross-sectoral perspective. It includes all funding activities where the majority of beneficiaries, men and women, are poor, and where target groups actively participate in project design and implementation. The old framework plan for 1999 had allocated

Germany

12.7% (DM370,3 million) of total bilateral commitments for technical and financial assistance to self-help poverty reduction.[5] The new Government has increased funds for this purpose to 14.3% (DM447.9 million) in the same year[6] – still less than the share in 1997, when actual commitments were 15.7%. However, in 1999 the cumulative share of all three poverty categories monitored by the BMZ fell from 54.9% (old administration) to 51.5% (new administration).

In continuity with the old administration, the new leadership has declared its support for the 20:20 Initiative on basic social services. A look at the budgetary figures, however, reveals the continuing gap between word and deed. The framework plan for 1999 includes commitments to basic social services of 17.3% (DM524.7 million); see Table 18. The old administration had allocated 18.3% (DM526.7 million) for the same year. While basic education and primary health go up, funding for the other categories declines. In 1997, actual commitments for basic social services stood considerably higher at 27%.

While support to basic education rises, overall funds for education go down. The old administration had set a target of 10.3% (DM302.2 million) for 1999. The new figure stands at 9% (DM281.7 million).

The new BMZ leadership has not yet taken an official position on the strategic DAC document *Shaping the 21st Century* (S21), which outlines specific targets for poverty elimination within a clearly defined time schedule. In order to provide an unambiguous data base for monitoring progress, the DAC has developed a comprehensive set of social and environmental indicators. DWHH and tdh commend the BMZ on the improvement of its statistical systems, according to DAC standards, and on its new openness in informing the public. Particularly welcome are the BMZ data on basic social services, which allow for a precise monitoring of the 20:20 Initiative. So far, however, the BMZ has not made any effort to relate its policies and programmes to the development targets of S21.

DWHH and tdh accept that the BMZ is not a 'poverty' ministry but poverty reduction is a crucial BMZ objective. The objectives of the poverty programme should be embedded in global structural policies. Some areas of global structural policies, such as supporting international regimes for the environment and for financial markets, are not directly relevant to poverty.

Since poverty reduction is not explicitly mentioned in the coalition agreement, DWHH and tdh request a conclusive statement by the BMZ on the relevance and financial volume of the poverty programme within the overall concept of global structural policies. For example, Germany is ready to allocate 0.7% of its GNP to global structural policies. One third of this will go towards poverty reduction. DWHH and tdh ask the new administration to increase the funds allocated to poverty reduction. They realise that the new BMZ focus on global issues, which they support, naturally limits the quantitative dimension of the poverty programme. In order to facilitate a better pro-poor targeting, especially towards women as the primary managers of family survival, the share of self-help oriented poverty projects should be raised. Also, support for basic social services should be substantially expanded, since financing needs for the implementation of the DAC's development targets are immense. The slight increase of allocations for basic education is an encouraging step in the right direction.

Gender equality – time to address systems, not symptoms

The new leadership of the BMZ (the Minister and the Parliamentary State Secretary are both women) has put strong emphasis on gender issues. Girls and women are mentioned as a special target group in the coalition agreement. The Minister is particularly committed to the fight against female genital mutilation.

The advancement of women was a prominent objective of BMZ policy statements under the old administration. However, implementation of a coherent gender approach has, inter alia, suffered from very limited staff resources. The number of projects in financial cooperation classified as potentially detrimental to women's interests and, therefore, in need of compensatory measures has increased. This could be interpreted as a sign of heightened gender awareness.

A cross-sectoral evaluation in 1998 by the GTZ, the German agency for technical cooperation, of 15 of its projects in 15 countries, underlined the low priority attributed to gender issues. In two thirds of cases, gender specific and poverty-reducing activities were not integrated. The identified reasons for this were the technocratic and quantitative orientation of projects as well as lack of gender competence of the project staff, which is also due to the inadequate provision of instruments such as gender training.

A positive development under the new Government is that financial assistance to women's projects can be given in the form of a grant in recipient countries that would normally only receive loans.

In practice, the politically established principle of gender equality is undermined. Project implementation is still largely oriented at fighting symptoms instead of promoting structural changes for equity and equality. Parallel to

Germany

Table 18 Share of basic social services in bilateral commitments 1999

| | Old government | | New government | |
	DM million	%	DM million	%
Basic education	89.5	3.1	115.0	3.7
Basic health	54.2	1.9	78.7	2.6
Family planning and reproductive health	144.5	5.0	137.5	4.5
Water and sanitation for the poor	238.5	8.3	193.5	6.4
Total basic social services	526.7	18.3	524.7	17.3
Total bilateral commitments (financial and technical assistance)	2,879.15	100	3,039.15	100

Source: BMZ, Referat 411, 20 October 1998 and 13 April 1999

interventions at the micro level, adjustments of the political and economic macro structures are indispensable.

DWHH and tdh welcome the new approach to macro-economics and gender within the DAC framework. In order to understand better the links between gender and poverty, DWHH and tdh ask for a systematic evaluation of the gender dimension to the BMZ's self-help oriented poverty projects.

Coherence must include military and trade policies

The coalition agreement states: 'The new government will ensure developmental coherence with other ministries.' There are some promising signs of how this ambitious target could be put into practice. Export credit guarantees are to be reformed according to social and developmental criteria. The Government wants to work for a similar transfor-mation of structural adjustment programmes within the IMF and the World Bank, and supports changes of international trade and investment regimes.

As a new member of the federal body dealing with arms exports, the BMZ can introduce development and human rights considerations into this policy field. In a number of cases, the BMZ articulated its opposition to military exports but was overruled by other ministries and the Chancellor. The German Government is determined to take on a more active role in multilateral debt relief.

DWHH and tdh see the need for wide-ranging changes in German policies towards the South in order to implement the Government's commitment to developmental coherence. In particular, they hope for a meaningful reform of export credit guarantees. DWHH and tdh call on the BMZ to take a strong stand against military exports to countries

of the South in the Federal Security Council. They expect the Foreign Office to join ranks with the BMZ and they ask for public transparency concerning such decisions.

DWHH and tdh welcome the German debt initiative but consider it inadequate as a long-term solution. The maximum quota for debt service in relation to export revenues should be set at 5% – the margin for Germany's debt forgiveness after the Second World War. As a structural solution to the debt trap, a legal insolvency regime needs to be established at the international level.[7]

DWHH and tdh ask the BMZ to increase its support for voluntary labels in international trade and foreign direct investment, which allow consumers to opt for products of high social and environmental standards. This relates to the certification of fairly traded, biological products and compa-nies in the South which observe core human and labour rights (for example Social Accountability 8000[8]).

Conclusion

The change of government has raised considerable hopes for a substantial reorientation of German aid policies and of foreign relations in general. The coalition agreement spells out a number of concrete commitments which, if properly implemented, would change the nature of German links to the South.

DWHH and tdh support the new framework for devel-opment policies. They are prepared to enter a new phase of meaningful dialogue and practical cooperation with the Government in development and foreign affairs, in a way that respects their specific mandates, functions and resources. DWHH and tdh welcome the initiative of the Foreign Office in setting up a civil society forum, to promote a continuous exchange of ideas and experiences with NGOs.

Germany

They ask the BMZ, in turn, to consider appropriate ways of institutionalising its channels of communication with NGOs in Germany. The coming years will tell to what extent the new administration is serious in implementing the ambitious and visionary principles set out in the coalition agreement.

Notes

1   See *The Reality of Aid* 1996, p126.
2   This book keeping exercise can be understood as a loan by the BMZ to itself, which augments present cash allocations at the cost of diminished resources in future years. The financial implementing agency KfW buys from the BMZ outstanding debts that the Ministry holds against the recipients of financial assistance. Cash appropriations and commitments in future years are reduced by the same amounts.
3   In judging the resources available for the German aid programme, one also has to consider the fact that the 1999 budget comprises a new expenditure item which the old government neglected to take into account. Beginning this year, the BMZ has to provide funds to the STABEX programme of the European Union in the order of DM400 million. This commitment must be met at the expense of regular programmes. The aid programme will be further squeezed by the fact that the US$ exchange rate has been set at the unrealistically low value of 1.6695 DM. Today the US$ stands at 1.84. This may cost the BMZ another DM50 million in 1999 if it is not compensated appropriately by the Finance Ministry.
4   Composite financing is a combination of funds from the financial aid budget and funds from the capital market which are guaranteed by the government. This is favourable to German suppliers as the ratio of aid to commercial credit can go up to 1:4. The credit costs for the borrower are still far below market interest rates. In its 1995 review of the German aid programme, the DAC underlined concerns shared by NGOs that composite financing may be used as an instrument of export promotion even though the credits are not tied formally to the purchase of German products.
5   BMZ, Informationsvermerk Nr 8/98 für den Bundestagsausschuß für wirtschaftliche Zusammenarbeit und Entwicklung zu den Vertraulichen Erläuterungen 1999 für die bilaterale Finanzielle und Technische Zusammenarbeit mit Entwicklungsländern, 27.8.1998.
6   BMZ, Informationsvermerk Nr 3/99 für den Bundestagsausschuß für wirtschaftliche Zusammenarbeit und Entwicklung zu den Vertraulichen Erläuterungen 1999 für die bilaterale Finanzielle und Technische Zusammenarbeit mit Entwicklungsländern (neu), 5.3.1999.
7   Germany should complement the HIPC initiative by a generous bilateral relief programme covering financial aid and loans taken over from the former GDR. Wherever appropriate, debt relief should include counterpart funds in local currency which are jointly controlled by state and non-state actors of creditor and debtor countries alike.
8   Social Accountability 8000 is a voluntary code of conduct for companies, developed by the New York-based Council on Economic Priorities. It defines operational standards with regard to core human and labour rights.

Ireland

Michael O'Brien, Concern Worldwide*

Aid grows but progress to 0.7% slows

In recent years the Irish Aid budget has grown steadily and substantially– from a low base of IR£40m (0.16% of GNP) in 1992 to IR£139.6m (0.31% of GNP) in 1998.This upward trajectory is set to continue.

The unprecedented continuous high rate of growth of GNP between 1992 and 1998 has meant that although ODA expenditure has more than trebled in that period, the increase in terms of percentage of GNP has not quite doubled. The ODA target 0.4% of GNP by 1997, set in the 1993 Irish Aid Strategy Plan, has not been met.

Even so, governments since 1993 have been in favour of moving towards the UN target for development aid of 0.7% of GNP. The current Government, in its *Action Plan for the Millennium*, is committed to reaching the target for ODA of 0.45% of GNP by the year 2002. This was reiterated by the Minister of State responsible for the Aid Programme in a speech at the launch of the 1998 Irish Aid Report in June 1999.

While NGOs acknowledge the relatively rapid rate of growth in the share of ODA to GNP over the period 1992 to 1998, they also note that the resources available to fund ODA at this time are unprecedented, due to the rapid growth of the economy and the resultant high rates of growth in Government revenues. Over the period of this growth in ODA, Ireland has received very large EU transfers, thus making it a substantial net recipient of development assistance.

Many NGOs now fear that the GNP target may become a receding horizon. They therefore call for the setting out of a specific growth path for ODA in relation to GNP so as to make steady progress towards realising the Government's own target of 0.45% by 2002. They call for a projected date for reaching the UN target of 0.7% of GNP.[1]

In November 1998, a new initiative in the Irish Aid budget was announced, namely multi-annual funding. The 'discretionary spending elements' of the Irish Aid budget will be increased by 66%, or IR£62.2m, over the three years 1999–2001. This figure is additional to the normal increases, which allow for inflation, and does not preclude extra spending on debt relief and multilateral aid.

Commitment to poverty reduction confirmed

Irish Aid's management objectives and plans were set out in the *Strategy Statement of the Department of Foreign Affairs 1998–2000*.[2] As outlined in this Statement, Irish Aid's overall policy aim is to work with the people and governments of developing countries (including LLDCs) and within the international community, to eradicate poverty and promote sustainable development.

Table 19 Ireland's ODA (IR£ millions)

	1992	1993	1994	1995	1996	1997	1998	1999*
Total ODA	40.0	55.6	75.2	96.8	112.1	124.1	139.6	178.3
ODA as % of GNP	0.16	0.20	0.24	0.28	0.30	0.31	0.30	0.35

Note: *estimate
Source: Annual Report of Irish Aid 1998, published June 1999

* Chapter based on research by Deirdre Farrell

Ireland

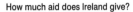

Percentage of national income spent on aid: a 30-year picture

How much aid does Ireland give?

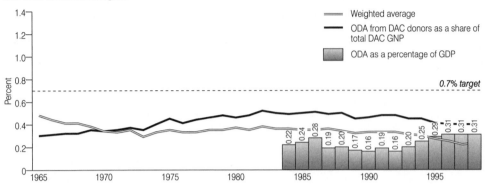

Legend:
- Weighted average
- ODA from DAC donors as a share of total DAC GNP
- ODA as a percentage of GDP

0.7% target

Bar values: 0.22, 0.24, 0.28, 0.19, 0.20, 0.17, 0.16, 0.19, 0.16, 0.20, 0.25, 0.29, 0.31, 0.31, 0.31

Where is Irish aid spent?

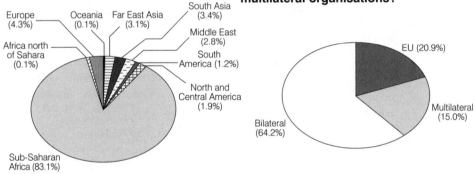

- Europe (4.3%)
- Oceania (0.1%)
- Far East Asia (3.1%)
- South Asia (3.4%)
- Africa north of Sahara (0.1%)
- Middle East (2.8%)
- South America (1.2%)
- North and Central America (1.9%)
- Sub-Saharan Africa (83.1%)

How much Irish aid is spent through multilateral organisations?

- EU (20.9%)
- Multilateral (15.0%)
- Bilateral (64.2%)

What is Irish aid spent on?

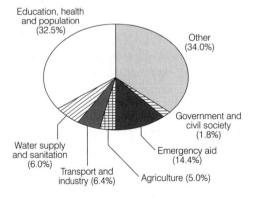

- Education, health and population (32.5%)
- Other (34.0%)
- Government and civil society (1.8%)
- Emergency aid (14.4%)
- Agriculture (5.0%)
- Transport and industry (6.4%)
- Water supply and sanitation (6.0%)

For notes on data and sources see page 286

How much Irish aid goes to the poorest countries?

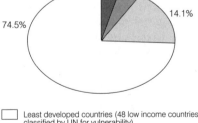

5.7%   5.7%   14.1%   74.5%

- Least developed countries (48 low income countries classified by UN for vulnerability)
- Low income countries (<US$765 annual income per capita in 1995)
- Lower middle income countries (US$766–US$3035 in 1995)
- Upper middle income countries (US$3036–US$9385 in 1995)
- High income countries (>US$9385 per capita in 1995)

Ireland

Box 23 Irish aid at a glance

How much aid does Ireland give?

Ireland gave	US$205m, IR£144 million in 1998*
that was	0.31% of GNP
and	0.78% of total government expenditure
which meant	US$56 or IR£39 per capita for 1998

Is it going up or down?

In 1998 Irish aid	rose by $18m, up 12% in real terms over 1997
Ireland was	level, remaining at 0.31% of GNP
The outlook is	that Irish aid is continuing to rise in real terms

How does Ireland compare with the other 20 donors?

Ireland ranks	19 out of 21 for its volume of aid
It is	10 out of 21 in the generosity league
It gives	88.6% of its aid to low income countries, a higher proportion than 19 other donors
Private flows	amounted to $136m, 73% of ODA
Total flows	to developing countries were 0.54% of GNP and rank 16 out of 21 in the DAC

What proportion of bilateral aid goes to basic education and basic health?

Ireland	has not yet reported to the DAC on its basic health and basic education spending

How important are commercial interests in aid?

Ireland reports that	it sees any commercial returns as a spin off. Irish aid is untied except for technical cooperation which is linked to Irish personnel

* The Irish government reported figure is IR£139.6m for 1998

Irish Aid supports a process of self-reliant, sustainable, poverty-reducing and equitable growth and development. Important principles that are fostered and advanced include respect for human rights, partnership, protection of the environment, gender equality, capacity building, and support for civil society and democracy. Hence, Ireland's aid programme is explicitly committed to concentrating on poverty reduction. Approximately 30% of the total Irish Aid budget is allocated to basic social sectors – primary education, health care and livelihood security.[3]

Bilateral aid is given to programmes and projects that meet basic needs in six priority countries in sub-Saharan Africa: Ethiopia, Lesotho, Mozambique, Tanzania, Uganda and Zambia. In 1998, more than IR£42m was allocated to spending on the priority country programmes, as compared to IR£6.5m in 1992.

Of the total Irish Aid expenditure of IR£139.6m for 1998, more than IR£84m, or 60%, was spent on bilateral assistance. However, in the 1999 allocations, bilateral assistance is planned for 56.5%, despite an increase in the overall budget of IR£38.7m (see Table 20). This is a cause of concern for NGOs who consider that Irish Aid must continue its policy, laid down in the 1993 Strategy Plan, whereby two thirds of Ireland's aid budget is bilateral and one-third multilateral. This was almost achieved in 1997 but has been lost in 1998 and 1999. The figure for 1999 is skewed somewhat by the introduction of a debt relief package in excess of IR£14.5m in the multilateral budget. This is mainly aimed at relief in two of Ireland's priority countries. When this debt relief is discounted from the total package, the bilateral percentage for 1999 rises to 60.2%, that is, the same figure as 1998.

Ireland

Table 20 Irish aid bilateral and multilateral assistance

	1997 (IR£ millions)	Percentage of BAP	1998 (IR£ millions)	Percentage of BAP	1999 (projected) (IR£ millions)	
Bilateral Aid (BAP)[4] includes:	60.5		66.2		70.1	
Priority Countries	35.6	58.8	42.3	64.0	41.7	59.5
Democratisation	0.9	1.4	1.0	1.5	1.3	1.8
Co-financing with NGOs	7.5	12.2	6.4	9.9	7.0	10.0
Rehabilitation assistance	4.0	6.6	5.0	7.5	6.0	8.6
Development education/information	1.1	1.8	1.1	1.6	1.0	1.5
Training/Fellowships	0.8	1.3	0.7	1.0	0.8	1.1
Other[5]	10.8	17.8	9.6	14.5	12.3	17.5
APSO	10.6		10.7		10.6	
Emergency humanitarian assistance	6		6.0		12.0	
Support to programme refugees in Ireland	1.50		1.1		6.0	
Total bilateral assistance	78.58	63.1% (of Irish Aid)	84.0	60.2% (of Irish Aid)	98.7	56.5% (of Irish Aid)
Irish multilateral assistance	43.2	34.8% (of Irish Aid)	52.8	37.8% (of Irish Aid)	76.1	43.5% (of Irish Aid)

Since the inception of the Irish Aid programme in 1974, Irish Aid has enjoyed a strong programme of collaboration with NGOs. However, the proportion of the bilateral aid programme spent on the NGO Co-financing Scheme, which is used for long-term development, has declined from a high of 14.3% of bilateral aid in 1995 to 9% in 1998 (see Table 20). This is counter to the trend towards increasing the percentage of the total aid budget spent through NGOs by increasing the amounts given to them for emergency work.

As the Irish Aid budget increases, NGOs call for an annual pro-rata increase in the co-financing line of the bilateral aid programme. They consider that NGOs have the capacity to spend increased amounts of money in developing countries, particularly in view of the fact that the Department of Foreign Affairs is revising administrative procedures to ensure appropriate accountability and reporting requirements for NGOs.

In 1998, the Department of Foreign Affairs organised the first Joint Forum with NGOs on Human Rights This was seen by many NGOs as a positive step. However, they also feel that there should be commitments to increasing the Human Rights and Democratisation budget line. These NGOs have prioritised support to building capacity with southern partners working for human rights and are convinced that such investment has a large multiplier effect

in promoting just structures in society.

The figure for refugees relates to first-year costs incurred by Government departments in Ireland, for example education, social welfare. Expenditure on refugees in developing countries is included under emergency, rehabilitation and other lines.

The rehabilitation assistance line is intended to continue funding beyond emergencies into rehabilitation, reconstruction and reconciliation efforts. Irish Aid had a budget for IR£5 million for this purpose in 1998 and this will increase to IR£6m in 1999. Irish Aid recognises that in the transition from an emergency situation it is important to lay firm foundations for sustainable social and economic development, good governance and respect for and promotion of human rights and fundamental freedoms.

The main objective of the programme is to assist the most vulnerable people in a selected number of countries to re-establish their lives and livelihoods. This involves helping to meet basic needs in areas such as shelter, food security and health. It also involves supporting governments to address institutional and human resource issues to create conditions that can lead to peaceful, just, inclusive and stable societies. According to the Annual Report of Irish Aid 1998: 'This assistance should not perpetuate existing inequities and must try to address the root causes of conflict.'

Ireland

Access and quality priorities for basic education

A priority for Irish Aid in its support to education is to assist partner countries in increasing access to basic education and ensuring that the quality of education provided enables people to participate fully in society.

Education accounts for approximately 20% of all priority country spending, of which 82% was spent on basic education in 1998, compared to 43% in 1993. Much of the increase has been achieved through sector investment programmes in priority countries. It is hoped that these will lead to improved capacity within government departments to manage national educational programmes.

Whole-school development programmes are a feature of Irish Aid support to education in priority countries. Improving the learning environment, the teaching/learning process and the management of education, and training of parents and communities in school development are all supported as essential to improving the quality of education. Irish Aid also endeavours to improve educational opportunities for vulnerable groups, particularly girls, and children with special needs.

Ireland's development cooperation programme has been moving away from supporting a wide range of individual projects, towards integrated sector-wide approaches to development. With the exception of Lesotho, Irish Aid is involved in sector-wide programmes in education in all of its priority countries. It considers this a highly effective way of delivering aid to education, as sector indicators such as access, equity, quality and efficiency are monitored on an ongoing basis. Sector-wide programmes also have the advantage of being able to support recurrent and capital costs in education, and can examine key capacity areas of need at second and third level, while keeping the focus on basic education.[6]

In 1999, the Irish Aid Advisory Committee (IAAC) published a report on Irish Aid and Non-Formal Education (NFE). While Irish Aid already funds some NFE programmes, for example increasing adult literacy rates in Mozambique, IAAC supports '…allocating a greater share of Ireland's bilateral budget to non-formal education and considers that a substantial part of that allocation should be delivered through NGOs.' It further recommends that Irish Aid should encourage learner-driven NFE projects in the areas of women's education, life-skills education, non-formal education for children and youth, and community health education programmes.[7]

Irish Aid was due to publish an education policy and guidelines framework in October 1999. This will give an overview of Irish Aid support to education throughout the 1990s and will outline operational guidelines for assessing the impact of education programmes in priority countries.

NGOs consider Irish Aid support for basic services, particularly education, to be the principal means of poverty alleviation and thus support both direct aid to education programmes and indirect mechanisms such as debt alleviation.

Box 24 Review of Ugandan programme: poverty focus

As part of Ireland's DAC review of 1999, a field visit was made in December 1998 to the Irish Aid bilateral programme in Uganda. While the full DAC Review is not yet complete, the review of the Ugandan programme is available. The report states: 'Through targeted actions in support of Uganda's own development strategy, Ireland is contributing to poverty reduction, social development and environmental sustainability, and is promoting democratic and accountable governance, the protection of human rights and respect for the rule of law. Gender concerns are integrated into programme activities.'[8]

Irish Aid, therefore, can be seen in practice to fulfil the commitment, set out in their Strategy Statement, of assisting the sustainable development of the poorest countries in the world. The Programme is also consistent with the vision of development cooperation contained in *Shaping the 21st Century*.

Although the report is generally positive, it does state that there needs to be more regular monitoring and systematic reporting against objectives. NGOs believe that Irish Aid is adopting a more strategic approach, with an overhauling of all procedures and a tightening of accountability. However, they also consider that at this time of rapidly expanding programmes, Irish Aid must continuously strive, in partnership with its southern partners, to ensure that all aid is effective, accountable and remains targeted on basic needs.

Irish Aid must also monitor the impact of support to the IMF's Enhanced Structural Adjustment Facility (ESAF) and HIPC (Heavily Indebted Poor Country) initiatives in Uganda, and the impact of Ireland's participation in structural adjustment programmes (SAPs) and their social impact.

Revised country strategies for Ethiopia, Tanzania, Lesotho and Zambia will be published in 1999.

Ireland

Many NGOs are prioritising basic education as an international advocacy issue for the next five years. They are lobbying Government – in advance of the proposed review, in 2000, of developments since the Jomtien conference – to adopt a strategic plan for achieving the UN and DAC target of primary education for all by 2015.

Debt relief principles agreed

Ireland has long been an advocate of a multilateral response to the debt crisis in the developing world.

In September 1998, the Irish Government complemented its advocacy role in relation to debt relief, with the announcement of a Debt Relief Package jointly agreed by the Departments of Foreign Affairs and Finance. The IR£31.5m package embraces multilateral and bilateral elements as follows:

- IR£15m for multilateral debt relief (IR£11m to World Bank HIPCs Trust Fund and IR£4m to IMF's contribution to the HIPC's Initiative);
- IR£9.5m to Mozambique and Tanzania in bilateral debt relief (1998 allocation);
- IR£7m to the IMF's Enhanced Structural Adjustment Facility (ESAF).

It was also agreed that debt relief should become 'an integral part of Ireland's overall overseas development cooperation strategy'. The Government, following representations from NGOs, also published a set of principles that will govern Ireland's policy towards developing country debt. The principles, which have been welcomed by NGOs, include the need for:

- Definitions of debt sustainability to take into account human as well as economic development;
- Greater transparency in the workings of the Bretton Woods Institutions;
- A greater degree of consultation and involvement of civil society in developing countries in the planning, design and implementation phases of IMF/World Bank programmes.

A wide range of Irish agencies, through the Irish Debt and Development Coalition (including NGOs, trade union groups, youth and religious bodies), have highlighted the discrepancy between the principles and the Government's decision to contribute to ESAF, which they actively oppose. Many NGOs consider that the IMF has not yet addressed the reforms needed in its policy package, in terms of ownership and transparency. They welcome the Government's

decision to provide an annual review of Ireland's participation in the Bretton Woods Institutions but believe that:

- There should be a moratorium on any Irish government contribution to ESAF until Spring 2000, when the results of pilot studies on the social impact of ESAF and its programme design will be available for assessment;
- Priority should be given to support debt funds established by debtor countries;
- Any Irish contribution towards the IMF's allocation to HIPC should only be made if HIPC is substantially improved and the IMF makes a significant contribution from its own resources.

Multilateral aid boosted

Ireland has a stated commitment to ensuring the implementation of high-quality expenditure programmes both directly to individual partner countries and also through the EU, the UN and other multilateral channels.

While meeting the mandatory multilateral contributions, Ireland also makes voluntary contributions to a variety of UN development agencies and programmes and contributions to these agencies have increased significantly in recent years.

In 1998, IR£52.8 of the Irish Aid budget was spent on multilateral assistance. The projected figure for 1999 is IR£76.1m, representing an increase of 44%. In 1998, IR£8.4m was spent on voluntary contributions to UN development agencies. This reflects a 14% increase over the 1997 figure and allowed for new contributions to be made to UNCTAD – World Association of Investment Promotion Agencies; Debt Management and Financial Analysis System – and to the Office of the Special Representative for Children and Armed Conflict. Ireland's other voluntary multilateral contributions include UNICEF, UNDP and UNHCR.

As well as committing a percentage of the Irish Aid budget to multilateral sources, Irish Aid is also committed to multilateral development cooperation at policy level; for example, Ireland is a member of the Executive Board of UNDP (for three years from January 1998). Ireland is also a member of the UNDP Bureau.

Ireland's objectives in terms of multilateral aid include:

- Participating in the development of the EU successor arrangement to the Lomé IV Convention;
- Working to strengthen coherence between all EU policies and programmes affecting developing countries, as well as pursuing increased coordination

Table 21 Irish aid grants to public information and development education (IR£)

Year	Grant from Bilateral Aid Fund to NCDE*	Grant from Bilateral Aid Fund for information on Irish Aid	Total	Percentage of bilateral aid fund
1995	880,221	97,199	977,410	2.5
1996	1,028,697	105,775	1,134,472	2.4
1997	992,854	71,369	1,064,223	1.8
1998	992,000	113,000	1,105,000	1.6
1999	1,023,000	150,000	1,173,000	1.8

Source: National Committee for Development Education

between the role of the Union in its development policies and programmes and those of member states.

NGOs have urged the Government to ensure that any successor to Lomé remains focused on sub-Saharan Africa, that it incorporates adequate debt analysis and allows for the development of regional approaches.

Coherence is also a key issue for NGOs and they continuously urge Government to ensure the operation of a coherent Development Cooperation Policy at national and international level, on such issues as EU trade policy, international environment issues, debt policy and food security.

Challenge to invest in development education

The 1994 DAC Development Cooperation Review of Ireland remarked on the strong support for the Irish Aid programme, both at the political level and among the general public. High levels of public support continue to be evident in Ireland and there is strong voluntary support for non-governmental development organisations.

Irish Aid recognises the importance of development education as a means of promoting better awareness and understanding of development issues, and has been supporting development education since 1985. The National Committee for Development Education (NCDE) is funded by Irish Aid and administers a funding scheme whereby grants are distributed annually to organisations for development education activities.

Despite this commitment, the share of the Irish Aid budget to development education has remained stagnant since 1995 (see Table 21). Between 1995 and 1998, the development education share of the Bilateral Aid Fund decreased from 2.5% to 1.6%; and in 1998, the budget for development education and information remained below its 1996 level in real terms.

NGOs and opposition parties have recommended that funding for development education be increased to 5% of

the Bilateral Aid Fund, in a staged series of increases, with an interim target of 3% to be allocated by 2002. Many believe that Irish Aid support for development education in Ireland is now more necessary than ever, given the growing professionalism of development education, the genuine thirst for more knowledge on development issues, the low level of awareness of long-term development and the rise in racism and xenophobia that has accompanied the increased number of asylum seekers coming to Ireland.

Some commentators point to the need for ongoing qualitative and quantitative research into public attitudes to development, in order to ensure sustained critical support for development and improved effectiveness of development education.[9] There has also been a call for more money to be allocated to policy analyses given the growing complexity and range of issues regarding development aid.

Notes
1 Recent Opposition Party development policy has committed to ODA reaching 0.7% of GNP by 2007.
2 Promoting Ireland's Interests: Strategy Statement of the Department of Foreign Affairs 1998-2000.
3 See Irish Aid Annual Report 1997.
4 Irish Aid Bilateral Assistance includes funding for the Bilateral Aid Programme, APSO, Emergency Humanitarian Assistance, and Refugees.
5 Under the Bilateral Aid Programme, the following elements are funded: Priority Countries, Democratisation, Co-financing with NGOs, Rehabilitation Assistance, Development Education, Training/Fellowships, Funding for Countries other than Priority Countries, Co-financing with multilateral Agencies, Grants to Organisations and Courses, and Programme Support.
6 Irish Aid continues its traditional area-based projects and believes that what Ireland can contribute to sector programmes is its ability to bring to the policy dialogue the knowledge gained first-hand from experience in district programmes.
7 Irish Aid and Non-Formal Education, A Report to the Minister for Foreign Affairs by the Irish Aid Advisory Committee, February 1999, pp19-22.
8 Ireland's Aid Programme in Uganda – DAC Peer Review (DCD/DAC/AR(99)2/10), p10.
9 L. Wegimont and P. Quigley, Development – Who Really Cares? 1998.

Italy

José Luis Rhi-Sausi, Marco Zupi,[1] *Movimondo*

Annual increase cannot reverse downward trend

In 1998 Italy gave 0.2% of national income to ODA; that is a net improvement from 0.15% in 1997. But this figure cannot be considered the beginning of a new positive trend, because it simply reflects the obligatory periodical replenishment of multilateral funds by the Treasury Ministry that occurred in 1998, after delayed Parliamentary approval.

Compared to the 1997 figure, 1998 saw the contributions to multilateral organisations double (see Table 22). But if we take a broader view, we get a clearer picture: after the period 1986–89, which was the highest point of Italian ODA,

peaking in 1989 (0.42% of GNP), the first half of the 1990s represented the most evident declining trend of ODA volume, which fell from 0.31% (1990) to 0.27 (1994). This worrying decline continued, from 0.27% (1994) to 0.15% (1997).

In terms of projected figures for Italian ODA, the 1999–2001 resources will be around 0.15% of Italian GNP (the 1999 committed funds are US$1,700 million; of which US$350 million is the grant share, plus another US$120 million from past grant residuals – that is, unspent money from previous year's budgets). Even if the government has committed itself to progressing towards the current DAC donors' average, that is 0.22–0.23% of GNP, there is no specified timing and no evidence of concrete steps to reach this.

Table 22 Italian ODA disbursements (US$ millions)

	1997	1998
ODA, net disbursements	**1,265.55**	**2,355.55**
a) to LLDCs	239.01	590.20
b) to sub-Saharan Africa	278.63	531.69
Bilateral grants	**360.78**	**332.43**
Of which:		
a) technical cooperation	57.79	40.42
b) Food aid	16.11	39.43
c) Emergency	50.25	16.57
Bilateral loans (including debt relief)	92.95	431.50
Contributions to multilateral organisations	811.83	1,591.62
Of which:		
a) United Nations	163.60	172.31
b) EC	613.76	713.35
c) World Bank Group	17.43	498.78
d) Regional development banks and funds	1.35	193.31
c) Other	15.69	13.87
ODA commitment	**1,232.54**	**1,739.75**

Source: Italian General Direction for Development Co-operation (DGCS)/MFA, preliminary data

Italy

Table 23 Disbursements of Italian aid to poor countries

	1996				1997			
	committed	%	disbursed	%	committed	%	disbursed	%
LLDCs and LICs	888,941	77	712,584	64	408,349	73	321,523	51
LMICs	229,131	20	300,419	27	142,242	25	249,949	40
UMICs	39,124	3	102,591	9	8,808	2	58,911	9

Source: MFA, 1999

Thus, the objective of reaching 0.7% of GNP seems to have been abandoned, despite the fact that it was repeatedly stated as the quantitative objective of Italian political commitment during the 1980s and the first half of 1990s.

Most of the characteristics described in last year's *The Reality of Aid* have been confirmed: the emphasis on multilateral cooperation (bilateral/multilateral ratio reached 30:70 in 1998) and geographical concentration continue to be the most notable elements.

Data analysis confirms the importance of the LLDCs, which have received some 40% of Italian aid. If one includes the 40% of Italian aid that goes to the Northern Africa, Middle East and Balkan region, where LDCs are lower middle income countries, the result is that around 80% of Italian aid is concentrated in the low and lower-middle income groups of countries. The upper-middle income group receives only 2–3% of Italian ODA, most of it going to South Africa, where aid is specifically targeted to reaching the poorest people. Considering the more appropriate grouping of LLDCs plus LICs, the most recent data show that some 51% of disbursed Italian aid went to poor countries in 1997.

Another important element to be considered is the relevance of the Food Aid sector. After the FAO Summit in Rome, November 1996, Italy committed itself to making food security a first priority in ODA policy. At the end of 1997, the Italian parliament ratified the London Convention, and the first consequence of this has been that funding lines to food aid reopened. In 1998, Italy allocated US$110 million for food aid – both emergency and non-emergency – most of it going to sub-Saharan Africa. Food aid is a specific component of the national Budget (different from grants and loans) and 'emergency aid' can be provided under grants or food aid. Pending legal reforms should remove this confusion.

Poverty reduction central to policy

The approach implemented by national cooperation policy shows that Italy has definitely placed efforts for reducing poverty at centre stage in its development concerns, both at bilateral and multilateral levels. The specific foci of Italian interventions seem to be relief, rehabilitation and peace-building activities. The underlying idea is that managing the critical post-conflict crisis phase is the precondition to designing the economic and social policy needed to fight poverty. This is clearly important, considering the geographical priority areas of Italian intervention – the Middle East, the Mediterranean Basin and the Balkans, and Horn of Africa. All of these regions are suffering the destabilising effects of war, in terms of social cohesion, institution building and economic development.

A review of the Italian strategy for poverty reduction shows that its approach is not in fact made in the context of post-conflict crisis management, but rather promoting social cohesion and community life, within a well-defined local development framework. Hence, development aid is aimed at reducing poverty by promoting a peaceful environment at local level. This is a very complementary tool to diplomacy and security interests.

The idea of considering ODA as a tool to guarantee the local preconditions to promote social-economic development and poverty reduction also underlies the emphasis that the Italian Government has put on debt relief recently. A solution to the chronic debt overshadowing the world's poorest countries is part of the Italian agenda, both at the multilateral level (within the context of the HIPC initiative) and the bilateral level.[2]

Seeking peace and development close to home

With its focus on relief, rehabilitation and peace-building, Italian aid policy towards poverty reduction requires a strategy that strictly and coherently links emergency and development aid.

At a bilateral level, the bulk of Italian aid to Angola, Ethiopia, Mozambique, the Great Lakes region of Africa and Bosnia-Herzegovina is channelled to relief, rehabilitation and peace-building activities, as a way of mainstreaming a poverty focus into ODA.

Italy

Percentage of national income spent on aid: a 30-year picture

How much aid does Italy give?

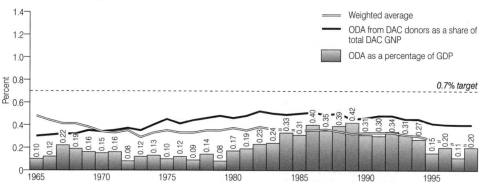

Where is Italian aid spent?

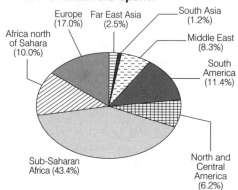

Europe (17.0%)
Far East Asia (2.5%)
South Asia (1.2%)
Africa north of Sahara (10.0%)
Middle East (8.3%)
South America (11.4%)
Sub-Saharan Africa (43.4%)
North and Central America (6.2%)

How much Italian aid is spent through multilateral organisations?

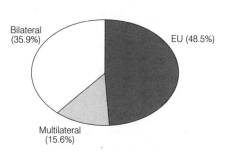

Bilateral (35.9%)
EU (48.5%)
Multilateral (15.6%)

What is Italian aid spent on?

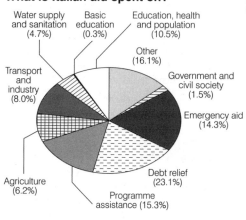

Water supply and sanitation (4.7%)
Basic education (0.3%)
Education, health and population (10.5%)
Other (16.1%)
Transport and industry (8.0%)
Government and civil society (1.5%)
Emergency aid (14.3%)
Agriculture (6.2%)
Debt relief (23.1%)
Programme assistance (15.3%)

For notes on data and sources see page 286

How much Italian aid goes to the poorest countries?

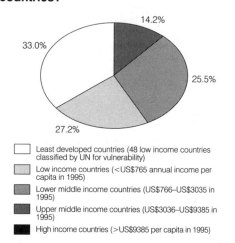

14.2%
33.0%
25.5%
27.2%

Least developed countries (48 low income countries classified by UN for vulnerability)

Low income countries (<US$765 annual income per capita in 1995)

Lower middle income countries (US$766–US$3035 in 1995)

Upper middle income countries (US$3036–US$9385 in 1995)

High income countries (>US$9385 per capita in 1995)

Italy

Box 25 Italian aid at a glance

How much aid does Italy give?

Italy gave	US$2,356m, 4,090 billion lire in 1998
that was	0.2% of GNP
and	0.41% of total government expenditure
which meant	US$41 or 71,935 lire per capita for 1998

Is it going up or down?

In 1998 Italian aid	rose by US$1,093m, up 84.5% in real terms over 1997
Italy was	more generous in 1998, rising from 0.11% GNP to 0.2%
The outlook is	for a general trend in ODA of around 0.15–0.16% of GNP. The 0.7% target has not been a real issue for the Italian political agenda for some years now

How does Italy compare with the other 20 donors?

Italy ranks	7 out of 21 for its volume of aid
It is	20 out of 21 in the generosity league
It gives	60.2% of its aid to low income countries, a lower proportion than 12 other donors
Private flows	amounted to $5,889m, 4.65 times ODA
Total flows	to developing countries were 0.71% of GNP and rank 13 out of 21 in the DAC

What proportion of bilateral aid goes to basic education and basic health?

Italy committed	0.1% of bilateral ODA to basic education, 0.9% to basic health and 0.4% to population and reproductive health

How important are commercial interests in aid?

Italy reported that	54.4% of its bilateral aid commitments were tied to the purchase of goods and services from Italy

---

During 1997, former Yugoslavia was a priority recipient area in terms of grants and emergency aid. In particular, Bosnia was the main recipient of emergency aid flows (US$3.5 million) and grant aid (US$11.5 million).

Table 24 Italian aid to Bosnia-Herzegovina in 1997 (US$ millions)

Emergency aid	Total grants	Loans	Other
3.5	11.5	n/a	2.5

Source: Italian MFA

Since the outbreak of crisis, Albania has received an increasing part of Italian aid and continues to attract important flows (which are not – strictly speaking – all items of

ODA budget, but come from different items and imply different Ministries' involvement). In 1997, Albania received US$32.5 million from Italian MFA and became the main recipient of Italian ODA funds.

What makes the Albanian case particularly interesting is the strong link between financial crisis and instability (and the migration emergency) on the one side, and development aid on the other. It means that Italy, in a reactive way, has searched to coordinate security, migration and development aid policies.

Nevertheless, until recently the absence of a proactive approach has meant the lack of a clear strategy and the prevalence of extraordinary (emergency) aid over ordinary development aid. By 1998, however, the picture changed: a three-year plan was introduced, and the MFA activity is now linked to:

Italy

Table 25 Italian 1997 Aid to Albania (US$ millions)

Emergency aid	Total grants	Loans	Other
2.7	10	11.5	8.3

of which:
1.1 to finance micro-projects (health, environment, food)
0.9 to recover health and sanitation
0.4 to provide food to the poorest
0.3 to support vaccination campaign against hepatitis

Source: Italian MFA

- The activities led by the Extraordinary Commissioner for Albania;[3]
- The programme 'Direct aid to people', of the Social Affairs Department of the Prime Minister's Office;
- The movement towards decentralised cooperation through regions and municipalities and NGOs.

In administrative terms, these activities are not considered part of ODA and are handled by separate ministries. In terms of projected figures, the 1998–2000 plan for Albania estimates a minimum sum of US$120 million (with a grants/loans ratio of 1:6) to be added to the presently committed US$50 million. Most of the resources should be devoted to basic infrastructure programmes in Tirana (some US$60 million for provision of water and electrical power), including some 'quick impact' initiatives.

Albania will be a crucial test case for translating principles into action, to demonstrate how practical this approach is.

The very importance given by Italian ODA policy to Albania, which will continue to be the main recipient country in coming years, shows the nature of the approach of Italian ODA at the end of the 1990s: the Italian targets are not the poorest countries, but those countries (in transition as well as developing) that are a short distance from Italy – in the broader sense, the whole Mediterranean basin and, particularly, the Balkans.

In order to implement its approach of poverty reduction focused on relief, rehabilitation and peace-building, Italy has some challenges to accept. One of these is the need to coordinate the health sector and socio-economic interventions: in fact, Italy's specialisation in health has traditionally emerged, at international level, in the peace-building process. The main areas of intervention through health sectoral policy have been:

- The promotion of national health service systems (Ethiopia, the Palestinian Territories, Mozambique, and Eritrea are the most interesting cases, because of the coordination activities carried out in close cooperation with donor countries and international organisations).
- The promotion of decentralised local health service systems, through NGO activities (Sao Paolo in Brazil, Sofala in Mozambique, the PCREV programme in Colombia and Uganda).
- The promotion of the Geographic Information System, health information systems and epidemiological surveillance (Swaziland, Zimbabwe and Salcedo province in Dominican Republic).
- The promotion of sustainable health infrastructure and bio-medical technologies at local level (Lebanon, Uganda, Egypt, Syria, Eritrea, the Palestinian Territories, Tunisia and Algeria).
- Basic health assistance, to control endemic diseases (AIDS, malaria, tubercolosis, leprosy), to promote policies for family and reproductive health and nutrition (targeted at the most vulnerable groups: children and mothers), and to promote prevention and rehabilitation activities to the advantage of people with disabilities.

Thus, Italy must search for a coherent approach to link these health activities to other sectoral interventions, reinforcing the mainstreaming of poverty reduction.

Building on the experience of human development programmes at local level is a way to establish this link: after the experience of PRODERE in Central America, Italy and UNDP are now promoting similar projects elsewhere. At multilateral level, they have promoted, since October 1995, the 'Trust Fund for sustainable social development, peace, and the support of countries in special situations'. This fund is specifically aimed at promoting a participatory approach in development initiatives to fight poverty. Bosnia-Herzegovina, Cuba, Mozambique, South Africa and Tunisia are now implementing the multilateral local level programmes for human development (PDHL).

Refugees are the target group of some other specific interventions in Sudan, Kenya, Uganda, Lebanon, Mozambique and the Palestinian Territories.

Italy has participated in several other donor coordination mechanisms at country level, since 1993. These include:

- The working group on poverty and social policy of the Special Programme of Assistance for Africa (SPA), which is helping the World Bank to define methodological guidelines for poverty assessment and link them to country assistance strategies.

* The DAC coordinating working group on policies for poverty reduction.
* Co-financing for the World Bank Social Funds in Albania, Ethiopia and Eritrea (ie countries whose post-conflict crisis is evident) to combat poverty.
* Operational coordination with the European Commission, at country level, particularly in countries where the volume of disbursed Italian ODA has produced a leadership role (such as in the case of Albania, Angola, Ethiopia, Eritrea and Mozambique).

Strategy faces obstacles on all sides

Obstacles to implementing this strategy and achieving the proposed results emerge both from the recipient country and the Italian administration.

The main obstacle in recipient countries is the LDC governments' attitude of giving priority to internal political concerns (particularly middle-class consensus and support for the civil service).The lack of effective democracy and real participation in LDCs makes it difficult to orchestrate a real process of ownership of development cooperation, and poverty reduction strategies. In terms of the Italian institutions' capacity to implement the poverty reduction guidelines, the Ministry of Foreign Affairs is still searching to close the gap between the very broad guidelines (the 1995 New Cooperation Policy Guidelines, yearly updated by the Minister in the Provisional Planning Act) and field activities by the project officers. Up to 1999, Italy lacks any operative guidelines at intermediate level.

Another constraint on the Italian administrative side is the absence of a methodical approach based on the use of a Country Programme Strategy. As of 1999, Italy had realised only one Country Programme. This was in Albania, where the current crisis has clearly modified the context. It is now negotiating a programme with the Ethiopian government.

Looking at these experiences, the difficulty of implementing a broad-based negotiation process is evident: the representatives of civil society have not been clearly defined in Albania, while in Ethiopia the government prevents any efforts of involving other actors. Yet it is precisely this lack of broad-based participation which prevents a more effective negotiation process as well as real ownership.

Another basic constraint on translating commitment to poverty into practice is the lack of specific professional profiles of people skilled in poverty reduction strategy and devoted to advising about project implementation in the field. This implies a problem of coherence between the

Administration's human resources (its organisation) and the theory of how aid should work. The projects aimed at reducing poverty are not properly supported by specialised technical advisors or training activities provided by the Ministry structure.

In 1995, a reform process was set in motion to change Italy's cooperation organisation structure; in 1998, after approval of a Bill at the end of 1997, this started to be discussed by parliament. The main thrust, in organisational terms, is a shift from a ministry-based management of ODA to the creation of an external agency to manage aid, which should guarantee a more professional management structure.

Italian evaluation activity is based on a single-project approach, attaching a preliminary assessment of the impact of aid on poverty reduction. 1998 saw the completion of the first external evaluation, clearly including the impact of aid on poverty, that is the evaluation of the Integrated Rural Development Programme in Ader Doutchi Maggia, Niger. The final report (an internal MFA document) was not available for review at time of writing.

The Government's 1997–99 plan to monitor and evaluate activities considers 'environment, gender, and poverty reduction issues as mainstream in development cooperation and to be evaluated in every activity'; and its implementation will require 'the adoption of an evaluation approach that must be coherent with DAC principles'.

Currently, three main areas of activities of Italian ODA policy are going to be evaluated: Aid to sub-Saharan Africa, Education and Training, and Promotion of Joint Ventures.

Critical components in confronting poverty

Mainstreaming gender equality

The 'Guidelines on the role of women and on the promotion of a gender perspective' established by the MFA in 1998 have, as their main objective, 'the promotion of men and women participation, as individuals of equal dignity, in the definition of sustainable development'.

The MFA intends to adopt gender perspectives in the conception, planning and implementation of all cooperation activities, and in the definition and implementation of cooperation policies. Particular attention is given to gender perspectives during the monitoring and evaluation phases, and in the definition of development indicators.

In pursuing these themes, in 1997 Italy began by identifying some precise actions of gender mainstreaming into the human development programme at local level, in Angola, as well as in South Africa. These actions should be part of the mainstreaming procedure in programmes due to be implemented in Bosnia, Tunisia and Mozambique.

Italy

The Italian Government intends 'to realise initiatives promoting women's full participation in the decision-making process at all levels and to enhance the gender perspective in the political, economic and cultural fields', in poverty eradication and conflict prevention activities.

Promoting micro and small enterprises

During 1997 and 1998, the Government committed itself to increase Italian ODA policy orientation towards the promotion of the private sector, which is now one of the principal concerns of the Italian debate. One recent indicator of this interest has been the Government document 'Promoting Local Development through Small-Size Enterprise Clusters: the Role of Migrants'. This was prepared on the occasion of the 1999 G8 Köln Summit. This debate, involving the Public Administration, research centres, enterprises and the NGO community, focused on effective tools to promote, in a systematic way, micro and small enterprises in LDCs. This can be seen as a useful step on the way to improving the coherence of aid.

At the end of 1997, the MFA started to introduce a new data base on Italian aid programmes on micro and small enterprises promotion, which they hope will make project identification, monitoring and assessment easier.

Between 1995 and 1997, Italian aid supported 24 programmes on micro and small enterprise promotion: seven were focused on micro-enterprises and cost US$12 million; the other 17 were for small enterprises, and cost US$155 million. With regard to the instruments, soft loans accounted for US$120 million and grants constitute the remaining US$47 million. Most of these programmes are channelled through the multilateral agencies (the World Bank, UNDP/OPS, ITC, UNCTAD, UNIDO).

During 1997, MFA approved seven additional projects on micro and small enterprise promotion: they cost US$12.8 million, of which two thirds went to micro-enterprises projects and the remaining third to small enterprise. The improvement of micro-enterprise projects' share demonstrates that Italian cooperation is considering the dynamism of the private sector as an important component of poverty reduction policy. Italian aid is promoting a more favourable environment for micro and small enterprise, with the creation of services centres, technical assistance, training, credit and micro-credit schemes.

Particularly important, in terms of poverty reduction, are those programmes supporting micro-entrepreneurship through micro-credit schemes: in Albania and Bosnia-Herzegovina, Italy participates through the World Bank Trust Fund; in Bangladesh through NGO activity; in Egypt through a bilateral programme, involving both a micro-credit line and a guarantee fund.

Strengthening support to basic education

Italian cooperation is traditionally weak in the sector of basic education. More activities are being carried out in the professional training and university cooperation sectors, in which Italy specialises.

In recent planning activities, more attention has been paid to this issue. The promotion of basic education is included in the guidelines for interventions concerning childhood. But currently Italian aid is far from becoming very active and specialised on this DAC issue.

NGOs are likely to remain the more crucial actors in basic education practice, because of their tendency to interact mainly with local counterparts, their flexibility and their primary interest in human resources and basic social services.

Reviving investment in NGOs

Financing of NGOs started again in 1996 and in 1997 the MFA approved 20 new projects promoted by NGOs. Four were based on self-financing sources; the other 16 requested a MFA co-financing line of some US$8 billion.

After the 1995 suspension of government funds to NGOs, 1997 confirmed the 1996 increment, and the revision and simplification of the procedural mechanisms seem to facilitate this trend.

In terms of geographical distribution, in 1997 the NGOs' preferences confirmed the priority given to Latin America. Cultural, linguistic, religious links, and the existence of a dynamic socio-economic fabric in Latin American society help to explain this.

Table 26 Geographical distribution of NGO programmes

Region	%
Latin America	55
Africa	20
Mediterranean basin	15
Asia and Pacific	10

Source: MFA

Considering the sectoral distribution, education and training continue to be the main field of NGO intervention.

Italy

Table 27 Sectoral distribution of NGO programmes

Region	%
Training	45
Multi-sectoral	20
Health	15
Food and agriculture	5
Trade and handicraft	5
Water provision	5
Industry	5

Source: MFA

Notes

1   The authors were assisted in preparing this chapter by Alberto Mazzali and Deborah Rezzoagli.
2   The Italian Government proposed, during the Köln G8 Summit, in 1999, through the Ministry of Treasury, the relief of foreign debt for the poorest countries. The preliminary estimates indicate an Italian commitment of around US$1,200 million (export credit) plus US$400 million (ODA loans).
3   General Angioni, who led the Italian mission in Lebanon, is in charge of managing assistance to Albania, mainly focused on institution building (support to customs and police agencies are the main areas of intervention).

The Netherlands

Caroline Wildeman, NOVIB

Concentrating on quality

In search of greater efficiency and quality, and driven by the goal of effectiveness within a limited budget, the Minister for Development Cooperation has proposed a radical change in bilateral development aid policy.

When the new cabinet took office in 1998, it soon became clear that the new Minister for Development Cooperation, Eveline Herfkens, wanted a change in direction, even though she was from the same political party (Social Democrats) as her predecessor. The most important arguments for changing the policy were the facts that Dutch aid had become too fragmented and dispersed, and that, given the additional pressure on the Development Cooperation (DC) budget, the resources available had to be used more efficiently.

While the previous minister, Jan Pronk, decided, for political-strategic reasons, to support many countries and allowed his policy to depend on demands, Minister Herfkens decided on a more pragmatic approach. As a former member of the Board of Governors of the World Bank, she was inspired by the World Bank report 'Assessing Aid: What Works, What Doesn't, and Why'. The most important conclusion of this report is that development aid can only be effective if the receiving government follows a sound policy. According to the report, this involves a well-balanced budget policy, trade liberalisation and combating corruption.[1] The World Bank authors warn that providing aid with the intention of positively affecting the policy followed is an illusion and does not lead to the result desired.

Focus on effectiveness

Within a few months of taking office, Minister Herfkens presented her plans for a new bilateral aid policy and announced that she would aim for a structural bilateral aid relationship with 20 countries. Her review of bilateral policy focused on 78 countries that received more than one million Dutch guilders (NLG) in bilateral aid in the previous year. The heading for bilateral aid accounts for 20% of the DC budget, or NLG 1.3 billion. Cooperation with countries that were not eligible for long-term structural bilateral aid were to be considered for continued assistance in a more limited form, through the application of specific thematic bilateral aid instruments. Where activities in certain countries or sectors were to be scrapped altogether (except for emergency assistance and small embassy support), an exit strategy would be developed to prevent an unwarranted destruction of capital.

The idea behind the policy change was to increase the efficiency and quality of Dutch aid by restricting the number of countries and sectors receiving structural aid. In addition to limiting the number of countries, a sectoral approach rather than project-based finance was decided on. The central element in the aid relationship for Minister Herfkens is ownership, with the government of the recipient country playing a leading role and bearing responsibility for its own sectoral policy. Sectoral support means that the receiving country draws up a policy for specific sectors (eg health-care, education), to which all the parties involved commit themselves on a multi-annual basis.[2]

Another reason for the concentration on a smaller number of countries was the limited Dutch executive capacity and the budget available. According to the Minister, tough decisions had to be made as to which countries, sectors and channels were to receive aid. New obligations taken up by the Department of Development Cooperation in the areas of international environmental policy and the reception of refugees from developing countries, as well as a commitment (made since the new Government came to office) to contribute to debt relief to Indonesia necessitated this.[3]

The list of countries that would apply for structural bilateral aid was based on three criteria: the level of poverty; the quality of socio-economic policy; and the quality of governance.

The Netherlands

'The level of poverty and the need for aid' were measured in terms of countries that qualify for soft loans from the World Bank (IDA). These countries are unable to borrow money on the international financial market because their GNPs are too low. The limit for the World Bank loan is a GNP of US$925 per capita per year. In addition, the added value of Dutch development aid compared to other donors was considered.

'Quality of socio-economic policy' depended on the quality of the particular government's macroeconomic, economic structure and social policies. With regard to social policy, the poverty reduction objectives were considered in particular.

'Quality of governance' was judged by the integrity of the administration, the prevention of corruption, transparent management of public resources, supervision of government spending, the level of participation by the population, the separation of powers, legal certainty, democratisation and observance of human rights. The relative level of the defence budget was also taken into account.

The selection was not just based on figures but also on fairly 'untransparent' qualitative data for which the embassies and multilateral organisations, in particular the World Bank, were consulted. Sound policy and good governance were put in a long-term context, in which positive trends were rewarded.

In early 1999, Minister Herfkens presented her list to the national parliament. That list included 19 countries: Bangladesh, Bolivia, Burkina Faso, Eritrea, Ethiopia, Ghana, India, Yemen, Macedonia, Mali, Mozambique, Nicaragua, Pakistan, Sri Lanka, Tanzania, Uganda, Vietnam, Zambia and Zimbabwe.[4]

With three countries – South Africa, Egypt and the Palestinian Territories – a time-bound bilateral relationship was proposed. In addition to the country list for structural bilateral cooperation, three theme-specific instruments were defined within which aid may be provided outside these 19 countries. These are: environmental programming; activities in the field of human rights, peace-building and good governance; and the private sector programme (mainly Dutch export promotion). Another 30 countries qualify for aid in this context.

Public supports new policy

The policy change has received a great deal of publicity. In general, the pragmatic approach of the new Minister won a positive response from the public. Limiting the number of countries from 78 to 19 was experienced as a fresh wind through development cooperation. Previous policy was

labelled paternalistic and interfering; providing aid on the basis of political motives, such as influencing internal governance, was also viewed as ineffectual since good governance is not for sale. The result of this approach was that many different initiatives were supported in an unspecified number of countries, rendering the policy unmanageable.

The national parliament agreed to the change in approach. The priority given to the poorest countries was considered particularly positive. After a public hearing, some changes were made to the proposal of 19 +3. Parliament removed Pakistan and Zimbabwe from the list and proposed Rwanda and Benin as aspirant candidates, to be decided upon within a year.

The change in direction of the bilateral policy evoked questions about the other channels, such as multilateral support and channelling through Co-Financing Organisations (CFOs). The new Minister, who attaches great value to multilateral cooperation, has announced that she will send a note to the national parliament about the quality of multilateral aid. She has already openly questioned the quality of assistance given by the EU and UNDP.

The role of the CFOs, which receive a fixed percentage of the development budget to support NGO activities in developing countries, was eventually raised as well. The Minister wanted to establish closer working relations with CFOs, both to assist the exit strategies and to strengthen the comparative advantage private organisations have in promoting community participation, especially in those countries where good governance is lacking. New working principles of the CFOs and the Ministry reaffirm, however, the autonomy of CFOs. Regular consultations should determine what division of labour will help to enhance their complementary roles. The 10% of the annual budget earmarked for cooperation through CFOs will remain the fixed percentage for coming years.

Political direction lacking

The choice of sectors within the concentration countries will depend on the outcome of a policy dialogue in those countries. For this purpose, the embassies in the now 17 countries, plus the three countries, have been given a fairly flexible mandate. The Minister does not wish to put her own priorities for sectors on the table beforehand, out of fear of a donor-driven dialogue and lack of ownership by the recipient country.

Novib and others have criticised the Minister's lack of political direction. It would not be sensible to give these countries a 'blank cheque'. Governments in the South are

The Netherlands

Percentage of national income spent on aid: a 30-year picture

How much aid does The Netherlands give?

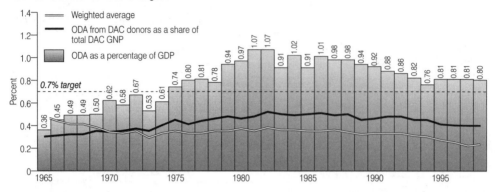

Where is Dutch aid spent?

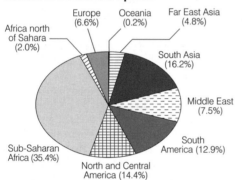

- Europe (6.6%)
- Oceania (0.2%)
- Far East Asia (4.8%)
- Africa north of Sahara (2.0%)
- South Asia (16.2%)
- Middle East (7.5%)
- South America (12.9%)
- North and Central America (14.4%)
- Sub-Saharan Africa (35.4%)

How much of Dutch aid is spent through multilateral organisations?

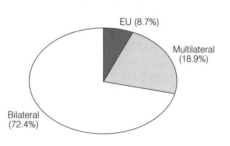

- EU (8.7%)
- Multilateral (18.9%)
- Bilateral (72.4%)

What is Dutch aid spent on?

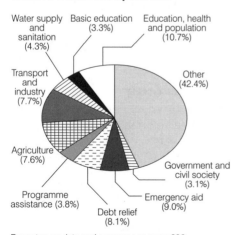

- Water supply and sanitation (4.3%)
- Basic education (3.3%)
- Education, health and population (10.7%)
- Transport and industry (7.7%)
- Other (42.4%)
- Agriculture (7.6%)
- Programme assistance (3.8%)
- Debt relief (8.1%)
- Emergency aid (9.0%)
- Government and civil society (3.1%)

For notes on data and sources see page 286

How much of Dutch aid goes to the poorest countries?

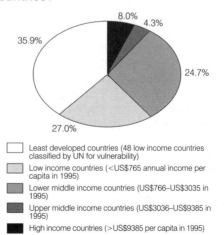

- 8.0%
- 4.3%
- 35.9%
- 24.7%
- 27.0%

- Least developed countries (48 low income countries classified by UN for vulnerability)
- Low income countries (<US$765 annual income per capita in 1995)
- Lower middle income countries (US$766–US$3035 in 1995)
- Upper middle income countries (US$3036–US$9385 in 1995)
- High income countries (>US$9385 per capita in 1995)

The Netherlands

Box 26 Dutch aid at a glance

How much aid does The Netherlands give?

The Netherlands gave	US$3,049m or 6,051 million guilders in 1998
that was	0.8% of GNP
and	1.71% of total government expenditure
which meant	US$197 or 391 guilders per capita for 1998

Is it going up or down?

In 1998 Dutch aid	rose by $102m, a rise of 3.5% in real terms over 1997
The Netherlands was	less generous in 1998, falling from 0.81% of GNP to 0.8%
The outlook is	that the target will remain at 0.8% of GNP until 2002

How does The Netherlands compare with the other 20 donors?

The Netherlands ranks	6 out of 21 for its volume of aid
It is	3 out of 21 in the generosity league
It gives	62.9% of its aid to low income countries, a higher proportion than 10 other donors
Private flows	amounted to $5,310m, 1.8 times ODA
Total flows	to developing countries were 2.21% of GNP and rank first out of 21 in the DAC

What proportion of bilateral aid goes to basic education and basic health?

The Netherlands committed 0.9% of bilateral ODA to basic education, 1.7% to basic health and 0.1% to population and reproductive health

How important are commercial interests in aid?

The Netherlands reported 5.6% of its bilateral aid commitments were tied to the purchase of goods and services from The Netherlands

---

party to international agreements reached in the 1990s at various UN conferences. The Minister should call the recipient countries to task with regard to the implementation of these agreements (eg in the fields of the position of women, investment in basic social services and sustainable development). The implementation of the 20:20 Initiative should form an integral part of this policy dialogue with the recipient country

The Minister stated that she believed that the policy for basic social services in the 17 countries was carefully considered, and that she did not, therefore, see the need to discuss the 20:20 Initiative in advance. However, it is doubtful whether this may be assumed without question as little data is available. From a study by UNICEF and UNDP on basic social services spending by governments in 30 developing countries, it appears that expenditures are low. Average spending is 12–14% of national budgets. Very few of these countries spend less than 10% and very few reach 20%. Particularly low allocations occur in Benin, Cameroon

and Zambia in sub-Saharan Africa, in Bangladesh and the Philippines in Asia, and Brazil, Dominican Republic and Nicaragua in Latin America. Only a few countries in Latin America and sub-Saharan Africa (Belize, Burkina Faso, Namibia, Niger, Uganda and Peru) allocate close to 20% to basic social services.[5]

In response to criticism from Novib and parliament, the Minister emphasised that reference to international meetings could be raised by embassies to guide the dialogue with recipient countries. If the promise of 20% of ODA for basic social services will not be met in the bilateral programming, she will give higher priority to BSS in multilateral programming to ensure that the Netherlands spends overall 20% of its budget on BSS.

Main objective of poverty eradication

What does the Netherlands do to achieve the poverty eradication objective? This question takes a central place in *The*

The Netherlands

Reality of Aid report. The Dutch aid policy has highlighted poverty eradication as its principal objective. Scientists have recently questioned the emphasis on indirect over direct poverty eradication. Where priority is given to promoting economic growth and economic self-reliance, too little is done to reach poor people directly with poverty eradication programmes.[6] The authors criticise the objective of poverty eradication by stating that no one has ever produced a good analysis of who are the poorest people and what their needs are.[7] They also criticise the lack of information on what is actually spent by the Ministry on direct compared to indirect poverty eradication.[8] Others have questioned the variety of objectives in addition to driving back poverty, such as the reinforcement of the position of women, protection of the environment, support to Suriname and the Netherlands Antilles and Aruba, and increasing Dutch export promotion.[9]

From 1 January 2000 some aspects of this will change as the Netherlands Antilles and Aruba will no longer qualify for ODA under DAC criteria. As a result, NLG230 million should then become available for pure ODA. However, this opening will be filled by costs for hosting asylum seekers in the Netherlands, economic cooperation with Indonesia and debt relief in the context of export credit insurance. These are all headings that do not fit into the objective of direct poverty eradication.

Prior to the annual budget debate in parliament, Novib criticised the interpretation of the objective of poverty eradication by pointing out the inappropriate use of ODA. At the formation discussions for the new Government, ODA was fixed at 0.8% of BNP. However, resources formally classified as ODA were used to solve domestic problems. Firstly, costs involved in compliance with international agreements to reduce CO_2 emissions have been classified under the development budget, through the financing of the Clean Development Mechanism, whereby developing countries can be supported to develop cleaner industry so as to reduce CO_2 emissions. However, at the international climate conference in Kyoto, it was agreed that no funds intended for poverty eradication should be used for this purpose. At a follow-up conference in Buenos Aires, the Netherlands was reprimanded for departing from this agreement. Within the EU also, it has been agreed that the application of the Clean Development Mechanism may not be at the expense of funds intended for poverty eradication.

The second additional encroachment on the budget for development cooperation involves the hosting of asylum seekers in the Netherlands. In the government policy statement it was agreed to reserve NLG244 million for the first-year reception of asylum seekers from DAC countries

with an A-status, ie recognised refugees, from 1999 onwards. This means that spending on this area will be doubled in comparison with the former situation. It is expected that the costs for receiving asylum seekers will turn out to be even higher for next year's budget: an additional NLG100 million was mentioned, to be financed with funds earmarked under 0.8% of BNP for ODA. The policy statement has been stretched in this respect; the agreement refers to asylum seekers with A-status, while the Government is now referring to refugees *appealing* for this status. The needs of the extra influx of asylum seekers should not be met at the expense of funds for poverty eradication – nor classified as ODA.

In its response to the draft budget for 1999, Novib also pleaded for a higher investment in basic social services. The 20% as agreed at the Social Summit has been incorporated in the budget. However, achieving the objectives as they have been laid down internationally – reducing absolute poverty at least by half; primary education for everyone; reduction of child mortality and access to medical services and reproductive healthcare – requires more than 20% of ODA funds.

Private money bypasses the poorest

Another concern is that commercial private money streams are passing the poorest countries by. Poverty eradication policy should be aimed at supporting the poorest countries in attracting foreign investment and establishing an enabling environment. This requires measures for promoting social development and investing in a country's political and economic stability.

According to Novib, the current private sector programme, mainly ORET (Development-Relevant Export Transactions, now merged with the Programme for Environment and Economic Self-reliance), insufficiently meets the need of the poorest countries to promote private investment. The ORET programme provides for financial support to the Dutch business sector in exports to developing countries.

The catalysing effect of export promotion for poverty eradication was often questioned, even by the former Minister. As discussed in the parliamentary debates, the exports involved seem rather ad hoc, with limited effect on long-term investment or growth. The funds for the private sector programme increased substantially during recent years (NLG185 million in 1997, 340 million in 1998 and 365 million in 1999). Novib therefore pleaded in 1998 for a thorough evaluation of the ORET programme, no further increase in funds for the private sector programme and in

The Netherlands

the meantime a shift in the programme from funding export promotion to funding investment promotion. The outcome of the evaluation and debate in parliament on the ORET programme was expected in late 1999.

Primary education goal needs priority funding

This year, in the context of Oxfam International's initiatives on basic education, Novib has started a campaign aiming to stimulate political willingness to generate the resources and policy measures necessary to fulfil the international agreement that all children should be able to go to school by the year 2015. The campaign shows that this objective can be achieved through a shift in funds to primary education. For the Netherlands to contribute its fair share towards this, the current reservation for primary education in the budget for development cooperation should be increased from 4.5% (Novib estimate) to 8%.

Novib urges the Minister to give priority to primary education in her policy of providing structural support to a limited number of countries. Worldwide, 125 million children are not in school, most of them girls. Others receive education of a poor quality that is not in line with their needs. Governments of the countries on the list for structural bilateral aid have developed plans to reform and extend primary education. Specific support for these plans through Dutch aid could mean an enormous contribution. Bilaterally financed activities are currently taking place in only 12 of the 17 countries. The effective extension of Dutch aid for primary education requires more experts at the Ministry and embassies, ideally one education specialist at each embassy in the countries on the list of structural bilateral aid. The Ministry currently employs ten educationalists (three in The Hague and seven at the embassies).

Earmarked budget support in combination with specific debt relief can provide the recipient governments with the means to enable access to good primary education. The Netherlands should support the idea – in an international context – of giving extra debt relief to those developing countries that wish to invest more in primary education and other social priorities, but whose public finances are seriously constrained by foreign debt payments.

In addition to governments and donors, local civil society organisations can also play an important role in realising the objective of universal access by the year 2015. Good and accessible education is primarily a task of the state. Primary education is, therefore, firstly an area of aid from government to government. However, local organisations have also proved that they can make an important contribution to providing access to primary education, especially with regard to groups that are difficult to reach, such as working children and women, and minority groups, to whom they offer education in their own language.

Often governments have taken insufficient measures to reach the poorest people, especially in rural areas. In those situations in particular, NGOs have added value to education. They have developed innovative teaching models that involve both parents and the wider community, thus motivating people to send their children to school. In addition, NGOs, together with other social organisations such as teaching unions, can put pressure on the government within the country to enable accessible and good education for everyone.

Notes

1 World Bank Report 'Assessing Aid: What Works, What doesn't, and Why' by David Dollar and Lant Prichett, Washington, November 1998.
2 Letter to the Lower Chamber on country policy for structural bilateral aid, 26 February 1999.
3 Idem.
4 For some countries in this list of 19, reservations were mentioned. For Eritrea and Ethiopia there are indications of concern about the border conflict. ODA to Ethiopia and Eritrea will be partly frozen as long as the armed conflict continues. Other reservations are made for Pakistan, Zambia and Zimbabwe. Because of the unstable situation in those countries a new assessment will be made within a year.
5 Letter to the Lower Chamber on country policy for structural bilateral aid, 26 February 1999.
6 'Country experiences in assessing the adequacy, equity and efficiency of public spending on basic social services' by UNICEF/UNDP. Paper for Hanoi meeting on the 20:20 Initiative, 27-29 October 1998.
7 Research commissioned by the DAC Informal Network on Poverty Reduction, DAC Scoping Study of Donor Poverty Reduction Policies and Practicies: The Netherlands' L Schulpen and P Hoebink, University of Nijmegen, July 1999.
8 'Netherlands Aid Policies for Poverty Reduction', P Hoebink and L Schulpen in ODI Working Paper 115, December 1998, London.
9 Research commissioned by the DAC Informal Network on Poverty Reduction, DAC Scoping Study of Donor Poverty Reduction Policies and Practicies: The Netherlands' L Schulpen and P Hoebink, University of Nijmegen, July 1999.
10 'Vernieuwing in de Nederlandse ontwikkelingshulp', J W Gunning and T de Ruyter van Stevenink in the *International Spectator*, February 1999.

Portugal

Maria do Céu Ferro, OIKOS

Welcome effort to streamline aid

The main destination of Portuguese Development Aid is still, almost exclusively, and mainly for historical reasons, the five Portuguese-speaking African countries (Angola, Guinea-Bissau, Mozambique, Cape Verde and S.Tomé and Prince), all classified among the Least Developed Countries (LDCs).

This concentration is in part a response to the difficulties these countries are experiencing but also takes into account the strategic objective of consolidating and reinforcing the Portuguese-Speaking Countries Community (CPLP), and affirming it in the international system. Given that Portuguese has a cultural presence in so many parts of the world, there is a strong argument for extending development cooperation beyond these countries. Certainly Portugal should formulate a policy for cooperation in Latin America and Asia, without ignoring its responsibilities to the Central and Eastern European countries that want to strengthen relationships with Portugal.

Portuguese development cooperation has suffered years of management deficiency, lack of coordination between sectors and limited resources, particularly when contrasted to other countries' performance. Everything that concerns cooperation policy is in an embryonic state but this Government is making a big effort to improve the mechanisms of coordination, control and evaluation. In fact, 1998 revealed itself as a quite remarkable year in this regard, mainly for the formulation, for the first time, of a development cooperation programme and an integrated budget.

While development cooperation will continue to fall under a secretary of state in the Ministry of Foreign Affairs and Cooperation, there was an important step forward, in August 1998, with the creation of a Ministerial Council to specialise in cooperation matters. This was the form found by the Government to deepen political consensus about the principles of cooperation and to endow this cross-cutting policy with the necessary legal and institutional mechanisms to coordinate the development cooperation policy more effectively.

The Ministerial Council will settle, each year, the volume of the budgetary resources for development cooperation, having as a base the target ODA/GNP ratio and the macroeconomic forecasts underlying the budget. It will also determine distribution in line with strategic objectives.

Among the other changes that took place in 1998, the creation of 'desks' for different themes such as poverty, education and gender equality, is notable. These desks, created by the ICP-Portuguese Cooperation Institute, which is a department of the Foreign Affairs Ministry, are still being established. However, at the ICP level, technical experts from all the desks participate in the meetings and studies organised by the DAC/OECD and European Union, including the DAC/OECD Poverty Network and Poverty Evaluation (DFID).

A document called Portuguese Cooperation on the Threshold of the 21st Century, prepared by the Foreign Affairs Ministry and recently approved by the Ministers' Council, Portugal's main governing body, aims to provide the guidelines for Portuguese development cooperation.

This document proposes a significant change in the target for aid – increasing to 0.36% of GNP in the 2000 budget, with predicted growth up to 0.7% by 2006, in line with the commitment made at the Rio Conference, in 1992.

Since 1992, Portugal has been erratic in its support of the development aid effort. In terms of ODA/GNP ratios, its contributions fell from 0.36% in 1992 to 0.21% in 1996, went up to 0.25 in 1997 and down to 0.24 in 1998. These oscillations are mostly explained by the relative importance of the flows associated with the external debt management in the receiving countries, in the total public development aid. As the rearrangement of the recipient countries' debt cancellation follows a specific calendar, it has not been possible to

Portugal

keep the ratio ODA/GNP on a desirable, solid growth course. It is clear that the 0.7% is quite far from being realised.

Taking account of the need to respond to the war in Guinea-Bissau and a quite recent government decision to help Timor with a programme of poverty reduction, it is likely that the 0.36% target will increase for 1999 and 2000. The government intends to revise its targets annually to achieve 0.7% through progressive growth.

The political reasons for acting on this commitment to progressively increase ODA are detailed in the resolution establishing the Ministerial Council. This articulates a need for Portugal, 25 years after it began its decolonisation process, to define its place in the European Community and in the community of Portuguese-speaking people throughout the world. Portugal sees its own sustainable development in terms of its strategic approach to political, economic and cultural relations with these communities.

It is within this frame that the development cooperation policy, an essential vector of foreign policy, acquires its particular strategic meaning; it differentiates and affirms a particular identity that values the country's historical and cultural heritage.

In this context, it is necessary to imbue the cooperation policy with greater strategic rigour and coherence, more effective politic leadership, a more rational organisation and an adequate finance system. This is the sense of the reform and adjustment measures adopted by the Government.

Poverty seen in a broad context

Poverty reduction can only be possible through a collective coordination effort by all countries – donors and recipients – and in each country, between NGOs and the Government.

While the more developed countries have a greater responsibility to devote resources to human development, all countries, both developed and in development, share a real interest in a more equitable wealth distribution, in a socially fairer world.

For all this, cooperation for development is more and more an effort of the Portuguese Government to support education, the productive sectors and the building of markets for goods and services, health, food security, access to potable water and financial aid, among other things.

The distribution of Portugal's aid is spread over a vast range of sectors, particularly in infrastructure and social services – which account for about US$50 million, or some 32% of bilateral ODA.

There are priorities for Portuguese cooperation policy – education, social services, food security and health come

first. Indeed, education is top priority, with a special budget and support of the Education Ministry for several projects, including sending teachers to African Portuguese speaking countries.

Efforts to reduce poverty in developing countries are greatly hampered by debt, which is strangling already precarious economies. However, another obstacle is the lack of coordination of aid and development programmes, and of real knowledge of people's problems and needs. On the side of receiving countries, the unrestrained corruption of some governments and the destabilisation caused by ethnic conflicts and civil wars delay and often obstruct fieldwork by NGOs and other agencies.

Reducing poverty and promoting economic and social development among the most disadvantaged populations in the least developed countries are seen as part of the answer to these obstacles. In addition, the Government supports efforts to reinforce democracy and governance. It is also promoting dialogue and regional integration, and European partnership for human development. This may not be enough but Portugal is trying to do its best.

Planning for integration

Portugal is a member of a DAC group working on Poverty Reduction Evaluation. During the last two years, and after an annual audit of Portugal's global cooperation effort, there was an attempt, although not exhaustive, to bring together projects/programmes which were connected, directly or indirectly, with poverty reduction.

In 1999, for the first time, a Portuguese Cooperation Integrated Programme was formulated, which makes provision for integrating all Ministries' programmes/projects for this year.

The 22 indicators set out in the core set of OECD documents from the Development Progress Indicators Seminar, in February 1997, were sent to NGO, ministries and embassies, and to universities offering courses in the field of development cooperation.

The Portuguese Cooperation Institute (ICP) has been training specialised statisticians in the area of evaluation and poverty indicators.

Drive towards gender equality

Portugal is part of the DAC/OECD Working Group on gender equality, which shares expertise and provides guidelines on improving approaches to gender equality in development cooperation programmes. At the CPLP level (Portuguese-speaking countries), there has been a concern to sensitise people to the importance of women's rights.

Portugal

Percentage of national income spent on aid: a 30-year picture

How much aid does Portugal give?

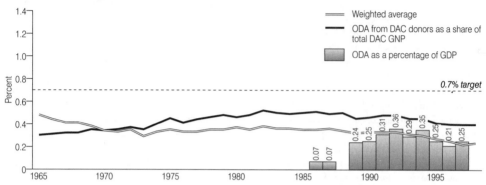

Legend:
- Weighted average
- ODA from DAC donors as a share of total DAC GNP
- ODA as a percentage of GDP

0.7% target

Bar values: 0.07, 0.07, 0.24, 0.25, 0.31, 0.36, 0.29, 0.35, 0.25, 0.21, 0.25

Where is Portugal's aid spent?

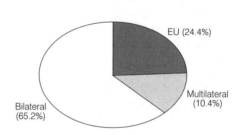

- Europe (0.3%)
- South America (0.4%)
- Africa north of Sahara (0.1%)
- North and Central America (0.1%)
- Sub-Saharan Africa (98.9%)

How much of Portugal's aid is spent through multilateral organisations?

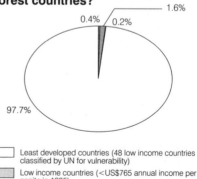

- EU (24.4%)
- Multilateral (10.4%)
- Bilateral (65.2%)

What is Portugal's aid spent on?

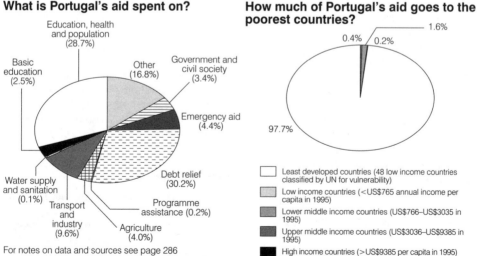

- Education, health and population (28.7%)
- Basic education (2.5%)
- Other (16.8%)
- Government and civil society (3.4%)
- Emergency aid (4.4%)
- Debt relief (30.2%)
- Water supply and sanitation (0.1%)
- Transport and industry (9.6%)
- Agriculture (4.0%)
- Programme assistance (0.2%)

For notes on data and sources see page 286

How much of Portugal's aid goes to the poorest countries?

1.6%
0.4% 0.2%
97.7%

- ☐ Least developed countries (48 low income countries classified by UN for vulnerability)
- Low income countries (<US$765 annual income per capita in 1995)
- Lower middle income countries (US$766–US$3035 in 1995)
- Upper middle income countries (US$3036–US$9385 in 1995)
- ■ High income countries (>US$9385 per capita in 1995)

Portugal

Box 27 Portuguese aid at a glance

How much aid does Portugal give?

Portugal gave	US$259m, 46,576m Escudos in 1998
that was	0.25% of GNP
and	0.56% of total government expenditure
which meant	US$26 or 4,681 Escudos per capita for 1998

Is it going up or down?

In 1998 Portuguese aid	rose by US$9m, a rise of 3.4% in cash terms over 1997
Portugal was	the same in 1998 at 0.25% GNP
The outlook is	that ODA is to reach 0.36% of GNP in the medium term and 0.7% by 2006

How does Portugal compare with the other 20 donors?

Portugal ranks	18 out of 21 for its volume of aid
It is	18 out of 21 in the generosity league
It gives	97.9% of its aid to low income countries, more than any other donor
Private flows	amounted to $1,004m, 4 times ODA
Total flows	to developing countries were 1.33% of GNP and rank 5 out of 21 in the DAC

What proportion of bilateral aid goes to basic education and basic health?

Portugal committed	0.7% of bilateral ODA to basic education, 1.1% to basic health and 0.2% to population and reproductive health

How important are commercial interests in aid?

Portugal reported that	none of its bilateral aid commitments were tied to the purchase of goods and services from Portugal

---

It is also worth noting that in the Working Group on Poverty and Social Policy, in the ambit of the SPA (World Bank), Portugal has been following the debates concerning gender equality, which it regards as a cross-cutting objective implicitly present in all its cooperation activities. The ICP has created a Gender desk, which is supposed to work on all aspects of gender equality related to the cooperation policy. In 1998, Portugal gave a US$20,000 USD voluntary contribution to UNIFEM (Emergency Fund).

At times of restructuring, Portuguese cooperation moves slowly towards new forms of action. While there has been a real effort to work towards gender equality, until now very little has been done. What is encouraging is the obvious will to improve performance in this area.

Basic education seen as key to poverty reduction

The establishment of the Ministerial Council was part of Portugal's efforts to improve the articulation and coherence of all its programmes and projects with the PALOP (African Portuguese-speaking countries). This body analysed the present cooperation situation, with a view to creating adequate strategies for implementation – and bridging the huge gaps between the different sectors of the country's cooperation policy. In the orientation proposed for the cooperation policy, approved by the Ministerial Council's Resolution 102/98, in August 1998, basic education was considered as the priority area. Education is a privileged sector because it is seen as an essential factor in combating poverty.

That Resolution defines strategic orientations for Portuguese cooperation and sets out an Integrated

Portugal

Cooperation Programme for 1999, in which basic education receives special attention at the budget level. There is a significant increase in the percentage of GNP spent in 1998/99 in the education sector, through the concession of education scholarships, teacher-training, institutional support and sending didactic materials to the Portuguese-speaking African countries. It is estimated that 0.07% of GNP, or US$130,000 goes to basic education.

Building local capacity

The aid programme's management is mainly done in Portugal, but in many programmes/projects there is a partnership in the management of the resources between the Portuguese NGOs and other cooperation agencies, and the ones in the receiving countries.

The Portuguese NGOs use their budget and human resources mainly in projects involving poverty reduction and basic education. Very few of the Portuguese NGOs are involved in development education. The role of NGOs is of interest to the Government and there is regular consultation. Below is a general view of some of the most important aid programmes developed by the Portuguese NGOs, with the support and knowledge of the Government.

The non-governmental movement is quite recent in Portugal, in terms of development cooperation. Its growth only started when Portugal joined the European Union. Although at the end of 1998 there were 130 NGDOs registered in the Portuguese Cooperation Institute, most of them were inactive.

In spite of its youth and fragility, the Portuguese NGDO sector has been demonstrating a great vitality, being the most active and dynamic among the decentralised cooperation agents.

The NGDOs introduce, in partnership with the institutional cooperation, irreplaceable qualities, namely reinforcing the level of cooperation and participation through their field work capacity to mobilise populations. This helps to give structure to civil society in receiving countries and strengthens their self-reliance.

The Portuguese Government has not been giving due support to NGDOs. This situation must be corrected. The NGDO contributions from the Portuguese Cooperation Institute are still very low, about US$750 000 in 1997, although there have been some significant increases in 1998 – about US$1.9 million – 1.05% of ODA.

However, some measures have been taken. For example, the ICP, together with the NGDO platform, produced in 1997 a document that settles the financing, disbursement and evaluation norms of the NGDO activities

and projects. The ICP is also granting the platform an annual subsidy which assures its coordination functions. The ICP keeps regular and systematic contacts with the platform, and supports some concrete NGDO activities. Examples of the range of activities these NGDOs are involved in, which complement the cooperation efforts of government are given below.

ACEP (Association for Cooperation between Peoples) works in partnership with the PALOP NGOs in the fight against poverty. It runs a programme of cross-national sensitisation about the PALOP/NGO partnership, which provides a forum for sharing knowledge and evaluating the work developed by these civil society organisations. It aims to transmit a true image of development in Africa and challenge negative, pre-conceived ideas. It encourages contact between people and organisations involved in development cooperation in different ways, and aims to enable future partnerships for education for development and cooperation. This project was delayed by the war in Guinea-Bissau and ACEP was busy supporting and promoting the integration of the Guinea-Bissau refugees. ACEP developed an educational project called Questioning underdevelopment: education in sub-Saharan Africa – a case study of Guinea Bissau. This aims to link civil society organisations involved in basic education in the North and South, with a view to promoting understanding of the issues.

ILAC/CT – the African/Portuguese Institute for Scientific and Technological Cooperation – develops projects/programmes in the Portuguese-speaking countries in Africa. An example is the 'Open School' in Mozambique, which provides integrated training of young people in civil construction to rebuild some of Mozambique's 2500 degraded schools. The trainees can go on to become assistants and managers to help ensure the sustainability of the schools.

ILAC/CT works with youth associations in Mozambique and S.Tomé and Prince. It also runs an integrated health programme involving several projects (sensitisation, post-graduate training of doctors and nurses, implementation of basic sanitary measures).

Marquês de Valle Flor Institute is starting an Education for Development project, Odyssey 2000, which aims to sensitise, raise awareness and reward young people in Portuguese schools for their interest in Africa, and particularly the Portuguese-speaking countries. The project operates through an internet site which aims to generate materials about Africa (history, tales, traditions, recipes, drawings, photos, songs, etc), and promotes links between schools and African associations both in Portugal and in Africa.

Portugal

Table 28 Geographical distribution of Portuguese bilateral ODA to principal beneficiaries

Country	US$ millions
Angola	23.93
Cape Verde	23.09
Guinea Bissau	10.76
Sao Tome and Principe	10.77
Mozambique	61.53
Portuguese sub-Saharan Africa (PALOP)	32.33
Portuguese speaking countries and others (CPLP)	13.99

Table 29 Portuguese ODA in 1998

	US$	Percentage of Total
Bilateral ODA	176.4	68.2%
Multilateral ODA	82.14	31.8%
Total ODA	258.54	100%

OIKOS receives support from the Ministry for Education in the form of a small grant and the secondment of teachers to work in OIKOS education projects. These cover all levels, from kindergarten to university, and give Portuguese children and youth a better knowledge of the world they live in.

OIKOS supports the Programme of Communal Development Promotion in Lichinga, Mozambique. This is a project of food security involving social reorganisation with the creation of 'agrarian houses', which were fundamental elements of reactivation of agricultural production after the war. Through these houses, people organise themselves in peasant associations, having received agricultural implements and seeds, and other support, such as programmes of saving and credit.

In close cooperation with Mozambique's programme for rehabilitation of the rural economy and reconstruction of basic infrastructure, OIKOS developed a programme of communal health, orientated towards maternal and infant protection, environmental health, nutrition, prevention and detection of endemic disease.

OIKOS also has projects in partnership with MOC (Community Organisation Movement), in north-east Brazil, and with COPROFAM (Family Promotion Committee) in Lima, Peru. OIKOS also has projects in Guinea and Angola, dealing with serious problems due to the latest conflicts.

Spain

Gonzalo Fanjul, Intermón[1]

Reforms needed to effect new policy

For the third year in a row, the Spanish official aid system is going through a period of transition, in an attempt to advance towards a mature, coherent aid policy on the same level as other donors' policies.

The transition has been marked by the approval of the Cooperation Law (June 1998) and by its subsequent parliamentary development,[2] which includes a Quadrennial Directive Plan and the reform of key institutions, such as the Spanish Agency for International Cooperation (AECI).

This is an interesting moment: although these measures represent Spanish aid's most serious effort to plan and quantify its actions in the mid-term, there is still significant work to be done to adapt existing executive institutions to cope with the policy changes. Until now the lack of economic resources and professional capacity has been a chronic problem in the Spanish aid system. It is therefore essential to launch deep institutional reforms to ensure that the policies proposed in the Directive Plan are made a reality.

Contributions undercut commitments

Year after year Intermón has denounced the limited increase in official resources allocated to aid. ODA has been at a standstill between 0.23% and 0.28% of Spain's GNP since the beginning of the 1990s. In 1998, however, an encouraging development took place. Aid resources went beyond two hundred thousand million Spanish pesetas (ptas), for the first time (208,100 million ptas, approximately US$1.300m).[3] Although this only brought ODA to 0.25% of Spain's GNP, the rise reflected a commitment to continuous increases in coming years and represented a 13% increase in real terms.

While Intermón appreciates this effort, we believe that the Spanish aid system must work towards greater increases in the future, if it intends to respond to its own commitments as well as to the message, voiced time and time again by Spanish civil society, that Spain should actively pursue the 0.7% target. We are still far below the average in relation to the rest of Europe (0.34% in 1998).

We hope that the final approved version of the Directive Plan will establish an environment favourable to future growth and will set specific, accountable targets for the coming years. As regards the original proposal for this Plan, Intermón has supported reaching 0.35% in the year 2002.

Directive Plan suffers unexplained delays

The Multiannual Plan's preparation and legislative process has been stop-and-go from the start. The Administration's responsible body (Planning and Evaluation and Office of the Ministry of Foreign Affairs) promoted a participatory decision-making process and entrusted a group of academics with the first written proposal. This draft[4] was then discussed both in the Ministry of Foreign Affairs and the Ministry of Economy and Finance.

The Government promised to have fully discussed the first draft and placed a Bill before Parliament by the end of May, so that the Cooperation Council (a consultative body of representatives from civil society, the Administration and independent experts) and other responsible bodies could prepare their own reports on it before the end of June. This would have enabled parliamentary groups to discuss the Plan's budget during Parliament's annual budgetary preliminary negotiations during July. This was the only way to ensure that the Plan would be fully in action by the beginning of the year 2000.

Unfortunately, various factors have hindered the process. For unknown reasons, the Ministry of Economy has taken more than three months to present its opinion on the draft and has blocked further discussion. Considering that the legislative process for the Cooperation Law was initiated a year ago, this is obviously not a good start. Besides, fears have been expressed in relation to the Government's plans to introduce significant changes to the original proposal.

During the negotiating process, there was consensus on the need to reform the concessional credits (FAD) system. Although no major changes have been introduced, there appears to be a will to increase the poverty focus of FAD and to make this instrument complement the rest of ODA. Last minute changes could also be expected in the lights of the opposition to the proposal from the Ministry of Economy.

Table 30 summarises the most relevant aspects of the original proposal (before the Administration's amendments):

Logically, the Plan has its weaknesses; for example, its lack of definition in some areas (such as multilateral aid or debt relief) and the absence of key elements such as policy coherence among aid's general goals. However, the proposal entails very important improvements in Spain's official aid policy and is an essential working tool for future developments.

Implementing ODA: the Spanish Agency for International Aid (AECI)

In the Spanish aid model, the institution that holds political responsibility for Spain's Official Development Assistance (ODA) is the Secretary of State for International Cooperation and Latin America (SECIPI). The AECI is the SECIPI' s executive branch and, as such, is in charge of implementing specific aid programmes and policies.

In addition to this political-executive axis, there are other bodies within the Administration with responsibilities concerning aid policy. The most important is the Ministry of Economy and Finance, which manages concessional credits, debt relief programmes and Spain's contributions to international financial institutions, as well as to the European Union. These contributions amounted to 61% of Spain's total aid budget in 1997.

Added to the problems caused by the ill-defined distribution of responsibilities – and the consequent lack of unity in the direction of aid (which, according to the law, falls on the Ministry of Foreign Affairs) – in Intermón's opinion, the structure of the Spanish Administration cannot manage aid appropriately.

The AECI exemplifies the model's weaknesses. The Agency was created in 1988 and has undergone minor reforms over the past ten years in order to adjust its managerial structure to changes in the nature of Spanish aid. Despite these alterations, there are still significant weaknesses within the institution that prevent it from playing a leading role in Spain's aid system. These weaknesses can

be summarised as follows:[5]

- It has an inappropriate legal status, which imposes unnecessary hindrances on the institution's management (both budgetary and administrative) and is incompatible with its activities. For example, no project can be approved over a period of more than a year.
- Its organisational structure does not fit in with the Directive Plan's requirements.
- It provides insufficient staff training.

Considering all the points mentioned thus far, we can conclude that Spanish aid is making important steps towards maturing its proposals, as well as trying to improve its planning, managerial and evaluation instruments. Nevertheless, the institutions responsible for implementing these measures are not in a position to do so, therefore profound changes are needed.

Policy needs to highlight basic education

The amount of Spanish aid allocated to basic education in 1997 was approximately 3% of all bilateral ODA. Expenditure on basic education was only a fifth of the total amount allocated to the education sector. The lion's share has been consistently spent on the university education system, which absorbs 45% of Spain's total bilateral aid destined to the education sector (mainly, through scholarships and concessional credits for infrastructure).

Although it may appear that the Government's low level of interest in basic education responds to a defined policy, in fact it does not. As in most areas of Spanish aid, priorities in the education sector are determined by contextual circumstances in each country rather than by a systematically planned strategy.

The new Directive Plan can and must correct this tendency. Education appears in two of the Plan's priority sectors: basic social services and investment in the human being. The former affects investments in basic education projects directly, whereas the latter refers to education at secondary school and university levels.

According to the first draft of the Plan, 'investment in the human being' (which covers higher education, cultural and research projects) should amount to 18% of bilateral ODA within four years; while investment in basic social services should attain 25%.

Although a percentage specifically for basic education remains to be defined, Intermón has proposed that at least 8% of bilateral aid should be allocated to this area, in accordance with UNICEF's calculations.[6]

Spain

Percentage of national income spent on aid: a 30-year picture

How much aid does Spain give?

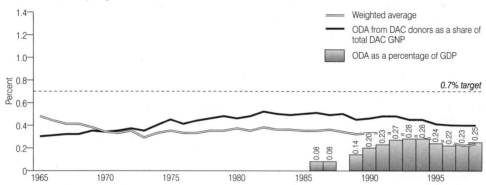

Legend:
- Weighted average
- ODA from DAC donors as a share of total DAC GNP
- ODA as a percentage of GDP
- 0.7% target

Values shown: 0.08, 0.08, 0.14, 0.20, 0.23, 0.27, 0.28, 0.28, 0.24, 0.22, 0.23, 0.25

Where is Spain's aid spent?

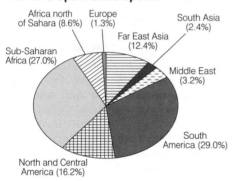

- Africa north of Sahara (8.6%)
- Europe (1.3%)
- Far East Asia (12.4%)
- South Asia (2.4%)
- Middle East (3.2%)
- Sub-Saharan Africa (27.0%)
- South America (29.0%)
- North and Central America (16.2%)

How much of Spain's aid is spent through multilateral organisations?

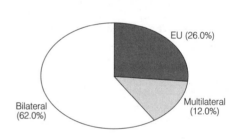

- EU (26.0%)
- Multilateral (12.0%)
- Bilateral (62.0%)

What is Spain's aid spent on?

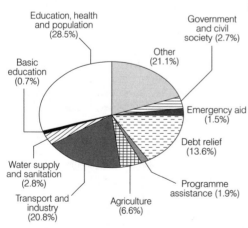

- Education, health and population (28.5%)
- Government and civil society (2.7%)
- Other (21.1%)
- Basic education (0.7%)
- Emergency aid (1.5%)
- Debt relief (13.6%)
- Water supply and sanitation (2.8%)
- Programme assistance (1.9%)
- Transport and industry (20.8%)
- Agriculture (6.6%)

For notes on data and sources see page 286

How much of Spain's aid goes to the poorest countries?

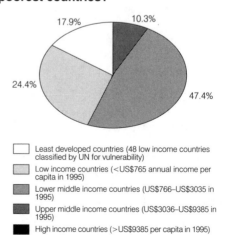

17.9% 10.3% 24.4% 47.4%

- ☐ Least developed countries (48 low income countries classified by UN for vulnerability)
- Low income countries (<US$765 annual income per capita in 1995)
- Lower middle income countries (US$766–US$3035 in 1995)
- Upper middle income countries (US$3036–US$9385 in 1995)
- ■ High income countries (>US$9385 per capita in 1995)

Box 28 Spanish aid at a glance

How much aid does Spain give?

Spain gave	US$1,383m, 208,108 million pesetas in 1998
that was	0.25% of GNP
and	0.6% of total government expenditure
which meant	US$35 or 5,292 pesetas per capita for 1998

Is it going up or down?

In 1998 Spanish aid	rose by $149m, a rise of 11.8% in real terms over 1997
Spain was	more generous in 1998, rising from 0.24% GNP to 0.25%
The outlook is	improving. For the first time in five years there are signs that aid volume may increase with the government seriously considering a number of different scenarios to improve the GNP ratio.

How does Spain compare with the other 20 donors?

Spain ranks	11 out of 21 for its volume of aid
It is	17 out of 21 in the generosity league
It gives	42.3% of its aid to low income countries, a lower proportion than 18 other donors
Private flows	amounted to $6,177m, 5 times ODA
Total flows	to developing countries were 1.39% of GNP and rank 4 out of 21 in the DAC

What proportion of bilateral aid goes to basic education and basic health?

Spain committed	1.3% of bilateral ODA to basic education, 4.7% to basic health and 0.2% to population and reproductive health

How important are commercial interests in aid?

Spain reported that	100% of its bilateral aid commitments were tied to the purchase of goods and services from Spain

---

Hurricane crisis sparks major relief effort

Spain's massive relief effort in response to Hurricane Mitch is unprecedented. The media bombardment of news and images of the hurricane's disastrous consequences spurred the Spanish public to send more than Ptas 22,000 million (about US$150m) to NGOs and institutions working in the affected area.

Spanish society has always tended to respond rapidly to emergency crises. In fact, Spaniards have always been more willing to respond to these situations than to make serious commitments to long-term development programmes. However, the reaction to the situation in Central America clearly marked a milestone in the history of Spanish aid.

Noting the degree of public response, the Spanish Government also reacted swiftly. Unfortunately, it immedi-ately encountered the official aid system's limitations and lack of coherence. On the one hand, the Ministry of Economy and Finance prepared a package of Ptas 17,500 million (US$117m) in concessional credits, and postponed debt repayment until 31 December 2001; on the other hand, the AECI offered an additional emergency aid package of Ptas 1,800 million (US$12m). As usually happens, the Ministry of Foreign Affairs was tied to a very restrictive budget, while the Ministry of Finance could immediately allocate thousands of millions of pesetas. In the end, lack of political will to mobilise these funds meant that only an extra Ptas 850million (US$5.5m) were allocated to the reconstruc-tion of Central America during 1999. This clearly disappoints Spanish society's high expectations of Spain's official response to the crisis. Although information was still sparse at the time of writing, there had also been worrying news

Spain

Table 30 Critique of key aspects of proposal for Spain's new Directive Plan

Topic	Proposal	Improvements in relation to the current situation
Priorities by sector	The text sets out an allocation of resources by sector, in accordance with the following priorities: basic social sectors; education, culture and research; infrastructure development and economic activities; strengthening of civil society, institutional development and good governance; environmental protection; conflict prevention and peace process support. In addition, it establishes three cross-cutting themes (poverty eradication, gender and the environment) that must be taken into account throughout the preparation phase of every single project.	Up until now, there has been no defined policy on sectional allocation of resources covering the whole of Spanish ODA. Although Spanish aid had gathered considerable experience in some areas (such as governance and institutional development), it suffered from an excessive fragmentation of resources across many sectors. The inclusion of three cross-cutting themes is intended to reduce the lack of quality and coherence that characterised Spanish aid programmes in the past.
Geographical priorities	The proposal divides receiving countries into two groups: preferential countries and others. Preferential countries (around 25, mainly in Latin America and sub-Saharan Africa, but also in Asia) will receive the lion's share of resources. Various instruments and a defined aid policy will establish a country plan and a budget plan for each state. Actions in 'other' countries will be minor and very specific, depending on the needs in each case.	The proposal seeks to solve another of Spanish aid's problems: an excessive geographical dispersal. The suggested group of preferential countries breaks the traditional hegemony of Latin America and countries with commercial potential. Under the new plan, Spain increases its aid flows to sub-Saharan Africa (which have been very low in recent years) and will expand aid to Asia beyond concessional credits.
Budget frameworks	The Plan envisages four different frameworks for future aid increases. These range from pessimistic visions (increases parallel to the evolution of Spain's GNP) to more optimistic expectations (0.35% by the year 2000). Each plan includes suggestions for each preferential country's evolution and the role of each aid instrument, taking into account the geographical and sectoral priorities defined above.	For the first time, this proposal establishes concrete goals which consider Spain's predicted patterns of economic growth and the promises made by members of government over the years. On the one hand, this implies that decisions concerning budgetary frameworks will depend almost exclusively on the government's political will. On the other hand, it gives Spanish civil society concrete commitments to back up its demands.
Multilateral Aid	The Plan aims to develop Spain's contribution policies towards multilateral financial and non-financial institutions much further. It establishes a set proportion for multilateral contributions (40% of total aid). Possible priorities for Spanish support will be defined from among the different multilateral agencies, in accordance with the experience and capacities of Spanish aid programmes.	In this area, the Plan reveals the lack of definition of Spanish aid. Despite the amount of resources allocated to multilateral aid over recent years (an average of 37%), Spain has not had a defined policy for its relationships with multilateral agencies.

Spain

Table 30 (continued)

Topic	Proposal	Improvements in relation to the current situation
Instruments	The proposal revises and assesses the instruments that constitute the Spanish aid system, and suggests how they could be integrated and made part of a coordinated and coherent aid policy. The main instruments are: • Projects, Programmes and Technical Cooperation • Food aid • Emergency aid • FAD credits • Debt relief • Grants to NGOs • Research and development education • Microcredits	The key improvement to be found in the proposal is its concept of integrating existing aid instruments. Up until now, some programmes (such as concessional credits and debt relief) worked independently, without being part of a broader intervention strategy specific to each country. Likewise, the Plan introduces various important advances: it considers debt relief as yet another instrument within aid policy that must be managed by common criteria and which is able to take action beyond the pace marked by other creditors; it introduces Development Education as a priority area; and finally, it defines criteria for a recently-established micro-credit programme.
Actors	The Plan insists on the need to unite the political direction of Spanish aid (according to the Cooperation Law, this responsibility lies in the hands of the Ministry of Foreign Affairs). This requires objective decision-making and coordination mechanisms. Likewise, the Plan argues that all bodies with responsibility for ODA should have sufficient resources and capabilities to enable them to manage aid programmes appropriately. The important role of decentralised institutions (local governments) in promoting aid programmes, as well as that of NGOs and firms, is also analysed.	The text reveals two important weaknesses in the Spanish aid system: the lack of precise objectives and clearly allocated functions between ministries and agencies, and the lack of capabilities within existing executive bodies. The structural problems in the AECI (theoretically, the aid system's main executive body) are analysed later in this chapter. At this point, it is important to stress that the existence of overlapping responsibilities within the aid system can cause tensions between administrations. Current organisational weaknesses are clearly detrimental to the quality of Spanish official aid.

from the first ODA projects approved by Spain, including FAD credits for parts of Nicaragua which have not been affected by the Hurricane.

It is fair to acknowledge, however, the Spanish Government's effort in other areas of Central America's reconstruction process. During the second meeting of the World Bank's Consultative Group on Central America, which took place in Stockholm in May 1999, Spain demanded concrete mechanisms to evaluate the end-use of resources, as well as insisting on the participation of civil society in all decision-making procedures.

Spain has also supported a deepening in existing debt relief mechanisms, by softening the conditions of the HIPC initiative and by proposing a moratorium for repayments scheduled over the next three years. We hope that this first step will be followed through with an international agreement for faster and deeper debt relief for Honduras and Nicaragua.

In Stockholm there was a generalised consensus concerning the need to make use of the current situation in Central America to go beyond mere reconstruction and to promote a profound transformation in the area. Although some political basis for this was introduced – for example, a focus on civil society participation – there is a need for practical steps to establish such initiatives.

Spain

Notes

1 The author would like to thank Raúl Rodriguez for his valuable contribution to this chapter, as well as Paloma Escudero, Marta Arias and José María Vera for all their comments and insights.

2 The Law's wording is very vague. Therefore, its capacity to move the Spanish aid system forward or backward will be strongly influenced by subsequent norms.

3 US$1 = 160 ptas.

4 José A. Alonso, *Estrategia para la Cooperación Española. Estudio para el primer Plan Director*, Ministerio de Asuntos Exteriores (SECIPI). Madrid, 1999.

5 Intermón has drafted a proposal that analyses these weaknesses and suggests possible solutions. This document was presented and discussed with representatives from the Administration during June and July 1999 (Intermón. *Propuestas para la reforma de la AECI*. Madrid, June 1999).

6 See Oxfam International's campaign, Education Now: Breaking the Cycle of Poverty, March 1999.

Sweden

Svante Sandberg, Forum Syd

A lot of new policy, little new practice

Redefinition of the Swedish Government's development cooperation policy continued this year. The policy is now formulated around four central areas: gender equality, environment/sustainable development, democracy/human rights and poverty eradication, in a series of documents passed through Parliament.

As a sort of summing up of this process, the Government announced just before Christmas 1998 that it would name a parliamentary commission to review the whole development policy. The commission was due to start in the first half of 1999 but was delayed, probably because the Minister for Development Cooperation, Mr Pierre Schori, left his post in June, after being elected as the leading Swedish Social Democratic Member of the European Parliament. The parliamentary commission is now expected to start work by the end of 1999 and continue for at least one year of the new millennium.

The NGOs have expressed some positive expectations of this commission, and at the same time are demanding that Government make it work in close contact with civil society. They argue for its mandate to be as broad as possible, so that it covers not only traditional aid policy but the whole spectrum of overall development policy. The broad approach is important as the NGOs often find reason to criticise the lack of coherence between the Government's actions in the field of development cooperation and its policies concerning Swedish interests in international trade or investment regulations. This discrepancy is becoming more worrisome the closer we get to the millennium round of WTO.

Generally, the new policy documents have been received rather positively by the NGO sector, although they see the slow implementation of the new policy as problematic.

Budget ceiling knocks back rise in aid

In 1999, the Swedish aid budget was going up moderately, due both to the decision to increase slightly the percentage of ODA (from 0.7% in 1998 to 0.705% in 1999) and to the economic growth in the Swedish economy in general. That means an overall aid budget of 12,840 million Swedish Krona (SEK) in 1999, compared to SEK 12,418 million in 1998.

Paradoxically then, there was a rather sharp cut in aid during 1999, due to the system of strict budgetary control of overall government spending. When the Government noted in April that the overall budget ceiling was going to be reached, it made a harsh but short-term budget adjustment. In its need to reduce total spending by SEK 8,000 million during 1999, the Government decided that about 40% of the total, or SEK 3,000 million, was to be taken from the ODA.

This sum was not part of the actual aid budget for this year, but came from reserves from previous years that the Government had authorised to be spent during 1999. Although the Government promised that the funds would be available immediately at the beginning of 2000, the cut affected some programmes in 1999 quite notably, including the emergency programmes to Central America after Hurricane Mitch. This cut was, therefore, heavily criticised by the NGOs.

Despite this, it is considered certain that ODA will be increased again during coming years, at least if the current, rather positive economic outlook for Sweden is maintained.

'The rights of the poor' and the imperatives of growth

In 1998, the Government presented to parliament its new programme on poverty eradication, 'The Rights of the Poor – Our Common Responsibility'. The programme has a focus on structural issues and argues that poverty is a lack of rights due to a complexity of reasons.

Sweden

Percentage of national income spent on aid: a 30-year picture

How much aid does Sweden give?

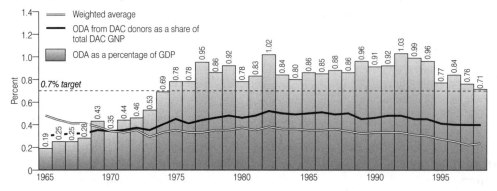

Where is Swedish aid spent?

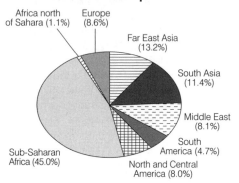

Africa north of Sahara (1.1%)
Europe (8.6%)
Far East Asia (13.2%)
South Asia (11.4%)
Middle East (8.1%)
South America (4.7%)
North and Central America (8.0%)
Sub-Saharan Africa (45.0%)

How much Swedish aid is spent through multilateral organisations?

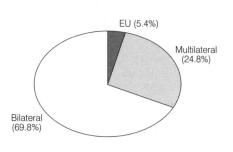

EU (5.4%)
Multilateral (24.8%)
Bilateral (69.8%)

What is Swedish aid spent on?

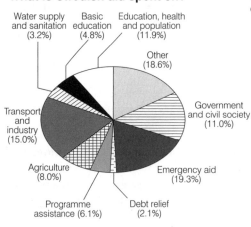

Water supply and sanitation (3.2%)
Basic education (4.8%)
Education, health and population (11.9%)
Other (18.6%)
Government and civil society (11.0%)
Emergency aid (19.3%)
Debt relief (2.1%)
Programme assistance (6.1%)
Agriculture (8.0%)
Transport and industry (15.0%)

For notes on data and sources see page 286

How much Swedish aid goes to the poorest countries?

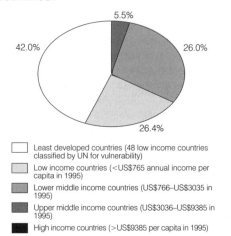

42.0%
5.5%
26.0%
26.4%

Least developed countries (48 low income countries classified by UN for vulnerability)

Low income countries (<US$765 annual income per capita in 1995)

Lower middle income countries (US$766–US$3035 in 1995)

Upper middle income countries (US$3036–US$9385 in 1995)

High income countries (>US$9385 per capita in 1995)

The **Reality** of Aid 2000

Sweden

Box 29 Swedish aid at a glance

How much aid does Sweden give?

Sweden gave	US$1,551m, 12,326 million Swedish Krona in 1998
that was	0.71% of GNP
and	1.12% of total government expenditure
which meant	US$175 or 1,393 Swedish Krona per capita for 1998

Is it going up or down?

In 1998 Swedish aid	fell by US$180m, down by 7.5% in real terms over 1997
Sweden was	less generous in 1998, falling from 0.79% of GNP to 0.71%
The outlook is	that the actual budget for ODA is to increase to 0.73% in 2001

How does Sweden compare with the other 20 donors?

Sweden ranks	10 out of 21 for its volume of aid
It is	4 out of 21 in the generosity league
It gives	68.4% of its aid to low income countries, a higher proportion than 13 other donors
Private flows	amounted to $360m, 0.21% of ODA
Total flows	to developing countries were 0.96% of GNP and rank 9 out of 21 in the DAC

What proportion of bilateral aid goes to basic education and basic health?

Sweden committed	5.1% of bilateral ODA to basic education, 5.2% to basic health and 0.8% to population and reproductive health

How important are commercial interests in aid?

Sweden reported that	36% of its bilateral aid commitments were tied to the purchase of goods and services from Sweden

The main theme of this programme is much more on 'growth with equity' than 'basic social investments'. Gender equality in this context is not only seen as a human rights issue, but also as a means for poverty eradication. Therefore, the new Policy Division, directly under the General Director, is working in an integrated way on three areas: poverty eradication, economic growth and gender equality.

As stated in previous issues of The Reality of Aid, the Swedish Government has been quite reluctant to relate its development policy and programmes to the International Development Objectives set out in the Plan of Action from the Copenhagen Summit, or to Shaping the 21st Century. Therefore, we are quite pleased to find that the Government, in its central document on development cooperation – the budget proposal for 1999 – included the goals from the OECD/DAC document in its main set of objectives. The Reality of Aid has argued strongly that these objectives

should be more central to Swedish development policy. This new focus on the development objectives from UN conferences and the OECD/DAC document now also forms an important part of the rationale of Sida's own programme proposal for the year 2000.

Still, the Swedish Government continues to be quite sceptical about the 20:20 Initiative and, therefore, makes very little mention of it. It shows no signs of trying to relate its development plans to the 20:20 concepts.

Apart from some reservations about the actual content of the new poverty policy, a main issue for Swedish NGOs at this stage is its analysis that not very much of the new policy can be traced through to the practical work of Sida. Basically, the results of the policy so far are related to Sida's internal work.

In its Annual Report for 1998, Sida presents quite a lot of information about how the environmental policy and, to a slightly lesser extent, the policy on gender equality, is

Sweden

reflected in the programme of Sida. On poverty eradication, the references are mainly on internal educational aspects or policy dialogue within the World Bank (in relation to the World Development report 2001 on Poverty) or OECD/DAC. The report has very little to add on how the new policy is borne out in concrete bilateral development programmes; there are merely brief references to dialogues about partnerships for poverty eradication with the Governments of Uganda and Namibia.

The focus on internal work within Sida, and especially on its Working Group on Poverty Issues, largely has to do with the findings of a baseline study made in 1996, as part of the policy work. The study aimed at measuring how poverty was prioritised in Sida's country strategies and evaluations. The findings of the study were not very encouraging, as poverty analysis and strategies were basically absent except in very general terms. Therefore, it was decided to start this internal process of capacity building that, among other things, has resulted in guidelines for how the poverty policy shall be translated into the different programme activities. It has also, hopefully, resulted in an enhanced capacity within Sida to address the lack of poverty strategies so far. One step will be a follow-up in 1999 of the 1996 baseline study, to see if there are any significant changes within programmes and evaluations three years later.

Another step will be a handbook, developed by Sida and the Ministry of Foreign Affairs, on how to incorporate the poverty policy into the elaboration of the Country Strategies, which constitute the basic planning tools for Swedish Development Cooperation. The handbook, which only exists as a draft, will also relate to the indicators of the development objectives from Copenhagen and OECD/DAC.

As a result of this process, Sida has announced, in its plans for 2000, that its own action plan on poverty will be modified before the year 2001. It says this will be based on the integration of the poverty programme with the other policy areas, and in that sense gives poverty eradication the central role in the whole policy framework.

Considering such a role for poverty issues within the general policy, it is worth noting the clear focus on growth in this poverty strategy. The Sida proposal for 2000 says: 'Without sustainable economic growth it is not possible to see a long-term rise out of poverty for broad sectors of the population. The main task for Sida is to create the conditions for such a sustainable development.'

The document also points to some common factors in countries that have been successful in poverty reduction. It cites the need for a well-functioning market economy that gives space for small producers and the informal sector, as well as for a dynamic balance between social and economic development, where social investments – especially in basic education and basic health – tend to be of critical importance for sustainable economic growth.

More developed is the implementation of the gender equality policy, which has been in place since 1996, when equality between women and men in partner countries was established as one of six overall goals of Swedish development cooperation. Since 1998, the guidelines on gender for the processing of Country Strategies have been applied, which has been especially the case in the elaboration of strategies in South Africa and Namibia.

New kinds of national 'Gender Profiles' are being produced, with an emphasis more on macro-economic and juridical aspects, mentioning health and education only as part of the poverty complex. Sida has also established 'the special initiative' for Tanzania, Namibia and Nicaragua, the objective of which is to give gender equality issues a high political profile, aiming at supporting the three countries in implementing the Plan of Action from the Beijing Conference.

Gender equality is also an important issue in the poverty policy. In Sida's Annual Report 1998, there are numerous mentions of gender dimensions in the overall reporting, which can be seen as a proof that the mainstreaming process has been fairly successful. When it comes to gender disaggregated statistics, however, the situation is completely different: there are very few available data with such content in the overall reporting.

Basic education – more on objectives than outcomes

Basic education has traditionally played a significant role in Swedish Development Cooperation. Part of the reason for this is that different forms of popular education systems constituted significant aspects of the Swedish model of welfare society. When the modern era of development cooperation started in the late 1950s, a lot of its pioneers came from this sector of the education system.

According to the latest OECD/DAC data, Sweden gives one of the highest shares of basic education as part of total ODA (among those who report basic education as distinct from other parts of education) and it is also increasing (3.1% in 1995 and 4.8% in 1996).

In its policy for basic education and education reform from 1996, Sida clearly underlined that its policy was guided by the overall objectives of the World Declaration on Education for All at Jomtien 1990. As in the case of how the

Sweden

development cooperation programmes relate to the International Development Objectives of Copenhagen and *Shaping the 21st Century*, there is very little about the outcomes of the educational programme in relation to the Jomtien objectives. In fact, the reporting on basic education is poorer in Sida's Annual report of 1998 than in that of 1997.

One of the central issues in the policy on basic education is the particular attention paid to equity issues regarding the education of girls and women. Part of that includes new methodological aspects, especially underlined in the Annual Report, such as the special support in 1998 for the Forum for African Women Educationalists.

About half of Swedish support to primary education goes as direct budget support, which of course highlights the question of aid dependency within the educational systems of many southern partner countries. There is a general attempt by the Government to find ways of tackling the problems of aid dependency but, as far as we can see, there are no real solutions in sight in the short term to the funding of the basic education system.

According to the programme, Sida basically supports production of education materials, curriculum development, environmental education, education on HIV/AIDS, special-needs education, teacher training, literacy and adult education, a diversity of programmes for greater gender equality, school construction and maintenance. It also makes an input on more general education planning, management research and evaluation.

The balance of priorities in Sida programmes is based on two strategies for supporting basic education. One is more general support in poor countries such as Ethiopia, Mozambique, Tanzania and Bangladesh. This aims at qualitative improvement within the activities of the Ministries of Education, for example through support for national teacher training programmes, the provision of education materials and adult literacy. The other strategy is more direct support to specific poor sectors, such as rural workers within countries such as Sri Lanka and Zimbabwe. That direct support includes the targeting of girls.

The special programme, with a broad capacity and competence focus, announced by Sida last year, is continuing. One of its main strands is an overall increase in support for all kinds of education and research, from basic education to universities. The ambition is to develop more broad-sector support programmes for the different parts of the education system. As noted in last year's edition, there is a risk that this approach will also lead to a less sharp focus on basic education and more general support to different levels of the education system. At the same time, it could lead to an overall strengthening of education support, which would then also favour the basic level.

United Kingdom

Mark Curtis and Anna Jefferys, ActionAid

Global agenda at odds with progressive policy

The UK Government's 1997 White Paper on development – the first comprehensive government statement on development for over two decades – aims to:

- Refocus aid on poverty eradication;
- BGuild partnerships with developing countries and the private sector;
- Strengthen public understanding and support for development;
- Ensure that the full range of government policies affecting developing countries takes account of sustainable development.

Nearly two years on, how have these aims been implemented, and to what extent is the UK promoting a positive development agenda in the context of globalisation? In summary, ActionAid's view is that DFID has become one of the most progressive donors, with a number of significant policy changes over the past year. At the same time, however, the UK government as a whole remains a champion of a global liberalisation agenda that systematically works against the interests of poor people.

Welcome focus on poverty reduction

1998/99 has seen a number of welcome DFID policy changes. These are:

- An intention to link activities to the International Development Targets (IDTs) with poverty eradication as the central stated goal;
- A wide-ranging consultation exercise with civil society;
- A shift towards prioritising working with governments committed to promoting poverty eradication;

- An increase in aid, announced at the last budget and a commitment to reach 0.3% of GNP by 2001;[1]
- Steps to ensure greater coherence in development policy across the Government;
- A commitment to a rights-based approach to development and steps taken to articulate and implement it;
- A greater focus on influencing the multilateral institutions and in seeing the UK as a lever in securing wider change;
- Steps to transform DFID from an aid delivery agency to a broader development organisation.

The new emphasis on poverty-focused development is reflected in greater UK support for *sector-wide* initiatives. These offer budgetary and technical support to an entire sector – particularly in health, education and natural resources – in coordination with other donors and led by the national government. DFID is also pursuing an integrated approach to gender, incorporating gender equality objectives into a range of activities, including its education and health programmes, improving women's access to productive assets, and lobbying the multilateral institutions. This extends to influencing other Government departments, including the women's unit in the Cabinet Office and the human rights department of the Foreign Office. However, DFID has not yet evaluated the impact of these gender policies, and our understanding is that there has not yet been a significant attitudinal change within DFID to incorporate a commitment to gender equality into all policy and programmes.

Civil society consultation

As part of its partnership approach, DFID stresses the need for transparent dialogue with northern and southern CSOs. While this new ethos has not yet infiltrated every corner of DFID, change can already be seen.

United Kingdom

DFID established a Development Policy Forum in 1998 to consult with a wide range of CSOs at home and in developing countries in order to explore how it could work more effectively with them and build stronger alliances for the elimination of poverty. Topics for discussion included: DFID's approach to partnerships; aid effectiveness; sustainable development; globalisation, humanitarian aid and conflict, and building public support for development.

In another consultation process on DFID's engagement with civil society, 28 DFID departments and more than 550 organisations – 60% northern and 40% southern – were consulted. Among the recommendations proposed by CSOs were that DFID could modify its funding mechanisms to give more support to southern groups and should work more closely with well-established southern and international NGOs in its capacity building support for southern NGOs.[2]

DFID raises advocacy profile

DFID increasingly sees itself as an advocate – both for change within the UK Government and internationally. It has, for example, helped to set up an inter-departmental working group on development, with members from more than half a dozen other Government departments. This meets twice a year to discuss development issues. DFID has also launched several joint initiatives – on debt relief with the Treasury, on trade and investment with the Department of Trade and Industry, on introducing core labour standards with the Department for Education and Environment, and on security sector reform with the Foreign Office and Ministry of Defence.

DFID is working to influence the multilateral institutions and produces Institutional Strategy Papers setting out policy towards each of the major ones. In 1998, the UK helped secure endorsement for international ownership of the International Development Strategy at the G8 summit in Birmingham and agreement that the World Bank, the United Nations, and the OECD will cooperate in assembling and publishing regular data on the 21 IDT indicators, to clarify the extent of progress towards them. The Development Ministers of Britain, Germany and France led the calls for the appointment of one EU Commissioner for Development and a single EU development policy.

Box 30 Difficulties of implementation: Kenya country study

Basic Rights in Kenya[3]
In 1997–98 UK aid to Kenya totalled £28.4m, making it one of the largest donors. Commitment to natural resources, health and population, and education comprised the bulk of sectorally focused aid, most of which was channelled through DFID-led programmes.

In line with the IDTs, DFID's most recent Country Strategy Paper pledges to reduce the numbers of Kenyans living in extreme poverty by 2015. However, while recognising the need for health and education programmes, the need to improve livelihoods and to care for the needs of disadvantaged social groups, the CSP falls short of identifying those needs within a basic rights and entitlements framework.

Other than channelling direct support to poverty-reducing projects, UK assistance to poor people in Kenya is found in Participatory Poverty Assessments. These attempt to expand the definition of poverty beyond income-based indicators to include concepts of power, inequity and injustice. The Kenyan Government's National Poverty Eradication Plan helped to produce a document that places the fight against poverty within a basic rights framework. It remains to be seen whether the recently appointed Commission for Poverty Eradication can catalyse Government, private corporations and voluntary organisations around this plan. DFID recently hosted a round-table between the donor community and a coalition formed to enshrine basic and group rights within the Kenyan constitution.

DFID continues to channel resources towards legal and human rights programmes which promote legal awareness, judicial reform and the promotion of group rights such as children and women. The Denver pledge of 1997 to raise support for basic health care, education and clean water in Africa by 50% is seriously constrained by DFID's reluctance to channel aid through the Kenyan government. DFID has assumed a 'low case' approach to aid which severely limits aid allocations. Movement to a 'high case' scenario will require Kenyan government compliance with a range of conditionalities, particularly in the area of budgetary reform. This form of aid embargo is likely to have a direct negative impact on poor people. It remains to be seen whether support to civic institutions and NGOs can produce the necessary internal pressure for accountable, pro-poor and inclusive forms of governance. Should the aid embargo extend to non-state agencies and delivery systems, this would leave poor people with few options for support in future.

United Kingdom

Percentage of national income spent on aid: a 30-year picture

How much aid does the UK give?

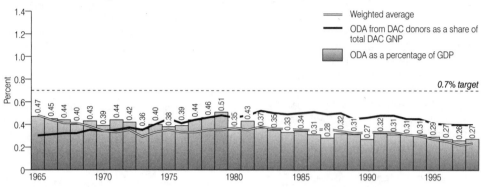

Legend:
- Weighted average
- ODA from DAC donors as a share of total DAC GNP
- ODA as a percentage of GDP
- 0.7% target

Where is the UK's aid spent?

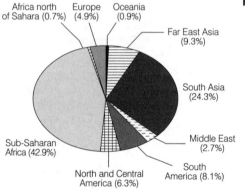

- Africa north of Sahara (0.7%)
- Europe (4.9%)
- Oceania (0.9%)
- Far East Asia (9.3%)
- South Asia (24.3%)
- Middle East (2.7%)
- South America (8.1%)
- North and Central America (6.3%)
- Sub-Saharan Africa (42.9%)

How much of UK aid is spent through multilateral organisations?

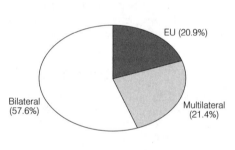

- EU (20.9%)
- Bilateral (57.6%)
- Multilateral (21.4%)

What is the UK's aid spent on?

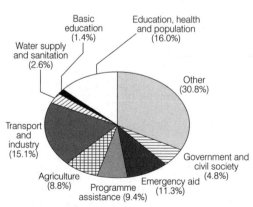

- Basic education (1.4%)
- Education, health and population (16.0%)
- Water supply and sanitation (2.6%)
- Other (30.8%)
- Transport and industry (15.1%)
- Government and civil society (4.8%)
- Agriculture (8.8%)
- Programme assistance (9.4%)
- Emergency aid (11.3%)

How much of UK aid goes to the poorest countries?

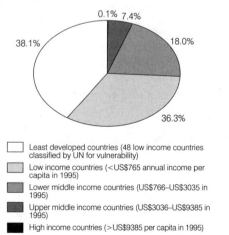

- 0.1%
- 7.4%
- 38.1%
- 18.0%
- 36.3%

Legend:
- Least developed countries (48 low income countries classified by UN for vulnerability)
- Low income countries (<US$765 annual income per capita in 1995)
- Lower middle income countries (US$766–US$3035 in 1995)
- Upper middle income countries (US$3036–US$9385 in 1995)
- High income countries (>US$9385 per capita in 1995)

For notes on data and sources see page 286

United Kingdom

Box 31 UK aid at a glance

How much aid does the UK give?

The UK gave	US$3,835m, £2,315 million in 1998
that was	0.27% of GNP
and	0.69% of total government expenditure
which meant	US$66 or £40 per capita for 1998

Is it going up or down?

In 1998 UK aid	rose by $402m, a rise of 7.8% in real terms over 1997
The UK was	more generous in 1998, rising from 0.26% to 0.27% of GNP
The outlook is	more optimistic as the Government begins to reverse the decline in the aid budget.

How does the UK compare with the other 20 donors?

The UK ranks	5 out of 21 for its volume of aid
It is	14 out of 21 in the generosity league
It gives	74.4 % of its aid to low income countries, a higher proportion than 15 other donors
Private flows	amounted to $16,338m, 4.76 times ODA
Total flows	to developing countries were 1.5% of GNP and rank 3 out of 21 in the DAC

What proportion of bilateral aid goes to basic education and basic health?

The UK committed	1.2% of bilateral ODA to basic education, 1.0% to basic health and 1.5% to population and reproductive health

How important are commercial interests in aid?

The UK reported that	13.9% of its bilateral aid commitments were tied to the purchase of goods and services from the UK

Debt and aid: a coherent approach

Treasury Minister Gordon Brown and Development Minister Clare Short have argued for a fundamental review of the HIPC Initiative so that it will deliver more relief to countries committed to the IDTs. They have addressed aid and debt together by:

- Challenging the international community to agree to increasing debt cancellation to US$50 billion;
- Supporting the call to sell US$1 billion of IMF gold to help finance debt relief;
- Boosting UK ODA from 0.26% to 0.27% eventually aiming to reach 0.3%.

The UK has been one of the more progressive actors on debt but its proposals could be more far-reaching. ActionAid would like to see it:

- Write off all the outstanding bilateral debts of developing countries;
- Support Jubilee 2000's aim to cancel all unpayable debts by 2000;
- Help to remove the conditionality associated with traditional structural adjustment programmes (ie, policies that adversely affect poor people) in the HIPC initiative.

ActionAid has also proposed an International Debt Commission to act as an independent international watchdog in debt negotiations, to encourage transparency in debt policy and help prevent accumulations of unpayable debts in the future.[4] While ActionAid welcomes pledges to increase aid, the UK is committed merely to reaching the 1992 aid levels.

United Kingdom

Global liberalisation undermines poverty focus

DFID policy must be seen in the context of global liberalisation. Prime Minister Tony Blair has identified 'spreading the benefits of globalisation' as the government's first main priority.[6] DFID is committed to curbing the worst excesses of global liberalisation and promoting the interests of developing countries in a number of policy areas. However, it is the priorities of other Government departments – notably the Department of Trade and Industry (DTI) – which often determine policy. It is also the case that DFID policy itself is often at odds with promoting the interests of poor people under globalisation. There is a big assumption at the root of DFID policy for which it, and others, has little real evidence: that global liberalisation will indeed work to the benefit of poor people. ActionAid sees at least three areas that need addressing, as follows.

Trade with developing countries

UK policy on trade with developing countries appears too heavily determined by the interests of the DTI and, on agricultural trade, the Ministry of Agriculture, Fisheries and Food. DFID policy is welcome in several areas but often does not go far enough to promote the interests of poor people. And it – along with other OECD countries – has hitherto refused to commit itself to undertaking and support-

ing impact assessments of the current trade agreements before the new round of trade negotiations begins, even though this is required under the WTO agreement.

The UK's view is that 'the multilateral system operated by the WTO offers all countries the opportunity of participating on an equal basis in setting the rules of trade'.[7] But it is clear that, in reality, the US and the EU set such rules. One rule under discussion concerns patenting under the Trade-related Intellectual Property Rights (TRIPS) clause in the WTO agreement on agriculture. In the inter-departmental debates currently taking place, DFID appears to be acquiescing in the UK government's overall support for TRIPs, which increases the ability of TNCs to secure monopoly rights over plants and animals. The UK government's belief in integrating poor countries into the global economy glosses over the fact that the global economy systematically excludes and exploits the poorest countries, while continuing unfairly to protect northern companies and agriculture. In this context, UK aid cannot compensate for the progressive marginalisation of the world's poor from the global economy and the growing disparities in wealth that result.

DFID is supporting (through UNCTAD, the World Bank, the Commonwealth Secretariat and the WTO Secretariat) capacity building of southern governments to help them play a fuller role in trade negotiations. This is an important

United Kingdom

task, but the international community needs a much more coherent and better-resourced engagement in this process if the position of developing countries is really to be improved. It is a welcome trend that the UK has been one of the strongest critics of the Common Agricultural Policy (CAP). However, as long as the CAP's domestic and export subsidies continue to have adverse impacts on poor people, it appears disingenuous for the UK to oppose as 'protectionism' southern policies designed to support and protect farmers from this unfair competition.

ActionAid identifies several policy barriers to developing countries prioritising agricultural production for food security, including the removal of import controls on cheap food from the North, declining public sector support to agriculture, and the increasing concentration of power in the hands of transnational companies. Reducing by half the number of people living in extreme poverty by 2015 depends on much more equitable economic and political governance of agricultural and food markets.[8]

Reform of structural adjustment programmes (SAPs)

UK policies in this regard also appear quite modest in intent. This is surprising given that the IDTs – to which the government is strongly committed – will probably not be met unless SAPs are designed more to address questions of redistribution of resources and power. DFID states that its aim is only to ensure that SAPs 'take account of the impact on the poor' and asserts that 'future programmes will be designed to protect social sector spending for the poorest, most vulnerable groups'.[9] However, there is still a way to go for World Bank statements on reformed policies to be implemented on the ground – although the UK government has been pressing the World Bank to implement its rhetoric, more persuasion could be forthcoming.[10]

ActionAid has seen in Malawi how the market liberalisation pushed by major donors is continuing to exacerbate poverty, especially in terms of food security. The results have included the reduction or withdrawal of food, seed and fertiliser price subsidies and crop price fluctuations. The World Bank social safety net programme in Malawi does little to protect poor groups from the adverse consequences of its broader policy.[11]

Reform of the global financial regime

Such reform is clearly needed, as demonstrated by the massive increases in poverty in some Asian countries as a result of the financial crisis. The UK Chancellor has taken an international lead in calling for social principles to be developed to encourage countries to prioritise social improvements alongside economic development and as a means to ensure that the IMF considers social impacts when responding to short-term crises. He has also called for the IMF to be more publicly accountable.[12] The UK has outlined its view of the 'need to modernise the international financial system' and to help 'put in place reforms to minimise the risks of disruption, protect the most vulnerable and capture the full benefits of global markets in order to deliver greater prosperity for all'.[13]

However, it is questionable whether such proposals go anywhere near far enough if poor people really are to benefit from a new global financial regime. The case for the real benefits to poor people of increasing financial liberalisation has not been proven, although the UK, among others, is a strong advocate of such liberalisation. Much more effective, transparent, democratic and well-resourced institutions capable of effective regulation are surely required.

Box 33 Loosening ties and liberalisation

Despite strong lobbying by the British government, donors failed to reach agreement on untying aid to LLDCs at the DAC High Level Meeting in mid-May. Work will continue to reach a compromise agreement by December 2000 that will meet the concerns of France, Japan and other donors currently dragging their feet. In response, some like-minded countries wish to develop reciprocal arrangements to untie aid. A weak agreement may have been worse than no agreement since the breakdown of the consensus approach plus the continuing political process provides new opportunities to press for full untying and for aid procurement and contracting to support development objectives more effectively. ActionAid strongly supports DFID's promotion of multilateral untying and believes it should now be using whatever levers it has at its disposal to press for full untying. ActionAid is concerned, however, about EU countries' strong support for fully liberalising government procurement at the WTO, which would open up procurement to powerful northern companies and undermine private sector development in developing countries. This is hypocritical when donor countries cannot even agree to untie a proportion of their aid.

United Kingdom

Conclusion

ActionAid's view is that the UK government overall is in effect promoting two different development paradigms. One prioritises partnership, poverty focus, and the IDTs and could be understood as the Rights approach; the other prioritises international rules (such as trade, patenting and investment) that discriminate against poor people and is the Global Liberalisation approach.

There is naturally a big difference between these two approaches: the first could promote a genuine international-ism of shared moral responsibility for sustainable development within a more democratic order of global governance; the second signifies a widening of disparities between the powerful and powerless, and rich and poor, within global regimes that discriminate in favour of the privi-leged. DFID's ultimate challenge is to ensure that the totality of British policy moves in favour of the former but it is still often hamstrung by other government departments and some of its own priorities. Although the UK has made more strides on ensuring such coherence in policy-making than others, there is still a considerable way to go.

Notes

1 DFID, *1998 Departmental Report,* HMSO, London, April 1998, p10.
2 See *DFID Civil Society Consultation: A Submission by ActionAid*, September 1998.
3 Written by Irungu Houghton, ActionAid Kenya.
4 ActionAid, 'Beyond Crisis Management: Southern Perspectives on the Future of Debt, *ActionAid Policy Briefing no 3*, June 1998.
5 Arthur van Diesen and Karen Walker, 'The Changing Face of Aid to Ethiopia: Past Experience and Emerging Issues in British and EC Aid', *Christian Aid*, January 1999.
6 DFID, *Departmental Report 1999*, p.83.
7 DFID, *Departmental Report,* p.83.
8 See ActionAid, 'WTO and Food Security: Opportunities for Action', *ActionAid Policy Briefing no 4*, January 1999; and ActionAid, 'Patents and Food Security: Options for Research and Action', *ActionAid Policy Briefing no 5*, January 1999.
9 Ibid, p72.
10 For excellent analysis of World Bank and IMF policies, see Bretton Woods Project *Updates* briefings and its website: www.bretton-woodsproject.org
11 Sarah Collinson, 'External influences on poverty in Malawi', Internal ActionAid paper, September 1998.
12 Speech by Chancellor Gordon Brown at the Annual Meetings of the IMF and World Bank, Washington DC, 6 October 1998.
13 DFID, *Departmental Report*, p22

Part III
Perspectives from the South on Development Cooperation

Latin America: the economy and the environment collapse on the region's poorest people

Humberto Campodónico, DESCO, and Mariano Valderrama, CEPES

For Latin America, the period 1997–99 has been a difficult one. The entire region suffered the impact of the economic crisis. The rate of economic growth fell and poverty indicators regressed. The region of Central America suffered the scourges of Hurricane Mitch and several countries (including Brazil, Ecuador and Peru) felt the ravages of the El Niño phenomenon.

Between 1990 and 1997, in many Latin American countries, positive capital flows allowed increased consumption and investment, low inflation and macroeconomic equilibrium. Nevertheless, this equilibrium was not built on a solid foundation, but coexisted with a systematic imbalance in the external account (due to a considerable deficit in the balance of trade and the payment of foreign debt). High interest attracted foreign investment and overrated local currencies allowed for imports, which brought inflation down. But with the decline of foreign financing, the equilibrium collapsed.[1]

The rate of growth of the GDP plunged by 50%, from 5.2% in 1997 to 2.3% in 1998. Furthermore, forecasts for 1999 indicated that GDP growth would fall to –0.8% and saw it recovering to only 2.5% by 2000, a figure far from the 3.3% average for 1991–98. The rate of growth is far below the rate needed to reduce the number of people living on one dollar a day[2] and the situation is worsened by the highly unequal distribution of income. Latin America is the region with the greatest inequity in the world.[3]

In Argentina, poverty has increased notably throughout the country. A study by the National Institute of Statistics and Censuses (INDEC), published on 5 June 1999, asserts that over more than three million inhabitants of Buenos Aires and its periphery fall below the poverty line, which means an increase of 63% since October 1998. According to the World Bank, in Argentina there are 13 million inhabitants – one third of the total population – living in absolute poverty. CEPAL indicated, in a report distributed through local

companies, that Argentina is one of the Latin American countries in which the distribution of income worsened between 1990 and 1997, despite the explosive expansion of the economy during those same years.[4]

In the case of Brazil, the crisis has again increased poverty: according to a World Bank report, between October 1998 and January 1999, close to 50% of the people who had risen out of poverty since the Real Plan was implemented in 1994 fell back below the poverty level.[5]

In Chile, the crisis has plunged the country into a heavy recession, increasing levels of unemployment. Unemployment in Chile rose to 8.7% of the economically active population between February and April, its highest level of the last 8 years. At one point data from the national statistics institute, INE, showed that 505,000 of Chile's economically active population of 5.3 million people were out of work. Between February and April of last year, the rate was 5.3%. In one year, 200,000 jobs were cut.[6]

The Washington Consensus pushed for structural adjustment, arguing that economic stability and economic growth were the basis for social welfare. In the case of Latin America, growth in the 1990s didn't solve problems of unemployment, poverty or low wages. Even worse now, with the financial crisis there is no economic growth in sight and fewer possibilities of dealing with poverty. Now even the World Bank acknowledges the limitations of the previous economic adjustment policies[7] and speaks of a transition from the Washington Consensus to the Santiago Consensus.

All of the above calls into question the neo-liberal economic models applied in the region and proposes new demands and challenges for development policies and international cooperation. It also shows the limitations to the strategy of social investment or emergency programmes applied in Latin America with the technical advice and financial support of the multilateral and bilateral agencies. For example:

Latin America

- The crisis clearly reveals the influence of macroeconomic policies on the evolution of poverty.
- The programmes have the nature of charity and do not lead to sustainable solutions. They must address the generation of employment and more sustainable mechanisms for regional development.
- Social compensation programmes, envisaged as transitional, emergency programmes, are turning into permanent programmes, but have very specific local effects.
- Unequal distribution of income in Latin America is a major obstacle to development and to the struggle against poverty. The situation of poor people could be solved through redistribution mechanisms without the need for foreign aid.
- Many of the social programmes financed with the support of international cooperation end up as programmes for proselytising, or gaining a political following for the current administration.
- Many programmes are administered in a highly centralised manner, without any coordination between the different, local or regional bodies, and without participation of society.

Social programmes hit by decline in cooperation funds

Flows of international cooperation towards Latin America have tended to decline in the last few years, following the general trends in foreign aid. Between 1993 and 1997 (the most recent year for which statistics are available) cooperation varied as follows:

The restriction of financial resources worsened; not only did flows of technical cooperation decline, but official financing through the multilateral banks stagnated and private flows fell markedly. According to Global Development Finance 1999, net concessional flows are now one third below the 1990 level in real terms.

It was thought that, in the case of Latin America, technical cooperation (ie, donations) was limited to the poorest countries and that the relationship with the larger and more dynamic countries was moving into the field of investment. With the crisis, the private flows that had been increasing between 1990 and 1997 have declined. There is also a tendency to use the public credit from multilateral agencies for adjustment programmes, to the detriment of social programmes, just at the moment when the demand for support in these areas is growing.

For 1998, the OECD estimates a slight rebound in global foreign aid (an increase of 8.9% over the previous

year), but it will still fall short of the 1996 levels. The World Bank's estimates offer a less encouraging outlook for 1998.[8] For 1999, we will see the emergency support for areas hit by Hurricane Mitch reflected in increased figures for aid to Central America and also implied a greater concentration of aid to the region of Central America.

There is a tendency for technical cooperation to be concentrated on the poorest countries. The Netherlands, for example, made the decision to concentrate its cooperation programmes on fighting poverty in Nicaragua and Bolivia.

Main recipients and donors of aid in Latin America

The countries of Latin America that received the largest volumes of foreign aid in 1997 were, in decreasing order: Bolivia (US$717 million), Peru (US$488 million), Nicaragua (US$421 million), Brazil (US$487 million), Haiti (US$332 million), Honduras (US$308 million), and Guatemala (US$302 million). Cooperation, as a percentage of GDP, is significant only in a few countries. This is the case in Nicaragua (22.6%), Haiti (13.6%), Honduras (6.7%) and Bolivia (9.4%). For other countries such as Argentina, Brazil, Chile, Mexico and Peru, it is far below 1%.

As a bloc, the European Union (European Commission +15) is the main donor. Individually, by country, the United States is the largest donor, followed by Japan, Germany, The Netherlands and Spain.

The following variations were registered for 1998: The total amount given by DAC countries to Latin America was reduced by 46.8%. The United States, while remaining the major donor reduced its contribution by more than 100%. Japan reduced its aid budget to the Latin American region by 37% and the European Union by 27.9%. Even Spain, which in recent years had been increasing its aid programme to Latin America reduced its flows more than 30%.

While the decrease of aid given by the European Union and its members to Latin America, as well as by Japan, between 1996 and 1997, reflected some budget cuts, it was also related to the devaluation of European and Japanese currencies as compared to the US dollar.[9]

The decrease in the European Commission's contribution between 1996 and 1997 also fell by 20%, in comparison to a steady increase in the previous decade. The outlook is not good. Consider, for example, the Commission's recent agreement, concerning finances for the period of 2000 to 2005, to apply a 20% budget cut in the area of foreign activities. There is also an evident interest in allocating a larger amount of aid funds to Eastern European nations.

Table 31 People affected by Hurricane Mitch: Central America

Indicators	Honduras	Nicaragua	Guatemala	El Salvador	Total
Dead	7,007	2,863	268	240	10,378
Missing	8,052	948	121	19	9,140
Wounded	11,998	388	280	N/A.	12,666
Affected	4,753,537	867,752	734,198	346,910	6,702,397
Total population	6,203,188	4,492,700	11,645,900	6,075,536	28,417,324

Source: CEPAL

The summit of the heads of state and of government of Latin America and the European Union, held in Rio de Janeiro in June 1999, reveals Europe's interest in having some political and commercial influence in the region. It also shows Latin America's interest in having another inter-locutor to establish some counterweight in its dialogue with the United States, either through the Commission or the member nations. Nevertheless, this mutual interest seems to have little impact on aid flows.

Hurricane Mitch mobilises international cooperation[10]

Hurricane Mitch seriously affected the population of Central America. A total of 10,378 people died, 9,140 went missing and 12,666 were injured. Close to seven million people – a quarter of the population – were affected.

Mitch set the affected countries back by two decades. The magnitude of the damage caused by the hurricane is better understood if we bear in mind the extreme poverty and the marginalisation in the region.

For a good number of poor people, the hurricane meant the loss of all means of survival; farmers even lost their farmland. One of the dilemmas in allocating aid resources is whether the reconstruction will reproduce the previous inequalities.

The international community responded in solidarity: emergency aid, condoning or restructuring of the debt. The summit held in Stockholm in May convened many of the international (bilateral, multilateral and non-government) cooperation agencies, along with representatives of the governments and NGOs of Central American countries. The purpose was to present and discuss the 'Reconstruction and Development Plans' of the countries affected by Mitch, and to see who would contribute how much and for what. The final figure agreed in Stockholm was US$9 billion for all of Central America. The aid from NGOs of the North is also impressive.[11] NGOs and civil society are organising within the affected countries themselves. In Honduras, the Inter-Forum Spaces gathered networks of Honduran NGOs. In Nicaragua, 320 organisations formed the Civil Coordination for the Emergency and Reconstruction.

The support for the emergency reconstruction also revealed some of the limitations to international cooperation. The European Union, instead of using the teams already existing in the region to design the emergency programmes, formed new teams. In addition, at that very moment, it decided to undertake a reorganisation of its offices in Central America, all of which has hindered the timely imple-mentation of the programmes.

In Honduras, for example, there is no 'real' setting for coordination. There are many meetings here and there, but

Table 32 Social Indicators: Central America

	Guatemala	El Salvador	Honduras	Nicaragua	Costa Rica
% of poor families	86.0	50.0	65.0	74.0	17.0
% Unemployment and underemployment	39.4	55.0	40.0	62.0	21.0
% Literacy	55.7	70.9	72.0	65.3	94.7
Child mortality (per 1000 live births)	40.0	51.0	53.0	30.0	13.0
GDP per capita in US$	1,360	1,680	660	440	2,720

Source: Comisión Centroamericana de Ambiente y Desarrollo

Latin America

Table 33 Total net foreign ODA to all Latin America (current US$ millions)

	1990	1991	1992	1993	1994	1995	1996	1997
EU Members total	1965.07	2283.09	2386.61	2428.84	2069.02	2440.41	2549.99	1993.32
France	205.87	311.74	195.65	281.61	209.54	376.82	241.47	173.69
Germany	558.64	492.06	556.92	572.63	440.78	607.92	853.93	472.71
Japan	561.24	846.91	772.18	737.02	832.18	1141.55	985.86	715.03
Netherlands	357.98	273.12	402.47	389.04	317.81	467.92	496.65	450.37
Spain	169.94	317.54	433.46	478.58	401.11	397.8	368.0	284.16
United States	1343.00	1397.00	790.00	821.00	1355.00	928.00	1917.00	924.00
DAC countries. total	4188.41	4856.68	4293.65	4263.85	4549.95	4798.69	5757.44	3920.9

Table 34 Total net foreign ODA to all Latin America (percentage of donors' total)

	1990	1991	1992	1993	1994	1995	1996	1997
EU Members total	36.7	38.1	55.6	43.3	33.6	35.6	31.2	31.8
France	3.8	5.2	4.6	5.0	3.4	5.5	3.0	2.8
Germany	10.4	8.2	13.0	10.2	7.2	8.9	10.4	7.5
Japan	10.5	14.1	18.0	13.1	13.5	16.6	12.0	11.4
Netherlands	6.7	4.6	9.4	6.9	5.2	6.8	6.1	7.2
Spain	3.2	5.3	10.1	8.5	6.5	5.8	4.5	4.5
United States	25.1	23.3	18.4	14.6	22.0	13.5	23.4	14.7

Table 35 Variation of total net Foreign Aid to Latin America (%)

	1991	1992	1993	1994	1995	1996	1997
EU Members total	16.2	4.5	1.8	−14.8	18.0	4.5	−21.8
France	51.4	−37.2	43.9	−25.6	79.8	−35.9	−28.1
Germany	−11.9	13.2	2.8	−23.0	37.9	40.5	−44.6
Japan	50.9	−8.8	−4.6	12.9	37.2	−0.136	−0.3
Netherlands	−23.7	47.4	−3.3	−18.3	47.2	6.1	−9.3
Spain	86.9	36.5	10.4	−16.2	−0.8	−7.5	−0.2
United States	4.0	−43.5	3.9	65.0	−31.5	10.7	−51.8
Total DAC							−30.6

nothing concrete. Each organisation needs to 'quickly spend' the money provided by the contributors to their countries and that is what they do. The other great problem is the limited local capacity to join the effort to design and execute the reconstruction projects. Many cooperation organisations have decided to send 'experts' or hire them from other countries. In other words, thousands of consultants are trying to do everything quickly, without consulting anyone and with highly passive 'participation' from local institutions.

Table 36 Official Foreign Aid to Latin America 1993–97 (in current US$ millions)

1993	1994	1995	1996	1997
5,605	6,150	6862	8,185	6,271

Source: OCDE Report 1999

Latin America

Notes

1   Humberto Campodónico, 'Entre el 2,000 y los límites de la Ortodoxia,' in Quehacer, no 116, Lima, November 1998.

2   Jornal do Brasil, 3 June 1999.

3   Economic Policies of Latin America, IV Quarter, 1998, Office of the Chief Economist of the Inter-American Development Bank. Latin America is the region with the largest inequalities in income distribution in the world.

4   Diario 'Gestión', 7 June 1999, Lima.

5   IBASE, Social Watch Brazil, May 1999, Rio de Janeiro.

6   Folha de Sao Paulo, 1/jun/99

7   Joseph Stiglitz, Senior Vice-president and Chief Economist of the World Bank: Distribution Efficiency and Voice: Designing the Second Generation of Reforms, Conference in Brazil 14 July, 1998. Stiglitz criticises the Washington Consensus as having been too narrowly focused on low inflation and private enterprise. Important factors to be considered in the future: establishing institutions, the effective functioning of organisations and social networks, and the creation and maintenance of social capital. History also shows the role of the State in successful development, neglected in the Bank neoliberal policies. Nevertheless the self criticism is theoretical. Adjustment policies still have the lead in addressing situations such as the Brazilian crisis.

8   According to Global Development Finance 1999, only three countries: Ireland, Sweden and the United Kingdom, announced increases in aid budgets for 1998. The largest donor, Japan, decided on a 10% cut.

9   Christian Freres; 'La solidaridad de la Unión Europea con América Latina de Cara a la Cumbre Eurolatinoamericana,' paper presented at the XIII General Assembly of ALOP, Montevideo, May 1999.

10 We thank Oscar Azmitia, Brian Tomlinson and Felix Bombarolo, who provided us the information for this section. Additional information is available on the website http://www.rcp.net.pe/cti

11 The most apparent are the USA church organisations: Save the Children, CARE, Mennonite and Evangelical churches of all types, Ladies of Charity, etc. Among the international NGOs there are Oxfam/Intermón, Doctors without Borders and the Red Cross. There was a civil society campaign in other countries. Collections and solidarity meetings were promoted by Voice, Eurostep, the Forum Syd (Sweden) initiative and Whola (USA) at the summit in Stockholm.

Latin America: cooperation and basic education

Latin American Association of Promotion Organisations (ALOP)

The need for quality and social equity[1]

José Rivero, UNESCO Regional Office for Education in Latin America and the Caribbean[2]

This overview of the status of basic education in Latin America focuses on issues of quality and social equity, as well as the roles of international cooperation. There are a number of general observations that can be made about basic education in the region and these are summarised below.

Universal access

In the last few years, Latin America has made significant progress in the coverage of primary education. Access to primary education is almost universal.

Poor performance

The progress in coverage contrasts with indicators of quality. The standard of performance and results obtained are unsatisfactory. At the beginning of the 1990s, out of a total of 75 million children registered in the primary schools, 22 million had to repeat the year. Of the nine million children who entered first grade each year, around four million failed to pass the grade. The percentage is so high that some countries have decided to automatically pass the students who attend.

Studies done in Nicaragua, El Salvador, Brazil, Colombia, Honduras, Guatemala and the Dominican Republic show that the degree of repetition in the early years is much higher than indicated in official statistics. The real regional average of repetition in the first six grades of primary would be 30.9% and not the 15.3% declared by the countries. This average is higher than that of other regions. The cost of repetition is great. It is estimated at US\$4.2 million per year, for the region as a whole, a cost that limits the possibility of using the budget to incorporate into the educational system the ten million children who are still outside of it, or to achieve adult literacy or promote supplementary adult education.

Rural schooling suffers

The differences within the Latin American educational system are high. In Brazil, for example, the richer states spend six times as much as the poorer states per student registered. Generally, the rural communities and the indigenous people have progressed much less in the matter of education than the urban areas and the dominant ethnic groups. Colombia is an exception for the high level of its rural education, influenced by the experience of the Programa Escuela Nueva (New School Programme) that has been applied for the last 25 years in that country.

Poverty affects quality

The problem lies not only in the quality of teaching, but also in the physical environment and context (poor school infrastructure, malnourished children, children of illiterate parents with clear limitations to supporting their children's learning). In some cases, the probability that children will reproduce their parents' low level of education can be as high as 60%. At least seven out of ten children of professionals also enter university, compared to only two or more of every ten children of parents with low levels of education. This reveals that to improve the level of education in the poorest areas it is not enough to improve the quality of the teaching. Social policies must also be developed. Improving nutrition among poor children, improving their health check-ups and achieving higher levels of education and access to employment for their parents, will give education a more equitable and solid foundation.

Importance of pre-school

The importance of pre-school education as a foundation for ensuring success in primary school has been proven; the children who have access to pre-school education programmes display a better emotional, mental and physical preparation that allows them to perform better in school. There are studies that show that poor children can benefit more from this initial education than their more privileged peers. Therefore, pre-school education merits being incorporated as a key aspect of educational strategies in impoverished areas. In practice, however, there are limitations to the access to early education of poor sectors of the population. In Chile, only 19% of the poorest fifth of people enjoy an early childhood education, in comparison to 43% among the richest fifth; in Argentina the figures are 42% and 81%, respectively; in Chiapas, Mexico, only 38% of the children access early education as compared to 82% in Mexico City.

Targeting investment

Programmes that are able to channel investment into poor areas have potential importance. Chile's experience, aimed at benefiting the 900 low-performance schools in poor areas, is one of the more interesting 'positive discrimination' programmes. One limitation of some of these programmes is that the complementary support concentrates on emulating the educational patterns of the middle-class cities, instead of strengthening the cultural characteristics, needs and potentialities of the poorer population.

Adult education overlooked

Education of young people or adults as a means of overcoming poverty has generally been neglected by educational policies and in the allocation of the funds from the State and international finance agencies. This line is fundamental, both because it supports the poor and informal sectors in resolving problems associated with their activities, and because it generates mechanisms of self-esteem and motivation. The family environment improves when the parents are involved in educational activities and have a better perception of the importance of their children's education. Adult training and literacy places the parents in a better situation to support the education of their children.

Reforms reflect economic, not educational priorities

Today, the World Bank is the leading financier of education and even the leading formulator of basic education policies in the last five years. The present change in education has been generated with obvious influence of economists, using as a basic reference (at least until the recent Asian crisis) the educational model of countries in South-East Asia. The present rhetoric of educational reforms is in line with the idea of *human capital*, reflecting the economic development model that associates quality with competitiveness and makes market rules prevail in a context of globalisation of capital.

External influences problematic

In the emphasis on quality, some of the dominant efforts are the push to extend the school day (Chile) and to change the teaching curriculum (Argentina, Brazil, Colombia, Chile, Mexico, Peru, the Dominican Republic, and others). In the case of curriculum changes, some of these efforts have been clearly influenced by extra-regional experiences such as Spain's. Some cases have been hindered by communication barriers between reformers and teachers; the somewhat theoretical language of the experts is often incomprehensible to the teachers, which makes it hard to put into practice the new curriculum objectives, methodologies, materials and programmes.

Salaries and incentives low

Teachers have not been at the centre of the reforms. The cases of teachers' unions in Colombia and the Dominican Republic promoting the educational changes along with the official agencies are an exception. In some cases (such as Chile's) there have been incentives. Chile created a system of scholarships for the best teachers to do internships or attend courses in other countries. Two central problems make this teacher participation difficult: their salary conditions and the weakness of their training.

The income of Latin American teachers is so low that it does not differ from that of other workers who are not required to educate or bear a teacher's responsibility. In the 1980s, the salaries of the teachers in basic education decreased in real terms by an average of 14%. Over 20% of the teachers of basic education have no teaching certificate and the least qualified are those who work in the rural areas. The possibilities of salary and professional promotion are low and the degree of feminisation in this profession is high. This situation and the low participation of teachers explain the open opposition among teachers to the majority of the processes of educational change that have been initiated.

Trends in public participation

There are interesting experiences in society's participation in educational issues. In Peru, the Educational Forum has

Latin America

been formed as a plural group of experts in educational issues who formulate proposals to improve education. It includes a wide range of former ministers, directors of private schools and leaders of NGOs specialising in education. In Mexico, there is an Educational Observatory formed as an extensive platform that publishes twice monthly a page in the daily, *La Jornada*, examining different aspects of education and offering educational authorities a space in which to express their points of view concerning any criticism. In Colombia, FECODE (Federación Colombiana de Educadores) is taking an active part in the discussion of educational reform and it sponsors the specialist magazine *Educación y Cultura*.

Evaluation finds reform means more than funding

The results of a recent comparative evaluation of performance in language and mathematics indicate that the present educational systems achieve better results in countries where there is a greater political determination, or where there are educational reforms that combine teaching and administrative innovations (Argentina, Chile, Brazil and Colombia). That is, efforts to improve the quality of teaching are more likely to succeed in a situation where there is also support for planning, decentralisation, infrastructure and teachers' salary improvements.

In this evaluation, Cuba's highly favourable results over the other 12 participating countries also indicate that more international funds are not a sufficient condition for success and that the preparation and supervision of teachers and directors continue to be determinants. These results seem to indicate stagnation in countries such as Costa Rica, with a history of solid teaching, and advances in countries such as Bolivia, where the effects of the present changes in education are beginning to be evident.

Priorities for improvement

If we were to delineate some priorities for improving the quality and equity of education in Latin America, we could highlight some central elements:

- There is a need for a policy of equity that concentrates resources in critical areas, choosing a clear strategy of positive discrimination to address the effects of growing poverty.
- Quality must be addressed systematically. Measures such as curricular changes, lengthening the school day, introducing technologies, training and updating teachers, and giving schools autonomy must take

place within the framework of long-term strategies. All relevant actors and agents should be involved in the search for lifelong education of similar quality for all children, young people and adults.

- Greater national investment and international cooperation in education is required. Without sufficient financing is it hard to improve education. The impact of education projects needs to be monitored by the recipients themselves.
- The teachers are the key players in any attempt to improve the quality of education. Without a real policy for enhancing the professional abilities of teachers it will be impossible to achieve lasting results.
- Citizen oversight is important. The people's participation helps to improve the results of education. It is also important to have an independent and transparent information and evaluation system that allows for monitoring the quality of education.

The Achilles' heel of education: bypassing the teachers

One of the main limitations to educational modernisation projects, or educational reform, lies in the little importance given to teachers, both in public policies and in international cooperation programmes. Priorities are generally placed on infrastructure, preparing teaching materials, planning programmes, etc. In contrast, aspects such as teacher training, salaries and living conditions, updating of their knowledge, and their role in designing educational programmes, tend to be neglected. The role of teachers and their relationship with the State have been the most divisive issues in the educational reforms of several countries.[3]

Certainly, the credit awarded by multilateral banks and cooperation agencies has included only a small portion for teacher training. Furthermore, this usually consists of short courses that can do little to counteract cumulative structural deficiencies.

This is why the report on basic education in Guatemala maintains that the training of primary school teachers promoted by the World Bank is insufficient. The fundamental strategy is based on quality circles. These are undoubtedly useful, but they have limited potential for realising improvements in service. One significant dynamic is that more teachers are graduating than the educational system can absorb. However, the quality of their training leaves something to be desired and the type of training is not oriented towards the requirements of the educational system. (Of the 226 formal, mainstream, teacher training schools in Guatemala, only 26 were training teachers for rural areas and bilingual teaching). The number of schools could be reduced, using the funds to improve quality and to reinforce the training of the personnel currently in service.

Studies promoted by the United Nations Economic Commission for Latin America (CEPAL) also emphasise the important role of teachers. One fundamental reform that is needed to improve the educational system in Latin America is the empowerment of teachers, within the State's education apparatus and the schools, to take an active part in formulating, implementing and evaluating educational projects. More active participation from teachers can also help them to become links between formal education and the culture-based learning taking place in the community. At present, the teachers' performance in rural areas is characterised by their own insecurity, which leads them to cling to standards and programmes, distancing themselves from the community. Many teachers of rural origin do not see their own culture as an advantage.[4]

María Amelia Palacios' diagnosis of the role of teachers in Peru is illustrative. The following is a summary of her work.

Do teachers matter?

Maria Amelia Palacios, Tarea, Perú

Although improving quality is a commonly held objective, to be made a reality it requires certain conditions. Without these it is illusory to attempt any real, qualitative transformation in basic education.

One of these conditions is meeting the development needs of the corps of teachers. The national goal of reforming and improving the quality of basic education is impossible to achieve without the voluntary participation of the teachers, and without policies to support their professional and work development. This has not been given sufficient weight in public policies for education, or in international cooperation programmes.

In 1995, working teachers represented 4.6% of Peru's economically active population (EAP). The majority of teachers (77%) were working in public and private, graded schools that provided pre-school, primary and secondary education for children. As many as 80% of them were teaching in State-operated schools. In the last few years, we have observed the following trends among Peruvian teachers:

1   A corps of mostly urban teachers, with those in rural areas employed almost exclusively in State schools;

2   A significant percentage of pre-school teachers (52%) and primary teachers (40%) teaching in one-teacher and multi-grade schools;

3   Young teachers (70% with nine years of service or less);

4   An increasingly female teaching corps;

5   A growing number of certified teachers in the cities.[5]

The country doesn't yet have an integrated policy of teacher development that works simultaneously to improve the precarious living and working conditions of the teaching corps, and to raise their degree of professionalism. It is a mistake to isolate training, for example, from other dimensions that are equally vital to the quality of teachers' work, such as salaries, working conditions, career development, initial training or teachers' participation in the discussion of public policies for education.

The Government continues to neglect policy regarding the teaching profession, which has been its Achilles' heel in every assessment of educational policy of the 1990s. Efforts in mass training carried out through national plans, with the participation of civil society institutions, and financed by foreign (World Bank) credit, have spurred the process of changing the traditional approach to teaching. The change is expressed in the motto, 'from a teaching-based model of education to a learning-based model'. This joint effort has energised the work in classrooms and generated interest among the majority of teachers, whose needs for ongoing training have long been abandoned by the State.

Nevertheless, this effort requires a more sustained and diversified process of continual training for the teaching profession. The last national examination to cover teaching positions yielded very poor results: only 16% of the candidates achieved passes, although the test, which was the sole instrument used for selecting the candidates, has yet to be analysed.

The Teacher Training Modernisation Plan was begun in 1996, with very few funds, and has basically centred on curricular reform. The training of the trainers in the pedagogical institutes that implement this curricular modernisation received an initial start in 1997, but it has not continued. Some of the main weaknesses of the teacher training system are:

1   *The quality of academic and pedagogical training.* The divorce between theory and practice has been one of the most constant criticisms of teacher training in Peru. Universities are blamed for emphasising theoretical and academic training to the detriment of practical

Latin America

abilities. Higher pedagogical institutes are accused of giving priority to the instrumental aspects of teaching at the cost of a solid training in the subjects to be taught.

2   *The disjunction of pedagogical institutes and universities with pedagogical innovation and investigation*. The trainers must initiate the students in social investigation rather than in pedagogical investigation and, with a few exceptions, the trainers do not act as investigators of their own actions. Detached from creation, analysis and reflection, the teaching profession loses prestige and lacks intellectual stimulus.

3   *The absence of incentives for teacher improvement.* The present teacher pay policy turns out to be a principal limitation (of time and money) to teachers taking improvement courses with their own funds, after working hours. The higher pedagogical institutes do not have the budget to pay for the continual training of their teaching team. Meanwhile, the State does not have a policy of providing continual training for teacher trainers, nor of giving preferential attention to those who work outside of the large cities and who have fewer opportunities for improvement.

4   *The inorganic growth of the supply of teacher training.* The rapid and disproportionate expansion of the private supply of regular teacher training since the early 1990s has not been accompanied by mechanisms for evaluating its pertinence and quality.

5   *The continuation of uncertified teachers in service.* The system still has a significant percentage of teachers who are uncertified for the levels and types of education they offer. Among pre-school teachers, 43.3% are uncertified; among primary teachers, 40.9%; and among special education teachers, 55.3% are uncertified. Many of these uncertified teachers have only secondary level education.

6   *The quality of teacher training is not evaluated.* Such an evaluation would:
    *   Indicate the availability in training establishments of qualified human resources and support materials (up-to-date libraries, teaching resources, access to computers);
    *   Measure how pertinent the training is to the educational reality of the population to be educated (quality of diversification);
    *   Assess how effective the training is in developing, in the students, the teaching competencies established in the professional profile (pedagogical quality).

One of the great obstacles to developing teachers – who are such an important factor in education policies – is their present pay situation and the conditions in which they perform their professional work. The level of pay and professional status of the teachers serving in public education is a constant social demand. The gross monthly pay of a young, certified teacher just entering the career (first level) with a 24-hour teaching week is US$215. The net pay after legally fixed deductions is US$185.

Educational reform in Brazil: market and social inequity

Sergio Haddad, Acción Educativa[6]

Education has been one of the priorities of the Government of Fernando Enrique Cardoso, who has held the office of President of Brazil since 1994. The Minister of Education, an economist with work experience in multilateral banks and education, enjoys the President's full confidence and is committed to the State's model for reform.

During the last four years, the federal Government's actions have been aimed at reforming the educational system – without increasing spending in the education sector – and trying to adapt the educational system to the market's priorities and needs. Among all of Brazil's social reforms, the educational reform seems to have achieved the best performance and greatest public visibility.

The policy of the Ministry of Education and Culture has generally aimed at:

*   *Reform*, with the least amount of resources, to increase productivity by applying resources based on a cost-benefit analysis.
*   *Seeking foreign financing*, particularly from the World Bank and the Inter-American Development Bank, institutions that, in addition to financing projects, also influence educational policy.
*   *Focusing its actions*, prioritising basic education.
*   *Deregulating the system* to make it more flexible, reducing limitations established by previous legislation and strengthening some of the social rights already gained.
*   *Decentralising* responsibility for basic education and putting it under the municipalities, with the Ministry of Education directing curriculum development and performing evaluations.
*   *Privatising* some teaching sectors in order to create a market for private initiative.
*   *Seeking different types of associations* with institutions of civil society (NGOs, business foundations).

Table 37 Indicators of Spending in Education: Brazil 1998 (US$ millions)

Indicator	Value	% of GDP
GDP	804	100
Public spending in education	36.430	4.53
Spending in basic education	9.000	1.1
Technical cooperation	0.112	0.01
Credit from multilateral agencies	0.297	0.04
Total foreign financing (donations, credit)	0.409	0.05

Table 37 provides an overview of the relative weight given to the education sector as a portion of the GDP and the national budget, as well as the relative weight of international technical cooperation and financing from multilateral banks.

As seen in the table, the weight of cooperation and foreign financing in relation to public spending in education is insignificant. Nevertheless, the multilateral banks exercise a considerable influence on the formulation of education policy. In terms of volume and in comparison with other nations, Brazil is one of the main recipients of credit from multilateral banks (from a US$1 billion portfolio of multi-year programmes, US$297 million was approved for 1998) and the credits it receives for education have been increasing.

It must also be remembered that Brazil allocates most of its public spending to personnel, while the foreign funds are allocated to education 'policy' (contracting technical studies, designing curriculum, training and evaluation). The influence of agencies such as the World Bank in education policies is disproportionate to their share of the allocated funds. This is the strategy established by these institutions. The Bank itself indicates that:

'The World Bank is strongly committed to supporting education. It is currently aiming one quarter of its placements to education in developing countries, but its contributions represent only about 0.5% of the spending on education of the developing countries. That is why the World Bank's most important contribution should be to provide advisory services conceived to help governments develop education policies adapted to the specific characteristics of their countries. The Bank's financing, in general, will be delineated with a view towards influencing changes in the spending and policies of the national authorities.'

(World Bank Report, 1995: XXIII)

The projects agreed to with the multilateral banks have diverse problems, such as:

- Little transparency and meagre social control. There is scant information on how the funds are handled and how effective they are in realising the objectives. Greater knowledge, participation, follow-up, monitoring and control of these funds on the part of civil society – which will ultimately have to assume the costs – could help to ensure their effective use.
- Problems in monitoring the projects. The project agreements are based on contract models used for economic loans, which define quantitative indicators for evaluation, whereas education requires qualitative indicators. This implies problems and delays in the development of projects.
- The projects with multilateral banks are generating an onerous foreign debt, which is becoming difficult to manage.
- Problems of autonomy arise at the time the countries define their education policy. On borrowing funds, they also buy a model. They buy a system for monitoring how these funds are used, which restricts their autonomy for building a national model of education reform.

On the threshold: basic education in Guatemala

Werner Fernando Ramírez Avila[7]

Contributions from international technical cooperation and loans from multilateral banks have been increasing in Guatemala. However, because the issue is complex and they represent a minor component of the education budget their impact is limited, and they are unable to break some of the inertia in Guatemalan education policies.

The average level of schooling among the population of Guatemala (2.3 years according to the national statistics institute, INE) reveals the educational deficit accumulated

Latin America

among young people and adults. CONALFA estimates that, in 1998, 1.9 million Guatemalans over the age of 15 (32% of the population) were still illiterate. Of every ten illiterate people, eight live in rural areas, six are indigenous people and six are also women.

The gross rate of coverage (GRC)[8] for the pre-primary level was 59% in 1998,[9] 26% higher than in 1995. Despite the important effort to expand the coverage at this level, in 1998 more than 300,000 children between the ages of five and six were not served by the education system. At primary level, the GRC rose to 99%, an increase of 14% during the three years from 1995 to 1998, considerably greater than the 3% increase observed in the period of 1992 to 1995. Nevertheless, the GRC of primary schools achieved in Guatemala continues to be below the Latin American average of 113%.[10] Considering that, in 1996 and 1997, the difference between the gross and net rates of coverage was an average of 16 points, in 1998 some 200,000 children of primary school age failed to receive school services.

Intense efforts are being made to expand the coverage of basic education among children, which is commendable but still insufficient. Approximately half a million children received no schooling in 1998. That same year, the national literacy committee, CONALFA, served 405,696 people.[11] Given this state of affairs, in Guatemala we are still generating more illiterate than literate people for the future.

Along with the deficits in coverage, we have problems with the continuity and quality of education in the country. The phenomenon of 'withdrawal' is common. Improperly called desertion, as if the children dropped out of school simply to escape it, in the majority of cases, withdrawal is caused by poverty or other problematic circumstances in the family. In pre-primary, withdrawal rose from 4% in 1996 to 9% in 1998,[12] while in primary, for the same period, it rose from 5% to 8%.

The lack of coverage is the first line of discrimination in education, because the indigenous population receives the least coverage, although the Ministry of Education is expanding the coverage significantly. The total number of children registered in primary school rose by 11% in 1998 over the previous year. Where there *are* schools and teachers in the indigenous communities, another line of discrimination becomes patent: the lack of cultural relevance in the educational system. If the former hinders access to universal knowledge, the latter permits it, but with pressures towards acculturation.

The main programme for school service for the indigenous population, using their own languages and elements of their culture, consists of the schools operated by the

General Office for Intercultural Bilingual Education (DIGEBI). These schools provide pre-primary and primary education. They cover 13 linguistic communities, in 11 of the 18 departments with indigenous populations. However, these schools continue to be insufficient for the potential needs of indigenous communities (when you compare the proportion of DIGEBI schools to the proportion of indigenous communities in the total population). In addition, not all of these schools provide complete primary schooling.

The bilingual education is limited and, furthermore, its intercultural nature is aimed only at the indigenous people. This is a third line of discrimination: the *Ladino* or *mestiso* people know little of the other peoples of Guatemala. This is why the Educational Reform Design affirms the purpose of an intercultural system for all, in order to foment unity amid diversity, and proposes additive multilingualism, so that everyone can learn one or more other languages without having to neglect their first language.

Attitudes change more by the dissemination of improved practices and the opening of new possibilities of interaction, than by theories and debates. In the area of changing curriculum, there are innovative experiences and, in addition to the orientations of the Reform Design, there are proposals such as *Lineamientos curriculares para la educación primaria bilingüe intercultural*, (curricular guidelines for intercultural bilingual primary education) prepared by CNEM, DIGEBI, PEMBI-GTZ, UNICEF and USAID in 1998.

Because *real quality* in education is a socio-political matter, participation is essential as a means of enabling new interactions. Hence the importance of the provisions of Article 76 of the Constitution of the Republic, that the educational system must be decentralised and entrusted to the regions. In Guatemala, decentralisation of education has progressed with the creation and reinforcement of the departmental offices of education. Other catalysts have been the creation of 2841 COEDUCA institutions and 503 School Boards, up to 1998, and the integration of the municipal, departmental and national Opposition Juries, which appoint the teaching personnel. Regionalisation, on the other hand, has stagnated. The Regional Education Offices were barely functional for many reasons, one of which is that the law is inconsistent in delineating the preliminary regionalisation. The Indigenous Rights Agreement proposes that regionalisation be adapted to the population's linguistic and cultural characteristics. This criterion is sound but in reality regionalisation and decentralisation are still goals rather than achievements.

One problem is that the country is not training the teachers it needs to provide this intercultural education. In

Latin America

studying the characteristics of teacher training, the Maya Intercultural Bilingual Education Project (PEMBI), financed by the GTZ, made the following findings in the bilingual pilot schools in Guatemala's Region VI:

- Overload of general courses and the inclusion of courses on leadership and community development and the teaching of trades;
- Insufficient time for the numerous assignments and excessive homework due to a lack of coordination between professors;
- Scant attention to pedagogical issues, which, along with the lectures, only had a general focus;
- Minimal content on the Maya culture;
- Teaching of languages without pedagogical grammars, which brings disadvantages for improving the students' communication abilities;
- A disjunction between the teacher training institutes and the schools where teachers apply the skills and knowledge they have learned. Teachers are often assigned to jobs based on needs of the receiving establishment and not training needs.[13]

Several of these findings are also certainly present in the other normal schools.

Investment and innovation lacking in Peru

María Amelia Palacios, Tarea, Peru

In view of the magnitude and complexity of the educational problems in Peru, the efforts and funds currently invested by the State, as well as by civil society, to improve the quality and equity of basic education for the poorest people, are still clearly inadequate.

The State's priorities – and the funds it devotes to improving coverage and quality in basic education – continue to be heavily influenced by the desire to strengthen the role of central government, and by the policies of the

multilateral credit agencies (the World Bank and the IDB), from which the Peruvian government has contracted loans.

The main government programme in basic education is undoubtedly the MECEP (Programme to Improve Quality in Primary Education), begun in 1995 with funds from the Public Treasury and a US$146 million loan from the World Bank. The base costs of the programme (US$253.9 million) are being invested in improving the quality of education (US$88.1 million), developing institutions (US$44.8 million) and improving infrastructure (US$121.8 million).

The loan from the IDB is distributed among pre-school, secondary, higher technological and higher pedagogical education. As seen in Table 38, 40.77% of both loans was due to be paid out in 1999. This is also a key year for completing the commitments with the World Bank and negotiating a second phase.

An analysis of the destination of the loans from the World Bank and the IDB reveals that the most important component has been the improvement of infrastructure, which has included rehabilitation and maintenance of school buildings, furniture, the preparation of a 'school map', and an infrastructure monitoring system.

The provision of educational materials and the training of teachers in basic education, on the contrary, have received much lower sums. Furthermore, institutional development, where the proposed priorities were the modernisation of the educational administration, a plan to promote autonomy in public schools, a management information system and a system for evaluating learning, have been neglected. The lack of attention given to strengthening the school institution and the intermediate agencies at the local level of the sector is consistent with the Government's general policy, little inclined to strengthening institutional democracy or to calling on other players to participate in the general or sectoral policy decisions.

Added to this is the Ministry of Education's proposal, made public in late 1997, to change the structure of the educational system.[14] The initiative returns to the concept of basic education, seeking to unite what the system now

Table 38 Loans for improving the quality of education in Peru (US$)

Institution	Total	1996	1997	1998	1999	Balance
BIRF	146,400	2,396,876	16,492,054	42,731,597	66,533,000	18,246,473
IDB	100,000	–	1,301,000	21,643,000	33,930,000	43,126.000
TOTAL	246,400	2,396,876	17,793,054	64,374,597	100,463,00	61,372,473
Percentage	100	0.97	7.22	26.13	40.77	24.91

Source: 1999 Education Budget (currently in debate in Congress); prepared by S Chiroque

Latin America

Table 39 *Destination of international loans by percentages: Peru 1999*

Areas/projects	BIRF	IDB
Development of curriculum	0.2	–
Educational materials	3.0	4.4
Teacher training	4.8	0.4
Measuring student performance	0.5	1.2
Infrastructure and furniture	84.4	85.9
Quality circles	–	0.7
Modernisation of higher pedagogical and technological institutes	–	2.5
Capacity building in institutions	6.2	
Modernisation of administration	2.1	
Information systems	3.9	
Consolidation of the OINFE	0.2	
System to improve teacher performance	–	0.8
Planning and evaluation system	–	2.2
Coordinating Unit	0.9	2.0

Source: 1999 budget of the Ministry of Education; prepared by Sigfredo Chiroque

separates into primary and secondary, to cut secondary education by one year and to create a new, non-mandatory, post-secondary level of two years, called the Bachelor's Degree. This latter is to be a prerequisite for continuing higher studies. The result is a reduction of the basic education (primary and secondary), which is mandatory and free to everyone, to ten years of studies.

This year, the Ministry of Education began to pilot the Bachelor's Degree in 200 of the nation's schools and has announced that the programme will be applied in all schools by the year 2000. It has done so without first generating a social consensus concerning these changes and has diverted to the Bachelor's Degree project funds that it could have devoted to improving the quality and coverage of mandatory basic education, and secondary education in particular.

These programmes and proposals have left some populations without the educational services to satisfy their basic learning needs. These non-serviced populations include 47% of adolescents between the ages of 12 and 16, who are not registered in any year of secondary, and the approximately six million young people and adults over age 15 who were unable to complete their basic education during the standard years. Peru is far from fulfilling the commitments it made to Education for All.

The greatest progress achieved to date by the process of modernisation of basic education directed by the State lies in the field of curricular reform. However, basic education continues to present serious problems that affect its equity and quality. These include:[15]

- *Deficits in service.* The deficits in basic education service are a clear expression of the inequities in education. Among children aged 6–11, 5.7% (more than 200,000 boys and girls) do not attend school. The deficit is greater among girls (6.2%) than among boys. Among adolescents aged 12–17, 17.0% do not attend school and, again, women are the most disadvantaged (18.2%). The situation of poverty and extreme poverty increases absenteeism. Among poor adolescents, 19.5% do not attend school and among those who live in extreme poverty, non-attendance rises to 23.2%. Official figures indicate that, of every 1000 students who enter school, 173 withdraw before reaching sixth grade of primary and 328 do not complete secondary schooling.

- *Low levels of learning.* In Peru we do not have a consolidated system for measuring learning, to complement the evaluation done by the schools. The issue of educational achievement indicators and the public responsibility for the results is only beginning to enter the teaching and public administration culture.

Neither is there a tradition of government agencies rendering accounts to the citizens on their fulfilment of national goals. The Ministry of Education has not publicised the results of the learning evaluation tests given to a sample of students in the fourth grade of primary in 1997, nor the results of the measurements done by UNESCO through the Quality Measurement Laboratory.

- *Inequity between urban and rural, and private and public environments.* A small-scale study[16] of vocabulary, reading and arithmetic performance of boys and girls in fourth and fifth grade of primary level showed differences among urban (Lima and Huaráz) and rural (Huaráz) schools. Between urban schools in Lima, there was also a gap between the private and public schools, in favour of the former.

  The report of UNICEF and Peru's national statistics institute (INEI), called 'The Situation of Children, Adolescents and Women – 1996', presents eight variables for measuring the educational development level in the departments of Peru. This report reveals wide gaps and the existence of educational inequity throughout the entire country.

- *The precariousness of rural education.* The greatest precariousness in basic education is observed in one-teacher schools and in incomplete, multi-grade schools, mostly in rural areas, in which one teacher serves two or three grades. In 1997, there were 27,174 primary schools in the country, of which 8,600 were one-teacher schools and more than 12,000 were incomplete, multi-teacher schools.

  In 1998, the Ministry of Education began a project with cooperation funds from the European Union for the development of rural basic education. The Ministry's 1999 operating plan foresees, for this year, training 2,700 teachers of schools with a vernacular-speaking population and providing educational materials in the vernacular to the schools with intercultural, bilingual education.

- *High rate of repetition.* The rate of repetition has been very high in the first grade of primary, largely as a result of the low quality of the education. This requires an investment solely to keep repeaters in the system, an expense that does not contribute to dealing better with learning difficulties. In recent years we have seen a significant reduction of repetition in primary, from 31.84% in 1990/1991 to 27.28% in 1994/1995. The largest variation occurred between 1995 and 1996, when it fell to 12.63% (Miranda, 1999). The reestablishment of 'automatic promotion' from first to second grades of primary must have influenced this, but the State's greater initiative through the MECEP programme, may also be a factor.

- *Reduced learning time.* Another important indicator of quality is the effective time of learning. The effective hours of learning in rural schools are 226 per year; in the marginal-urban areas it is 450 hours per year, while in private schools, boys and girls study 1,100 hours per year. This is another indicator of the extreme differences in quality between rural schools and private schools in Peru, and of the reduced number of hours of learning in the schools in urban, popular neighbourhoods.

  One official report based on data from the Office of Planning, Strategy and Measurement of Educational Quality of the Ministry of Education (1996) indicates that the number of effective hours of class may be only 50–80% of the school hours scheduled. In the rural area on the border, in one-teacher or multi-grade schools, the proportion of effective hours of learning may not reach 30%.

Peru is a multilingual and multicultural country. According to data from the latest census (1993), 3,750,492 people over the age of five living in Peru have Andean or Amazon languages as their mother tongues. Of these, 3,199,474 speak varieties of Quechua, 420,215 speak varieties of Aimara and 130,803 speak various other vernacular languages.

Bilingual education is an officially recognised means of education within the educational system, although it presently reaches only a section of the indigenous language speakers of the Andes and the Amazon basin, who are in pre-school and primary levels. Despite this progress, resistance to bilingual education persists within the Ministry of Education. There is not a shared conviction among public officials of the importance and relevance of intercultural, bilingual education to improve the quality of education and of learning.

Notes

1. This section is based on a summary of the presentations and conclusions of the workshop organised by the ALOP (Asociación Latinoamericana de Organizaciones de Promoción) international cooperation group, along with FASE and Acción Educativa de Brasil. The workshop was held in Río de Janeiro, May 28-29 1999. It was sponsored by Ayuda en Acción and ActionAid. Mariano Valderrama, coordinator of the work group on ALOP international cooperation, was responsible for editing the material.
2. The author's opinions are not necessarily those of UNESCO.
3. Martínez, Juan. *Reformas educativas comparadas. Bolivia-México-Chile-España.* Centro Boliviano de Investigación y Acción Educativas (CEBIAE), La Paz, 1995, p129.
4. *Educación, eficiencia y equidad*, edited by Ernesto Cohen, Santiago de Chile CEPAL/OEA/SUR, 1998. See especially the article by John Durston: 'La participación comunitaria en la gestión de la escuela rural.'
5. María Amelia Palacios and Manuel Paiba (1997) *Consideraciones para una política de desarrollo magisterial.* Foro Educativo, Lima, Perú.
6. Sergio Haddad is president of the Asociación Brasileña de ONG (ABONG) and director of Acción Educativa.

Latin America

7   Investigator with training in economics; national advisor to Germany's GTZ project to support the Ministry of Education; consultant to the Consejo Nacional de Educación Maya (CNEM).

8   The GRC is obtained by dividing the total number of students registered by the total population in the corresponding age group (for primary school, the latter is the child population between the ages of 7 and 12).

9   MINEDUC *Informaciones cuantitativas de la preinscripción, información año 1998*, Guatemala, March 1999.

10   World Bank *Guatemala basic education strategy: equity and efficiency in education*, Report no 13304-GU, 20 January, 1995, p5.

11   Comité Nacional de Alfabetización (CONALFA). *Informe gerencial de alfabetización (presentación preliminar)*. Guatemala, March 1999, p6. The figure refers to the total number of people attending and includes literacy and post-literacy, as well as services for over-age children.

12   The data for 1996 and 1997 come from the respective statistical annuals of MINEDUC.

13   PEMBI-GTZ. *Malla curricular para la formación de maestros de la escuela primaria bilingüe intercultural*; Versión resumida; Xe'lajuj No'j (Quetzaltenango), November 1998, pp1-3.

14   Ministerio de Educación (1997). *Nueva estructura del sistema educativo peruano. Fundamentos de la propuesta*; Lima, Perú.

15   Manuel Iguiñiz (1999) *La educación primaria en la política educativa peruana*, Tarea, Lima, Perú.

16   See: Pollit, Ernesto, Jacoby, Enrique y Cueto, Santiago. Desayuno Escolar y Rendimiento, Editorial Apoyo, Lima 1996.

Africa: aid, debt and development

Twisema S Muyoya, MWENGO

The increasingly familiar picture of declining aid flows from OECD countries has become a reality that many in sub-Saharan Africa have come to accept as the continent's inescapable plight. Equally obvious, but perhaps not inescapable, is the unprecedented level of unemployment, rising poverty and the proliferation of conflicts and wars across the continent.

By mid-1999, no fewer than 12 African countries[1] were embroiled in wars, experiencing turmoil or engaged in civil wars within their own countries. A number of countries were on the verge of war with their neighbours. Even the relatively peaceful Southern Africa region was increasingly facing the spectre of war, outside the war in the former Zaire.

During 1999 there was rising border tension between neighbours Namibia and Botswana over the Caprivi Strip. Angola fell just short of declaring war against its eastern neighbour, Zambia over allegations that the latter was assisting Jonas Savimbi's Unita rebels to procure arms, as their traditional route through the former Zaire had been closed following the outbreak of war in Laurent Kabila's Democratic Republic of Congo.

The border conflict between Ethiopia and Eritrea continued despite many attempts at negotiated settlement. The cease-fire in Sierra Leone still hangs in delicate balance. Civil war is looming yet again in neighbouring Liberia.

Conflict and war leave in their wake only destruction, desolation, and the displacement of masses of people. The absence of peace threatens not only the democratic rights of citizens but also their personal safety. Without peace and stability, progress and development are held up as conflict and war use up vital resources that could promote human development.

Those countries that have been spared the ravages of war have had to contend with other problems. Some of these have been the result of crippling corruption, bad governance and weak civil society. Poor commodity prices on world markets and unfair terms of trade have been cited as the cause of lack of economic growth in many sub-Saharan countries.

In spite of all these difficulties, the Economic Commission for Africa (ECA)[2] reports that the continent registered a 3.3% growth in GDP in 1998 compared to 2.9% in 1997. Though such growth was not evenly distributed among the continent's 49 countries, this is a significant development, given that much of the previous decade had seen mainly negative growth.

Even more significant was the 4.1% growth in GDP (up from 2.4 in 1997) recorded by the 33 Least Developed Countries (LLDCs). This surpassed growth in the continent's largest economies – Algeria, Egypt, Morocco, Nigeria and South Africa- which averaged 3.1% growth in their GDP.

It is important to note sub-regional differentiation indicates that only North Africa and Central Africa recorded a GDP growth rate of 3.1%, an improvement of 1.1% from 1997. The other regions experienced a decline in the GDP

At country level, topping the growth rankings were Botswana, Republic of Congo (Brazzaville) and Equatorial Guinea which all registered an impressive 7% growth in their GDP.

However, the trouble with statistics is that they look good on paper. In the short- to mid-term, it is hard for the average man or woman in the street to feel the impact and see the benefits of the growth in GDP. There may be many reasons for this. When governments are corrupt or embark on military adventures, there is a direct competition between, on one hand, unbridled greed or big military spending, and the allocation of resources to social services and development financing.

Further, a considerable amount of the earnings from this growth are inevitably diverted to the servicing of external debt. Oxfam, in its *'Education Now Campaign,'* observes

Africa

that 'each year sub-Saharan Africa spends $10 billion in debt repayments'.

This has obvious implications for social spending by African governments. For example, 10% of Zambia's GDP went to the servicing of debt while spending on primary education did not exceed 2% of the GDP. Other examples include Ethiopia and Niger whose debt servicing expenditure is twice that of primary education.

Under Structural Adjustment Programmes (SAPs), liberalisation and reduced spending by governments are standard IMF panaceas for developing economies. These SAPs, which often result in cuts in social sectors, are increasingly meeting with the disapproval of African citizens, who are yet to see any benefit accruing from these policies. But despite this declining popularity with local people, these IMF policies and programmes remained largely intact in 1998.

1998 saw no significant progress in terms of moving towards sustainable alternatives to foreign aid and investment. Africa remains highly dependent on these inflows – a dependence which continues despite the steady decline in ODA flows to the continent.

Although sub-Saharan Africa has 80% of the poorest and most indebted developing countries,[3] only Mozambique was among the top ten[4] recipients of Official Development Assistance in 1996/7 – receiving 1% of total ODA (around US$600 million).

It is against this background that the increase in global financial flows to developing countries by 8.9%[5] in 1998 must be understood. This increase may be cause for optimism in broad foreign aid terms. However, the impact of this modest development is still far from being felt across the continent.

Net resource flows to sub-Saharan Africa actually fell in 1998 by a third from US$4.5 billion in 1997 to US$3 billion. The increase in global aid flows therefore has little or no meaning for African economies; more importantly, for the masses of the poor. A positive difference for African countries will only be possible if the reversal in the downward slide of foreign aid can be permanently arrested and aid flows to Africa are increased significantly over the coming years.

African economies remain vulnerable to the volatile political climate; to the vagaries of weather and natural disasters; unfavourable world commodity markets and an increasing marginalisation by the international donor community.[6]

The African continent is entering the new millenium with 44% of the population of sub-Saharan Africa still living under the poverty line. The effects of economic liberalisation and other IMF prescriptions will continue to be felt well into the next millennium.

Rather than equip African economies to take up their place in the global economy, IMF policies have further weakened the continent and left it unprepared for globalisation. Aid policies, as they stand, offer no real hope for economies that so desperately need to 'bridge the resource gap in order to hasten development'. At the same time with sound national policies and institutions, economic growth and development will become more achievable. Where these sound policies and institutions are not developed or where they do not exist, aid can be used to facilitate the development of such policies and nurture such institutions.[7]

Widespread conflicts and prolonged wars mean that many parts of Africa enter the new millennium unstable, more divided and more troubled than ever before. Millions are still displaced internally or externally.

Yet in the shadow of all this seeming hopelessness, there is a glimmer of light, of hope. The shift to open and more democratic systems of governance, holds hope that African countries are moving towards greater transparency and accountability.

As civil society organisations take on the challenge of playing an expanded role in the transformation from stagnation to sustainable development, the democratisation process across the continent has led to the opening up of political space for non-state actors.

Grassroots communities and their organisations are deservedly demanding their own space, increasingly confident in the knowledge that their destiny lies in their own hands. Outsiders, however well-meaning and committed, can only facilitate (catalyse) and not shape those destinies.

Although the relationship between the state and civil society remains an issue of concern, new horizons are beginning to emerge. There is a significant growth in the levels of consultation between some institutions of the state and civil society organisations. The improving relations can no doubt, be enhanced if the capacity to collaborate, network and manage cross-sectoral relationships is addressed appropriately and adequately.

The emerging commitment by African leaders to the search for home-grown solutions to the continent's problems, is one clear indication that time has come for everyone, politicians in particular, to look beyond their own pet ambitions and preoccupations and see the wider picture.

The opening up of political space through democratisation and the emerging desire to find African solutions to the continent's problems both represent opportunities for which civil society organisations must strategically position themselves.

The growth and development of civil society is likely to ensure good governance. With a stronger civil society, greater transparency and accountability, the diversion of resources or misuse of foreign aid will be reduced significantly. In more transparent societies with a tradition of public accountability, the frequency and extent of grand corruption are bound to decline and the prospects for effective aid which has a lasting impact on poverty will increase.

Notes

1 At the last count, Angola, Democratic Republic of the Congo, Eritrea, Ethiopia, Namibia, Rwanda, Uganda, Zimbabwe were involved in cross-border wars. Angola, Burundi, Congo Brazzaville, Somalia and the Sudan remain divided by internal strife. In Sierra Leone a shaky ceasefire had just been agreed by the Tejan Khaba government and rebels led by Foday Sanko. Even the small mountain kingdom of Lesotho has had more than its fair share of social unrest and political upheavals.

2 Economic Report on Africa 1999: the Challenges of Poverty Reduction and Sustainability.

3 51% of the sub-Saharan population live below the poverty datum line of $ 34 per month – Economic Report of Africa.

4 OECD statistics.

5 OECD News Release, June 10, 1999, Paris.

6 Since the birth of the independent states in the aftermath of the fall of the Soviet Union, resources which, many believe, would have benefited Africa have been diverted to Eastern Europe. Africa has lost out.

7 *Assessing Aid: What Works, What Doesn't, and Why*, November, 1998, World Bank Report.

Uganda: poverty and basic education

Tumutegyereize Kennedy, Uganda Debt Network

What is poverty?

The Uganda Participatory Poverty Assessment Project
(UPPAP, 1999) has defined poverty as lack of means to
satisfy basic material and social needs, as well as a feeling
of powerlessness. It is a dynamic process of social,
economic, cultural, political and other deprivation, which
affects individuals and communities. The Poverty
Eradication Action Plan (PEAP) has defined poverty as 'lack
of basic necessities of life (food, shelter, and clothing) and
other needs like education and health'.

People living in poverty do not form a homogeneous
class. They include:

- Those who are too handicapped to work by reasons of
  physical or mental disabilities or by reason of old age
  or tender age;
- Children especially orphans;
- Disadvantaged urban dwellers especially the
  unemployed, informal sector workers and slum
  dwellers;
- People in remote areas who lack access to services
  and markets for their products;
- those who live in insecure environments;
- Those affected by natural disasters such as drought
  and earthquakes;
- Women, especially those who are less educated and
  those under absolute control of their husbands, and
  those who have no access to gainful employment;
- Those with insufficient food;
- People who lack social support networks;
- Households with too many dependants;
- Those affected by insecurity and people suffering from
  geographical isolation.[1]

Poverty assessment

The Government of Uganda, analysed poverty in 1997 using
for the first time, a national absolute poverty line and a food
poverty line. The absolute poverty line reflects the monthly
monetary cost per person of obtaining both food and non-
food basic requirements. The food poverty line reflects the
monthly monetary cost of obtaining the recommended 3000
calories per person per day. Using the 1993/94 household
survey data, the national poverty line and food poverty line
were calculated at Uganda shillings 16,400 and 11,500
respectively. In 1992/93, 55.6% of the population were poor
as compared to 45.6% in 1995/96.

Since 1997, a number of initiatives have been undertaken to assess and increase the understanding of poverty.
The Poverty Eradication Action Plan was drawn up in 1997
to provide a framework to deal with poverty in a holistic
manner. The Uganda Participatory Poverty Assessment
Project was started in the Ministry of Finance to improve
understanding of poverty but most importantly to capture
the views of the poor on how they view themselves and the
possible options for reducing poverty. The Poverty Status
Report (1999) has been produced, and it is hoped this will
be an annual report.

The recent poverty assessments have indicated that
poverty goes beyond the traditional poverty indicators of
incomes, expenditure, consumption, health and education,
derived from the household surveys. A broader set of
indicators used to define poverty, including the previously
unconsidered dimensions such as risk, vulnerability, powerlessness and insecurity, have been highlighted as key
concerns to the poor themselves. These key concerns have
emerged from direct consultations with people living in
poverty in a participatory manner. This has highlighted the
fact that people living in poverty understand their own situation and are capable of highlighting their concerns. They
can appraise government anti-poverty programmes and set

Uganda

their priorities, which are in most cases different from those of Government programmes. It further recognised that poverty is a complex multi-dimensional, cyclical and seasonal phenomenon. The factors influencing poverty are interlinked and often interdependent. For example, poor health may be a consequence of poor education, which may be a cause and a consequence of poverty.

Challenges of poverty eradication in Uganda

The Government's top priority is poverty eradication. At the macro level, structural reforms have been instituted, including restructuring of the civil service, liberalisation, maintaining macro-economic growth, promotion of private investments and decentralisation of public services. The 1997 Poverty Eradication Action Plan (PEAP) integrates poverty issues into the national development plan instead of drawing a separate plan for the poor.

The adoption of the PEAP led to the revision of sectoral programmes and re-orientation of the public expenditure allocation to effectively address the needs of the priority sectors. The priority areas considered key to poverty eradication are roads (feeder roads and main roads), micro-finance and agriculture. These three areas are considered critical for increasing the incomes of poorer people. The other critical areas are education and health (directly concerned with improving the quality of life of the people) and improved efficiency in the utilisation of the resources available. However, according to the Uganda Human Development Report 1998[2] the PEAP is unrealistic given the activity load, time frame and availability of resources. In 1998, after the HIPC debt relief initiative, the freed resources were channelled through the Poverty Action Fund (PAF). PAF provides additional resources for expenditure in the priority sectors such as agriculture extension, water and sanitation, primary school classroom construction, feeder roads, and primary health care. Ushs 83 billions have been channelled through the PAF. The additional expenditure has alleviated the pressures on social sector expenditure. The quarterly PAF meetings have further brought transparency and accountability

Growth

The impressive economic growth rates experienced in the last 12 years have not trickled down to the majority. Since the poor are mostly located in rural areas, the Government has encouraged the production of non-traditional export crops, provision of micro-finance to give people start up capital, improved road networks so that small farmers in rural areas can access markets. Parliament passed the land

act (1998), with the hope of giving poorer people security of tenure, and the Government has formulated the Education Strategic Investment Plan (ESIP) for 1998–2003 and is in the process of drawing up the agricultural modernisation plan. However, it remains to be seen whether these reforms and policies will have a significant impact on poverty eradication.

Perhaps, the biggest challenge to poverty eradication has been lack of clear understanding of the dynamics of poverty. Until the UPPAP Project and the Poverty Status report (1999), the general view of the Government was that poverty was reducing. The definition of poverty was narrow and did not take account of the key concerns of the poor. Good governance, decentralisation, protection of human rights, the rule of law, transparency and accountability, gender equality, access to basic social services, are the key challenges to poverty eradication.

Policy environment and institutions to fight poverty

The Government of Uganda has refocused public expenditure directly linked to poverty eradication, and is therefore using a three-pronged approach to poverty eradication:

- Increase incomes.
- Strengthen good governance institutions.
- Improve the quality of life of the people, as recommended by the PEAP.

Maintaining and consolidating the existing macro-economic policies will not only put the country on the road to growth and encourage the participation and expansion of the private sector by creating an enabling environment but also will be the source of poverty eradication. In fact more than 90% of the success in poverty eradication registered so far is attributed to GDP growth.

A number of policies and institutions, have been put in place to achieve the objective of poverty eradication. They include formulation of the PEAP, Poverty Monitoring Unit, in the Ministry of Finance, Planning and Economic Development, and the Poverty Action Fund to mobilise additional funding and increase accountability.

Donor coordination in poverty eradication.

The donors (bilateral and multilateral) are coordinated through the aid coordination unit in the Ministry of Finance, Planning and Economic Development. Until 1997, the nature of interaction was between the government and donors. There was little or no interaction between the donors and the larger civil society. However, in 1998, the trend of events

Uganda

Table 40 Matrix showing the levels of implementation of the Government anti-poverty programmes

Policies/ Structures	Plan of Action	Level of participation by the civil society	Constraints
Poverty eradication	• Increase household incomes • Strengthen good governance • Increase quality of life through education and health • Micro-finance to give households start-up capital • Maintain high rates of growth (above 7%) • Increase access to markets • Improve on the infrastructure such as roads • Increase understanding of Poverty (UPPAP)* • Provide timely information	Participatory	• Poor record keeping • Lack of reliable and timely information • Lack of clear understanding of poverty • Corruption undermines anti-poverty programmes • Insecurity in the northern and western parts of the country • Lack of social development plan • Lack of coordination of the various anti-poverty programmes • Large families prevailing in Africa
Poverty Eradication Action Plan (PEAP)	• Reduce poverty by 2017 • Tackle poverty in a holistic approach (education, health, gender equality, etc)	Participatory: it involved wide consultations with the NGOs and local Councillors	• Not all elements of anti-poverty programmes are implemented because of budget constraints • The cost outlay needed is three times higher than the national resources available • Not gender sensitive • The poor themselves were not reached except by proxy through NGOs and local council representatives
Poverty Action Fund (PAF)	• Availability of guidelines • Quarterly PAF meetings involving Government, NGOs, the media and donors	Civil society not involved in design	• Few resources are available for PAF • Lack of understanding about the PAF by the population • It is not gender sensitive • Not all sectors are included
Poverty monitoring	• Empower districts to monitor poverty levels • Empower the population to assess poverty • Develop reliable and timely statistics for all sectors • Build data bank on all sectors	Highly participatory	• The National Bureau of Statistics is under funded to collect, analyse and disseminate timely data. • Lack of National Planning Authority to coordinate the efforts of all planners (especially districts) • Lack of accurate data • Lack of coordinated planning • Lack of clarity on measured and perceived poverty
External debt management	• External debt management strategy • Consolidate the gains from HIPC • Involve civil society in future loan contraction	Only parliamentarians are involved	• Dominated by the interests of creditors and donors • Lack of international and national targets on debt cancellation • Only parliamentarians are involved

Note * Uganda Participatory Poverty Assessment Project (UPPAP), aims to understand the perception of poverty at a household level. It is a participatory project jointly run by the Government and the NGOs
Source: Various Government documents and interviews

started to change. A few NGOs were invited to attend the Government-donor consultative meetings, and some donors, such as Sweden, have started direct consultation with the larger civil society and the Government. Beginning in the financial year 1999/2000, all the donors to the education sector are channelling their resources through the Poverty Action Fund. Quarterly meetings are organised to discuss issues related to implementation and the monitoring of the Poverty Action Fund. These meetings are organised by the Government and are attended by the donors, civil society representatives and the media. Through this kind of interaction the process is becoming participatory.

Basic education and poverty reduction

Education is one of the basic building blocks of development. The formal education sector covers three levels: primary level (seven years), secondary level (six years) and tertiary level (two to five years). Basic education is defined to include primary education, pre-primary education, alternative education and adult education.

The Education Strategic Investment Plan (ESIP) 1998–2003 is a foundation for government policy on education, based in turn on the foundation of the Government White Paper on education. The policy and strategy reform within ESIP are linked to the broader objective and strategy of poverty eradication, securing and sustaining high quality universal primary education and the provision of a better educated workforce for economic diversification. ESIP is also a key ingredient in accelerating and implementing the 1992 Education White Paper The key broad priority objectives identified in the ESIP are:

- To make significant and permanent gains in achieving equitable access to education at all levels.
- To improve considerably the quality of education and net enrolment level in primary schools.
- To enhance capacity, in particular of the Ministry of Planning, to set overall policy, and of the districts, to manage the delivery of education services.
- Achieve full universalisation by the year 2003.

The ESIP notes that in order to achieve 100% universalisation of primary education by 2003, an extra 26,000 classrooms have to be constructed. The plan further recognises the urgent need for textbooks. All in all ESIP sets out 20 different programmes costing a total of about UShs 780 billions over a six-year period. Most of the costs fall on the development budget. If such an ambitious programme is to

be achieved the level of development expenditure should be increased from the current UShs 50 billion to about UShs150 billion a year. About 90% of the development budget is funded by donors.

Education for all

In an attempt to create education for all, a number of programmes have been initiated. They include primary education, alternative education and universal primary education.

Universal Primary Education (UPE)

'We are so many. We sit on the floor and the teachers don't come regularly. They say that they have lost relatives. We don't have text books to read. There is no water in school and we starve a lot'.
Children in Kumi as quoted by UPPAP

In 1997, the Government of Uganda introduced UPE. UPE aims to educate four children per family (at least two boys and girls), all orphans, and all peopleof school-going age with disabilities . When UPE was introduced, the enrolment jumped from about 2.3 million children in 1996 to 5.3 million children in 1997. By 1999 the number had jumped to 6.9 million children. With the influx of children, the teacher student level is estimated at 1:110 (for primary classes one and two) and 1:55 for the rest of the primary level. The pupil:text ratio is 1:5.

With UPE, the participation of the community in the education sector programmes is beginning to emerge. The community is expected to contribute labour, provide material such as sand for classroom construction and purchase school uniforms and writing books/exercise books. The Government on the other hand provides materials that are costly for the community to provide such as iron sheets, pays teachers' salaries, and buys text books, etc. In this kind of interaction, a sense of ownership is emerging. However, in policy design, the teachers, parents, children and the community in general are rarely consulted. Yet the parents and the community generally are supposed to be actively involved in the implementation of government programmes.

Alternative education

This programme was intended to promote access to basic education by vulnerable children such as homeless and street children. It is supposed to be carried out by different actors such as the NGOs, Ministry of Education and Sports (MES), the Ministry of Gender, Labour and Social

Uganda

Table 41 Showing plan of action and constraints to education for all

Policies/ Structures	Plan of action	Level of participation by the civil society	Constraints
Poverty Universal Primary Education (UPE)	• Full universalisation by the year 2003 • Decentralise education • Construct 26,000 new classrooms and rehabilitate 15,000 • Classroom construction to meet the high demand • Purchase of instructional materials • Teacher training, development and management • Ensure increased funding and timely leases of UPE funds • Develop curriculum that is child-centred • Education Sector Investment Plan • Increase the enrolment for all school-going children • Increased monitoring and supervision of schools • Develop national curriculum that is child centred	To a small extent	• Poor quality of education • High rates of school drop out • Lack of adequate scholastic materials • Irrelevant education system • Lack of enough trained teachers • Lack of tracking mechanism • Lack of accurate numbers of school-going children • Few resources available compared to demand • High costs of scholastic materials • Long distance to the schools • Lack of educational standards • All stakeholders (parents' teachers, pupils and community) not involved in curriculum development
Alternative education	• Target homeless and street children • Involve all stakeholders	None	• Lack of policy • Lack of coordination • Lack of adequate resources • Poor estimates of the numbers of students in this category • No minimum standards • No structure to coordinate
Adult Education	• Involve all stakeholders • Form National Adult Literacy Committee • National Machinery (Ministry of Gender, Labour and Social Development) to coordinate it • Train more adult educators	Participatory	• Lack of a national work plan • Not in all districts • High demand compared to supply • Poor funding • Lack of information

Source: DENIVA (1999)

Development (MGLSD) and Ministry of local Government (MOLG). However, this programme suffers from a number of setbacks. For example, the efforts are not coordinated, there is no specific curriculum, the number of children in the target group is not known, the programme is not adequately funded, and minimum standards are not set. There is no clear policy or structure for alternative education. As a result the programmes exist only on paper.

Adult education

This programme is aimed at promoting the acquisition, use and retention of functional literacy for more effective participation in development by all people. The major objectives of this programme are to improve the quality of life of the individuals and the community, create awareness among adult learners, integrate reading, writing and counting with practical skills. Adult education will help to improve the knowledge of individuals to make informed decisions and be able to communicate with others. The Ministry of Gender,

Labour and Social development (MGLSD) is responsible for functional literacy programmes.

Various adult literacy committees have been developed with specific functions stretching from the class level to the National Functional Adult Literacy Committee. The NFALC advises Government on policy matters regarding adult education, promotes the integration of Functional Adult Literacy (FAL) in all activities in all sectors, publicises FAL activities and monitors the implementation of FAL. Various interest groups and ministries are represented. The MGLSD provides the technical assistance, policy formulation, provision of support services and programme design, monitoring and implementation. It works with other ministries: Education and Sports; Local Government; Agriculture, Animal Industry and Fisheries (MAAIF); Department of Information (President's Office); Ministry of Health (MOH); NGOs and community based organisations, Nsamizi Institute of Social Development (NISD), and the Institute of Adult and Continuing Education (IACE) Makerere University.

Pre-school education

This is otherwise called nursery education or kindergarten. This is not officially recognised in the structure of formal education. However, to give children a smooth transition from home to school and to enable young children to socialise with others, it is becoming increasingly necessary to take all children through pre-primary education.

All in all, it is clear that basic education is being taken seriously. However, the efforts are fragmented in different line ministries and they therefore suffer from lack of proper coordination.

Gender inequality in the education sector

Notwithstanding anything in this constitution, the state shall take affirmative action in favour of the groups marginalised on the basis of gender, age, disability or any other reason created by history, tradition or custom, for purposes of redressing imbalances which exist against them.

Gender refers in socially constructed and defined characteristics of women and men, boys and girls. Gender also refers to changeable and changing social characteristics rather than the biological differences between men and women. The National Gender Policy was launched in November 1997. Its aim is to guide and direct at all levels, the planning, resource allocation and implementation of development programmes with a gender perspective. It is important to note that an activity referred to as the Gender Policy Development Exercise has been ongoing since 1991

and has covered five ministries namely: Ministry of Agriculture, Animal Industry and Fisheries; Ministry of Education and Sports; Ministry of Trade and Commerce and Tourism; Ministry of Natural Resources and Ministry of Local Government

Access to primary education

The trend in enrolment to primary education for the period 1990–97 ranges between 77–86% (for boys) and 61–75%(for girls). The gender gap has been high with the absolute boy/girl difference of 15%. This implies that each year, for every 100 boys enrolled, 85 girls are also enrolled. This conforms to the generally held view that boys have more access to education compared to girls. However, in some classes, especially lower primary levels, the girls outnumber boys.[3] Regional imbalances in terms of accessibility to primary education exist with the north and the east having wider gaps compared to the national averages.

Availability and quality of primary education

The average distance to the nearest school is 2 km. Some schools do not have sanitation facilities and safe water sources. The districts most affected by lack of safe water sources are Kalangala, Kapchorwa, Bugiri, Sembabule and Nakasongola. Poor sanitation at school is an issue in Moroto, Kalangala, Katakwi, Nakasongola and Bundibugyo.[4]

The education system in Uganda has been criticised for not being relevant to the needs of the country. The challenge of UPE is even worse because the available resources are too few to meet the influx of students. It is thus clear that the quality of education is set to be compromised. Although UPE is a step towards achieving international commitments, inadequate facilities and high numbers of pupils compared to the available resources (classrooms, teachers and books) undermine the quality of education. A situation where we have graduates from the education system who are still illiterate is steadily emerging.[5]

Completion of primary cycle of education

Primary Cycle Completion Rate (PCR) is defined as the ratio of new enrolment in primary seven in the present year to the total enrolment in primary one in the corresponding year. The education sector in Uganda is characterised by high school costs and high school drop out as can be seen in Table 42.

The education system in Uganda was characterised by high wastage as a result of repeat years and drop outs.

Uganda

Table 42 Completion, repeat and drop out rates in primary schools, 1990–97 (%)

| | 1990 | | 1991 | | 1992 | | 1993 | | 1994 | | 1995 | | 1996 | | 1997 | |
	M	F	M	F	M	F	M	F	M	F	M	F	M	F	M	F
Completion rate	42	29	36	37	41	28	31	24	30	25	34	22	38	30	43	34
Repetition rate	18	17	14	14	14	14	14	15	13	14	16	15	13	12	9	15
Drop out rate	16	21	12	12	22	23	14	15	8	14	14	22	–2	–24	–	–

Source: Statistical Abstract, Ministry of Education and Sports

Persistence in school, which can be measured by the completion rate, is rather low. From Table 42 it can be observed that for every 100 boys who entered primary school in 1991, 43 completed primary seven in 1997. For girls it was only 34. The national averages indicate that for every 100 pupils who entered primary one in 1991, about 39 completed the primary cycle. Of those who complete primary education, about 12% make it to secondary schools.

The performance in class is equally bad. This increases the failure rate and there is a sharp difference between the urban and rural schools. In 1997, for example, out of 211,749 pupils who sat for primary leaving examination, about 166,667 (or 78.7%) passed at least one of the four subjects. The rest failed all four subjects. Of those who failed all four subjects, about 90% were from rural schools.

Bali (1997), has blamed the morally weak family background, as the major cause of the poor performance in schools.

The levels of repetition of the individual classes is equally high. The repetition for girls ranges between 9–18% and shows no significant difference with boys. However regional disparities do exist with the northern and the eastern parts of the country having the highest proportions of repeaters.[6]

Expenditure on education

The education sector expenditure has consistently been increasing. Most of the resources go to finance primary education.

In 1998/99 additional resources to finance the education sector were provided by savings from debt relief. These

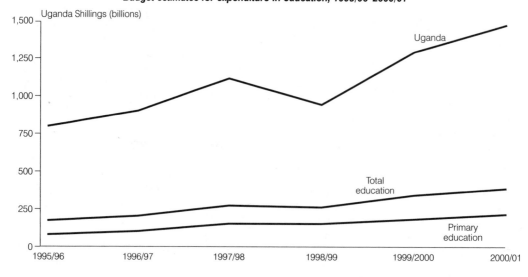

Budget estimates for expenditure in education, 1995/96–2000/01

Uganda Shillings (billions)

Uganda

funds are not reflected in the overall budget. However, a total of USch 45 billion were provided by the donors and the savings from debt relief.

References

Appleton, Simon (1998) 'Changes in Poverty in Uganda, 1992–1996'. A Report to the World Bank, Oxford, UK.

Appleton, S and Kagugube, J (1998) Poverty Trends in Uganda. A Paper Presented at National Planning Workshop for the Uganda Participatory Assessment Project, July, 1998.

Government of Uganda (1998) Background to the Budget 1998/99. Ministry of Finance, Planning and Economic Development, Kampala.

Government of Uganda (1998) Poverty Trends in Uganda 1992–96, Kampala, Uganda.

Government of Uganda (1998) Development Cooperation. 1996 Report, UNDP, Kampala.

Government of Uganda (1997) The Local Government Act 1997, Entebbe, Uganda.

Government of Uganda (1997) Poverty Eradication Action Plan. A National Challenge for Uganda, Vol 1, Ministry of Planning and Economic Development, Kampala.

Government of Uganda (1995) Constitution of the Republic of Uganda, Kampala.

Government of Uganda (1996) Demographic and Health Survey 1995. Ministry of Finance and Economic Development, Entebbe.

Government of Uganda (1996) Tracking of Public Expenditure on Primary Education and Primary Health Care. Ministry of Finance, Kampala.

Government of Uganda (1995) Uganda National Report for the World Summit for Social development. Ministry of Labour and Social Affairs and Ministry of Finance and Economic Planning, Kampala.

Ochieng Mary Kagoire T (1999) Status of Primary Education in Uganda. Paper Presented at a workshop, Meeting International development Targets. EPRC, Kampala.

Social Watch (1997) Social Watch no 1, From the Summit to the Grassroots.

Social Watch (1999) Social Watch no 3, From Summit to the Grassroots

UNDP (1998) *Human Development Report 1998*. Oxford University Press, New York.

UNDP (1998) Uganda Human Development Report 1998. UNDP, Kampala.

World Bank (1998) World Development Report 1998/99. Knowledge for Development. World Development Indicators 1998/99. Oxford University Press Washington, DC.

Notes

1   Appleton and Kagugube (1998); UPPAP, 1999; Uganda Poverty Statutes Report, 1999.
2   UNDP (1998), Uganda Human Development Report, UNDP, Kampala, p48.
3   Ministry of Gender and Community development and Ministry of Finance, 1998.
4   MFPED, 1998.
5   Tumutegyereize and Kamya, 1999.
6   MOS, 1995;1996.

Zambia: trends in donor support to education

Allast Mwanza

Introduction

Zambia is one of the most heavily indebted countries in the world with a total debt stock estimated at U$7,144 million in 1997.[1] The country's per capita debt is about US$714. During the early 1990s, donor support for Zambia rose tremendously, largely due to the change in the political system of the country.[2] But starting in 1994, donor support declined considerably as a result of donor disquiet over the state of governance. Since 1998, however, donor support has again risen in sympathy with the perceived positive changes in the human rights situation in the country.

This report attempts to discuss donor support to Zambia in general and to the education sector in particular. The main characteristic of Zambia's aid scenario is the erratic and unstable pattern it has exhibited over time. This partly reflects the impact of donor policies in response to the perceived changes (positive or negative) in the country's human rights situation.

Aid debt and conditionality

In 1997, total donor support to Zambia was US$486 million, of which US$321 million was project assistance and US$165 million was balance of payments support. However, balance of payments support declined from US$142 million in 1996 to US$133.5 million in 1997. This 5.9% decline reflected donor response to the non-fulfilment of conditionalities relating to good governance. The decline was also due to the appreciation of the US dollar against the SDR, which resulted in the reduction in the US dollar equivalent of the funds that had been originally denominated in the SDR.[3]

At the Consultative Group (CG) meeting held in May, 1998, the donor community had pledged a total of US$530 million of which US$230 million was for balance of payments support. However, due to the non-fulfilment of conditionalities such as those related to the sale of the country's mining holding company – the Zambia

Consolidated Copper Mines – no balance of payments support was released by December, 1998. Another cause of delay in the disbursement of the balance of payments support was the lack of progress in the public service reform programme.[4]

During the second half of 1999, the disbursement of project financing and balance of payments support was much better when compared with the latter part of 1998. Generally project financing was disbursed according to Zambian government expectations. Moreover, 1999 has witnessed a major improvement in the disbursement of bilateral balance of payment support. For instance by mid-1999, US$176.6 million had already been received from both bilateral and multilateral donors.[5] (The bilateral donors had disbursed US$17.748 million). In 1999, Zambia expects to receive a total of US$423 million as balance of payments support. The main reason for the improvement in the flow of balance of payments support is the improvement relating to issues of good governance, the progress in the privatisation of ZCCM and the conclusion of the Enhanced Structural Adjustment Facility (ESAF) programme with the World Bank.

The debt crisis

Zambia's external debt stock of US$7.1 billion (December, 1997), represented an increase of 7.5% over 1996 (31st December) when it was US$6.6 billion. The increase was due to the fact that the country had contracted new debt in 1996 from the World Bank for balance of payments support. As is shown below (Table 43), the largest proportion of Zambia's debt is owed to multilateral creditors, especially the World Bank and the IMF.

This debt stock presents serious development problems for Zambia in that a lot of finance has to be set aside for debt servicing. Thus in 1996 external debt service consumed US$173.5 million while in 1997, US$160 million was committed for the same purpose. The slight fall in debt

Zambia

Table 43 Debt stock by creditor as at December 1996 and 1997 (US$ millions)

Creditor	1996	1997
Bilateral	2,872	3,208
Paris Club	2,410	2,422
Non-Paris Club	462	786
Multilateral	3,253	3,294
IMF	1,180	1,180
World Bank Group	1,486	1,610
Others	587	504
Other creditors	446	642
	6,571	7,144

Source: Ministry of Finance and Bank of Zambia

service in 1997 was a result of the debt relief by the Paris Club under the so-called Naples terms which amounted to US$123.1 million. From Table 44 below we notice that the largest portion of debt was paid to multilateral creditors, particularly the World Bank group to which US$60.23 million was committed.

This means that Zambia has become heavily dependent on the preferred creditors (ie those institutions whose debt may not be easily rescheduled). The resource flow is clearly in favour of these creditors.

Donor flows

As already indicated above, Zambia enjoyed good relations with the donor community immediately after the attainment of multiparty democracy in 1991. From Table 45, we see that in 1991, total external assistance amounted to US$926 million while in 1992 and 1993 it was US$928 million and US$623 million respectively. Thereafter, donor flows fell to US$556 million (1994), US$559 million (1995), US$445

million (1996) and US$422 million (1997). This represents a fall of 54.4% in donor flows over the 1991–97 period. The biggest decline was registered in balance of payments support and debt relief. Project financing has not been subjected to massive cuts.

Table 46 presents a breakdown of external assistance by donor country or institution. The largest bilateral donors for Zambia are Sweden, Japan, Finland, the European Union, Germany and Norway. The World Bank is the largest multilateral donor while the African Development Bank (ADB) also plays an important role.

During the period under review, bilateral aid has either fallen or been subjected to a high level instability whereas multilateral aid has remained largely stable. Thus aid from Sweden, the UK, US, Germany and Japan has either fluctuated widely or declined during 1991–97. Zambia has therefore become more dependent on World Bank support.

Education sector support

Donor support to the various sectors is indicated in Table 47 below. External project financing to the various sectors was US$301.3 million in 1997, but rose to US$318.5 million in 1995 and to US$457.9 million in 1999. The social service sector received the biggest amount. Thus in 1997, these sectors received US$143.3 million which was 47.6% of total donor support in the form of project financing. In 1998, donor support to the social sectors was US$143.6 million which was 45% of total sectoral support. In 1999, it is projected that donor project finance will be US$166.1 million or 36% of support to various sectors.

Within the social sectors, health has received the largest share, followed by education and then water and sanitation. In 1997, education received US$40 million which was 28% of the total disbursed to the social sectors. This

Table 44 Debt servicing by creditor in 1997 (US$ millions)

Creditor	Principal and interest	Charges	Total
Bilateral	48.37	–	48.37
Paris Club	33.87	–	33.87
Others	14.51	–	14.51
Multilateral	10.30	8.65	111.6
World Bank/IDA	60.23	–	60.23
IMF	8.65	–	8.65
Others	42.78	–	42.78
Total	151.37	8.65	160.0

Source: Bank of Zambia Annual Report, 1999

Zambia

Table 45 Donor flows (US$ millions)

	1991	1992	1993	1994	1995	1996	1997	1998 pledged	1998 estimated	1999 potential	
Total external assistance	926	928	623	556	559	445	422	530	322	891	
BOP support	586	491	299	278	304	142	120	225	0	423	
World Bank	202	165	144	147	171	120	111	112	0	175	
Other	384	326	155	131	133	22	9	113	0	248	
Commodity support	74	246	90	26	40	34	0	10	3	10	
Drought maize	16	146	40	0	40	0	0	–	2	–	
Other	58	100	50	26	0	34	0	10	1	10	
Project financing	266	191	234	252	215	269	302	295	319	458	330*
Debt relief	1,158	551	359	260	234	310	159	118	122	219	
Total external financing	2,084	1,479	982	816	793	755	581	648	444	1,110	
Gross debt service	−1,841	−926	−710	−616	−578	−453	−352	−302	−289	−309	
Net transfer	243	553	272	200	215	302	170	346	155	801	

Note: * included in the macro programme
Source: Bank of Zambia

Table 46 External assistance 1991–99, breakdown by country (US$ millions)

	1991	1992	1993	1994	1995	1996	1997	1998 pledged	1998 estimated	1999 potential
Canada	19	22	19	12	3	4	5	7	7	7
Denmark	15	2	15	15	10	22	21	26	23	12
European Union	72	76	153	44	53	36	27	61	25	182
Finland	74	30	15	11	10	11	8	7	8	9
France	1	2	1					8	12	12
Germany	54	90	9	20	41	24	9	8	12	11
Ireland	4					9	9	10	8	8
Italy	14		6	5				7	3	
Japan	91	139	47	60	39	38	27	28	14	41
Netherlands	50	30	14	17	26	10	17	17	16	19
Norway	54	44	31	35	45	31	36	31	26	27
Sweden	109	47	33	37	20	30	19	19	16	18
UK	58	73	18	76	51	32	19	61	27	56
USAID	44	14	42	20	18	22	16	27	29	23
AfDB	55	35	30	13	15	31	33	30	26	39
World Bank	212	179	144	174	179	144	139	175	70	282
Others	–	9	14	8	31	25	5	5	–	–
Discrepancy	–	37	32	9	18	−24	−27	3	–	–
Total	926	928	623	556	559	445	363	530	322	746

Source: Bank of Zambia

Zambia

Table 47 Disbursement of externally-financed projects 1997–99 sector distribution (US$ millions)

	1997	1998	1999
Agriculture	74.1	47.0	61.0
Environment	7.0	2.5	6.9
Social sectors	*143.3*	*143.6*	*166.1*
Education	40.0	32.1	48.1
Health	51.2	63.2	59.1
Water supply/Sanitation	33.7	29.4	29.3
Other Social	18.4	18.9	29.6
Infrastructure	*52.2*	*60.9*	*137.6*
Roads	40.9	39.6	70.4
Other transport	8.4	4.7	28.3
Energy	2.9	16.6	38.9
Tourism	–	1.4	6.2
Public service reform	–	5.8	3.8
Governance	5.7	4.7	6.2
Private sector development	12.2	13.8	40.7
Other/Unidentified	7.8	43.2	29.4
Grand total	**301.3**	**318.5**	**457.9**

Source: Ministry of Finance.

declined to US$32.1 million in 1998 (or 22% of the total allocated to the social sectors. In 1999, education is projected to receive US$48.1 million or 29% of the total (Table 47).

Most of the aid to the education sector has been spent on rehabilitation of education infrastructure that has seriously deteriorated over time. Under the Zambia Education Rehabilitation Project (ZERP) the International Development Association (IDA) and bilateral donors have committed financial resources for basic school infrastructure rehabilitation. Most of the rehabilitation is coordinated by the micro-projects unit which is located in the Planning Section of the Ministry of Finance.

Since the early 1990s, government has concentrated on the repair or maintenance of existing infrastructure. As a result, there has been very little expansion or increase in public education facilities. Most investment in education has been undertaken by the private sector. Thus Zambia has registered a large expansion in private education infra-structure.

Donor support to basic education has also consisted of provision of technical support. Thus a number of bilateral donors, have supplied education materials or teaching aids and staff. Although empirical information is hard to get, it is obvious that a lot of financial and technical resources have been spent on the rehabilitation and management of Zambia's basic education sector.

Notes

1 Bank of Zambia, 1997: 18
2 In October, 1991, the Movement for Multiparty Democracy (MMD) defeated the ruling party (UNIP) in elections, thus beginning an era of multiparty politics.
3 op cit, note 1.
4 Bank of Zambia, 1999.
5 op cit, note 4.

India: because the market tells them so

Binu S Thomas, ActionAid India[1]

Official donors risk long-term aid goals for short-term gain

With the largest number of poor people in the world, India has for years been among the top recipients of Official Development Assistance (ODA). In 1997, India received US$1.6 billion in ODA, – only China and Egypt received more.[2] Yet, with aid constituting a minuscule portion of India's Gross National Product (0.6% of GNP), ODA has never quite been a subject of serious public policy debate within the country. Recent cutbacks in overall levels of development assistance to India have, however, created some ripples. Aid to India has been falling every year since 1994, when it reached US$2.3 billion.

The most dramatic cutbacks have been made by India's largest bilateral aid donor, Japan. Japanese aid to India, which peaked at US$886 million in 1994, has declined steadily, falling to US$492 million in 1997.[3] Following the nuclear tests conducted by India in May 1998, Japan suspended new yen loans, grant aid and technical cooperation, keeping open only its tiny grant assistance facility to NGOs. A year after the blasts, new Japanese aid to India remains suspended (existing commitments continue to be serviced). Yen loans, which are made available at an interest rate of 1.8% per annum, with a repayment period of 30 years and a grace period of ten years, constitute more than 90% of Japanese aid to India and have been overwhelmingly directed to building economic infrastructure.

A variety of other bilateral agencies have also suspended or curtailed their aid programmes to India in the wake of the nuclear tests.[4] Sweden terminated its three-year (1997–99) cooperation agreement with India. Norway decided to freeze all aid except that directed towards poverty alleviation programmes. Denmark decided to reverse the increase it had envisaged during aid talks held in January 1998. Germany, India's second-largest bilateral donor, cancelled the 1998 aid negotiations. Switzerland cut its aid budget by about 3 million Swiss francs and suspended one programme in which the Government of India was a partner.

Among the bilateral aid programmes that remained virtually unaffected by the nuclear blasts were those of the UK, France, Italy and Belgium. Indian officials are cautiously optimistic that some of the suspended aid programmes will resume soon, particularly in the light of better appreciation of India's security considerations following Pakistan's incursions into India-controlled Kashmir in early 1999. The distinct thaw in US-India relations, following the US initiative to get Pakistan to pull back its infiltrators from Indian soil, is likely to help put the international aid programme to India back on track in the near future.

Multilateral aid, particularly from members of the UN family (see Table 48), has also been falling in recent years.

While some of this decline has to do with the commencement of new funding cycles, UN sources point out that reductions to their overall budgets being experienced by leading UN agencies worldwide are beginning to tell on their funding in India. The UNDP, for instance, has been hit by major cutbacks to its budget effected by Denmark and Germany, although it hopes to receive higher contributions from Britain to its coffers.[5] In several UN agencies operating in New Delhi, there has a been a freeze on new recruitment, with some positions being axed when staff leave.

It is a sign of the times that, for the last two years, UNDP in India has suspended bringing out its annual development cooperation report, which reviews the activities and funding of various official donors. The nuclear tests, the preoccupation with survival politics of the rather fragile BJP-led multi-party coalition in New Delhi and the limited war with Pakistan over Kashmir have all contributed to the Government putting aid on the backburner. The India Development Forum, the annual get-together of India and

Table 48 Disbursements of some major UN system agencies in India (US$ thousands)

Agency	1991	1993	1995	1997	1998
IDA	1,342,200	3,353,000	942,393	892,300	798,000
UNDP	24,546	29,971	19,694	21,445	18,543
UNFPA	13,088	9,138	6,256	8,800	8,500
UNICEF	40,834	64,762	54,948	52,000	41,000
WFP	49,830	51,660	32,165	26,540	21,290

Source: United Nations System in India. www.un.org.in

her official donors, has not been held for two years, with the June 1998 meeting being postponed by the hosts, Japan, to protest the nuclear explosions.

Private capital shapes the 'aid business'

The general decline in aid volumes contrasts with a huge increase in private capital flows to developing countries. The situation in the late 1980s, when aid flows were larger than private capital flows, has been reversed with private flows now being nearly five times larger than official ODA. Most of the private capital flows to developing countries have gone to a handful of countries, most notably China. For the vast majority of very poor nations, aid – reduced as it is – still constitutes the major source of development funding. In Mozambique for instance, aid constitutes more than 60% of GDP.

Much more significant than the decline in aid is the change in the thinking of aid bureaucracies that the massive expansion of private capital has triggered. Aid administrators are under pressure as never before to show returns on investment almost along the lines of private capital. The induction of people with World Bank and IMF backgrounds into key positions in development ministries and aid agencies (for example the current Dutch Development Minister has a World Bank background as does the new chief of UNDP, Mark Malloch Brown) has no doubt contributed to this. But there are greater strategic reasons as well. With the end of the Cold War, the need to prop up allies in developing countries with dollops of aid has disappeared. The market orientation of aid has also been facilitated by the trend of private capital becoming a contributor to official aid budgets. UNDP, for instance, announced earlier this year that it was launching a Global Sustainable Development Facility with major transnational corporations contributing US$50,000 each.

Largely in response to the new market pressures to become more efficient, the UN Secretary-General has launched an initiative to get the various UN agencies to harmonise their work. The UN system in India has embarked on the ambitious task of preparing a single United Nations Development Assistance Framework (UNDAF) with common objectives and timeframes. India is one of 18 countries piloting UNDAF, which is a key component of the UN Secretary-General's Track I and II reform proposals. Final guidelines for the formulation of UNDAF were approved in April 1999 and include the preparation of a UN System Common Country Assessment (CCA). A key element is the provision of a mechanism for the joint follow-up by UN agencies of commitments made by UN member states at the international conferences of the 1990s.

A UNDAF task force, comprising representatives from key UN agencies in India, has been meeting every week with the aim of making public, following Government of India approval, the CCA and the UNDAF document on 24 October 1999 – the last UN Day of this millennium. But this has not been easy work. Staff of several UN agencies express a variety of concerns about the UNDAF process. While all seem to agree on the need to avoid duplication and get improved results through harmonising the work of various agencies, there are worries that UNDAF may lead to a loss of identity of individual agencies, cuts in budgets and staff lay-offs. 'To have joint programming is an attitude thing, and I don't think we are quite mentally prepared for it yet,' said a senior staff member of one of the specialist organisations of the UN, who did not want to be named.

It was also noted that, since individual agencies tend to work in a vertical, compartmentalised fashion, with one part of the organisation having limited or no links to the work of another, it was a bit ambitious to talk about harmonising inter-agency workplans and budgets.

There has been internal debate on the need to rotate the UN Resident Coordinator's post, which currently lies with the head of UNDP. Several agencies have, say sources, expressed the view that UNDAF should provide for the Resident Coordinator's post to be rotated among the various UN agencies.

India

A key UNDAF inter-agency working group has identified some 60 social, economic and demographic indicators that would underpin the CCA. Numerous discussions on how to focus the work of the UN have led to gender equality and decentralisation being identified as the two key themes around which UNDAF will be constructed. It is expected that the pilot phase will last until 2002 and the first fully fledged UNDAF will come into operation from 2003, by which time the exercise of synchronising the funding cycles of the major UN agencies in India would have been completed.

A lot would depend on the Government of India. Currently the UN agencies liaise with different line ministries and some degree of harmonisation would be required at the government level for UNDAF to work. India has some concerns about the unilateral manner in which the UN has pressed ahead with the UNDAF process. It is concerned that, by reducing duplication, a common development framework for UN agencies may also reduce the amount of money coming into the country.

In December 1998, India piloted a resolution in the General Assembly stressing the importance of the UN ensuring full government participation in UNDAF and its full ownership through the agreement of the recipient governments to the finalised framework. Following this, three advisers to the Planning Commission in India have been actively involved in screening the drafts of the CCA and the UNDAF that are being prepared by the UN task force in New Delhi.

Aid reform is also on the agenda of some bilateral donors, most notably of the UK, traditionally India's third largest bilateral donor, after Japan and Germany. The Department for International Development (DFID), which moved its entire South Asia Department to New Delhi a few years ago, has just completed an extensive consultative process – in both India and the UK – on its aid programme. This is to culminate in the release of a new Country Strategy Paper (CSP) for India in September 1999. 'Our new role is supporting and facilitating change towards eliminating poverty,' said Robert Graham-Harrison, Head of DFID in India.[6] Under the new CSP, DFID is to focus its aid programme on a small number of pro-reform state governments. To its existing list of target states, Andhra Pradesh, Orissa and West Bengal, DFID will add Madhya Pradesh, whose chief minister, Digvijay Singh, has been in the forefront of promoting pro-poor reform. He established an Education Guarantee Scheme under which the state government would by law provide a teacher and teaching materials at the request of any community with a minimum of 25

children eligible to go to school. This won him high praise not only in development circles but among his constituents, who recently gave him a rare second consecutive five-year term in office.

DFID's expansion into Madhya Pradesh is also being undertaken partly in deference to concerns voiced by the Government of India over too much attention being lavished by donors on too few of India's 25 states.

Among other priorities, DFID is to:

- Help promote accountable government;
- Invest more in education, health and water and sanitation;
- Provide for greater empowerment of poor groups, particularly women and scheduled castes and scheduled tribes;
- Promote better management of the natural and physical environment.

These priorities would fall under three broad categories that the new strategy would support – focused activities on poor communities (eg slum development), inclusive interventions where programmes include poor people (eg the District Primary Education Programme) and enabling activities (eg reducing subsidies and promoting privatisation of power production and distribution).

In recent years, DFID in India has been viewed positively by the development sector, for its pool of technical staff (the largest among bilateral donors operating in India), for being the largest contributor of grant aid to India, for moving away from infrastructure funding to more programmatic inputs and for significantly increasing spending on the social sector. DFID's staff strength of 160 in India has enabled it to start engaging in policy dialogues with various state governments, including such institutional set-ups as Orissa's Poverty Task Force, on an on going basis. It has also phased out from funding the mining sector, whose social and environmental impact continues to be of major concern to the NGO community. But DFID operations in India have their share of critics as well. Concerns have been voiced, inter alia, over the weak interface with civil society, the excessive reliance on European consultants, the considerable variation in fee structure for foreign and Indian consultants, and for major spending on power sector reforms – a sector in which British firms are major international players.[7]

Some steps have already been initiated to address these concerns. To improve transparency, a new website on DFID India is under construction and a press and public

---

Box 34 District Primary Education Programme (DPEP): some early results in reforming primary education

Perhaps the most ambitious of ODA-funded programmes in India in recent years has been the District Primary Education Programme. Since it began in 1994, DPEP has attracted some US$900 million in external assistance, largely from the World Bank, the European Union, DFID, the Netherlands and some other bilateral donors.

By 1998, DPEP was operational in 150 educationally disadvantaged districts (defined as those in which the female literacy rate is below the national average) in 14 states. It covered 180,000 schools, 600,000 teachers and 30 million children.[8]

DPEP is unique in that it was the first experiment of its kind in India, conceived by the government, where decentralisation and community participation was to be put into practice on a large scale. More than 70% of its annual budget is to be reserved for 'software', that is activities to improve the quality of education, community mobilisation and reduction of inequities (of gender, caste, tribe, disability, etc), rather than infrastructure.

The centrepiece of the programme is the creation of Village Education Committees (VECs), comprising 10–15 people, with at least a third of the membership being women. These are supposed to take the initiative in the community assuming ownership of the educational programme.

DPEP hoped in five years to achieve universal enrolment, drop-out rates of less than 10%, a 25% improvement in learner achievement and reduction of inequities to less than 5%.

Overall, donors admit that the DPEP marks a major improvement on earlier donor interventions in the area of primary education. 'There is good ownership of the programme and one sees greater questioning of the state level by the district level, which is not common in government programmes and is a healthy sign,' says Mervi Karikorpi, Education Programme Coordinator for DPED at the European Commission Education Programme Office. The EU is investing 150 million Euros[9] in the programme over a seven-year period. Greater financial autonomy at lower levels in the DPEP structure has facilitated local-level decision-making.

There are however some qualitative concerns. A study of Village Education Committees in 16 districts revealed that they were in many cases constituted in a top-down manner with the headmasters supported by project officials nominating the members.[10] The majority of VEC members also had formal educational qualifications up to secondary and post-secondary that created a distance between VECs and the bulk of the illiterate parents and families.

The Government of India is now seeking to extend DPEP to cover elementary education and has begun a dialogue with donors on the issue.

---

relations officer has been appointed. More printed material on DFID's work in India and its priorities is being made available.

A new 'Poorest Areas Civil Society Programme' will focus on providing assistance to NGOs working in the 100 poorest districts in the country, many of which are found in clusters in Uttar Pradesh and Bihar, which are not the focus states for DFID's aid programme in India. Care would be taken, says Graham-Harrison, to ensure that NGOs did not replace the work of the governments. 'The fundamental need is to work with government towards common objectives,' he says.

Efforts are underway to improve DFID's database of local consultants, which will to an extent reduce dependency on foreign consultants. As for funding power sector reforms, Graham-Harrison argues that the subsidies here are not well-targeted at poor groups and their elimination will help state governments redirect public expenditures to

areas that directly benefit poor people and on which DFID will maintain an ongoing policy dialogue with state governments.

DFID's heightened level of activity in India comes at a time when the overall British aid programme is expanding after many years of stagnation. Graham-Harrison expects funding for India to move up from just under £100 million per annum currently to around £130 million a year in a couple of years.

Reform is also on the agenda of the Dutch aid programme. Following a full aid review, the Dutch government has decided to reduce the number of recipient countries from some 80 to 19 eligible for comprehensive aid programme and some 20 others where the focus will be on one or two sectors. India is eligible for a full donor cooperation programme, while Nepal (the Royal Netherlands Embassy in Delhi also administers the Dutch aid programme in Nepal and Bhutan) will be eligible for support in some sectors. Bhutan,

India

along with Costa Rica and Benin, will remain in a third category as a Sustainable Development Country.

As in the case of the British programme, the Dutch will also be focussing on a few states – Andhra Pradesh, Gujarat and Kerala. These three have been selected on the basis of various criteria, including the existence of responsive state governments with capacity for implementation. While the approvals will still be sought from the central government in New Delhi, and the finance routed through it, the Netherlands hopes to start a direct policy dialogue and forge a much closer working relationship with the state governments.[11] The Netherlands provided about 85 million guilders as aid to India in 1998 and was expected to maintain that level of assistance in 1999. With the sharp reduction in the number of countries receiving Dutch aid, it is expected that more money may actually be available for work in India in the near future.

The rush among bilaterals to focus on a few reform-oriented states, rather than those with the largest concentration of poor people, signals a shift from directing aid where it is most needed to where it is likely to be most effective and indeed even profitable. This shift is likely to open up considerable business opportunities for corporations from the donor countries given that states like Andhra Pradesh, Orissa and Gujarat are in the forefront of market-led reforms in India. Both Andhra Pradesh and Orissa, in particular, have ambitious plans to privatise the power sector, and DFID, for instance, has already committed some £130 million to power sector reforms in both states.

In Indonesia a US$3 million investment by USAID in support of privatising the energy sector led to a US$2 billion award to a US firm for Indonesia's first private power contract.[12] Rapid privatisation of the infrastructure in developing countries can, however, turn into a 'horror story', as the head of the World Bank's Asia-Pacific region Jean-Michel Severino recently told the London *Financial Times* while describing the impact this strategy had in South-East Asia in the wake of the regional economic crisis.[13]

The country strategy for Danish aid adopted in 1997 involves withdrawing from the states of Tamilnadu and Orissa, to focus only on Karnataka and Madhya Pradesh. The choice of Karnataka over Orissa was surprising, considering that Orissa has the highest percentage of people below the poverty line of any state in India. Karnataka's per capita income is 50% higher than Orissa's. Besides the choice of Orissa would have been more appropriate as it shares a border with Madhya Pradesh and that would have opened up possibilities of cross-border interventions in poorer regions of both states. Commenting on this choice, a recent study on Danish aid to India[14] notes: 'It has probably been a good deal more important that Karnataka – and in particular the capital, Bangalore, widely projected as a dynamic city, the new electronic software capital of India – is much more interesting than Orissa from the point of view of Danish business interests. A Danida private sector adviser has been stationed in Bangalore since 1993 and several Danish firms are either established or on their way.'

Curiously enough, while many official donors have few problems divesting the state of its responsibilities in such sectors as power, transport, etc and handing the same over to the private sector, they sing a different tune when it comes to NGO involvement in the social sector. Here they emphasise that NGOs should not end up doing the job of the state but should instead serve as models for the state to do its job better.

In taking this dual stand, they tend to perpetuate a dangerous stereotype that the 'business of business' is best left to private business, while the state's role is limited to delivering services to the poor and the marginalised (whose numbers often tend to swell with unbridled private-sector expansion in infrastructure development in poor countries) as effectively and efficiently as NGOs can show them how. The NGO's role as a critic of policy shortcomings of both the government and the private sector is virtually ignored by official donors in their highly utilitarian conception of what NGOs ought to be doing. The struggles of various social movements to reshape both markets and states, and make them more responsive to the needs of poor and marginalised people continue to find little or no support in the aid strategies of official donors.

What works for whom?

The increasing tendency of official donors to pick on a few reform-minded states to direct their aid is in keeping with current notions of what constitutes effective aid. A recent World Bank paper, *Assessing Aid: what works, what doesn't, and why*, argues that the first condition for ensuring that aid is effective in tackling poverty is to target it at low-income countries with sound economic management. 'In a good policy environment financial assistance is a catalyst for faster growth, more rapid gains in social indicators, and higher private investment. In a poor policy environment, however, aid has much less impact. Clearly, poor countries with good policies should receive more financing than equally poor countries with weak economic management.'

The International Development Association, which is the single largest official aid-giver, has gone one step further. Among the recommendations for IDA 12 is that

---

Box 35 What's good for USAID is good for US trade

While most bilaterals go to great lengths to distance their aid spending from any commercial considerations, USAID actually trumpets how the US profits from assistance to India.[16] In a presentation titled 'US Assistance to India is a Good Investment', the agency states:

- Food aid is purchased from American farmers, processed by American agribusiness and shipped on US carriers.
- About 70% of economic assistance is channelled through American suppliers, NGOs and universities.
- USAID programmes facilitate US trade and investment.
- The Government of India returns to the US Treasury, in principal and interest on past loans, more than it receives in new assistance. In 1998, the Government of India will pay US$178 million to the US and receive US$125.3 million.

'lending to countries with weak governance should be scaled back or stopped entirely if necessary.'[15] This seems to be an extreme case of punishing the poor for the failures of their rulers. Unfortunately some bilaterals in India seem to be acting on such advice and neglecting states like Uttar Pradesh and Bihar, which are the poorest in the country and have weak economic management, in order to focus on the star performers. The Netherlands, for instance, has just removed Uttar Pradesh – India's largest state with a population equal to that of Indonesia, the world's fourth biggest country – from its list of priority states after the recent aid review. Uttar Pradesh and Bihar together account for 49.7% of India's poor population.[17]

At a time of dwindling aid budgets, it perhaps makes good practical sense for aid bureaucracies to concentrate their limited resources on where results can be shown and quickly. This will help protect, if not expand, existing aid budgets. Sadly, in the process, it appears that the aid effort, which drew its moral sustenance from the felt need to address pressing humanitarian and social concerns in developing countries, is increasingly coming to be directed by the politics of the market. The Government of India is reportedly worried by these trends but given the situation where the Indian economy is itself fast integrating into the transnational-driven and WTO-led global economy, it can do little more than occasionally murmur its concern.

If official donors operating in India are to stay true to their stated goal of poverty reduction, they need to redress the growing imbalance in favour of the so-called progressive states by directing a sizeable portion of their assistance to supporting institutional and policy reform in weaker Indian states – which are almost always the poorest as well. But in doing so they will have to focus on reform of institutions and policies that directly benefit poor people rather than those, such as the power sector, as the market would dictate. *Assessing Aid*, after examining the cases of success in diffi-

cult environments, recommends four things that donors ought to do:

- First, find a reform-minded champion among heterogeneous communities and perhaps even from government.
- Second, have a long-term (ten-year) vision of systemic change.
- Third, support knowledge creation through innovation and evaluation.
- Finally, support civil society either to pressure the government to change or to take service provision directly into its own hands.

Greater donor coordination would be necessary for supporting institutional and policy reform than was the case with the traditional donor function of 'moving money'. However, the experience with donor coordination in India has not been a happy one. In 1994 the UNDP set up Inter-Agency Working Groups dealing with themes such as Gender and Development, HIV/AIDS, Primary Education, etc, to improve coordination among UN agencies. It followed this up in 1996 with Multi/Bi-Sectoral Coordination Groups involving multilateral, bilateral donors and, in some cases, leading international NGOs.[18] However, the results of these interactions have been disappointing. Many groups have become dormant while others meet so irregularly and with such ill-defined agendas that there is little to show. More recently, some donors have begun advocating in favour of state-level donor coordination meetings, occasionally involving state governments, as that would be closer to where the assistance is being used and hence more productive.

Official Development Assistance to India today stands at a crossroads. Donors could take the low road and blindly route their assistance to the few fast-reforming states. This may bring them good results in the short-term, but could

India

take them further away from their overriding goal of eradicating absolute poverty. Or they could take the high road of encouraging pro-poor aspects of reform in the fast-developing states while proactively pushing pro-poor institutional and policy reform in the weaker states – no doubt a long, tedious enterprise and a less rewarding one in terms of quick results. Only the latter, however, would ensure the continued legitimacy of their aid programmes into the new millennium.

Notes

1   The author is Coordinator, Policy & Advocacy Unit, ActionAid India. The views expressed here are not necessarily those of ActionAid India.
2   DAC Statistics. OECD/DAC Statistical Reporting Systems. www.oecd.org.
3   Data provided by Japanese Embassy in New Delhi.
4   Indian Economic Survey 1998/99. Government of India.
5   Interview with Bhaskar Bhattacharji, Assistant Resident Representative, UNDP, New Delhi.
6   Interview with the author.
7   The Quality of British Aid to India. Arthur van Diesen, Christian Aid. July 1998.
8   Partnership for Educational and Social Transformation, European Commission Education Programme Office, New Delhi, 1998.
9   The Euro has replaced the ECU as the unit of the currency used by the European Commission.
10   Community Mobilisation and Participation in DPEP. Maya Pinto & Rajesh Tandon. PRIA. New Delhi. 1997.
11   Interview with Kitty van der Heyden, Deputy Head, Development Cooperation, Royal Netherlands Embassy, New Delhi.
12   The Politics of Aid: The Normatives of Giving and Receiving, Shobha Raghuram, *Development*, SAGE Publications, 1999.
13   IBRD Official speaks of Asia 'horror story', Reuters, London, 27 July, 1999.
14   Danish Development Cooperation with India – In a Poverty Reduction Perspective, CDR Working Paper 98.2, February 1998.
15   Additions to IDA Resources: Twelfth Replenishment, A Partnership for Poverty Reduction, 23 December, 1998, International Development Association.
16   From 'Snapshot USAID/India'.
17   Incidence of Poverty in India: Towards a Consensus on Estimating the Poor, Rajeev Malhotra, The Indian Journal of Labour Economics, Vol 40, No 1, 1997.
18   Breaking New Ground in Donor Coordination in India. Binu S Thomas, *The Reality of Aid 1997/98*, Earthscan.

Part IV
Donors Compared
At a Glance

Table 49 The outlook for aid

	ODA as % of GNP in 1998	Target for aid	Most recent affirmation of the target	Percentage change in real terms	Outlook
Australia	0.28	0.7	The newly re-elected Coalition Government states that it is committed to the 0.7% target 'as and when economic conditions permit' but no interim target has been set.	+10.4	Little likelihood of an increase for three years. Despite there being a large surplus in the 1999/2000 budget, the government has failed to increase the aid budget and forward estimates indicate no real growth for the next three years. The real terms increase noted for 1998 is largely due to exchange rate changes.
Austria	0.24	0.7	By the Austrian Government on signing Maastricht Treaty when joining EU.	−3.7	Poor. By 1991 Austria declared a target of the OECD average and in recent three-year programme the 0.7% has not even been mentioned and the Austrian percentage continues to drop. However there is some speculation that things may change for the better towards the end of 1999.
Belgium	0.35	0.7	June 1999 in a general policy paper of the new government.	+14.6	Improving. It appears that 1998 has been a turning point for Belgian aid. The combination of a restructured and better performing aid administration, increased budgets and increased ODA spending by other departments will increase the quantity of aid. It must also be borne in mind, that the ratio of ODA to GNP is being tempered by a fast growing GNP.
Canada	0.29	0.7	Finance Minister in the Federal Budget of February 1999.	−11.4	The 1999/2000 Budget announced retroactive increases to the 1998/99 budget and a small one-time increase of $50 million and $25 million respectively to the 1999/2000 and 2000/01 ODA budgets. But without similar retroactive increases to 1999/2000 ODA in the February 2000/01 Federal Budget, ODA for 1999/2000 will be less than 1998/99 and the possible diversion of funds for the Kosovo crisis and its aftermath may limit these retroactive increases to ODA for this year.
Denmark	0.99	1	Five-year Plan for 1999–2003 agreed by the present Government in 1998.	+4.1	Danish aid will be kept at 1% of GNP. The budget for 1999 is 11,399 million Krone compared with 10,720 million Krone in 1998 – a 6% increase. Added to this is a special appropriation for environmental protection and disaster.

The outlook for aid

	ODA as % of GNP in 1998	Target for aid	Most recent affirmation of the target	Percentage change in real terms	Outlook
					relief to be used in Eastern Europe, The Arctic, and the South which is planned to reach the level of 0.5% of GNP in 2002.
Finland	0.32	0.4	The government announced its present ODA level after the budget negotiations in autumn 1998. It was clear from this that the target of raising ODA to 0.4% of GDP would not be reached	+5.2	Very poor. The Finnish Government initially stated that the 0.4% target for 2000 was an interim target, and now says that even this will not be reached in time. Generally the outlook remains vague and non-committal. The positive climate of stabilising and allowing slight increases in ODA in recent years has often obscured the harsh reality that ODA spending is half what it was at the end of the last decade and is therefore taking place in severely reduced circumstances.
France	0.41	0.7	The objective of 0.7% of GNP has been abandoned. It was last officially affirmed by the former President Mitterand in 1992	-6.2	Future prospects related to French ODA are not hopeful. The current decrease will continue in percentage terms as well as volume terms. The Government has not given any objective in figures and merely commits itself to maintain 'a high level of public aid'. It does, however, recognise that budgetary constraints will be 'long-lasting'.
Germany	0.26	0.7	By the new Government that took over in October 1998. When referring to the volume of aid in the coalition document, it talks of approaching the 0.7% target.	-4.1	The new government has committed itself to an enhanced role for development cooperation – in quality as well as in quantity. German policies towards the South are to be guided by the principles of coherence, human rights, gender equality, ecology and cooperation with civil society organizations – in line with the overall aims of the coalition agreement. In 2000 the BMZ budget will be cut by 8.7% compared with the previous year. The medium-term financial plan shows further cuts for the years 2001–03.
Ireland	0.31	0.7	The target of 0.45% of GNP by 2002 was restated by the Minister of State at the Department of Foreign Affairs on November 26, 1998 and Ireland's commitment to reaching the UN target was restated by		Irish Aid continues to rise in real terms. However, between 1998 and 1999, ODA expressed as a share of GNP only increased by 0.02% due to a rapidly expanding economy and exceptional GNP growth. In November 1998, the Minister announced multi-annual funding for ODA

The outlook for aid

				Change	
			Minister O'Donnell on May 5, 1999 when she addressed the Joint Oireachtas Committee on Foreign Affairs.	+12	whereby the Irish Aid budget will be increased by 66% or £62.2m over the 3 years 1999–2001. This figure will be additional to normal increases for inflation and additional to spending on debt relief and contributions to international agencies. However, this level of increase will make it highly unlikely that the Government's interim target for Irish Aid of 0.45% of GNP by 2002 will be reached.
Italy	0.2	0.7	An official statement on the commitment to increase total ODA was made by Mr. Rino Serri (Under-secretary at the Foreign Affairs Ministry) at the Ambassadors Conference in Rome in September 1998.	+84.5	The general trend for Italian ODA is estimated at around 0.15–0.16% of GNP. The large increase between 1997 and 1998 is due to the unfreezing of funds by the Ministry of Treasury, for the re-settlement of banks and development funds capitals (about one third of the total fund), as a consequence of the approval of the law in Parliament, however, there is the long term intention by the Italian government to raise the amount of the ODA to 0.25% of GNP.
Japan	0.28	0.7	By Japanese Delegation to the Earth Summit in 1992.	+23.1	In 1997, the government decided to cut aid for three years starting 1998. In 1998, aid budget was cut by 10.4% and although another cut was scheduled in 1999, the aid budget will be increased by 0.2% in 1999. This is because the Japanese government considers that supporting the efforts of the revival of Asian economies is necessary for the revival of Japan's own economy.
Netherlands	0.8	0.8	The Minister of Development Cooperation presenting the 1999 budget, September 1998.	+3.5	The outlook will remain 0.8 per cent of GNP for 1998–2002 (the period of the current cabinet).
New Zealand	0.27	0.7	By New Zealand officials at Habitat II in 1996, but only the words 'striving to fulfil' were endorsed.	+2.6	Aid continues to increase at approximately 0.01% GNP per annum. These increases have been won despite continued cutbacks in government spending. There is an election in late 1999 and polls indicate that there will be a change of government to a centre left coalition. The parties involved are cautious about making spending promises although both have supported increases in aid in past policies and both have adopted the 0.7%GNP target.

The outlook for aid

	ODA as % of GNP in 1998	Target for aid	Most recent affirmation of the target	Percentage change in real terms	Outlook
Norway	0.91	1	Parliament made a renewed commitment to the target of 1% of GNP for ODA in 1996.	+8.4	Norway maintains the target of increasing development aid to 1% of GNP within the present four-year period. But in its budget proposal to Parliament for 1999 the Government declared that the planned increase had to be postponed by one year because of the economic situation. This makes it doubtful that Norwegian aid will reach 1% of GNP by 2001.
Portugal	0.24	0.7	The long-term target on aid is 0.7% of GNP, confirmed in a recent document, 'Portuguese Cooperation on the threshold of the 21st Century' prepared by the Ministry of Foreign Affairs	+ 3.4[1]	The 'Portuguese Cooperation on the threshold of the 21st Century' document sets out guidelines for national cooperation and has just been approved by the Ministers Council. There is a significant change in the target for Aid – in this document it is proposed that it will achieve 0.36% of GNP and the prediction is that it will grow up to 0.7% by 2006.
Spain	0.25	0.7	As a result of the Cooperation Law, passed by the Parliament in July 98, Spanish ODA will rely on a 4-year Directive Plan which will include targets and strategies (both quantitative and qualitative). In this plan, the 0.7 target is included as a long-term reference for Spanish ODA.	+11.8	For the first time in five years, there could be some significant changes in the perspectives of increasing aid volume. In the first draft of the document four different scenarios are considered, from the most pessimistic to the most optimistic. In the worst case, ODA would only increase in line with GNP, and in the best case Spain would reach 0.5% in year 2002. In fact, the Government is seriously considering the two in between – a commitment to either 0.35% in 2002 or 0.35% in 2000. NGOs have been pressing for the latter and formal discussions are scheduled for mid-1999, but there are no reasons to be optimistic yet.
Sweden	0.71	1	Government and Parliament are constantly reaffirming their aim to restore ODA to its 1% level as soon as the financial situation permits	-7.5	The outlook is that the actual budget for ODA is to increase to 0.73% in 2001. What is more complicated is the decision by the government in 1998 and 1999 of first authorising the use of reserves from the ODA budget of previous years, and then withdrawing the decision. In 1999 this had a considerable effect which led to serious constraints on ODA payments.

The outlook for aid

Switzerland[2]	0.33	In its 1998 annual report to parliament the Swiss Cabinet confirmed the target of 0.4%, noting that an implementation 'in the near future' is prevented by the financial situation.	−3.6	0.4	The Federal Council has never set itself the target of reaching 0.7%, stating only 0.4% by 2000. However, the volume of Swiss ODA has declined since 1994 due to measures adopted to stabilise the federal budget. In 1997 Switzerland spent only 0.32% of GNP on ODA, compared with 0.34 in 1994. If this trend continues ODA will drop to 0.29% of GNP in 2001, one third below the target set by the Cabinet of Ministers
UK	0.27	Since taking office in May 1997, the UK government has fulfilled its pledge to reverse the decline of aid. UK ODA will reach 0.3% GNP by 2001. The November 1997 White Paper affirms the UK's commitment to 0.7%, but the government has set no timetable.	+7.8	0.7	The Secretary of State for International Development and Chancellor of the Exchequer announced a four-matrixed debt relief and aid campaign in March 1999. In it, they announced they would: reduce Third World Debt by $50 billion through reform of the IMF/World Bank HIPC Initiative; increase aid flows to $60 billion or 0.26% of GNP; challenge NGOs to raise their aid levels to $1 billion by the end of the year 2000; and support the sale of $1 billion of IMF gold to fund enhanced debt relief.
USA	0.1	The US has not committed itself to the UN target of 0.7% but supports the DAC's 1995 Policy statement 'Development Partnerships in the new Global Context' which reaffirms its commitment to 'generating substantial resources for development cooperation to back the efforts of countries and people to help themselves'.	+17	None	The US does not consider the 0.7% of GNP target realistic. Moreover, budget constraints, expected increases in military spending, domestic issues, and a continued marginalisation of foreign aid by the US Congress will prevent any increase until after the Presidential and Congressional elections of 2000 and most expect the US foreign assistance budget to decline further. In addition, the US response to crises in Kosovo and in Central America following Hurricane Mitch may cause offsets in development assistance budget line items.

Notes
1 This increase is in cash terms
2 There are differences between the data quoted by the Swiss government and by the DAC on ODA volume and ODA as a percentage of GNP. Figures given in the 'Outlook' column on both targets and spending are from the Swiss Government. All other data is from the DAC

Donor responses

Table 50   Donor responses to international development goals and Shaping the 21st Century

Country	Government attitude	Government action
Australia	The government supports the DAC *Shaping the 21st Century* goals and is giving more emphasis to areas covered by the goals, however, it has not set any funding targets. The Government and AusAID like to talk about having the flexibility to meet needs depending on the situation of each developing country.	Australia's new aid priorities – health, education, rural development and agriculture, infrastructure and good governance – largely coincide with the DAC goals. While AusAID has not set specific funding targets for these areas it does refer to the goals in its statements and is taking account of them in the development of new performance measures for the agency. Over the last five years funding for basic social services has increased; however the rate of growth (an average of about 5% per year) needs to increase if Australia is to contribute its fair share to reaching the goals for 2015.
Austria	The Three-Year-Programme for 1999–2001 stated that Austria participates actively in the decisions of the DAC High Level Meeting. Austria has agreed to the targets and strategies set out in *Shaping the 21st Century*.	The Three-Year-Programme states that new strategies and instruments are necessary to implement *Shaping the 21st Century*.
Belgium	The Belgian government hardly makes any reference to *Shaping the 21st Century* in its policy statements. The general policy paper, now converted into and adopted by parliament as a law on international cooperation, makes rather general statements, but in the growing number of strategic policy notes (on countries as well as on sectors) attention to output goals is increasing. Furthermore the evaluation and policy preparation unit of BADC[1] is involved in DAC-working groups elaborating further criteria and specific targets such as gender and environment.	No output goals as such are mentioned within the general policy paper, nor is there evidence of them in country strategy papers, however, Belgian activities are increasingly integrated into the national programmes of recipient countries and multilateral programmes, so they will endorse eventual output goals.
Canada	The Canadian government has consistently endorsed the goals of *Shaping the 21st Century* and CIDA has integrated the goals within its policy framework for Basic Human Needs and for Basic Health. A policy strategy for Basic Education is also underway. Canada has played an active role in developing the goals at the DAC and is working multilaterally with the group on implementing the 22 indicators established to measure progress on the goals.	CIDA has neither strategic framework nor any specific Canadian ODA targets related to *Shaping the 21st Century* goals that demonstrate incrementally how Canada will contribute to their achievement. CIDA, in its 1999/2000 Expenditure Estimates, suggests that the international financial crisis since 1997 has 'led to some re-evaluation of the resources and time needed to meet the targets', although 'how much more difficult is uncertain'.
Denmark	The Danish government is committed to its own Strategy for 'Danish Development Policy Towards the Year 2000' and considers this more far-reaching than *Shaping the 21st Century*. It entails major	Danida has an approach to development and poverty reduction which is far more holistic than the International Development Targets. Danida constantly works at different levels with various concrete actions in order

Donor responses

	elements from *Shaping the 21st Century* like emphasising capacity building in the recipient countries and ownership of the development process by the recipient government. Danida is also very supportive of the idea of coordination of donor activities. The targets in *Shaping the 21st Century* are not used in the setting of objectives for Danish development assistance. Poverty reduction generally speaking is the most important goal in Danish aid policy. Indicators are being developed for measuring the output of Danish aid.	to achieve the targets. The strategy for poverty reduction is threefold and involves: 1 promotion of economic growth with redistribution of wealth 2 investment in social sectors and development of human resources 3 promotion of people's participation and good governance. In some areas, such as redistribution of wealth and promotion of good governance, there are serious obstacles.
Finland	In its recent statement on policy and relations with developing countries, the government has reiterated its strong support for the goals. According to the Decision-in-Principle, the government supports the development cooperation strategy adopted by the OECD in May 1996, which it calls 'the most important international development cooperation policy statement of the last few years'. However, at the practical level, there is much hesitation over, and even some resistance to, creating tangible International Development Targets with specific time frames. Finnish aid authorities and politicians seldom mention the *Shaping the 21st Century* targets in their statements and speeches.	Finland supports the specific contents of the targets, but has continued to avoid and even resist committing itself to fixed deadlines, emphasising instead that 'partnership as a basis of cooperation is a recommendation set forth in the OECD strategy.'
France	In an attempt to demonstrate a commitment to *Shaping the 21st Century*, France is focusing on Mali. A review of international aid to Mali will be the starting point with France wanting to put the views of a recipient country to the fore – their views being a desire for greater ownership without conditionality and greater notice taken of their opinion.	When it comes to quantitative targets, French aid has not yet achieved any form of integration (it is managed by a number of different ministries) and the government still has to translate the targets into sectoral policies.
Germany	The new leadership of the Federal Ministry for Economic Cooperation and Development (BMZ) has not yet taken an official position on *Shaping 21st Century* but may soon come out with a statement.	So far, the BMZ has not made any overt effort to relate its policies and programmes to the development targets of *Shaping the 21st Century*. This is certainly due to the fact that the old administration fundamentally rejected the notion of quantitative targets.
Ireland	Irish Aid is strongly committed to the goals outlined in *Shaping the 21st Century*. In this regard, Ireland considers monitoring, reporting and evaluation to have increasingly important roles. Ireland considers that the DAC will need to apply its energy to help the international community to move from awareness of the partnership concept to putting it into operation in a coordinated way.	Irish Aid's overall policy aim is to support a process of self-reliant, sustainable, poverty-reducing and equitable growth and development in the least developed countries. Irish Aid officials consider that the principles followed by Irish Aid in their bilateral aid programmes in priority countries are completely consistent with the goals of *Shaping the 21st Century* particularly in their recent shift towards basic interventions and focus on partnership with recipient country Governments. The recent DAC peer

Donor responses

Country	Government attitude	Government action
		review of the Irish Aid programme in Uganda stated that 'The priority country programme is…consistent with the vision of development cooperation contained in *Shaping the 21st Century*.'
Italy	Since 1997 the Italian government has been actively pursuing the goals outlined in *Shaping the 21st century*. The only area in which the Italian government is weak is basic education and it is difficult to foresee a substantial change of direction given the limited amount of resources and the search for maintaining its own specialisation in the international ODA task division.	The most important step is the definition of operational guidelines that apply the targets at an intermediate level, between the general targets defined by the CIPE (Interministerial Committee for Economic Planning) and field activities. The operational guidelines should follow those of *Shaping the 21st Century*. At present, guidelines regarding gender issues and childhood issues have been defined.
Japan	The Japanese government has continuously emphasised that it took leadership in the process of adoption of the document at DAC. *Shaping the 21st Century* is considered as one of the bases of Japan's aid policy. In Japan's ODA 1998 (annual report of the ODA programme) The Ministry of Foreign Affairs (MoFA) stated that Japan should take leadership in realisation of the goals.	In June 1998 the Japanese government sponsored the 'Tokyo Conference on the DAC's New Strategy'. Also at the Second Tokyo International Conference on African Development' (TICAD II) held in October 1998, *Shaping the 21st Century* was considered as the basis for discussion. In 1999, as one of Japan's efforts for expansion of aid in sectors related to the *Shaping the 21st Century* targets, Japan will more than double (from 2.5 billion Yen to 5.2 billion Yen) the budget for grants for children's health.
Netherlands	Dutch development cooperation is based on five quantified quality objectives: 1 20% of total development cooperation should be geared towards basic social services 2 4% to reproductive health care 3 0.1% of GNP to international environmental policy in developing countries 4 50 million guilders to the tropical rain forest 5 0.25 per cent of GNP to be spent on Least Developed Countries. All these targets were met during 1997, except for environment-related aid, which amounted to 0.092% of GDP.	The Netherlands favours the introduction of performance criteria to be able to measure the impact on poverty reduction. It works closely with the DAC to formulate these performance criteria. In its budget the Netherlands increased funds allocated to basic social services. This, combined with the allocation of development aid to countries that meet the good governance criteria, should increase the effectiveness of alleviating and reducing poverty.
New Zealand	NZODA supports the goals. They have been reflected in NZODA's programme and in its dialogue with partner governments. The goals are substantially reflected in the revised Fiji programme and provide a basis of reference in the current review of education programmes.	NZODA has concerns that adoption of targets will interfere with a partner driven agenda and also because they feel they are difficult to apply in the context of small island states where donors take responsibility for different sectors/priorities at the request of the partner government.

Donor responses

Norway	Despite criticising the DAC strategy's weak treatment of aid volumes and equality issues, Norway accepts *Shaping the 21st Century* as guidelines for all parts of the DAC's activities.	
Portugal	There are no Government statements on *Shaping the 21st Century*	Only in basic education and gender are direct actions observable in relation to the targets set in *Shaping the 21st Century.*
Spain	*Shaping 21st Century* goals have been included in the Directive Plan proposal, but concrete strategies are yet to be developed.	
Sweden	The Swedish government has been quite reluctant to refer to the development goals of *Shaping the 21st Century*. However, for the first time in the government's budget proposal for 1999 there is a very clear reference to *Shaping the 21st Century*, and already in the first part of description of the overall objectives for ODA there is a lengthy reference to the content of the *Shaping the 21st Century* goals.	It is not very clear how the government is planning to contribute to the fulfilment of the *Shaping 21st Century* goals. In the budget the government argues that donor coordination is a main issue if its goals are to be addressed. They are arguing that Sweden should push for better coordination within the UN system, DAC and the World Bank's Special Programme for Africa.
Switzerland	In its 1998 framework credit submission to parliament, the government referred to the *Shaping the 21st Century* strategy as an issue being above all the responsibility of developing country governments. International cooperation would support such internal processes in the South to encourage civil society and democratisation in particular.	For internal purposes, the Swiss Agency for Development and Cooperation (SDC) has made a comparison of the DAC Strategy for the 21st Century and selected major SDC policy papers. The results: 1 There is a far-reaching compatibility of the DAC and SDC approaches. 2 Whereas the DAC adopts quantitative targets in a clear-cut timeframe, SDC refrains from such an operationalisation. 3 The DAC strategy uses an income/consumption based poverty concept and emphasises economic growth, whereas SDC focuses much more on inequality and human development. The Federal Office for Foreign Economic Affairs (FOFEA) does not deal with the DAC strategy.
UK	The Comprehensive Spending Review set key targets to be achieved by the end of the current Parliament in 2002, which closely reflect the International Development goals agreed in 1997. DFID's principal aim is to halve the number of individuals living in extreme poverty by 2015. To help achieve this, DFID has stressed the primacy of poverty eradication across all of its programmes and has stressed that it is also up to the developing countries themselves to make the commitment to meet these targets.	Though the Government signed up to the DAC targets two years ago, only now is it preparing Strategy Papers, each of which describes how DFID will contribute to the international effort to achieve the specific goals. They will set out the goal statement, the present position, experience to date, and DFID's future strategy. DFID's whole development programme is directed towards achieving the DAC targets.

Donor Responses...

Country	Government attitude	Government action
USA	The goals that USAID set in its 1997 Strategic Plan were linked to, and, in many cases identical with those of the DAC. In 1998, as part of its Annual Performance Review, USAID examined all goals and data sources and determined that in some cases, no data was being collected on the DAC indicators. In these cases, USAID has sought other indicators that are more useful in tracking progress towards these goals. USAID does not believe that it should duplicate the efforts of other donors, particularly multilaterals and therefore, has few plans to establish mechanisms to measure DAC goals. However, in some situations, notably population and health, USAID has established extensive surveys to measure progress towards DAC goals. USAID is in the process of updating its 1997 Strategic Plan and there is no intention of abandoning the DAC goals.	USAID has established an extensive system of programme indicators that measure progress. In 1998, 69% of all USAID Strategic Objectives were reporting against pre-set targets. Since the DAC goals are very high-level countrywide goals, USAID, in most cases, does not consider it useful to monitor individual programme accomplishments against them. Nonetheless, all programme goals must be directed towards achievement of the overall DAC goals. There are some USAID programmes, notably Demographic and Health Surveys, that appear to provide the best available data on achievement in Child Survival, Child Nutrition, Maternal Mortality and Population goals.

Note: 1 BADC: Belgian Administration for Development Cooperation, responsible for about 60–70% of total Belgian ODA. The remaining 30–40% are being disbursed by the Ministry of Finance and other departments, and cover multilateral aid and debt relief.

Table 51 Donor government policies and poverty reduction

Country	Do government policies help world poverty reduction?	Linking poverty with global trends
Australia	There is room for improvement in Australia's policy coherence and the need for a more holistic approach to poverty reduction. For example there appears to be little consideration of the effects of APEC policies and other trade and economic reforms on poor communities in the region and there is minimal cooperation between Treasury, AusAID and the Department of Foreign Affairs on debt issues and how Australia could play a more active role in resolving these problems.	The government has taken some positive steps to ensure greater policy coherence between the aid programme and other government functions. This has been most apparent in relation to Australia's response to recent East Asian financial and social problems. For example Australia has taken a leading role in suggesting improvements to international financial architecture, has helped broker and support peaceful change in East Timor and Indonesia and has provided important loans to depressed East Asian economies.
Austria	While the development policy of the Department for Development Cooperation contributes to poverty reduction, there is still no overall, coherent government policy.	Issues of labour and employment in the global context are addressed through development information and development education.
Belgium	Since 1994, an 'Interdepartmental Working Group on Development Cooperation' has involved representatives from the Ministries of Development Cooperation, Foreign Affairs, Finance, Agriculture, Defence and in theory negotiates on policy themes and decisions affecting developing countries. However, this working group has been mainly responsive to the demands from world development campaigns, rather than taking a particularly proactive role. Key people on the committee who decide on allocation of concessional loans and export credits have recently said that more attention is being paid to the developmental relevance of these loans and credits. However, there has been no ex-post evaluation of these instruments.	The Minister for Development Cooperation launched the 'Brussels call for action' in October 1998, linking development and disarmament. For him, conflict management in general is an important issue linked with development cooperation and he has set up a specific programme for this. In addition, the government was challenged by 'Working up the World', a two-year campaign by development NGOs and trade unions, linking globalisation, labour conditions, uncontrolled capital flows and investments to development.
Canada	Canadian foreign policy priorities in the 1990s have been oriented strongly towards extending trade relations and the liberalisation of economic relations. Canadian NGOs have long suggested that aid's impact on poverty is conditioned by the coherence and cumulative countries and currently there are few levers to promote active coordination and coherence among them. Together with Norway, working with a small group of northern and southern countries, Canada's Foreign Minister, Lloyd Axworth, has been developing and promoting an agenda for "human security" and the International Cooperation impact of the full range of Canadian policies towards developing Minister suggests that poverty is not a	Human security has been elaborated as a central guiding framework for Canada's foreign policy that significantly broadens the traditional notion of 'national security' and is a current pillar in Canada's 'activist' middle power foreign policy. The implications of this policy are being played out in the Kosovo crisis. In a concept paper, the Department of Foreign Affairs suggests that human security does not create a 'right to intervene'. However, 'it does support the rights of populations affected by gross physical attack, coercive threats and intimidation. Human security provides the political basis upon which the international community can respond to crimes against humanity so that genocide, ethnic cleansing and terrorism can be deterred and reduced in frequency.' At the end of March 1999 the Prime Minister signalled some new

Donor government policies

Country	Do government policies help world poverty reduction?	Linking poverty with global trends
	subsidiary issue in human security, saying that "all development assistance is an investment in human security". Informal working groups inform policy making for key events, such as G7 meetings, but these often lack the potential for coordinated and timely input from interested parties outside government. Interestingly, Canadian policy implementation in support of NATO's response to the Kosovo crisis demonstrate an ad hoc, practical and well coordinated approach, with integrated but specific roles for many ministries which demonstrated that with a sense of urgency and political will, strong coherence in government policy and practice is achievable. To date this will seems possible only in response to immediate crisis management in the Balkans or in Rwanda.	initiatives for Canadian foreign policy, highlighting his pre-occupation with human rights, fair trade and investment regimes, and 'most pressing of all', global poverty. He also proposed that Canada should forgive debt and grant further credits to countries that increase spending on education and health care for their people and reduce spending on weapons and the military. A 'Millennium' Throne Speech in the Fall of 1999 is expected to identify a foreign policy framework and specific initiatives for Canada.
Denmark	Danida and the Minister for Development are very much aware of the importance of globalisation, trade, debt, and foreign investment for development processes in developing countries, and Denmark does take a pro-developing country stance in international negotiations. At the same time it can be seen that Danish business and interest groups are quite influential on Danish policy, and that ministers other than the Minister of Development pay less attention to the need of developing countries than to the need of immediate Danish interests. The agriculture and fishery sectors are not characterised by policies friendly to sustainable development.	The Danish government has a complex view on the present global situation and the interaction of different aspects, such as how the participation of civil society affects poverty, and how economic globalisation has a bearing on the global political power structure. The Danish government does express its views in international forums, but does not always obtain political results from them, because of both lack of political power internationally and conflicting Danish economic interests.
Finland	The new government policy line on relations with developing countries makes it clear that Finland views the fight against world poverty in holistic terms, as a leading concern for global, regional and national policy. Reference is made to a comprehensive approach that aims to thwart poverty both in the South and in Finland. In some aspects of Finland's domestic social, health and environmental policies, traces of this integrated approach can be seen but remain undeveloped.	The guiding concept of the new policy line on relations with developing countries is to lay out Finland's position on how these links are connected. The policy covers the interrelation between aid and economic globalisation and market integration, debt relief, labour and environmental standards and domestic policies. The overriding concern is to achieve security in its broad sense. Within this context poverty reduction, the pros and cons of economic globalisation, human rights, equity and civil society are all considered. Poverty in relation to employment, income distribution, investment and governance has also been given much attention. However, disarmament and reducing military spending are not properly addressed in terms of their potential impact on poverty.

Donor government policies

France	There is no specific mechanism to secure the coherence of French Government policy with any objective of poverty reduction. In a general way, questions related to cooperation and poverty eradication remain confined to those organisations involved in implementing ODA such as ministries, agencies and service organisations.	When it comes to trade issues, market liberalisation and military policy, French interests are (almost) exclusively given priority. For instance, when France left the negotiations on MAI, it was only to protect French interests and for political reasons. Issues related to development of southern countries were not taken into account.
Germany	The new government has committed itself to pay increased attention to the coherence of its policies towards the South. On this issue, the coalition agreement explicitly states: 'The new government will ensure the developmental coherence with other ministries'. There are some promising signs of how this ambitious target could be put into practice. Export credit guarantees are to be reformed according to environmental, social and developmental criteria and the government also wants to work for a change of structural adjustment programmes as well as international trade and investment regimes along these lines. As a new member of the federal body dealing with arms exports, the BMZ is now in a position also to introduce development considerations into this policy field and the German government is also determined. In January 1999, Chancellor Schröder announced a German initiative for improving the conditions of the HIPC programme at the upcoming Cologne G8 summit. NGOs welcome this step but consider it as inadequate for a long-term solution.	The new BMZ leadership is outspoken on the links between development cooperation and global issues. Their arguments on this are strong and credible. The Foreign Office also puts more emphasis on human rights and global problems in its public statements. At this stage it is, however, still too early to judge the extent to which German policies in global affairs are genuinely ruled by the desire to contribute most effectively towards cooperative efforts of the international community. The coming years will show whether the impressive guidelines which mark the start of the new government will effectively shape German policies at the operational level or whether narrow self-interest still rules in foreign relations. NGOs appreciate the initiative of the Foreign Office to establish a forum on global issues for dialogue with civil society organizations. The opening event took place in April of this year and German NGOs are now asking the BMZ to consider ways of expanding and institutionalising its channels of dialogue with them. Both sides could gain from deepening the exchange of views and field experiences while respecting different mandates and functions.
Ireland	Irish Aid considers that the operation of a coherent development cooperation policy necessitates Irish Aid working closely with other Government departments on such issues as EU trade policy, international environment issues, debt policy and food security. The Department of Foreign Affairs liaises with other Government Departments where relevant and appropriate.	Commitment to human rights is a vital part of Ireland's overall development cooperation policy and following the publication of the 1993 Irish Aid Strategy Plan, specific funding for democratisation and human rights was introduced into the Irish Aid programme. Support for human rights, democratisation and governance activities in priority countries are fully integrated within each of the country programmes and funded from the country programme budgets. A separate human rights and democratisation budget line was established for non-priority countries. This is used to fund, in the form of grant assistance, a wide range of projects and activities carried out by Irish NGOs, international NGOs and other international bodies. The Minister has recently stated that "In recognition of the importance of politics in the development process, a concern about democratic principles permeates all Irish Aid's actions".

Donor government policies

Country	Do government policies help world poverty reduction?	Linking poverty with global trends
Italy	The Italian government intends to raise the issue of the consistency of policies in international and EU forums, regarding the policies of donor countries as well as those of developing countries.	The Italian government commitment is based on the need to link international cooperation activities with conflict prevention and resolution. Linking development cooperation to the defence of human and political rights; the building of stable and democratic institutions and the rule of law are considered as the fundamental for development.
Japan	The newly published ODA Midterm Policy (August 1999) gives poverty alleviation and social development as one of the prioritised areas for the next five years. This takes the DAC Development Strategy and its goal of reducing by half the population living below the poverty line by 2015 into account. Japan will see the initiatives by recipient countries, their development efforts and their ownership of development projects as a basis for its assistance. The Midterm Policy also states that it intends to achieve the goals of the 20:20 Initiative. The Midterm Policy states that inter-ministry coordination will be strengthened by sharing information and facilitating communication. However, since trade, agriculture, environment and financial matters are all under different ministries, it may be difficult for the Government to establish coherent policy on poverty elimination, considering that, for example, ministries in charge of trade and agriculture policies reflect the interests of Japanese industries and farmers	It is considered that high military spending is bad for development and poverty reduction. Although the principles in the ODA Charter state that attention would be paid to democratisation and human rights there is no coherence in the adoption of this principle. Japan has frozen or suspended aid to some countries (most of them in Africa and Latin America) because of bad human rights records, but the principle has not been strictly applied to major recipients such as Indonesia and China.
The Netherlands	The Netherlands used its presidency of the European Union in the first half of 1997 to press the issue of coherent policies towards developing countries onto the international agenda. The European Commission subsequently adopted a Coherence Resolution that was supposed to report on the progress made in the first half of 1999. Thematic issues were to be evaluated along with institutional aspects. However, the European Commission failed to report on time. The revised date is the meeting of the Development Council in November 1999.	The Dutch authorities have continued to pay increased attention to conflict management and how it relates to development cooperation. A proposal for action on small arms proliferation will be presented during the Dutch Presidency of the Security Council. In June 1999, development ministers from the UK, Germany, Norway and the Netherlands announced their intention to adopt a common approach to poverty eradication and set out a prioritised agenda. Priority themes are improved donor coordination, increased ODA, untying aid, balancing the financing gap between humanitarian assistance and sustainable development, policy coherence, implementation of the HIPC Initiative and strengthening the multilateral system. A follow-up meeting is scheduled for 2000 in The Netherlands.

Donor government policies

New Zealand	The NZODA policy statement makes it clear that the government's approach to poverty alleviation is based on the belief that economic growth will lead to reduced poverty and increased social cohesion. MFAT states that economic growth is to be achieved by promoting an open international trading system (including ensuring successful outcomes in APEC in 1999). The government promotes integration into the global trading system as a goal of its aid programme. Economic growth accompanied by good governance and protection of human rights are all key factors in the programme.
Norway	Unfortunately, Norwegian concerns with poverty rarely focus on the external framework for poverty reduction, such as the global economy, trade and investments flows, migrations, capital transfers and the liberalisation of the financial markets – although the NGO and solidarity communities frequently address such issues. On the official level, the present emphasis is on internal economic and political factors. The Government has recently taken an international initiative to establish an independent legal advisory centre which may assist developing countries in managing trade disputes with resourceful opponents. It is also supporting a fund helping developing countries to benefit from WTO rules and it is joining alliances to support developing countries' efforts to improve their trade conditions through the next round of WTO negotiations.
Portugal	There are no effective mechanisms of coordination of policies concerning poverty elimination. Cooperation for development policy is a shared objective. It is based on the assumption that not only do the more developed countries have responsibility for a greater promotion of human development, but that developing countries also share a real interest in a more equitable wealth distribution. This goal can only be achieved through collective efforts of cooperation for development which is increasingly an effort of the State to support education, the productive sectors and the building of markets for goods and services, health, food security, access to drinking water and financial aid.
Spain	NGOs managed to get coherence objectives included in the Cooperation Act, that was passed last year. However, no further objectives or indicators have been settled in relation with this target. The only advances gained were linked to foreign debt and arms trade policies, but this cannot be deemed to be part of an overall coherenceinitiative. Spanish ODA has not reached a level at which this can be assessed. The Directive plan is currently being processed, and coherence objectives should be included (among others). Coherence is a mid-term aim for Spanish ODA policy.
Sweden	In the budget for 1999 there is an unusually explicit mentioning of the need for coherence between development and poverty reduction and other policy areas like security, trade, environment and migration. The example of the debate on MAI is referred to as something that illustrates the need of integration between trade and development. There are also examples of different coordination mechanisms between the Departments of Trade and of Development within the Ministry of Foreign Affairs. However, a lack of coherence between policies on trade and investment and of development is one of the main issues for the critique of the Government by the NGO community. Globalisation has been a main theme in the government's policy documents for the last few years.

Donor government policies

Country	Do government policies help world poverty reduction?	Linking poverty with global trends
Switzerland	Coherence has been a major issue for years in Switzerland. In 1994 the government presented North-South Guidelines to parliament which have served as a framework for debate and for coherent decisions. The Swiss political system is a "consultation culture", providing various opportunities and mechanisms to reconcile conflicting interests within the administration and in relation to business or civil society. The consultations are based on the legal aim of ODA to support "poor developing countries, regions and population groups". Beyond this general framework there are no additional mechanisms purely addressing poverty reduction. The policy guidelines are in place, appropriate mechanisms are also in place in most cases (apart from the refusal of NGO representation in decision making on export-risk guarantees), but these do not yet guarantee the necessary political will for coherent outcomes.	The government is well aware of potential global linkages mentioned and attaches particular importance to governance issues. SDC/FOFEA (the Ministries responsible for development assistance) have produced some guidelines on the Rule of Law. SDC has adopted guidelines on ODA and human rights and on corruption. Moreover, SDC has extended its programmes on human rights in recent years, and its support to civil society organisations.
UK	A key element of the White Paper was a commitment to seek greater coherence on all aspects of policy affecting developing countries. An Inter-Departmental Working Group on Development meets to consider development issues, bringing together Ministers from many departments with an involvement in development cooperation. According to DFID officials, there is now a strong culture of communication and interaction and an awareness that development objectives must not be undermined. Each country strategy paper now includes a section on future strategy, which discusses how DFID can ensure that British policies (ie trade, debt, and the environment) can maintain a development focus. DFID is also trying to be more open to ideas from civil society organisations to help push coherence. For instance, the Development Policy Forum has been established to encourage civil society contributions to the development debate, and DFID is now publishing more of its material regularly to encourage a more transparent dialogue on policy.	DFID works to promote its development partnership approach by ensuring that investment, trade and development are linked in a way that will help eliminate poverty. An aspect of this is the understanding that poverty involves vulnerability to shocks, lack of social and cultural rights and lack of opportunity; and that the way to address these issues is through inter-departmental consultation. DFID's approach is to support economic policies which encourage pro-poor growth. This entails working within the 'new international economic architecture' which provides links between investment, trade and development. DFID aims to achieve coherence between official and private, internal and external debt relief measures; military expenditure, conflict prevention, and the impact of policies on the environment. However, underlying all of this is DFID's promotion of global liberalisation – an example of this being its support for the WTO's Millennium Round.
USA	The introduction of strategic planning by all departments and agencies may bring some new harmonising discipline and improved coherence at the broad policy level, but it is too soon to evaluate. In the International	There have been no statements and limitations in US reporting systems and the diversity of US development coordination efforts make this difficult to answer. The US ascribes to the World Bank's findings that open economic policies tend

Donor government policies

Affairs budget, the leadership of the State Department, under the overall guidance of the Office of Management and Budget, has been stronger in recent years and mechanisms exist to improve coordination and coherence in budget, multilateral affairs, debt, trade and complex humanitarian crises. However, what this means for poverty elimination is unclear. In some countries as many as 30 different departments and agencies are represented in various US missions. Several reports show that the level of coordination among these many governmental entities is lacking. Recent trends in US trade with developing countries has shown large increases in two-way trade and shifts from primary products to capital and consumer goods. Developing countries receive over half of US agricultural exports although exports to sub-Saharan Africa have dropped significantly over the past four years. Despite US efforts to promote broad-based agricultural development in developing countries, tariff protection against food exports from these countries is high.

to correlate with broad-based economic growth and many USAID programmes focus on easing foreign exchange controls, eliminating obstacles to business ownership, and reducing bureaucratic delays and opportunities for official corruption. One of USAID's most widespread areas of activity is helping to improve policies, laws, and regulations that govern market activities and strengthen institutions and systems that support and reinforce markets. In the majority of countries where USAID is active, the expansion of access and opportunity for the poor, particularly women and other disadvantaged groups, is a major thrust of the programme as part of the broad base which is promoted for economic growth. In several countries, USAID has tried to expand opportunities of historically neglected areas with high concentrations of poor people. Democracy and governance is a strategic focus for 80% of USAID field missions and programme approaches centre on rule of law, elections and political processes, civil society and transparency and accountability in governance.

Making sure every aid dollar contributes

Table 52 Making sure that every aid dollar contributes to poverty eradication

Country	Progress towards mainstreaming poverty eradication as the goal of all aid	Progress towards ensuring that all aid spending contributes towards poverty eradication	Government policy on regional and sectoral aid allocation
Australia	Since 1997 poverty reduction has been a central goal of AusAID and to this end five key sectors have been prioritised: education, health, rural development and agriculture, good governance and infrastructure. There has also been a trend towards greater levels of funding for basic social services (although no specific commitments have been made in this area) as well as a focus on poverty reduction in country strategy plans. The rate of change, however, has been relatively slow. Total aid has continued to decrease as a proportion of GNP, and the geographic distribution of Australian aid is still not focused on the poorest countries.	AusAID and the current Australian government have a broad notion of how to achieve poverty reduction which places a strong emphasis on supporting general economic growth as well as funding some programmes which are specifically targeted at the poor. For this reason AusAID argues that almost all of its programmes are designed to reduce poverty and thus benefit the poor. There is a growing emphasis in AusAID to explicitly consider a project's effects on the poor and on disadvantaged groups such as women and indigenous people. This, however, is not subsequently evaluated unless it is a specific objective of the project. Measurement is therefore difficult.	In the last year the Australian government has reiterated its commitment to supporting East Asia during the financial and political crises in the region. It has also committed itself 'to doing whatever is necessary' to help Papua New Guinea during recent natural emergencies. Budgeted levels of aid to Africa have been maintained during this time; however, there has been a drop in total Australian aid to Africa as emergency and humanitarian funds have been allocated to East Asia and the Pacific.
Austria	None of Austria's aid is specifically classified as, or targeted towards, direct poverty reduction or basic needs. It is claimed that poverty reduction is mainstreamed as a goal of all aid, but the statistics do not support this.	There has been no further progress to improve the measurement and evaluation of aid to poverty reduction.	The three-year programme of the Department for Development Cooperation stated priority countries and regions as: Countries: Nicaragua, Cape Verde, Burkina Faso, Uganda, Ethiopia, Rwanda, Mozambique and Bhutan. Regions: Central America, West African Sahel, East Africa, Southern Africa, Himalaya Hindu Kush and Palestine.
Belgium	The conversion of the general policy paper (Kleur Bekennen) to law is an important step forward. For the first time in the history of Belgian development cooperation, the general objectives – which are pro-poverty eradication – are laid down in the long-term plan. These general	Within BADC, evaluation and poverty assessments are becoming increasingly established; however, a lack of personnel and severe financial control constrain further development. For other parts of ODA (bilateral concessional loans via the Ministry	The five priority sectors are health, education, basic infrastructure, agriculture and food security and capacity building. Combined with this are the three cross-cutting themes of environment, gender and social economy. The criteria for geographical focus are quite vague but based

Making sure every aid dollar contributes

	objectives are strategic papers for specific sectors and countries. However, this only applies to ODA managed by BADC which represents 60% to 70% of total ODA.	of Finance and aid to multilateral financial institutions) there is no formal evaluation foreseen. The Minister for Development Cooperation has put an end to tied aid, but again, this is only affects BADC controlled ODA.	on the Human Development Index and poverty Index. These choices have recently been repeated for a broader public in the leaflet published by the Government in March 1999.
Canada	The 1995 CIDA Policy on Poverty Reduction applies to all CIDA programmes and the degree to which this has been implemented is difficult to determine. CIDA uses a threefold classification of poverty programming: targeted poverty programmes working directly with the poor; poverty focused programmes that benefit a disproportionately larger number of poor than non-poor; and policy interventions that impact on the environment for poverty reduction. The Policy Branch coordinates an informal working group exploring how CIDA might better translate the Poverty Reduction Policy into practice. Throughout 1999, the Asia Bilateral Branch has been undertaking a widely consultative review of its programme with the aim of improving its contribution to poverty reduction. CIDA has also been an active participant in the DAC Informal Network on Poverty Reduction and contributed a study (yet to be published) on CIDA's approach and practice in poverty reduction.	Poverty profiles and reduction strategies are to be integrated into country and regional policy frameworks. However, there is little formal accountability to the Poverty Policy and implementation depends largely on the discretionary commitment of individuals involved in project and programme management. A 1996 internal CIDA study reported an overall 'perception [in CIDA]…that the policy has limited relevance to project design and exerts little influence in structuring, exploiting complementarities, or focusing programming work.' Other commentators have recommended stronger lines of accountability, career incentives related to results in poverty reduction, and explicit inclusion of expected poverty-based results in Country Programme Frameworks and related projects and their evaluation. The 1998 DAC review of Canadian ODA referred to the need to develop and disseminate guidelines and methodological tools and techniques to help CIDA staff implement the poverty mandate at the operational level.	The government and CIDA itself have a number of broad policy statements on the importance of basic human needs, including basic social services, for poverty reduction as well as sectoral strategies. In 1999 CIDA is undertaking a consultative process to develop a sector strategy for basic education. A 1998 assessment of Basic Human Needs highlights the importance of targeting to ensure benefits are concentrated on areas where the poor live and/or specific groups with high levels of poverty. Improved income for the poor must accompany improved access and use of basic social services to assure sustainability. It also considered the gender dimension central to the success of BHN programming. There are no explicit policies for aid allocation to sub-Saharan Africa, although the Prime Minister will be attending the Commonwealth Heads of State meeting in South Africa in 1999 where it is hoped he will address the development concerns of the region. CCIC calculates that this region has suffered disproportionate cuts in the 1990s (30.4%) compared to Canadian aid as a whole (21.2%), while (commercially-oriented) allocations to South America increased (by 33.5%).
Denmark	Poverty is mainstreamed in Danish aid. The current challenge is to keep the focus on poverty in a process where Danida is moving from project aid to sectoral programme aid. In the first case it is	All project documents have to deal with poverty reduction as the main objective of Danish aid, but there are no guidelines on the kind of poverty analysis to be made before embarking	The Danish Strategy aims at allocating around 60% of bilateral aid to sub-Saharan Africa, 30% to Asia and up to 10% to Latin America. The 1998 figures show that Africa received more

Making sure every aid dollar contributes

Country	Progress towards mainstreaming poverty eradication as the goal of all aid	Progress towards ensuring that all aid spending contributes towards poverty eradication	Government policy on regional and sectoral aid allocation
	easier to work with specific target groups for aid; in the latter, poverty orientation would mean influencing national policies in recipient countries to be more redistributive, for example, to promote land reforms when working in the agricultural sector.	on specific programmes. Indicators have been developed to evaluate the output of aid, focusing mostly on short-term physical results. The plan is to develop the indicator system into a tool for assessing the outcome and impact of aid as well.	than anticipated, namely 65.3%. In the Strategy for Danish Development Policy Towards the Year 2000 it stated that bilateral aid allocated to social infrastructure has been kept constant at around 30% whilst economic infrastructure and extension of the productive sectors have gone down from 64% to 38% from the mid-1980s to the early-1990s respectively. In the strategy Danida aims to increase the allocations for these two sectors to a level where they will once again play a prominent role in Danish aid. Emphasis is put on agriculture and physical infrastructure. The social sectors are planned to remain at the early 1990s level.
Finland	The new policy line on relations with developing countries released in October 1998 underscores poverty reduction as the priority for ODA. This builds on the approach taken by the government's 1996 Decision in Principle and offers a more coherent perspective on the relationship between poverty reduction and the overall thrust of relations with developing countries. There has also been a detectable shift in government policy toward emphasising the role of democracy and good governance as a goal of Finland's relations with developing countries, and this adds substance to the way poverty reduction is approached.	An assessment and evaluation of the impact of the poverty reducing content of spending and interventions has yet to be made. Currently, project appraisals do not assess the specific impact on poorer income groups nor on different income groups.	According to the 1996 Decision in Principle, Finland directs 'the bulk of its assistance to the poorest developing countries, particularly in sub-Saharan Africa.' There are, however, no recent statements on regional or sector-related allocations.
France	There is no formal classification and there has been no real progress in the measurement and evaluation of aid towards poverty reduction or towards mainstreaming poverty eradication into the overall goal of aid. A 1996 study found that 'poverty	For the French Government, all ODA contributes to poverty reduction, directly or indirectly. However, there are no specific policies for analysing or assessing French interventions against the objective of poverty reduction.	France has recently reaffirmed that sub-Saharan Africa is a priority for its bilateral as well as multilateral ODA. There is no real commitment to any one specific sector.

Making sure every aid dollar contributes

	alleviation is not listed as a practical priority by any aid institution; it has not been incorporated into the programming or evaluation; it is not the subject of any special strategy or policy statement; it does not appear as a development concept, as the subject of statistical analysis, or as a criterion for allocating aid'. However, the government's aim is to reduce poverty.		
Germany	The new administration's position on the goal of poverty reduction is not quite clear. It is somewhat disturbing that poverty reduction is not explicitly mentioned in the coalition agreement's section on development cooperation; however, much emphasis is put on redefining development cooperation in terms of global structural policies. This new orientation could also provide a suitable framework for more effective poverty programmes. The BMZ is now the lead ministry for habitat and the follow-up process of the World Social Summit and whilst the BMZ maintains important positions on the international stage, it would be useful for it to issue a policy statement clearly specifying how its additional responsibilities and activities on global issues directly or indirectly relate to poverty alleviation.	The new BMZ reporting system on all bilateral projects provides a systematic framework for assessing the poverty impact. In the planning process, as well as in evaluating the implementation of the plan, BMZ staff routinely review poverty aspects. A standard section of the questionnaire for evaluations directly addresses project impact on the poor with regard to participation, improvement of productive capacities and gender issues. As a new policy, short versions of BMZ evaluations are now available on the Internet.	The coalition agreement does not include a statement on allocations of aid to particular regions and Germany has not selected a specific group of concentration countries. Basic social services are explicitly referred to in the coalition document by a statement on increasing allocations to basic education and primary health care for girls and women. The new leadership has declared its support for the 20:20 Initiative on basic social services.
Ireland	In July 1998 the Minister of State at the Department of Foreign Affairs stated that '...I am determined to make certain that, at a time of rapid expansion in our programmes, Irish Aid...remains targeted on supporting basic needs in developing countries such as food, water, education and health'. The DAC Development Cooperation Report 1998 states that Ireland's aid programme is explicitly committed to concentrating aid on poverty reduction. All Irish Aid policy documents state that it will concentrate its resources on programmes to meet basic needs in food and livelihood security, clean water, access to primary health and education services.	There has been an increased monitoring of Irish Aid budgets to ensure that poverty elimination remains central to all programmes. Particularly in sector programmes all targets are reviewed in terms of the percentage spent on the basic social sectors. Also in sectoral programmes there is an important focus on the recipient government's economic and social policies as these are seen as affecting poverty and growth as well as ensuring that all aid resources contribute towards poverty alleviation.	The main focus underpinning the Irish Aid programme continues to be a concentration on assisting the poorest of the poor – with particular emphasis on basic health and primary education in a number of priority countries in sub-Saharan Africa. Direct funding is given to programmes and projects which meet basic needs in six priority countries: Ethiopia, Lesotho, Mozambique, Tanzania, Uganda and Zambia. In 1998, 31% of the Irish Aid budget was spent on direct support for priority country programmes.

Making sure every aid dollar contributes

Country	Progress towards mainstreaming poverty eradication as the goal of all aid	Progress towards ensuring that all aid spending contributes towards poverty eradication	Government policy on regional and sectoral aid allocation
Italy	The main progress of Italian ODA policy towards mainstreaming poverty eradication has been the definition of guidelines consistent with the DAC principles. In the guidelines related to childhood, poverty reduction is indicated as one of the priorities to be pursued.	Aid is not focused specifically on poverty reduction. However there has been progress in mainstreaming poverty in so far as programmes on basic needs and human development have been implemented. Evaluations of such interventions often foresee an assessment of the impact on the poorest groups. Moreover, in the planning document for evaluation activities for 1997–99, eradication of poverty was indicated as one of the issues always to be considered in project evaluation.	For 1999 the Italian government has confirmed its historical geographic priorities: the Mediterranean (and the Balkan region) and sub-Saharan Africa. The most important sectors are: small enterprise development, particularly micro-enterprises; the health sector; gender; environment; children; institution building related to conflict prevention and peace enforcement; stability; conservation of cultural heritage; agriculture and food security.
Japan	The government has continuously made commitments to achieving the goals in Shaping the 21st Century with poverty eradication and social development as priority areas. There is no consensus, however, within the government, as to whether poverty eradication should be mainstreamed in Japan's aid programme as the main thrust of Japanese aid is to build up economic infrastructure. A positive development is that there are increased opportunities for joint evaluation and learning between NGOs and the government. Missions composed of both NGO and government staff were sent to Bangladesh and Cambodia for evaluation of NGO and ODA projects in rural development with emphasis on poverty reduction.	While the government continues to assist the development of economic and social infrastructure, it has made poverty eradication and social sector development goals in the prioritised areas (the New Mid-term Policy).	The Japanese government is more committed to aid to Africa, as was evident in the sponsoring of TICAD II in October 1998 where the government prepared a list of project examples for the conference. Japan has also recently directed aid to countries affected by the Asian financial crisis. Japan is also trying to promote South–South cooperation, aimed at promoting exchanges between developing countries in Africa and the Asian economies that once showed rapid growth. In Japan's ODA 1998, there is a special chapter on aid in the health sector where it states that aid for basic medical care would be expanded.
The Netherlands	Poverty eradication is the principle objective of Dutch development cooperation. The Dutch government has however been criticised for its emphasis on indirect over direct approaches. Priority is given to promoting economic growth and	The Dutch government has poverty reduction as the main objective of its development cooperation policy but does not make specific assessments of how its development policy impacts on different income groups. However,	In line with the statement of the UN Secretary General, The Netherlands will allocate 50% of its overall development budget to Africa – which currently gets 45% of bilateral aid. The Netherlands has recently decreased the number

Making sure every aid dollar contributes

	economic self reliance with too little attention to reaching poorer people directly with poverty eradication programmes. The Dutch government has, up to now, failed to provide information on the distinction between direct and indirect poverty eradication in overall budget allocations.	three recent developments contribute to the objective to make development aid more effective in meeting the objective of poverty reduction. These are the criteria for good governance, in the belief that good governance will lead to 'aid spending benefiting the poor', a shift from project support to sector/ programme support and, decentralisation of support activities to the embassies in-country, enabling local initiatives to be supported.	of countries that receive structural bilateral aid to 17. There are three key criteria: 1) the degree of poverty – countries with a per capita income less than US $925; 2) quality of socio-economic policy; and 3) quality of governance. A further three countries will qualify for a time-bound relationship and another 30 will be funded under three themes: environment, human rights/ peace/good governance, and business support in cooperation with the Dutch business sector.
New Zealand	Poverty Reduction remains a principle purpose of NZODA and a primary focus for the guiding principles. The bilateral programme in Fiji has been reviewed with the intention of giving it a stronger poverty eradication focus and may provide a blueprint for other programmes. However, large amounts of bilateral funding, particularly in the Pacific, remain tagged for scholarship programmes.	NZODA has checklists and questions focusing on poverty aspects (including participation of beneficiaries and gender issues) of projects as part of all project and programme development. A poverty indicator is soon to be used in the approval process.	
Norway	According to a recent review of policies and strategies for poverty reduction in Norwegian development aid poverty reduction remains the overarching objective. However, this message tends to be modified by a number of other objectives, ranging from support to economic growth to good governance, gender equality, peace and environmental concerns. The challenge is to combine these objectives. Within the multilateral development organisations, Norway is using its influence, through ear-marked contributions, in a consistent effort to shift their programmes towards poverty reduction.	Currently there is no formal expertise on poverty reduction within NORAD and the Foreign Ministry. Although NORAD has a number of other monitoring mechanisms in place, the agency has neither feedback nor learning systems that routinely focus on poverty reduction issues. Lessons are, however, learned through country programming and practical experience in the field and through interaction with development partners and scholars.	The Government has declared that 50% of Norwegian bilateral aid shall be allocated to Africa. In a statement to Parliament in May 1999, the Minister of International Development and Human Rights launched a bid for increased Norwegian funds for the fight against corruption and for the promotion of democracy, both of which she saw as increasing people's possibilities to free themselves from poverty.
Portugal	The 22 indicators (of which poverty was one) resulting from the OECD 'Development Progress Indicators Seminar' in February 1997 were sent to NGOs, ministries, embassies and universities	An Evaluation Unit has been set up and evaluations of projects in the areas of health, youth training and law education have been conducted.	The main focus of Portuguese Development Aid continues to be the five Portuguese speaking African countries (Angola, Guinea-Bissau, Mozambique, Cape Verde and S.Tomé and

Making sure every aid dollar contributes

Country	Progress towards mainstreaming poverty eradication as the goal of all aid	Progress towards ensuring that all aid spending contributes towards poverty eradication	Government policy on regional and sectoral aid allocation
	involved in development cooperation. In addition, the Portuguese Cooperation Institute has been training specialised technicians in the poverty area on the use of indicators/markers (statistics area) and evaluation.		Prince), classified as least developed. The distribution of Portuguese aid is spread across a vast range of sectors, particularly infrastructure and social services – about 50 million US$, equivalent to around 32% of bilateral ODA.
Spain	When talking about Spanish ODA priorities for the next four years, Government officials have stressed its commitment to 20:20 Initiative. The new Directive Plan proposes that three cross-cutting themes (poverty, gender and environment), must be taken into account in the preparation of all projects.	No such measures are carried out by the Spanish Government.	As regards Directive Plan discussions, the NGO community has insisted on the importance of aid to Latin American least-developed countries and sub-Saharan Africa. It appears that the Government's proposal will increase ODA allocated to these countries, but no dramatic changes are expected. In a recent statement to the Parliament, the Secretary of State for International Cooperation expressed the desire to increase ODA to Africa.
Sweden	Poverty reduction is one of four main areas in Swedish ODA. The programme 'The Rights of the Poor' was passed by parliament in 1998 and is now to be translated into concrete policies. It is currently difficult at this early stage to judge how much has really been actioned.	Sida's poverty programme 'Reducing Poverty', released in 1996, contains many concrete methods of measuring and evaluating poverty issues within Sida's programmes. There is a permanent working group on poverty that follows up on a series of 'reference projects' where different methods of poverty reduction are tested. According to the programme, poverty analysis is to be integrated into the whole of Sida's activities. In their Annual Report 1998 there is a brief chapter reporting on poverty eradication. It states that in all new country strategies there is a clear reference to the 'Reducing Poverty' programme and it gives a series of areas of policy dialogue.	
Switzerland	A cross-sectoral external evaluation of the poverty orientation of all bilateral SDC operations has been completed and SDC has approved a 'Policy	SDC has made efforts to mainstream poverty reduction in country and sector programmes and project planning. A teaching aid is in	In 1998, the government had to renew its framework credit for technical and financial cooperation for the years 1999–2002. To get

Making sure every aid dollar contributes

for Social Development'. An internal working group is preparing proposals on how to action this policy. In contradiction to these positive efforts, the government's major 1996/98 ODA funding requests to parliament do not treat poverty reduction in an explicit way; and in the 1999 revised guiding principles ('Leitbild') poverty reduction is just one of eight priority areas. The emphasis on poverty reduction is now much weaker in the 1999 guiding principles than it was in the basic ODA law of 1976. FOFEA did not join SDC's policy and measurement efforts but considers its instruments such as budget aid, debt reduction, technology transfer, trade and investment promotion as indirectly contributing to poverty reduction.

preparation for relevant programme staff to facilitate the integration of poverty reduction into project design, planning, monitoring and evaluation; a training module will also be offered. Poverty orientation of sector policies is quite coherent with the exception of trade and industry and a study is being carried out on how the poor can benefit more from trade and industry promotion. FOFEA relies more on policy dialogue and positive growth effects than targeted interventions.

approval by parliament, it had to submit a comprehensive report which declared its intention to increase the priority of social development in the sense of the 20:20 Initiative. Africa's share of around 30% of total ODA will remain constant.

United Kingdom In the Comprehensive Spending Review, DFID's programmes were reviewed to ensure that resources were focused on eliminating poverty and key targets were set to be achieved by the end of this Parliament. Progress against these targets will be monitored in the Department's annual Output and Performance Analysis, which will take place in 1999 and be made publicly available. DFID's philosophy of eliminating poverty rests on its fundamental belief that economic growth combined with better distribution of resources, is the way forward.

In the last year, there has been a cultural shift within DFID from aid and service delivery towards long-term development and the onus has shifted from accounting for every DFID penny to assessing what DFID can achieve collectively with the international community. At the heart of the indicators against which performance is judged is a focus on outcomes and the international development targets. However, the new tripartite PIMS marker system still only focuses on intention rather than on tracking implementation. The evaluation department has recently commissioned independent work to assess the impact of British aid on poverty in four partner countries which should provide a framework for future evaluations. A new Performance Reporting and Information System for Managers (PRISM), trialed in 1998, is hoped to combine project monitoring information in accessible form. The

According to DFID the proportion of assistance directed towards Low Income Countries is expected to increased from 67% to 76% in 2001/02, reflecting DFID's focus on poverty reduction. DFID plans to increase the level of British commitments for basic education, basic health and water in Africa by 50% over a three-year period. Bilateral country programme aid to Africa is expected to increase from 41% to 48% between 1996/97 and 2001/02 to reach a total of UK£487 million. Aid to Asia and the Pacific will decrease from 39 to 35% to reach UK£356 million in 2001/02. Aid to Eastern Europe and the Former Soviet Union will decrease from 12 to 8% to each UK£87 million. Aid to the Western hemisphere will remain at a constant of 5% and aid to the overseas territories will increase from 3 to 4% amounting to UK£41 million in 2001/2.

Making sure every aid dollar contributes

Country	Progress towards mainstreaming poverty eradication as the goal of all aid	Progress towards ensuring that all aid spending contributes towards poverty eradication	Government policy on regional and sectoral aid allocation
		1998 report shows that about three quarters of all projects approved since 1990 were rated as successful or highly successful in achieving their objective. However, comprehensive disaggregation to evaluate the degree to which different income groups are benefiting, has not taken place.	
USA	USAID has a strategic aim to help reduce the proportion of the population in poverty by 25% by 2007. The objective of poverty reduction is explicit in one of USAID's six goals outlined in its Strategic Plan which calls for 'broad-based economic growth and agricultural development'. The poverty objective is also implicit in other strategic goals including those relating to strengthening democracy and governance, education and training, environment and disaster response. The US government places a premium on systemic approaches to assessing needs, projecting and tracking poverty reduction impacts (including gender differentiation) and evaluating the efficacy of different approaches. While these goals have been largely well received within the Agency, by host countries, and by USAID's partner organisations, it is still too early to assess the extent to which these approaches are impacting on poverty.	USAID's performance measurement systems are used to track the Strategic Plan by providing mechanisms to assess progress through the use of indicators for each programme result and efforts are made to derive lessons learned and collect best practices. Recently, implementing partner organisations, most notably NGOs, are participating in country 'strategic objective teams' working jointly with USAID mission staff on project planning, implementation and monitoring. The level of 'real' consultation between USAID missions and project partners varies greatly from mission to mission and is often attributed to personality or individual mission leadership. While USAID generally has been applauded for emphasising accountability and impact in its projects, it has received strong criticism from the US NGO community because it is perceived to stress management performance indicators over improving the lives of people in poverty.	In March 1998 President Clinton announced a ten-year African Food Security Initiative and the administration is again asking Congress for funding for the Development Fund for Africa to support programmes in child survival, economic growth and agriculture, human capacity development, population programmes, environment and democracy and governance. Supplementary funding is likely for humanitarian, migration and refugee assistance relating to the Kosovo conflict and a Central America Relief Bill was passed by the Congress for disaster relief in Central America. Spending is also being directed to the Middle East for peace efforts and to the Newly Independent States of the former Soviet Union for democratic transition.

Sources: NGO Reality of Aid questionnaire

Measuring aid for poverty reduction

Table 53 Measuring aid for poverty reduction

Country	Progress towards improvements in the measurement of aid for poverty reduction	Percentage of total ODA spent on basic social services[1]			Most recent government estimate of aid to basic needs/poverty reduction
		Basic education 1997 (1996)	Basic health 1997 (1996)	Water and sanitation 1997 (1996)	
Australia	It is encouraging to see that AusAID is putting more energy into monitoring and reporting the levels of expenditure in its five priority sectors and also in basic social service spending. In the coming year AusAID plans to carry out an evaluation of the effectiveness of the aid programme in alleviating poverty. It is hoped this study will help to increase the poverty-reduction focus of the programme.	5.6 (0.4)	4.7 (9.1)	2.88 (2.7)	In 1999/2000 AusAID expects that 14% of its funding allocated sectorally will go to basic social services, up from 13% in 1998/99. This is a 22% increase in real dollar terms since 1995/96.
Austria	Since the end of 1996 there has been a person responsible for designing guidelines for poverty alleviation measures within the Austrian Aid Programme and the DDC has presented a study to serve as a basis for guidelines for policy decisions which will be developed by a working group. The same person also has responsibility for assigning policy objective markers for poverty alleviation used in the DAC statistics	0.7 (0.2)	0.9 (1.5)	4.5 (7.1)	
Belgium	Within specific projects and programmes, a logical framework includes the evaluation of the results in relation to a whole range of parameters, including poverty reduction. Much effort is being made and more evaluations have been done in the past two years than in the previous decade, but it still seems difficult to reach the target. Progress is also constrained by severe financial control procedures which question the importance of evaluations.	0.5 (0.3)	5.5 (4.2)	2.6 (1.8)	In 1996, 17.7% of all BADC aid was invested in social services (10.5% of total ODA), rising from 10.4% of BADC (6.7% of total ODA) in 1994. The minister, when presenting the 1999 budget, said almost 35% of BADC aid would go to 'social infrastructure and services'. This is considered to be an over-estimate, but has yet to be confirmed.
Canada	In June 1999 CIDA implemented a new information management system that will	0.4 (1.2)	0.8 (0.4)	0.7 (2.3)	

Measuring aid for poverty reduction

Country	Progress towards improvements in the measurement of aid for poverty reduction	Percentage of total ODA spent on basic social services			Most recent government estimate of aid to basic needs/poverty reduction
		Basic education 1997 (1996)	Basic health 1997 (1996)	Water and sanitation 1997 (1996)	
	substantially improve the collection of data on Canada's aid disbursements. CIDA is adopting the DAC sectoral coding structure and poverty markers. CIDA is also one of six donors who have been reporting new bilateral commitments against a 'poverty marker'. However, this marker cannot be translated into an indicator of total disbursements for poverty reduction activities. While the marker is not related to disbursements, when combined with improved sectoral coding and identification of beneficiaries in later phases of the information system, a more complex understanding of poverty targeting will be possible.	(CCIC calculates that 2.9% of ODA was spent on basic education in 1997/98)			
Denmark	Danish aid generally is meant to be poverty reducing. Therefore, no specific figures exist on aid for poverty reduction. Danida has developed quantitative indicators which will be used to register the output and the outcome of specific programmes, notably the poverty reducing effect. The indicator system is to be further developed into a monitoring system, which will include qualitative data. Danish aid has been criticised for not targeting the poor directly, for not involving a thorough analysis of poverty, and for regarding the poorest of the poor as a group who cannot really contribute to development and therefore should not be addressed.	0.2	1.4	10.0 (11.7)	The overall aim of Danish aid is poverty reduction. Sustainable economic growth is seen as one important means of poverty reduction. This means that most economic infrastructure and productive sector allocations can be defined as poverty oriented in the long run. The allocations directly to the social sectors health and education were 21.6% of bilateral aid in 1998. If drinking water, sanitation, women projects, democracy, and a few others are included, aid given to social infrastructure amounted to 39.9% of bilateral aid in 1998.
Finland	Monitoring guidelines published in 1998 aim to create a minimum requirement for progress	3.0 (1.9)	0.2 (1.8)	7.2 (10.1)	No change. A full evaluation of the poverty orientation of Finnish

Measuring aid for poverty reduction

development cooperation has yet to be made by the DIDC.

and monitoring reports and must assess projects in terms of their compatibility with the strategic goals of Finnish development cooperation: the reduction of poverty being the first of these. However there are no criteria or indicators suggested for how an intervention is to be judged as reducing poverty.

Country		Has not yet reported	Has not yet reported	(6.5)	
France	There is no significant progress and the Government has no real strategy as such in this area.	Has not yet reported	Has not yet reported	(6.5)	There are no estimates
Germany	Last year the BMZ introduced a new measurement system for direct and indirect poverty reduction as defined from a cross-sectoral perspective. The BMZ has provided comprehensive figures to interested NGOs on commitments for basic social services (20:20 Initiative) as defined by the DAC.	2.1 (3.6)	1.8 (1.1)	8.7 (5.5)	The new government has increased funds for technical and financial assistance to direct poverty reduction defined from a cross-sectoral perspective to 14.3% of technical and financial assistance (DMmillion 447.9) in 1999. In 1997, actual commitments were 15.7%. The cross-sectoral approach to poverty alleviation is not limited to social sectors but comprises all funding activities where the majority of beneficiaries are poor and target groups actively participate. Planned commitments to basic social services, as defined by the DAC, amount to 17.3 (DM million 524.7) in 1999. In 1997, actual commitments to basic social services stood considerably higher at 27%.
Ireland	Irish Aid continues to adopt a more strategic approach to aid and efforts continue to improve performance measurement with a greater focus on results. The Minister stated in November	Has not reported	Has not reported	(6.0)	Pending international agreement on measurement standards related to the 20:20 Initiative, Irish Aid has made a provisional estimate of

Measuring aid for poverty reduction

Country	Progress towards improvements in the measurement of aid for poverty reduction	Percentage of total ODA spent on basic social services			Most recent government estimate of aid to basic needs/poverty reduction
		Basic education 1997 (1996)	Basic health 1997 (1996)	Water and sanitation 1997 (1996)	
	1998 that '…the whole area of policy and application has been fine-tuned and made more professional, effective and efficient'. While officials admit that it is difficult to measure poverty principles, it is clear that there has been a radical shift from higher-level to basic-level interventions and a more poverty-focused strategy, along with a shift from freestanding programmes to programmes fully integrated into local circumstances. Most elements are now in place for a poverty-focused approach.				expenditure on the basic social sectors to be in the region of 30%. Irish Aid are committed to continue to work with other donors with a view to arriving at internationally agreed standards of measurement in this respect. However, Irish Aid considers that they 'comfortably exceed the target established at Copenhagen for expenditure on the basic social sectors'.
Italy	Italy is involved in DAC and World Bank working groups on setting up a poverty reduction marker system. The Administration is going to implement the necessary studies to adapt its marker system to the DAC poverty reduction marker system. The planning document on the evaluation of ongoing and ex-post activities for the period 1997–99 indicates that government will adopt an evaluation policy consistent with the principles of the OECD-DAC. It will include a number of crosscutting issues, such as the environment, gender and poverty reduction.	0.1 (0.3)	0.9 (1.7)	9.4 (4.7)	There is no estimate. So far evaluation activities have always been carried out on single projects. Special attention has, however, been given to the impact on poverty reduction and on lower income populations.
Japan	The Japanese government's definition of aid to basic human needs is the total of aid in the sectors of social infrastructure, agriculture, food aid and emergency aid. This very broad definition is an obstacle for the measurement of aid directly targeted at poverty reduction.	1.0 (0.2)	0.5 (1.3)	10.5 (10.9)	The government says that 35% of ODA was distributed to basic needs in 1997. This is based on its broad definition (see column one). This is a slight drop from 35.7% in 1996. The government reported to the DAC that 0.3% was allocated to basic education and 1.7% for basic health, but these figures have not

Measuring aid for poverty reduction

The Netherlands	Poverty reduction, in the Dutch government's view, has a strong political dimension. Measurement of poverty reduction should therefore partly be the extent of materialisation of empowerment of the poor. Actions/policy targeting poverty reduction should aim at both institutional development and at increasing the quality of basic social services in developing countries. About 40 evaluations dealing with Dutch development programmes took place during 1997. These reports varied from country reviews to evaluating information material published by the Ministry of Development Cooperation.	0.9 (3.3)	1.7 (2.7)	4.3 (4.3)	been mentioned in publications available for the Japanese public. 1998:20%, 1999: 20%, and again 20% each year for the cabinet period up to 2002.
New Zealand[2]	No information has been received on progress in measuring aid for poverty eradication.	(0.1)	(0.7)	(0.5)	No new information received.
Norway	Norway's aid is mainly directed towards countries which actively pursue policies aimed at reducing poverty. Reporting on aid is being done according to the new DAC system. No monitoring mechanism is yet in place that specifically focuses on aid's impact on poverty; however, this year NORAD is introducing a new system for economic management, which is expected to improve general transparency.	3.7 (3.0)	2.2 (2.1)	0.0 (0.7)	In 1998, aid to the education sector increased to more than 11% of Norway's bilateral aid, and health was in the region of 10%. But aid to basic services in the areas of health, education and social measures amounted to 15% of bilateral aid the year before, and it had hardly reached the 20% mark in 1998.
Portugal	For the last two years, and after an audit of Portuguese cooperation, any projects and programmes connected, directly or indirectly, with poverty reduction were collated. Portugal is also a member of the DAC group for the evaluation of poverty reduction. The First Portuguese Cooperation Integrated Programme for 1999 has started collating information on all	0.7 (2.5)	1.1 (4.3)	7.4 (0.1)	Portugal's expenditure for basic education was 0.67% of bilateral ODA in 1998; basic health, including population and reproductive health 0.22% of bilateral ODA and water and sanitation 0.35%.

Measuring aid for poverty reduction

Country	Progress towards improvements in the measurement of aid for poverty reduction	Percentage of total ODA spent on basic social services			Most recent government estimate of aid to basic needs/poverty reduction
		Basic education 1997 (1996)	Basic health 1997 (1996)	Water and sanitation 1997 (1996)	
	projects/programmes being executed by the various ministries associated with overseas aid.				
Spain	No breakthroughs have been identified, and it has yet to be seen whether the Directive Plan will include concrete indicators to measure aid for poverty reduction. However, there is a feeling in the Development Community that classic indicators such as 20:20 or 0.15% of GNP are not sufficient to measure commitment to poverty reduction. The debate was initiated when the Government argued that all its institutional reform projects (mainly support for the settlement of fiscal systems) were in fact poverty-oriented aid and some academics agreed with them. The conclusion is a need for clearer indicators and a new information system.	1.3 (0.7)	4.7 (4.2)	0.0 (2.8)	There are no official figures available as yet, but a rough calculation is that 11.4% of Spanish bilateral ODA was devoted to basic social sectors.
Sweden	Poverty reduction is one of four main areas in Swedish ODA. Sida issued its programme on Poverty Reduction in 1996. The government itself issued the programme – 'The Rights of the Poor – Our common responsibility' passed by the parliament in 1998. This programme is now, according to the government, being translated into action. However, within the NGO community there are criticisms of what is considered too slow an implementation of this new programme into everyday practice.	5.1 (4.8)	5.2 (6.4)	1.2 (3.2)	Reporting on aid to direct poverty reduction is not clear. To some extent this has to do with the stance taken in 'The Rights of the Poor', that poverty reduction has more to do with empowering the poor and not so much to do with aid programmes for basic social needs. The DAC statistics, however, demonstrate an increasing and, relative to other donors, large amount of ODA spent on basic education, basic health and water and sanitation.

Measuring aid for poverty reduction

Switzerland	SDC has made a considerable effort to measure the impact of its interventions on poverty. A new statistical system was introduced in 1999 which should provide rough but more reliable estimates in future. FOFEA was not active in poverty reduction measurement.	(1.0)	(5.9)	1998 figures show that 18% of SDC's ODA had a direct impact on poverty, 46% had an indirect impact, 24% had no immediate impact, and 12 per cent remained uncoded. The reliability of these figures is doubtful, however, as there is much subjectivity and arbitrariness involved. FOFEA does not apply a poverty focused coding system at all.
United Kingdom	DFID's Policy Indicator Marking System (PIMS) has been revised and now has a tripartite structure which is designed to reflect the objectives of the Statement of Purpose, White Paper policy statements, and Government requirements. The markers are divided into: PIMS, PAMs (Poverty Aim Markers), and POMs (Poverty Objective Markers). PAMs indicate the relationship between the programme and poverty reduction. Programmes are labelled as having one of the following three functions – enabling actions which directly target pro-poor growth; inclusive actions which aim to benefit broad-based population groups; and actions that focus predominantly on the rights, interests and needs of poor people. POMs work by spenders indicating which one of DFID's three objectives is predominantly targeted by each individual project based on an assessment of the share of the commitment value directed to each objective.	1.2	1.0 Not reported	The most recent estimates of aid directed towards basic needs and direct poverty reduction (otherwise known as 'direct assistance to poor people') were: £287.1 million in 1997–98 out of a total aid budget of £2,292 million; and £192.3 million in 1996–97. In the Comprehensive Spending Review, DFID's programmes were reviewed to ensure that resources were focused on the overarching goal of eliminating poverty.
United States	USAID does not measure aid for poverty reduction as a whole and does not categorise its spending in this area. Annually, USAID field missions and US-based operating units prepare	1.1 (1.8)	3.3 0.7 (5.2) (1.6)	Approximately 25% of the foreign assistance budget is targeted to basic needs/direct poverty reduction.

Measuring aid for poverty reduction

Country	Progress towards improvements in the measurement of aid for poverty reduction	Percentage of total ODA spent on basic social services			Most recent government estimate of aid to basic needs/poverty reduction
		Basic education 1997 (1996)	Basic health 1997 (1996)	Water and sanitation 1997 (1996)	
	an 'R–4' evaluation report (Results, Review, and Resource Requests) to assess performance and progress towards strategic objectives and targets. There is a perception among many inside and outside the Agency that the system has resulted in an imbalance between reporting performance measurement as opposed to achieving meaningful development results. There is also a concern held by many USAID staff and implementing partner organisations (mostly US NGOs) that USAID is spending too much effort producing information that is of limited use to resource allocation and more general management decision making. Over the past year, the Agency has been working on a plan to streamline its performance, planning and monitoring systems.				

Note:
1 The percentages given in these columns show the total new commitments made in a year. Expenditure can be spread over many years so actual disbursements of aid for basic education, basic health and water/sanitation will include funds committed in previous years. At the time of writing, some donors had not reported their commitments, so the data is partial. The data is also, almost certainly, an underestimate since it only captures activities that have BSS as their primary purpose and omits the BSS components of larger sectoral programmes, multisector aid and , in some cases, aid through NGOs.
2 Figures for New Zealand are 1994 figures
Source: DAC Report 1998 Table 19, NGO questionnaires

Donor policies on basic education

Table 54 Donor policies and actions on basic education

Country	Specific policy commitments on education/basic education	When were these commitments made?	Development of implementation plan	Progress on implementation of plan	% education spent bilateral and % via multilateral organisations	Involvement in Sectoral-wide approaches to education
Australia	AusAID introduced a new education policy in 1996 which gives greater focus to basic and vocational education and emphasises greater equity in access to education and capacity building in the area. The policy does not, however, include any specific funding targets. Traditionally the agency has devoted most of its education funds to tertiary scholarships in Australia.	1996	AusAID is actively implementing the new policy through its Education Policy Group and through the development of new country strategies.	Funding for basic education has more than doubled since 1995/96 and now represents about 4.5% of total aid disbursements. Equity is increasing in the allocation of scholarships.	A tentative estimate is that 70% of education aid is bilateral. However, some projects are run in cooperation with multilateral institutions but not channelled through them.	AusAID is involved in sectoral approaches to education in Papua New Guinea and the Pacific countries where Australia is a relatively significant donor.
Austria	In 1999 the Department for Development Cooperation adopted an Education Sector Policy which now includes basic education as one of the main areas of work – apart from the education levels that have been traditionally funded (vocational training, academic-vocationally oriented education and training in science and technology). At all levels mentioned, measures focusing on institutional and capacity building are prioritised with the aim of supporting the reform of education systems.	1999			Figures for the percentage of education spending channelled multilaterally are not available. Approximately 17% of bilateral ODA was spent on education in 1997 but this excludes spending where education is part of an integrated programme. The DDC has started to work on the improvement of data on its educational work – both	The DDC is currently involved in sectoral approaches to education in two of its priority countries – Cape Verde and Burkina Faso – although in Burkina Faso it is vocational education only.

Donor policies on basic education

Country	Specific policy commitments on education/basic education	When were these commitments made?	Development of implementation plan	Progress on implementation of plan	% education spent bilateral and % via multilateral organisations	Involvement in Sectoral-wide approaches to education
					quantitative and qualitative.	
Belgium	Although Belgium has not made specific budgetary commitments to (basic) education, it is one of the five priority sectors in which aid will be concentrated. After a considerable decrease in the early 1990s, the percentage of aid for education is now more or less stable, with the basic education share increasing.	With the presentation of the 1999 budget in December 1998. It was also stated in more general terms in the policy paper of December 1997.	The strategic paper on the education sector is being completed and is awaiting ministerial endorsement.	A rather slow but clear move towards the new policy.	This is currently difficult to disaggregate as much of the education spending through multilaterals takes place within multisector programmes. It should also be noted that a considerable amount of bilateral education spending goes through NGOs and universities.	Involvement in sectoral approaches is being prepared, by information notes for aid officials. Involvement is envisaged in Uganda, Niger, Burkina Faso and Mali for the period 1998–2000.
Canada	CIDA currently does not have any specific policy commitments for basic education in place. It is included under Basic Human Needs to which the Government is committed to allocating 25% of Canadian ODA; however, the bilateral Africa /Middle East Branch is committed to allocating 30% of its funds to Basic Human Needs.	The commitment to Basic Human Needs was made in the policy outcomes of the Foreign Policy Review in 1995. It was subsequently expanded upon in a CIDA policy for Basic Human Needs adopted in 1997.	CIDA Policy Branch is currently under-taking intensive and wide consultations, leading to the elaboration of a Basic Education Strategy for the agency in the Spring of 2000. As part of this process, a CIDA	A recent review of CIDA's Basic Human Needs programming noted that CIDA's bilateral programmes had done little to date in the area of primary and secondary education; however, there have been a number of individual projects whose goals are the	CICC calculates CIDA's disbursements for 1997/98 as follows: bilateral US$33m, NGOs US$7m, multilateral US$10m, for a total of US$50m. The DAC statistics for Canada on basic education are misleading due	In general Canada does not participate directly in any sectoral approach for education. One possible exception is South Africa where Canadian and other donor commitments to education are closely coordinated by the Ministry for Education. It is felt that in some circumstances the cost associated with ongoing

Donor policies on basic education

	...education specialist is putting together a series of forums with experts and practitioners in the education field.	promotion of basic education. UNICEF, Canadian NGOs and other institutions have been the most important delivery channels for basic education programming.	to a difference in reporting methods.		country/donor dialogue seems to outweigh the resources available. In addition there is a degree of political pressure to assure country visibility through distinct Canadian contributions to projects.
Denmark	Within the education sector, Denmark focuses mainly on basic education. However, it feels it should include different levels such as pre-school education, secondary school and informal education and has pushed for support to levels other than formal primary education for children. Generally, Danida is not willing to support operational expenditure, but focuses on the development of educational materials, capacity building within Ministries of Education and restoration of schools.	Denmark's policy has been developed over the last decade. Commitments have also been made in the follow up process from Jomtien.	Aid is given through a sector programme approach, and in the particular countries where the educational sector has been selected for support; plans are being developed as an integral part of the recipient government plans for the education sector. Plans are also made in cooperation with other donors working in the same sector. Great emphasis is put on keeping the recipient government as the 'owner' of the process.	Progress is being made steadily. It is, however, a time-consuming process with many partners involved. As Danida has a policy of working in one social sector only within a given country, it does mean that if it is already working in the health sector, education is automatically precluded.	Truly disaggregated figures are not available. Overall, 50.7% of Danish aid is spent bilaterally, and 46% multilaterally. Within bilateral aid, 10.2% was spent on education in 1998. Within multilateral aid, 4.5% went to UNICEF with emphasis on children at risk, and 1% to UNESCO with emphasis on education.	In five out of 20 recipient countries the educational sector has been chosen as a sector for support. In the majority of them a plan for sectoral programme support has been developed; in the rest it is being developed in cooperation with other donors and the recipient government.
Finland	Basic education and education in general are strategic branches of development cooperation.	The November 1996 Decision in Principle and the	There are plans for implementing basic education	Progress on implementing the programmes has	There are no figures available for the percentage of	Finland is working towards sector-wide programmes. In a number

Donor policies on basic education

Country	Specific policy commitments on education/basic education	When were these commitments made?	Development of implementation plan	Progress on implementation of plan	% education spent bilateral and % via multilateral organisations	Involvement in Sectoral-wide approaches to education
		October 1998 Policy on Relations with Developing Countries.	programmes in Ethiopia, Mozambique, Tanzania, Zambia, Nepal, Palestine, Nicaragua.	been good and has received added impetus in the form of new agreements, for example with Tanzania and Nepal, to focus especially on basic education and some additional funding.	spending channelled through multilateral organisations; however, the percentages spent bilaterally are: 1997 education (total) 8% basic education 3% 1998 (provisional) education (total) 6% basic education 4.2%.	of countries Finland has adopted a two-level approach with the bulk of support going via traditional project types, but additionally some 'seed money' has been allocated for the sectoral process.
France	France has no obvious specific plan to make basic education a priority.			French cooperation is more concerned with basic education than in previous years when most of the aid for education was spent on universities and secondary education. However, there is little in the way of budgetary commitments.		
Germany	There is a commitment to increase support for basic education and education in general directed towards girls and women.	The coalition agreement of October 1998.	So far, no specific principles or guidelines for implementation have been issued.	BMZ support for basic education has declined continuously in recent years. However, the new government has raised the share of	While support to basic education rises, overall funds for education will decline compared to previous schedules. The new figure is 9% (DM	The BMZ at present rejects the concept of pooled funding for sector programmes where ongoing activities in social

Donor policies on basic education

Ireland	A priority for Irish Aid is support to education which assists partner countries in increasing access to basic education and ensuring that the quality of education provided is such that it enables people to participate fully in society. Ireland has repeated its commitment to poverty eradication through a focus on basic education at many international forums.	The last two Annual Reports from Irish Aid have stated that basic education is a cornerstone of Irish Aid policy. Irish Aid is developing an overview of Irish Aid and education entitled 'Irish Aid Education Policy and Guidelines' which will be available in October 1999.	Ireland is involved in sectoral approaches to education in Ethiopia, Mozambique, Uganda, Tanzania and Zambia.	Direct spending on education now stands at approximately 20% of the Irish Aid budget for priority countries, and approximately 82% of this is spent on basic education.	Irish Aid has become involved in sector-wide approaches to education which allow Ireland to impact on macro-economic, structural and social policy and planning in the area of education. The sector-wide approaches also provide significant gains in terms of donor coordination thus ensuring that Irish Aid expenditure on education is efficient and effective.
Italy	Italian cooperation is traditionally weak in the basic education sector. More activities are being funded for professional training and university education. The promotion of basic education is also included in the guidelines for interventions concerning childhood.	Guidelines on childhood issued by the Board of the Directorate-General for Development Cooperation (DGCS) of November 1998.	There is no specific implementation plan for basic education; however, it is a focus in the human development programme. Education and professional training – either as specific sector policy or as a part of multisectoral actions – is included in the cooperation	No data available	Italy does not participate in sector-wide approaches for basic education.

bilateral commitments million 281.7). The resources for education going to multilateral institutions or programmes is not known.

going to basic education to 3.8% (DM million 115).

services such as education or health. BMZ staff fear that effectiveness and efficiency of resource use cannot be adequately monitored in such cases. Furthermore, current administrative regulations in Germany act against pooled funding since it requires the earmarking of funds for specific projects.

Donor policies on basic education

Country	Specific policy commitments on education/basic education	When were these commitments made?	Development of implementation plan	Progress on implementation of plan	% education spent bilateral and % via multilateral organisations	Involvement in Sectoral-wide approaches to education
				sectors that have to be evaluated in the period 1997–99		
Japan	The New ODA mid-term policy emphasises the following: assistance in curriculum development and teacher training; aid to residents into project implementation; and active working relations with NGOs.	The Government announced the five-year ODA mid-term policy in August 1999.	Implementation plans are being prepared and agencies in charge are to be announced.	No information available due to the new policy.	No information available due to the new policy.	No information available due to the new policy.
The Netherlands	As a result of the debates in Parliament on basic social services, the Dutch government has increased its budget for basic education over the years. Nonetheless, at 175 million guilders, the basic education budget remains very limited compared with the 300 million guilder budget for higher education.	At the presentation of the 1999 budget.	The emphasis is on the quality and need for reform of national education systems, making them accessible and relevant for the whole population. The Dutch government stresses the need for ownership of these reforms by recipient governments. It therefore looks to national governments to manage and take responsibility for implementing these reforms.	The programme proposals for education are screened, both qualitatively and quantitatively, on their gender sensitivity. Programmes funded by the Dutch government should both support access of women to schools and completion rates by women.	During the 1990s an increase in funds for basic education has been witnessed. In 1999 2.5% is budgeted bilaterally (175 million guilders), 1% multilaterally (65 million guilders and 1% through non-governmental organisations (like Novib – 63 million guilders). The percentages of multilateral and the NGO channel are estimates.	Increasingly the Dutch government's emphasis is on financing through (sub) sectoral budget support or co-financing with the World Bank or other bilateral and multilateral donors. The Dutch government supports those countries that are willing to spend considerable funds which means that it provides those countries with programme or sectoral budget support as opposed to project support.
New Zealand	NZODA Policy Framework identifies education and human resource	The current policy framework was	Achieving a shift towards provision of	Although no formal implementation plan	Figures not available	NZODA is not involved in formal sectoral

Donor policies on basic education

	development as being central to the achievement of the aims of the programme. The bulk of education spending is on tertiary scholarships and vocational training in an attempt to redress skill shortages in partner countries. Despite this, NZODA is beginning to focus more on basic education needs.	developed in 1995 and revised in 1998.	increased resources for basic education has not been easy and the Ministry for Foreign Affairs and Trade is currently undertaking an evaluation of education support to examine the barriers and identify strategies for increasing support for basic education.	is in place there have been significant shifts towards increased support for basic education in bilateral and regional programmes.	approaches but does have strong informal networks. The administration participates in coordination and collaboration at project level in some instances.
Norway	The Norwegian Government has committed itself to increase the support for education to 10% of ODA before year 2000 with a further increase to 15% in the following years. The funding for basic education will primarily be directed to Africa and women's and girl's education is a priority.	These commitments were made in a White Paper passed in 1997 and prepared by the Labour Government of that time; however the same objectives are shared by the new coalition.	The Government has no detailed general plan for implementing education projects or programmes as implementation is decentralised and planned in close cooperation with national authorities.	NORAD has established a project for the social sector called The Social Sector Initiative which has an overall responsibility to develop a policy and a strategy that ensures coherence and coordination between the various projects in the social sector, as well as between multi- and bilateral initiatives contributed to by Norway.	The Norwegian Ministry of Foreign Affairs has earmarked additional funds of NOK70 millions for education purposes. The funds are channelled through NGOs, national and regional networks and multilaterals, including the World Bank. Bilaterally the percentage is approximately 10%. Multilaterally no figures are available at present. Norway is involved in sectoral approaches to education in several different countries. Among these are Ethiopia, Zambia, Pakistan, Tanzania, Nepal, and Uganda.
Portugal	There is no specific policy or commitment to basic education.				About 9% of Portugal's bilateral

Donor policies on basic education

Country	Specific policy commitments on education/basic education	When were these commitments made?	Development of implementation plan	Progress on implementation of plan	% education spent bilateral and % via multilateral organisations	Involvement in Sectoral-wide approaches to education
	However, Portugal does consider that education for all is one of the principle weapons in the fight against poverty.				aid is spent on education.	
Spain	No specific commitments have been made on this issue. As regards general education, Spain participated in the Jomtien Conference, so it implicitly accepted the objectives and commitments made there. As part of the DAC, it has also recognised the objectives included in *Shaping the 21st Century*. Although no concrete percentages have been settled as part of the 20:20 Initiative however, there are demands to allocate 8% of bilateral ODA to basic education before the year 2002.	Jomtien in 1990. *Shaping the 21st Century* in 1996, The World Social Summit in Copenhagen 1995.	One of the main problems affecting Spanish ODA to education in general and basic education in particular is the lack of a specific plan or strategy in this direction. Changes are expected in the Directive Plan which will be approved later this year.	In the year 1995, ODA to basic education underwent a large increase, Since then figures have remained mostly stable. During the approval process for the Directive Plan more specific benchmarks to meet particular targets towards the goal of 8% will be put forward.	Bilateral aid to basic education increased from 0.5% in 1994 to 2.3% in 1995. Multilateral figures are not available.	The Spanish Government is involved in a debt swap for education in Mozambique. Having sold to a Spanish NGO (Intermón) 17 million US$ at 8% of its nominal price, the operation will result in a basic education projects bag of about 3.5 million dollars. The identification of the projects has been done together with the Mozambican Government.
Sweden	Sweden shares the commitment of the 1990 World Conference on 'Education for All' at Jomtien to meet the basic learning needs for all people – children, youth and adults.	The commitments were made in 1990 at Jomtien and in different policy papers thereafter. In January 1996 Sida published new 'Guidelines for cooperation in basic education and education reform', replacing the old guidelines which had	In line with the World Declaration for All, Sweden has developed three main objectives for development cooperation on basic education: to support reform processes; to raise the quality of education at the basic level and to	No real evaluation has yet been made of the implementation of the plan.	No statistics available.	Sweden has been increasingly interested in sector programme support, in cooperation with other donors and the World Bank. In such programmes, the aim is to integrate all contributions to education programmes within a framework provided by a national education policy and implementation plan. Sida

Donor policies on basic education

(continued)		been in operation since 1986.	support the provision of basic education services for previously neglected groups and in previously neglected geographical areas.			participates at present in such joint-financed education programmes in Bolivia and is also involved in the preparation for such support in Mozambique, Tanzania and Ethiopia.
Switzerland	There are only commitments on a country and project level within a long-term perspective.	Not applicable as the focus depends on individual country programming.	Implementation plans are developed only if the commitment is part of country programming priorities.	No information is available.		Switzerland has not adopted sector-wide approaches in basic education. Coordination is ensured by the partner governments when SDC is supporting nationally run schools. SDC feels that a sector approach for informal education is not appropriate.
UK	DFID has stated its commitment to achieving the DAC target of universal primary education by 2005. In line with the commitment to poverty targets, DFID has recently made significant commitments to education programmes in Ghana (£51 million) and Uganda (£67 million) and is giving increased commitment to education. Global development assistance to primary education has increased by over 50% during the 1990s.	1997	At a country level, DFID has stated its commitment to working with governments and other major partners in the development of education policies and strategies and a goal strategy paper is under preparation which will focus on how to improve education for the poor.	According to the Departmental Report: the UK has pledged to increase support for basic health care, education and clean water in Africa by 50%.	DFID cannot give exact demarcations. In the widest sense education received 25% of bilateral spending in 1997–98. It is harder to compute multilateral spending since 16% of the EU budget comes from the UK. Overall, 3% of ODA, or £215 million, was spent on education last year. In 1998 DFID substantially increased the share	DFID has taken a lead in sector-wide approaches to education. It has adopted such approaches in East Africa, Ghana, Ethiopia, Zambia, Malawi, Mozambique, India and Pakistan.

Donor policies on basic education

Country	Specific policy commitments on education/basic education	When were these commitments made?	Development of implementation plan	Progress on implementation of plan	% education spent bilateral and % via multilateral organisations	Involvement in Sectoral-wide approaches to education
					of aid allocated to basic education as well as the absolute level of funding.	
USA	Pursuant to the Government Performance Results Act, USAID issued its Strategic Plan in 1997. This plan establishes six USAID goals under each of which is a framework of objectives and programme approaches. Performance goals are spelled out for each goal. Goal 3 calls for 'Human capacity built through education and training'.	USAID's commitment to basic education stems from the Strategic Plan adopted in September 1997.	USAID's main object-ive in improving basic education is to increase human productive capacity. Four performance goals have been established to support this goal: 1 The proportion of primary school-age population that is not enrolled should be reduced by 50% by 2007; 2 gender disparity in primary enrol-ment should be eliminated by 2007; 3 primary school completion rates should be improved 4 higher education enrolment should be increased.	USAID has 20 country programmes involved in basic education. One vehicle for education is the Girls' and Women's Education Initiative launched in 1995. USAID recognises that education of girls is strongly related to social and economic development and this initiative aims at decision makers in developing countries to find solutions to lower barriers to girls' education and mobilise resources to provide opportunities for girls in six countries.	Data not available.	Data not available.

Source: NGO Questionnaires

Table 55 Donor approaches to gender

Country	Status of gender policy and way that it is incorporated into aid strategies	Action to implement DAC guidelines on gender equality	The influence of gender on development thinking
Australia	Australia's Aid Commitment Policy Statement was announced by the Minister for Foreign Affairs March 1997 and includes a system of gender and development markers. There are continuing criticisms of the depth and consistency of AusAID's commitment to gender issues, but staff in the organisation have continued to work towards more effective and consistent application of the gender policy.	AusAID has been an active player in the development and implementation of the DAC guidelines with gender and environment being identified as the two major cross-cutting issues in all priority sectors. All current AusAID staff have been trained in gender and development issues and new staff are trained as they join.	AusAID has recently appointed a GAD advisor and she has been inundated with requests from project staff for advice. Many staff appear to be very keen to incorporate gender issues more fully in their work and expenditure on projects with a direct gender component has increased from A$34.5 m in 1998/99 to A$43.3 m in 99/00. It is also understood that recent DAC sector reviews on health, education and environment have noted a high level of gender sensitivity in Australia's aid programme and that significant improvements in the gender equity of Australia's tertiary scholarship programme are also starting to emerge.
Austria	Gender is claimed as an aim of the overall aid strategy.	A series of criteria has been developed for the assignment of gender markers in the DAC statistics.	In 1997 a consultant for gender was employed and since then gender has been more systematically included in the design of country programmes. Gender relevant programmes and projects are monitored regularly by the consultant.
Belgium	In August 1998, a strategic paper was published, and in February 1999 a report on gender was introduced in parliament. The latter indicates the way gender policy statements are not only increasingly integrated in strategic papers as an overall objective, but also gradually being translated into practice. However, the gender unit at BADC has not been enlarged nor does it have its own financial resources.	Considering there is only the equivalent of 1.5 people in the gender unit at the administration, much has actually been achieved. Included in a report to parliament is the incorporation of the gender element in strategic papers; introducing gender within the project management and evaluation process; follow up of specific projects and making gender visible in the budget and in ODA statistics as for example, the DAC 'marker on gender equality'.	As a result of the BADC gender unit, gender-awareness has now been established at least in people's minds, in policy notes, strategic papers and terms of reference for evaluation. However, much still remains to be done in order to make it visible in daily practice.
Canada	In 1999 a new Gender Equality Policy was published and CIDA has been a leader among	CIDA's Gender Equality Policy responds directly to the challenges to donors posed in the DAC	The 1996 Performance Review (published in 1998) commends CIDA for strengthening the

Donor approaches to gender

Country	Status of gender policy and way that it is incorporated into aid strategies	Action to implement DAC guidelines on gender equality	The influence of gender on development thinking
	donors in addressing gender policy dimensions of development cooperation since its first policy guidelines in 1976. A Performance Review of its gender policy published in 1998 points to some success but also raises a number of concerns regarding the mainstreaming of gender policies in CIDA. A review of projects reveals that bilateral projects where women are the prime beneficiaries increased from less than 1% in 1986/87 to 3.5% in 1994/95. In a review of CIDA programme performance in 1997/98, however, only 5% of total programme expenditures were coded to 'Women in Development and Gender Equity'. While serious limitations in the coding system under-report this priority these numbers clearly suggest that attention to the feminisation of poverty and women's rights seem marginal to CIDA's core programming.	Guidelines on Gender. It makes a substantial link between gender equality and poverty reduction and sets out examples of gender equality results for the six CIDA programming priorities. The policy provides guidelines for the practical application of gender analysis. The Policy sets out an outline of strategies and activities to support gender equality for policy dialogue, country programming frameworks, economic and sectoral programme assistance, capacity building, and bilateral, multilateral and Canadian partnership programmes and projects. The Gender Equality Division of Policy Branch will be establishing baseline benchmarks for the policy during 1999 to allow future assessment of progress in realising the policy goal and objectives.	institutional capacities but concludes that CIDA's policy 'does not inform the development action and decisions of CIDA as broadly as it should' and 'it is neither embedded nor incorporated into current corporate planning and reporting'. After 20 years of policies relating to gender issues, there is still significant misunderstanding of the implications of the policy and resistance to applying it to all development initiatives. Accountability is a key concern. Similar to the poverty policy, implementation 'depends on individual initiative (rather than professional accountability)' and 'there are few rewards for innovative work in WID and Gender Equity programming'. In response to the Performance Review, the 1999 Gender Equity Policy provides clearer objectives and strategies to translate these objectives into practice, with a commitment to monitor results.
Denmark	Danida's WID policy was first formulated in 1987 and revised in 1993. The overall aim of Danish development policy is gender specific poverty reduction – meaning that any work for poverty reduction has to be based on the different roles and needs of men and women. What is lagging behind in Danida is not gender policy, but implementation and mainstreaming. Danida is undergoing a process of monitoring implementation of the gender policy and continues developing new tools and training courses for this.	The Ministry of Foreign Affairs reports that efforts will be made to implement the DAC Gender Action Plan and Denmark will continue its active participation in the DAC expert group on women's empowerment and gender equality. Danida constantly develops its own tools for gender analysis and practices with a focus on women's empowerment and gender equality.	An evaluation of WID in Danish aid from 1994 showed that only a few projects were WID-specific, and that WID had not been integrated in the majority of the Danida projects and a policy for mainstreaming gender in Danish aid was therefore created. The implementation of the policy is still weak, but work is going on to train personnel and develop tools. The sectoral programme approach poses new challenges, opportunities and threats to mainstreaming gender and national women organisations in recipient countries will have a major role to play in promoting gender sensitive national policies and equal rights and opportunities for men and women.

Donor approaches to gender

Finland	The new policy line on relations with developing countries does not advance the DIDC/Foreign Ministry's handling of gender. The lack of input on gender in a policy which otherwise aims to take a fully integrated and coherent approach to development cooperation in the context of globalisation is startling, and reflects the neglect this 'cross-sectoral' issue receives within the DIDC, despite certain non-policy oriented initiatives taken on gender, such as expert studies and training events.	The reorganisation of statistical data in the DIDC along DAC guidelines has still to result in usable information on the gender and WID content of cooperation.	Although the concepts of gender and gender analysis are well known amongst staff, integrating these into the project planning and implementation requires continual training. Even though the Finnish guidelines have already required the use of sex disaggregated data in all project documents for some time, this advice is often poorly followed. The DIDC reports that in 1998 15.8% of all bilateral commitments were WID-integrated in a broad sense, and that 0.6% were WID-specific. This information is unreliable, however, because of the imprecise methods of assessing commitments. DIDC has noone currently working on gender but the department has been drawing on outside expertise to assess various aspects including the (as yet unrealised) commitment to gender mainstreaming.
France	Although there are no precise figures, France appears to be gradually integrating gender into its development policies. However, there is no significant change over last year.		
Germany	The new leadership of the BMZ (the minister and the parliamentary state secretary are both women)has put strong emphasis on gender issues. Girls and women are mentioned as a special target group in the coalition agreement. The minister is particularly committed to the fight against female genital mutilation.	The German government is contributing to the Gender and Development Committee of the DAC, contributing knowledge on macro-economics and gender. The DAC Guidelines have been distributed to 60 GTZ offices and 100 projects.	So far, there has been no systematic effort to evaluate the gender dimension within the BMZ's self-help oriented poverty projects.
Ireland	From the outset, Irish Aid has viewed the role of women as a central issue in all aspects of development cooperation. Gender is now an integral part of all Irish Aid projects, from planning to implementation, monitoring and evaluation. Formalised Gender Guidelines, adopted in 1996, set the context.	Irish Aid has an integrated gender dimension in all projects. There are also projects with a specific focus on women. As part of the Joint Donor Government reviews of the education programmes in Tanzania and Mozambique, Irish Aid employed a consultant on gender and submitted a report on gender within programmes.	The recent (1999) DAC Peer Review of Ireland's aid programme in Uganda, stated that '...gender concerns are integrated into programme activities'. However, the Report also states that '...there is scope for sharpening the focus on gender equality objectives with district partners'.

Donor approaches to gender

Country	Status of gender policy and way that it is incorporated into aid strategies	Action to implement DAC guidelines on gender equality	The influence of gender on development thinking
Italy	The 'Guidelines on the role of women and on the promotion of a gender perspectives' established by the Directorate-General for Development Cooperation (DGCS) in 1998 have, as their main objective, 'the promotion of male and female participation, as individuals of equal dignity, in the definition of sustainable development'. The DGCS intends to adopt gender perspectives in the conception, planning and implementation of all cooperation activities and in the definition and implementation of cooperation policies. Particular attention is given during the monitoring and evaluation phases and in the definition of development indicators.	The Italian aid administration considers the DAC guidelines on gender equality and women's empowerment as priority activities. The Italian government intends 'to realise initiatives promoting women's full participation in the decision-making process at all levels and to enhance the gender perspective in political, economic, cultural field and in poverty eradication and conflict prevention activities.	There still is resistance among officials and in order to promote gender perspectives, it has been agreed to enhance the role of gender experts, to adopt innovative methodologies for planning activities, to encourage greater awareness and to train the internal and external aid administration operators.
Japan	The government announced the 1995 Women In Development Initiatives and continuously focuses on three areas including education, health, and economic and social participation. The mid-term policy states assistance on the areas of family planning, micro-financing, job training and improvement in working conditions.	The new ODA mid-term policy makes it necessary for both men and women to participate equally in the process of development in order to achieve balanced and sustainable development in LDCs.	As JICA has played an active role in promoting gender consideration, the number of both staff and projects in Women in Development has been constantly increasing for the past nine years (the available data is from 1990 to 1998).
The Netherlands[1]	Gender equality and women's autonomy are officially a priority for development cooperation. The WID Division of the Ministry of Foreign Affairs is implementing several pilot projects to contribute to operational policy development based on the priority themes of the Beijing Platform for Action. Gender issues are also to be mainstreamed at two levels: in the Ministry at policy level and at country level through a network of twenty gender specialists in embassies.	Gender equality has been adopted as a strategic objective. In practice however, the process of mainstreaming is not easy. An important evaluation of the effects of ten years of Dutch WID policies showed that despite progress in terms of women's participation in the execution of projects and relative increases in the amounts of aid reaching women, development assistance still discriminates between men and women and fails to reach the poorest women. An important conclusion is that strong policy support is needed to keep Women and	Work on mainstreaming gender has focused on macroeconomic issues, sectoral approaches, multilateral cooperation and gender policy. Selected policy themes from Beijing are being operationalised in four clusters: 1 Women's rights (including violence against women, reproductive health rights, access to water) aimed at developing quality criteria and influencing government and donor policy. 2 Contribution of women to conflict prevention and solution based on the experience and

Donor approaches to gender

Donor			
		Development high on the policy agenda. The evaluation noted positive results in terms of human resources, gender experts in the field and Ministry and the availability of a special WID fund. There are eight full time staff members in the WID Division of the Ministry. The budget is 40 million guilders of which 33 m is spent at country level. Remaining funds are used to develop and operationalise policy and support multilateral and regional activities.	perspectives of women involved in peace processes. 3 Poverty alleviation aimed at developing best practice for gender and micro credit, and gender and the role of the private sector. 4 The participation of women in policy decision making and good government.
New Zealand	NZODA is seen by DAC to have some effective methods for mainstreaming gender from a donor perspective which 'are worth sharing with other donors'. Policy dialogue on gender issues is common in programme discussions and a number of partner countries have agreed gender strategy papers.	A gender policy is in place and operational. The approach is very structured with gender being an integral part of policy, action plans, monitoring and reviews. There are gender policy 'markers' on policy approvals and gender 'prompts' are integrated into model Terms of Reference. There is ongoing training for staff, consultants and NGOs on gender issues.	DAC conducted an evaluation in 1998 which showed positive progress is being made. Significant progress has been made in the area of scholarships where 50% women targets have been met in many countries.
Norway	The aid administration has taken some initial steps towards implementing the DAC guidelines but the DAC system will not be operational before year 2000.	In 1997 The Norwegian Ministry of Foreign Affairs presented its Strategy for Women and Gender Equality in Development Cooperation. It states that mainstreaming a gender perspective at all levels in aid and international development cooperation is an official Norwegian policy and based on this document, NORAD have developed an Action Plan and a Handbook. The gender focus is on agriculture and ground level education, to ensure women's rights within these sectors. The focus within education is towards agricultural education and the priorities within agricultural aid are subsistence and food security. NORAD is also working together with the Institute of Women's Law at the University of Oslo towards educating lawyers and officers within the state administration, on the subject of the strength of women's law according to the UN Women's convention.	NORAD are continuously doing evaluations where the gender issue is implemented, and particularly on women's access to credit, evaluations have shown good results within the projects.

Donor approaches to gender

Country	Status of gender policy and way that it is incorporated into aid strategies	Action to implement DAC guidelines on gender equality	The influence of gender on development thinking
Portugal	Portugal participates in the DAC/OECD Working Group for Gender Equality, and at the CPLP (Portuguese speaking countries) level there as been a groundswell for women's rights. Portugal has also been following the debates within the Working Group for Poverty and Social Policy at the World Bank on Gender Equality. Portuguese cooperation is still in a phase of reconstruction and many aspects are still awaiting clarification. However, it is considered that Portugal has already shown a commitment to gender issues in the creation of the gender equality desk.	Gender equality is implicit in all the actions promoted and supported by Portugal.	There are currently no evaluations that permit a conclusion as to how gender has influenced development thinking and practice.
Spain	In 1997, 750 million pesetas were devoted to gender projects, 6% of total bilateral ODA. Gender has been included in the Directive Plan proposal as one of the three cross-cutting sectors for projects carried out by Spanish ODA. However, it has yet to be seen as to how this will translate into implementation.	The Spanish Agency for International Cooperation (AECI – official executive development agency) has recently employed a specialist on gender issues. As yet, no specific strategies have been settled in relation to this issue; major improvements are not expected for the moment.	There are no assessments which provide any information as to how gender has affected development thinking and practice.
Sweden	Since the end of 1998 issues of gender equality are no longer handled separately but come under the auspices of the Policy Division, which works in an integrated way on three prioritised areas: Poverty Eradication, Economic Growth and Gender Equality. On the basis of the 1997 'Action Programme for Promoting equality Between Women and Men in Partner Countries', each department and division prepare separate Action Plans. The Policy Division continues to produce high quality thematic documents on gender issues and also finances thematic studies of strategic	The promotion of gender equality was already set as one of four prioritised issues within Sida in 1995. It was followed by the establishment of the new overall goal in 1996 and the integration of the gender equality issue into Sida's Policy Division in 1998. The Swedish goal of Gender Equality is in line with the DAC guidelines endorsed in 1997, but the DAC guidelines have no official status within Sida's work.	Sida has not yet developed a comprehensive system to collect relevant information or economic data that would give a true picture as to the extent to which the gender equality policy is implemented within the organisation, or what impact this policy has had in the aid-receiving countries.

importance and gives financial support to organisations doing research on the gender aspects of international trade and macro economy. New kinds of Gender Country Profiles are being produced, the main difference being that the macroeconomic and legal aspects are emphasised whilst issues such as health and education are mentioned as part of the poverty complex. As part of the mainstreaming strategy a gender sensitive version of the Logical Framework Approach is used for planning and evaluation within Sida.

Switzerland	The revision of the SDC concept of 'gender-balanced development' has been postponed as the basic principles are still valid. This revision is more of an update and extension than a complete change of direction. Steps to implement the policy are being undertaken by the different SDC organisational units, mainly by the department of bilateral cooperation and Eastern Europe, with the support of the SDC gender unit. In addition to the gender unit, in some of the geographical divisions and SDC coordination field offices there are individuals who have responsibility for gender issues as part of a wider portfolio.	SDC participates in the DAC working party on Gender Equality and endorses the DAC guidelines. Their implementation is taken seriously. No additional steps have been taken as the SDC gender strategy is already in line with the DAC guidelines. FOFEA, however, does not treat gender relations as a priority.	Assessments of selected experiences are being finalised and efforts are being made to include gender in evaluations. There are new initiatives such as regional exchanges and networking. Gender training has been a key resource for many years.
United Kingdom	The White Paper states that gender equality is an 'integral and essential' part of its development approach and commits DFID to help reach the DAC target to eliminate gender disparity in primary and secondary education by 2005. DFID has taken a proactive role in a dialogue with government on gender policy issues to try to mainstream gender in domestic policy thinking. It also supports the	In 1997–99 DFID approved 124 new activities worth £266 million, which held gender equality as a principal or significant objective. This year an evaluation study of DFID's gender work is to be completed in order to get a firmer grip on the benefits of assistance in this area. DFID is continuing its twin-track approach to gender and development to promote gender equality in as many of its mainstream activities as it can. This	The Social Development Division and the Evaluations Department have undertaken a number of evaluations of gender policy in the last year aimed at gauging to what extent gender policies are being implemented and incorporated in projects. DFID also undertook a rapid review in 1998 to gauge the extent to which gender was taken into account in its overall programme evaluation reports. The conclusion was that

Donor approaches to gender

Country	Status of gender policy and way that it is incorporated into aid strategies	Action to implement DAC guidelines on gender equality	The influence of gender on development thinking
	efforts of multilaterals stressing that gender evaluation must be a part of the review of donor poverty work being undertaken for the OECD and DAC Poverty Network. DFID realises that the interests and needs of women must be systematically pursued in the formulation of all government policies and programmes, but recognises that it has not done enough to support this.	approach attempts to address inequalities between men and women in all of the strategic areas of DFID's work while supporting specific initiatives to enhance women's empowerment.	gender has not been sufficiently integrated into the project implementation or the evaluation process. At present DFID is undertaking a thematic evaluation of gender within its development programme which will involve evaluating CSPs and specific projects within them. Finally, DFID is preparing an internal website to give guidance to employees on how to incorporate gender awareness throughout DFID policy.
USA	In 1973, the US Congress passed the 'Percy Amendment' which directed foreign aid efforts to consider women's productive as well as reproductive roles and to assess the impact of projects on women. A governmental review in 1993 indicated that progress had been minimal. As a result of the review and the momentum of the Fourth World Women's Conference, in March 1996 the Administrator of USAID announced a new Gender Action Plan as 'an Agency-wide blueprint designed to ensure that gender considerations are institutionalised through USAID development programmes and projects' which includes more than fifteen specific actions. Among federal department and agencies, USAID has one of the only plans for addressing gender equity in programmes and organisational structures, rather than focusing on special programmes or services for women.		In January 1999, USAID issued an internal review of the Gender Action Plan, which reported gains in the impact of field programmes on girls and women and in incorporating gender in the agency's R–4 (Results, Review, and Resource Request) process. As a means to gather broader perspectives on the Plan's implementation, the Advisory Committee on Voluntary Foreign Aid (ACVFA) has contracted a consultant to carry out an independent review to be completed by the end of 1999.

Source: NGO Reality of Aid questionnaires

Table 56 Political and public opinion in donor countries

Country	Public attitudes to aid and poverty	Building public commitment
Australia	No new survey since June 1998 when 84% of respondents approved of Australia giving overseas aid, while 78% said that the government should spend the same or more than they currently spend. 36% of Australians said that the government should spend more.	AusAID and Australian aid NGOs have begun to work more closely together to assess opinion and to inform the Australian community about aid and development. Total AusAID funding for this area will grow from A$1.3m in 1998/99 to A$1.8m in 1999/2000. Total fundraising by Australian aid NGOs increased 8% in real terms between 1997 and 1998.
Austria	Opinion polls attest a constantly positive attitude towards development cooperation (around 80%). However, compared to other EU countries the percentage of those against development cooperation is also high (around 10%).	Development Information, Public Relations and Education have become important issues in Austria's development policy. The DDC has outsourced the task of promoting a broader public awareness of development cooperation to KommEnt – the Society for Communication and Development. On behalf of DDC KommEnt supports NGO initiatives in development information and education. An information office for development cooperation has been established and an informal working group has been set up to discuss the issue of public support scientifically.
Belgium	A new poll is being prepared by the NGO-umbrella NCOS for September 1999. The latest published survey states that The Belgian public has the least confidence in development cooperation in Europe but nonetheless 51% of the public is in favour of more Belgian official aid, 72% think it is important but one out of every two Belgians doubts the accuracy of information provided on development aid.	The Minister for Development Cooperation initiated several actions to raise awareness of development cooperation – a 'Kleur Bekennen' campaign through schools, a broad cultural programme on Africa and the opening of an 'International House'. He also emphasised the high flow back of aid resources to Belgium, calling this a 'double return' or a win-win situation which NGOs were far from happy with, preferring to emphasise the implication of southern people, goods and services. In addition, NGOs and trade unions celebrated the end of their combined campaign 'Working up the World', with a high profile day in Brussels with media coverage where the Prime Minister presented the Government's response to the campaign. In Spring 1999, NGOs start their fourth combined campaign. This year's theme is a broad and general youth campaign, in collaboration with several youth movements.
Canada	A September 1998 Environics poll found that 58% of Canadians thought that the right amount or not enough (12%) is being spent on aid. This is down from 68% in 1997, when 20% thought that not enough was being spent, but up from 1993 (50%) and 1995 (49%). A sizeable proportion (33%) thinks Canada spends too much on aid. Only 31% could estimate correctly the amount Canada does spend on aid. When informed about the correct level, overall support (the	In 1995, the government cut all funding to community-based development education. Education activities by international programming NGOs, who also faced several years of funding cuts from CIDA, have also not increased, and in some cases have diminished. During 1998 and 1999 CIDA carried out consultations to initiate and implement a new *Approach to Public Engagement through Partners*. The strategy will be finalized in 1999 and will guide CIDA's renewed funding for public engagement. In 1998/99 and again in 1999/2000,

Political and public opinion

Country	Public attitudes to aid and poverty	Building public commitment
	right amount or not enough) goes from 58% to 74% (77% in 1997). Overall support for a Canadian aid programme remains high at 75% (52% strongly and very strongly support aid). However, the proportion of people who very strongly support aid went down 13% from 1997. Humanitarian reasons for supporting aid remain the strongest at 46%, with 15% identifying emergencies, 17% a moral obligation as a rich country, and only 3% economic benefits to Canada, as their reasons to support the aid programme.	new resources ($1 million and $1.5 million respectively) were added to ODA for innovative projects in public engagement.
Denmark	There is a generally a very positive attitude amongst the Danish public towards development aid. For the past years 73–80% of the population asked about their support to Danish aid said that they supported it. They were told beforehand, that the level of aid spending amounts to 1% of GNP In 1998 45% said that the level of aid was appropriate, while 38% said that it is too high. They were told beforehand, that each Dane pays about DKK 2,000 per year in development aid. This shows that there is a high degree of general support to aid, but that if people are confronted with facts and figures on what this means in real terms some are less supportive.	The Government tries to build public commitment to poverty eradication by emphasising the importance of this in their own policies and actions; and by encouraging Danida to be more precise in documenting the poverty reducing effect of Danish aid. NGOs, as well as Danida, make major efforts in educating a wider public on issues of poverty and its causes. The education partly aims at creating a feeling of solidarity with poor people in the world and at encouraging further support for development aid and poverty reduction.
Finland	According to the results of a new opinion poll, released in mid-March, there is broad public support for Finland's current policy of development cooperation and increased satisfaction with the country's response to development needs. The poll surveyed people's attitudes to Finnish ODA and their need for more information about development policy. 80% of respondents said they are content with the government's responsiveness in ODA, 69% think the level of aid is adequate and 78% support the choice of recipient countries. Public views about the amount, form and targets of Finnish ODA are roughly the same as those recorded in a survey conducted at the end of 1997. The poll shows that more people – 51% compared to 34% in 1997 – view Finnish ODA as an essential part of the country's foreign policy. However, the poll shows a slight decrease in people's interest in development aid, which may reflect the need for more widespread information about development cooperation and Finland's policy as a whole.	A number of initiatives have taken place in Finland in the last year that have helped focus attention on poverty in ways that link the issue with developments in Finland as well as further afield. The government's support of the Jubilee 2000 debt relief effort has given the campaign much leverage in mustering public backing for the need to tackle developing countries' debt and to link it with the wider issues of the causes of poverty. The debate on the effects of economic globalisation has also moved forward in Finland, with two sizeable international events held: a conference of the International Group on Grassroots Initiatives in September 1998, and a conference on civil society and development organised by the DIDC in March 1999. These saw a fair mix of NGO, official and expert exchanges on the negative impact of globalisation, and the problem of targeting poverty world-wide received much attention. These and others focusing on issues such as the Lomé process and the behaviour of the international financial institutions have helped stimulate debate on poverty.

Political and public opinion

France	French people remain concerned about public aid for development, as shown by a survey conducted in February 1999 in which 64% of respondents were in favour of an increase in ODA (the highest since 1993 and two points higher than 1998), although more than half put as a condition that it should be better used. 30% thought aid should not be increased but put to better use, and only 3% thought it should be reduced. It appears that France is entering a period where support for international cooperation and the desire to fight world poverty are strong.	The only important action undertaken by the Government, in relation with NGOs and civil society, was the organisation of a National Conference of Cooperation in October 1997. As preparation conferences were organised in nine regions and both governmental and non-governmental organisations concerned with development cooperation took part.
Germany	The latest opinion survey commissioned by the BMZ dates back to April 1994. Until 1987, a survey funded by the BMZ was published every other year. At present, the BMZ is considering reintroducing opinion surveys at regular intervals every two or three years whilst NGOs are requesting that the BMZ commissions opinion surveys every other year.	NGOs have used the recent federal election campaign to lobby candidates intensively at the local level and a number of useful materials were produced to inform the public about pressing issues in development cooperation with the intent that this information be used to question those running for office. The response of local groups has been stronger than anticipated. In addition, the strength of reactions of the former government towards critical assessments of their aid policies has demonstrated that public opinion on this issue does have an impact.
Ireland	The 1994 DAC Development Cooperation Review of Ireland remarked on the strong general support for the Irish Aid programme both at the political level and among the public at large. There are also high levels of voluntary support for non-governmental development organisations. In order to build public commitment to development aid and global poverty eradication, Irish Aid has established an information unit and there is now a more active information policy on Irish Aid.	The Government's Strategy Statement has a commitment to enhance appreciation by the public of issues affecting poor countries. The National Committee for Development Education is funded by Irish Aid and development education is available in both the formal education sector and the non-formal sector. In November 1998 the Minister stated that 'Informed debate provides the foundation for the democratic mandate for our development cooperation policy and promotes a sense of public ownership of the Aid programme.' There has also been sustained NGO action to build public opinion towards poverty eradication as well as some NGOs entirely dedicated to development education. NGOs consider, however, that more needs to be done to educate the general public about long-term development issues in order to build public support for Government spending on overseas aid. Dochas (the umbrella body for NGOs) has called for an increase in spending on development education to 3% of the bilateral aid budget by 2002.
Italy	There is no opinion survey on public attitudes towards aid and poverty. Every year, there are some 100 initiatives on education and information, most of which are developed in the schools through training programmes for teachers and student, or through seminars for teachers, media operators, or relating to specific issues such as	Information and the activities to increase public support for development initiatives are promoted by the NGOs and financed by MFA. In the last two years, the MFA has supported associated initiatives of groups of NGOs at national level, in order to realise a better coordination of activities and to concentrate efforts. Current NGO campaigns on sub-Saharan Africa and poverty reduction

Political and public opinion

Country	Public attitudes to aid and poverty	Building public commitment
Japan	According to the opinion poll in December 1997, • 15.6% responded that aid should be increased • 46.0% favoured maintaining the current level of aid volume • 14.8% said aid should be reduced • 1.8% called for stopping all aid programme • 21.9%: don't know Because of the prolonged recession, increasing unemployment and the huge government budget deficit, the trend of declining public support for aid is continuing.	women or children. In recent years many education and information activities have been organized in collaboration with the local authorities, however, despite this, the general public remains insufficiently aware of aid issues, due to the lack of organisation among NGOs and to lack of interest from the media in general. Maintaining public support for poverty eradication and aid is becoming increasingly important for both the government and NGOs. The government opened an 'information plaza' in October 1993 in Tokyo, and 17 smaller information centres have been opened (as of September 1998) in collaboration with local governments around the country. An 'International Cooperation Festival', participated in by governmental agencies, NGOs, international organisations and the business community was held in Tokyo on the weekend of October 2 and 3 1999 (International Cooperation Day). The NGO community is going to host the first nationwide campaign named 'Global Citizenship Week' to coincide with the festival.
The Netherlands	The Netherlands has a strong tradition of public support for development cooperation. There have been no recent opinion surveys, but public commitment to voluntary donations in the case of natural disasters can be inferred from the high level of donations to the victims of the hurricane 'Mitch' in Central America.	represent a priority area of interest: the COCIS (Coordinamento delle ONG per la Cooperazione Internazionale allo Sviluppo) NGOs federation organised a nationwide campaign named 'Lomé 2000'. The Dutch government builds public awareness of development cooperation issues through a number of different instruments. The NCDO (National Committee for International Cooperation and Sustainable Development) receives funds to organise public awareness activities and development education. The department of development cooperation publishes a monthly magazine and a magazine for a younger audience. The Dutch government focuses special attention to youth under the age of 18 years and uses interactive media to involve youth in decision-making around development issues. A 'Youth Council' was established in March 1997 to advise the Minister on development cooperation and the Ministry also organised a 'Move your World' campaign targeted at youth.
New Zealand	A survey of public opinion on overseas aid is currently underway. This is the first comprehensive survey since 1987.	The Administration publishes regular newsletters aimed at a general and business community readership to promote ODA activity. There is, however, no specific campaign to promote ODA. NGOs are currently running a low key 'Aid Works' campaign that has the dual goal of promoting the values of ODA while campaigning for a stronger poverty eradication focus but this campaign is hampered by lack of funding. Other current NGO campaigns that promote poverty eradication are Oxfam's basic education campaign and the Jubilee 2000 debt relief campaign. All campaigning on ODA suffers from poor media coverage.

Political and public opinion

Norway	An opinion poll in 1996 showed that 84% of the population was for development aid, as compared to 85% in 1986 and 1993. Support is therefore strong and stable. One half of the respondents felt that the present level of aid is reasonable, whereas 12% called for increases and 30% for reductions. The last figures represents a set back from 12% in 1986 and 26% in 1993.	
Portugal	There are no opinion surveys on ODA in Portugal.	There is no concrete data, however, the Portuguese public do respond well to calls for donations for emergency appeals.
Spain	The most recent survey, by the Institute for International Affairs and Foreign Policy published in May 1998, shows that in 1997 72.8% of the population supports or strongly supports the 0.7% aim. This is compared with 66% in 1996.	Apart from Ayuda en Acción and Intermón's initiatives on basic education, Intermón and Caritas Española have recently launched a report on Copenhagen's Summit Commitments from the Spanish perspective. Regarding the commitment relating to ODA policies, this report has stressed the importance of poverty eradication as a major objective for ODA programmes. The report had a considerable impact on public opinion, and gave rise to the issue of poverty eradication in relation to public policy.
Sweden	The annual survey commissioned by Sida on public opinion on aid had an all time low in 1996 for the support of Swedish Aid programmes. In 1997 the survey showed increasing support for aid; in the last survey of December 1998 this upward trend was maintained. The proportion that wanted to maintain or increase the current aid levels was 52.9% in 1997 and 56.9% in 1998. Sida also made a more comprehensive survey on public attitudes, where 71% agreed it important that Sweden supports development in the South.	There has been a joint working group between the Sida Information department and major NGOs to analyse the situation of public support for development issues. There is better coordination between the different actors, and Sida has issued new regulations for its financial support of NGO Development Education and advocacy, with the intention of stimulating campaigning rather than spawning isolated projects.
Switzerland	Since 1984, both the Swiss Coalition (NGOs) and SDC (Government) carry out opinion polls at five yearly intervals. The 1999 survey shows that 56% endorse the present ODA volume, 20% support an increase, 17% ask for a reduction; a majority overestimates Swiss ODA substantially. 63 percent see direct aid with Southern partners as most effective, 54 percent endorse also the cooperation with the United Nations as efficient. Cooperation between the World Bank and the Swiss Government, however, is seen as effective by only 37% of respondents. Aid by Swiss NGOs is more highly valued than the governmental programmes. 64% support changing life styles in the North to enhance development in the South.	The Swiss Coalition of Development Organisations led a three year 'North/South Campaign for Sustainable Development', culminating in 1998 in a conference held in the National Parliament with prominent representatives from the South and North present. The Swiss Coalition had discussions with leaders of political parties on aid and development policy and organised trips for MPs and journalists to selected southern countries. A people's petition with 86,000 signatures was submitted by the Swiss Coalition to government and parliament, requesting an increase in ODA, the creation of a Swiss Foundation for Solidarity, and the inclusion of Sustainable Development in the federal constitution. SDC/FOFEA have also recently published jointly a 10-year cooperation report on lessons learnt 1986–95.

Political and public opinion

Country	Public attitudes to aid and poverty	Building public commitment
United Kingdom	DFID's last opinion survey was in January 1998. Participants felt that targets to halve the number of poor by 2015 are too ambitious; that although Britain does have a moral obligation to help developing countries, its obligation is no more than any other country's; and that people need to know where their money is going. The most pressing needs that the public saw were to halve the number of poor by 2015, to share the benefits of globalisation, to encourage business which respects human rights, the environment and international labour standards, to deliver education to all, to provide access to water, to reduce conflict, and to take a partnership approach. There is little awareness of the decline in global development aid, and a growing awareness of the role of business in developing countries.	DFID has set up a Development Awareness Working Group (DAWG), made up of representatives from government, education, business, and the media. Its purpose is to increase public understanding of mutual dependence between North and South, and the need for international development. DAWG has also set up a Development Awareness Fund (DAF) which supports development awareness projects, predominantly in the formal education sector but also in trade unions, the workplace, and throughout Britain's working sector and civil society organizations. Out of 107 applications 25 are being taken forward. It aims to spread its development messages in schools through every discipline from biology to physical education. DFID has also set up a consultancy which is undertaking an audit of all the development-related materials available to the formal education sector so that gaps can be filled. In May 1999 questions on development awareness will be included in a national statistics survey to enable DFID to evaluate these projects. DFID is also engaging more and more with civil society organisations – for instance voicing its support to coalition organisations like Jubilee 2000, or supporting ActionAid's Development Education Campaign.
USA	Several studies conducted over the past few years have shown that the American public does not realize that the United States has the lowest level of effort among DAC Member countries. Most Americans still seem to overestimate the amount of US foreign assistance believing it to be over 15% as opposed to less than one percent.	Most actions have centered on building support for disaster response initiatives to meet humanitarian needs with the American public being generous in its donations and support of these emergencies. USAID remains the only active US government player in promoting public and private support for programmes. Senior policy officials and a handful of Congressional representatives occasionally advocate for sustainable development programmes but tend not to get involved in their planning or policies. Much attention is paid to globalization, but neither USAID nor the American NGO community have had success in using this as a vehicle to generate concern for world poverty. An ambitious ten-year *Global Interdependence Initiative* aimed at addressing US public opinion on foreign assistance will involve private foundations, NGOs and government and is to be launched in mid-1999.

Note: For Public Attitudes Column, entries for Australia, Belgium, Norway and Spain are based on last year's information
Source: NGO questionnaires

Table 57 Donor government funding for information, public relations and development education

Country	Total government funding for information, public relations and development education		Total government funds for development education (US$)	
	Year	Volume (US$m)	Year	Volume (US$m)
Australia	1999/00	1.13	1999/00	0.25
	1998/9	0.817	1998/99	0.25
	1997/8	0.89	1997/8	0.3
Austria	1998	5.65	1998	4.3
Belgium	1999	10	1999	6.89[1]
	1996	9.6[2]		–
Canada	1999/00	9.7	1999/00	5.59
	1998/99	9.9	1998/99	5.66[3]
	1996/7	7.3	1996/7	2.82
Denmark	1999	N/a	1999	5.97
	1998	N/a	1998	5.97
	1997	N/a	1997	5.6
Finland	1999	1.0	1999	0.94
	1998	1.0	1998	0.94
	1997	2.2	1997	1.19
	1996	2.2	1996	0.91
France	–	–	1998	2.6[4]
Germany	1999	3.27		–
	1996	4.4[5]		–
Ireland	1999	1.7	1999	1.45
	1998	1.6	1998	1.41
	1997	1.5	1997	1.39
Italy	1999	3.5		–
	1998	2.3	1998	10
Japan	1998	3.25	1998	2.83
Netherlands	1999	14.6	1999	10.07
	1998	14.9		
	1997	14.9	1997 & 1998	10.25[6]
New Zealand	1998/99	–	1998/99	0.15
Norway	1998	6.2[7]		–
Portugal	–	–		–

Donor government funding

Country	Total government funding for information, public relations and development education		Total government funds for development education (US$)	
	Year	Volume (US$m)	Year	Volume (US$m)
Spain	1996	7.0	1996	1.97
	1995	6.3	1995	1.52
Sweden	1998	17.3[8]	–	–
	1997	13.6	–	–
Switzerland	1998	4.6	1998	1.37
	1997	4.2	1997	1.26
United Kingdom	1997/8	2.13[9]	1997/8	1.31[10]
		–	1999	$0.75
USA		–	1998	$0.5
		–	1997	$0.75
	1996	PR and information functions of USAID have been subsumed by the State Department. Data is not available for PR related to humanitarian assistance alone	1996	$0.75

Note on exchange rates: The relevant OECD produced exchange rates have been used for 1995, 1996, 1997 and 1998. 1999 and 2000 figures have been converted to US$ from national currency using 1998 exchange rates

Notes:
1 through NGOs
2 $7.5 million through NGOs
3 Development Information Programme
4 spent by NGOs
5 on information, $2.8million of which went through NGOs
6 spent through National Committee for International Cooperation and Sustainable Development
7 Excluding Public Relations
8 $10.5 estimated to be channelled via NGOs
9 Centrally managed DFID expenditures only
10 centrally managed DFID expenditures only
Source: NGO questionnaires

Part V
Reference Section

Participating agencies

AUSTRALIA
Australian Council for Overseas Aid (ACFOA)
Private Bag 3
Deakin Act 2600
Tel: + 61 2 6285 1816
Fax: + 61 2 6285 1720
email: acfoa@acfoa.asn.au

AUSTRIA
Arbeitsgemeinschaft Entwicklungszusammenarbeit (AGEZ)
Bergasse 7
A –1090 Wien
Tel: + 43 1 317 4016/4020
Fax: + 43 1 317 4016
email: agez@magnet.at
Web: www.oneworld.at/agez

and

Osterreichische Forschungsstiftung fur Entwicklungshilfe
(OEFSE)
Bergasse 7
A –1090 Wien
Tel: + 43 1 317 4010
Fax: + 43 1 317 4015
email: office@oefse.at
Web: www.oefse.at

BELGIUM
Nationaal Centrum voor Ontwikkelingssamenwerking
(NCOS)
Vlasfabriekstraat 11
B–1060 Brussels
Tel: + 322 536 1150
Fax: + 322 536 1902
email: rudy.demeyer@ncos.ngonet.be

BRAZIL
FASE
email: jdurao@fase.org.br

CANADA
Canadian Council for International Cooperation/Conseil
canadien pour la cooperation internationale (CCIC/CCCI)
1 Nicholas Street
Suite 300
Ottawa
Ontario K1N 7B7

Tel: + 1 613 241 7007
Fax: + 1 613 241 5302
email: btomlinson@ccic.ca
Web: www.incommon.web.net; www.net/ccic-ccci

CHILE
SUR
email: urprof@netline.cl

DENMARK
Mellemfolkeligt Samvirke
Borgergade 14
DK–1300 Copenhagen K
Tel: + 45 7731 0000
Fax: + 45 7731 0101
email: ms@ms-dan.dk
Web: www.ms-dan.dk

EUROPE
Eurostep
115 rue Stevin
1000 Brussels
Belgium
Tel: + 322 231 1659
Fax: + 322 230 3780
email: sstocker@eurostep.org
admin@eurostep.org
Web: www.oneworld.org/eurostep

FINLAND
Kehitysyhteistyoen Palvelukeskus ry /Servicecentralen foer
Utuccklingssamarbete (KEPA)
Soernaeisten Rantatie 25
FIN–00500 Helsinki
Tel: + 358 9 584 233
Fax: + 358 9 584 23 200
email: kepa@kepa.fi

FRANCE
Centre de Recherche et d'Information pour le
Developpement (CRID)
14, passage Dubail
75010 Paris
Tel: + 331 4472 0771
Fax: + 331 4472 0684
email: crid@globenet.org

Participating agencies

GERMANY
Deutsche Welthungerhilfe
Adenauerallee 134
D–53113 Bonn
Tel: + 49 228 22 88 00
Fax: + 49 228 22 07 10
email: dwhh_gs@compuserve.com

and

terre des hommes BRD
Ruppenkampstrasse 11a
D–49084 Osnabruck
Tel: +49 541 71 01 0
Fax: +49 541 70 72 33
email: terre@t-online.de

GUATEMALA
PRODESSA
email: prodessa@gold.guate.net

IRELAND
Concern Worldwide
52–55 Lower Camden Street
Dublin 3
Tel: + 353 1 4754162
Fax: + 353 1 4757362
email: howard.dalzell@concern.ie

ITALY
Movimondo
Piazza Albania 10
1–00153 Rome
Tel: + 39 06 573 00 33 0
Fax: + 39 06 574 48 69
email: molisv.movimondo@flashnet.it

JAPAN
Japanese NGO Center for International Cooperation (JANIC)
5F, Saito Bldg
2–9–1 Kanda Nishiki-cho
Chiyoda-ku
Tokyo 101–0054
Tel: + 81 3 3294 5370
Fax: + 81 3 3294 5398
email: janic@jca.ax.apc.org

LATIN AMERICA
Centro Peruano de Estudios Sociales (CEPES)
Av. Salaverry 818 Jesus Maria,
Lima 11
Peru
Tel: + 51 14 336610
Fax: + 51 44 331744
email: cepes@cepes.pe
Web: www.rcp.net.pe/cti

and

ALOP
Casilla Postal 265 1350
San Jose de Costa Rica
Tel: + 506 283 2122
Fax: + 506 283 5898
email: info@alop.or.cr

NETHERLANDS
Netherlands Organisation for International Development
Cooperation (NOVIB)
PO Box 30919
2500 GX The Hague,
visiting address: Mauritskade 9
Tel: + 31 70 342 1621
Fax: + 31 70 361 4461
email: admin@novib.nl

NEW ZEALAND
Council for International Development/Kaunihera mo te
Whakapakari Ao Whanui (CID)
PO Box 12–470
Wellington
Tel: + 64 4 472 6375
Fax: + 64 4 472 6374
email: cid@clear.net.nz

NICARAGUA
FACS
email: facs@facs.org.ni

NORWAY
Norwegian Peoples Aid
PO Box 8844 Youngstorget
N–0028 Oslo 1
Tel: + 47 22 03 77 00
Fax: + 47 22 20 08 70
email: Gunhild.oerstavik@.npaid.org
Web: www.npaid.org

Participating agencies

PERU
DESCO
email: humberto@desco.org.pe

PORTUGAL
OIKOS Cooperacao e Desenvolvimento
Rua de Santiago 9
1100 – 493 Lisboa
Tel: + 351 21 882 3630
Fax: + 351 21 882 3635
email: edu.oikos@oikos.pt

SPAIN
INTERMON
Alberto Aguilera 15
28015 Madrid
Tel: + 34 91 5480458
Fax: + 34 91 5591667
email: gfanjul@intermon.org

SWEDEN
Forum Syd
Box 17510
S–118 91 Stockholm
Tel: + 46 8 702 7700
Fax: + 46 8 702 9099
email: forumsyd@forumsyd.se

SWITZERLAND
Swiss Coalition of Development Organisations
Monbijoustrasse 31
PO Box 6735
CH–3001 Bern
Tel: + 41 31 381 1711
Fax: + 41 31 381 1718
email: mail@swisscoalition.ch

UGANDA
Uganda Debt Network
C/o PO Box 11224
Kampala
Tel: + 256 41 543974/534856
Fax: + 256 41 235413
email: udn@infocom.co.ug
Web: www.uganda.co.ug/debt

UNITED KINGDOM
ActionAid
Hamlyn House
MacDonald Road
London N19 5PG
Tel: + 44 171 281 4101
Fax: + 44 171 281 5146
email: markc@actionaid.org.uk

UNITED STATES
American Council for Voluntary International Action
(InterAction)
1717 Massachusetts Avenue NW
Suite 801
Washington DC 20036
Tel: + 1 202 667 8227
Fax: + 1 202 667 8236
email: jzarafon@interaction.org

URUGUAY
CCU
email: guarino@chasque.apc.org

VENEZUELA
CESAAP
email: Cesap@eldish.net

ZIMBABWE
MWENGO
PO Box HG 817
Highlands
Harare
Zimbabwe
Tel: + 263 4 721469
Fax: + 263 2 738310
email: ts@internet.co.zw

Glossary

20:20	An Initiative to provide 20% of ODA and 20% of public expenditure in developing countries to enable universal access to Basic Social Services (BSS)
ABOS	Algemeen Bestuur voor Ontwikkelinssamenwerking (Belgian Ministry for Development Cooperation)
ACEAD	Advisory Committee on External Aid and Development
ACEP	Association for Cooperation between Peoples
ACFOA	Australian Council for Overseas Aid
ACP	The African, Caribbean and Pacific states, currently 70 in number, parties to the Lomé Convention of the EU
ACVFA	Advisory Committee on Voluntary Foreign Aid
ADB/AsDB	Asian Development Bank
ADEA	Association for the Development of Education in Africa
AECI	Spanish Agency for International Cooperation
AfDB	African Development Bank
AFRODAD	African Forum and Network on Debt and Development
AGEZ	Arbeitsgemeinshaft Entwicklungszusammenarbeit
AIDS	acquired immune deficiency syndrome
ALA	Asia and Latin America
ALOP	Latin American Association of Promotion Organisations
APEC	Asia Pacific Economic Cooperation Forum
APIC	Association for Promotion of International Cooperation
APSO	Agency for Personal Service Overseas
ASEAN	Association of South East Asian Nations
ATS	Austrian Schillings
AusAID	Australian Agency for International Development
BADC	Belgian Administration for Development
BAP	Bilateral Aid Programme
BeF	Belgian Francs
BHN	basic human needs
BIRF	International Bank for Reconstruction and Development (World Bank)
BJP	Bharatiya Janata Party (India)
BMZ	Ministry for Economic Cooperation and Development (Germany)
BNLS	Botswana, Namibia, Lesotho, Swaziland
BOP	balance of payments
BOU	Bank of Uganda

BRAC	Bangladesh Rural Advancement Committee
BSS	Basic Social Services (Basic Education, basic health and nutrition, safe water and sanitation) defined for the purposes of the 20:20 Initiative
BTC	Belgian Techical Cooperation
CAP	Common Agricultural Policy (of the EU)
CARICOM	Caribbean Community
CBO	community based organisation
CCA	Common Country Assessment
CCFD	Catholic Committee against Hunger and for Development
CCIC	Conseil canadien pour la cooperation inter-nationale
CEC	Commission of the European Community
CEE	Central and Eastern Europe
CEEC	Central and Eastern European countries
CEPES	Centro Peruano de Estudios Sociales
CFA	African financial community franc
CFO	Co-financing Organisation
CFSP	Common Foreign and Security Policy
CGGP	Commonwealth Good Governance Programme
CID	Council for International Development
CIDA	Canadian International Development Agency
COCIS	Coordinamento delle ONG per la Cooperazione internationale allo Svilluppo
CONALFA	National Literacy Committee (Guatemala)
COPROFAM	Family Promotion Committee (Peru)
CPLP	Portuguese-Speaking Countries Community
CRID	Centre de Recherche et d'Information pour le Developpement
CSO	Civil Society Organisations
DAC	Development Assistance Committee of the OECD. The DAC defines a list of developing countries eligible to receive ODA. In 1996 a number of countries, including Israel, ceased to be eligible for ODA. A second group of countries, 'Countries and Territories in Transition' including Central and Eastern Europe are eligible for 'Official Aid' – not to be confused with 'Official Development Assistance'. OA has the same terms and conditions as ODA, but it does not count towards the 0.7% target, because it is not going to developing countries
DAF	Development Awareness Fund
Danida	Danish International Development Assistance, Ministry of Foreign Affairs
DAWG	Development Awareness Working Group
DC	Development Cooperation

Glossary

DCD	Development Cooperation Division of the DAC
DDC	Department for Development Cooperation
DEV	Development Cooperation Division of the Ministry of Foreign Affairs
DFID	Department for International Development
DG	Directorate General
DGIS	Directorate-Generale for International Cooperation
DIDC	Department for International Development Cooperation
DIGEBI	General Office for Intercultural Bilingual Education
DIP	Decision in Principle
DKK	Danish Krone
DM	Deutsch Mark
DPEP	District Primary Education Programme
DTI	Department of Trade and Industry
DWHH	Deutsche Welthungerhilfe
EAC	East Africa Community
EAP	Economically Active Community
EBRD	European Bank for Reconstruction and Development
EC	European Commission
ECA	Economic Commission for Africa
ECHO	European Community Humanitarian Office
ECLAC	Economic Commission for Latin America and the Caribbean
ECU	European Currency Unit
EDF	European Development Fund, the main financing mechanism for EU aid under the Lomé Convention
EFA	Education for All
EIB	European Investment Bank
EMU	economic and monetary union
ERG	export risk guarantee
ESAF	Enhanced Structural Adjustment Facility
ESDP	Education Sector Development Programme
EU	European Union
FAD	Development Aid Fund
FADES	Bilateral programme for local social sector in Nicaragua
FAL	Functional Adult Literacy
FAO	Food and Agriculture Organisation (of the UN)
FDI	Foreign Direct Investment
FECODE	Federación Colombiana de Encadores
FIM	Finnish Markka
FOFEA	Federal Office of Foreign Economic Affairs
FTA	Free Trade Agreement
FY	financial year
G7	The group of seven main industrial countries
G-24	Group of 24 developed nations meeting to coordinate assistance to Central and Eastern Europe
GAP	Oxfam's Global Action Plan
GATT	General Agreement on Tariffs and Trade
GDP	Gross Domestic Product – the total value of a country's output per year
GDR	German Democratic Republic
GEF	Global Environment Facility
GNI	Gross National Income
GNP	Gross National Product – GDP plus income from economic activity overseas
GRC	Gross Rate of Coverage
GSP	Generalised System of Preferences
GTZ	German Agency for Technical Cooperation
HIC	High Income Countries with an annual per capita income of more than US $ 9385 in 1995.
HIPC	Heavily Indebted Poor Country debt initiative
HIV	human immunodeficiency virus
HPI	human poverty index
HSD	Human and Social Development
IAAC	Irish Aid Advisory Committee
IACE	Institute of Adult and Continuing Education
IADB	Inter-American Development Bank
ICICD	Interministerial Committee of International Cooperation and Development
ICP	Portuguese Cooperation Institute
IDA	International Development Assistance – the part of the World Bank that offers loans at very concessional rates to poor countries
IDB	Inter-American Development Bank
IDT	International Development Targets as outlined in the DAC document *Shaping the 21st Century*
IFAD	International Fund for Agriculture and Development
IFC	International Finance Corporation
IFI	International Financial Institution
ILAC/CT	African/Portuguese Institute for Scientific and Technical Cooperation
ILO	The International Labour Organisation (part of the UN)
IMF	International Monetary Fund
INDEC	National Institute of Statistics and Censuses
INE	National Statistics Institute
INEI	National Statistics Institute
JANIC	Japanese NGO Centre for International Cooperation

Glossary

JICA	The Japan International Cooperation Agency
JOCV	Japanese Overseas Cooperation Volunteers
KePa	Kehitsyhteistyoen Palvelukeskus ry / Servicecentralen foer Utuccklingssamarbete
KfW	Bank for Reconstruction (Kreditanstalt fur Wiederaufbau)
LIC	Low Income Countries – with an annual per capita income of less than US$765 in 1995
LLDC	48 poor and vulnerable countries defined by the United Nations with an annual per capita income of less than US $765 in 1995
LMIC	Lower Middle Income Countries, with an annual per capita income of between US$766 and US$3035 in 1995
MAAIF	Ministry of Agriculture, Animal Industry and Fisheries
MADCT	More Advanced Developing Countries and Territories comprise countries which transferred to Part II of the DAC List of Aid Recipients in 1996 or 1997
MAI	Multilateral Agreement on Investment
Med	Mediterranean Basin
MEP	Member of the European Parliament
MERCOSUR	A regional agreement for promoting trade and investment in the 'Southern Cone' countries of Latin America
MES	Ministry of Education and Sport
MFAT	Ministry of Foreign Affairs and Trade
MGLSD	Ministry of Gender, Labour and Social Development
MINEDUC	Ministry of Education
MMD	Movement for Multiparty Democracy
MOC	Community Organisation Movement
MoFA	Ministry of Foreign Affairs
MOH	Ministry of Health
MOLG	Ministry of Local Government
MWENGO	Mwelekeo Wa NGO
NAFTA	North American Free Trade Agreement
NAO	National Authorising Officers
NATO	North Atlantic Treaty Organisation
NCDE	National Committee for Development Education
NCOS	Nationaal Centrum voor Ontwickelingssammenwerking
NFALC	National Functional Adult Literacy Committee
NFE	Non Formal Education
NGDO	Non-Governmental Development Organisation
NGO	Non Government Organization
NIP	National Indicative Programmes

NIS	Newly Independent States – refers to the countries of former USSR
NISD	Nsamizi Institute of Social Development
NLG	Dutch Guilders
NORAD	The Norwegian official aid agency
Novib	Netherlands Organisation for International Development Cooperation
NZODA	New Zealand's Overseas Development Assistance Programme
OA	Official Aid. This is government assistance with the same terms and conditions as ODA, but which goes to Countries and Territories in Transition which include former aid recipients and Central and Eastern European Countries and the Newly Independent States. It does not count towards the 0.7% target.
ODA	Official Development Assistance (often referred to as 'aid'), of which at least 25% must be a grant. The promotion of economic development or welfare must the main objective. It must go to a developing country as defined by the DAC
ODF	Official Development Assistance
ODI	Overseas Development Institute (UK)
OECD	Organisation for Economic Cooperation and Development
OECF	Japan's Overseas Economic Cooperation Fund
OFSE	Oesterreichische Forschungstiftung fuer Entwicklungshilfe
ORET	Development-relevant Export Transactions
PAF	Poverty Action Fund
PALOP	African Portuguese-speaking Countries
PCR	Primary Cycle Completion Rate
PCREV	Promotion of Decentralised Local Health Service Systems
PEAP	Poverty Eradication Action Plan
PHARE	EU grant finance initiative for Central and Eastern Europe (originally Poland–Hungary Assistance for the Reconstruction of the Economy)
PNG	Papua New Guinea
PRISM	Performance Reporting and Information System for Managers
PRODEGA	Bilateral programme for Nicaraguan Livestock and Rural Development
Ptas	Spanish Pesetas
real terms	A figure adjusted to take account of exchange rates and inflation, allowing a 'real' comparison over time
REPA	Regional Economic Partnership Agreements

Glossary

RIP	Regional Indicative Programmes
S21C	*Shaping the 21st Century* – DAC donors' statement of Development Goals
SACU	South African Customs Union
SADC	Southern African Development Coordination
SAL	Structural Adjustment Loans
SAP	Structural Adjustment Programme
SCE	Common Service
SDC	Swiss Agency for Development and Cooperation
SDFC	Swiss Development Finance Corporation
SDP	Sectoral Development Programme
SECIPI	Secretary of State for International Cooperation and Latin America
SEK	Swedish krona
SICHE	Solomon Islands College of Higher Education
Sida	The Swedish official aid agency
SILIC	severely indebted low income country
SIP	Sectoral Investment Programme
SIRES	Bilateral Programme for Nicaraguan People with Disabilities
SME	small- and medium-sized enterprise
SPA	Special Programme for Africa
SPP	Swiss People's Party
SSA	sub Saharan Africa
SSDP	Swiss Social Democratic Party
STABEX	Non-programme EDF Finance to stabilise export revenue
SWAp	Sector Wide Approaches
TACIS	EU Programme for Technical Assistance to the Commonwealth of Independent States.
Tdh	terre des hommes
TEU	Treaty on the European Union
TICAD	Tokyo Conference on African Development
TNC	transnational corporation
TOM	French Overseas Territories
TRIPS	Trade-related Intellectual Property Rights
UEMOA	West African Economic and Monetary Union
UMIC	Upper Middle Income Countries with an annual per capita income of between US$3036 and US$9385 in 1995
UN	United Nations

UNCED	United Nations Conference on Environment and Development (Rio 1992)
UNCTAD	United Nations Conference on Trade and Development
UNDAF	United Nations Development Assistance Framework
UNDP	United Nations Development Programme
UNESCO	United Nations Educational, Scientific and Cultural Organisation
UNFPA	United Nations Fund for Population Activities
UNGASS	United Nations General Assembly Special Session
UNHCR	United Nations High Commissioner for Refugees
UNICEF	United Nations Children's Fund
UNIDO	United Nations Industrial Development Organisation
UNIFEM	United Nations Development Fund for Women
UNIP	United National Independence Party (Zambia)
UNSCAP	United Nations System Conferences Action Plan
UPE	Universal Primary Education
UPPAP	Uganda Participatory Poverty Assessment Project
Uruguay Round	Last round of multilateral trade negotiations under the GATT
USAID	United States Agency for International Development
VASS	Voluntary Agency Support Scheme (New Zealand)
VEC	Village Education Committees
WDR	World Development Report (World Bank)
WFP	World Food Programme
WHO	World Health Organisation
WID	Women in Development
WSSD	The World Summit for Social Development held in Copenhagen in March 1995
WTO	World Trade Organization
ZERP	Zambia Education Rehabilitation Project

Source notes

Notes on data used in icon graphs and Aid at a Glance pages

Country X gave
US$ source: OECD DAC Press release 10 June 1999 (1998 figures);

national Currency source: OECD 1998 exchange rates used with above press release figures;

percentage of GNP source: OECD press release 10 June 1999 (1998 figures);

percentage of public expenditure source: Data for ODA from OECD Press Release June 10, 1999. Data for total government outlays from OECD direct. Please note that this calculation is done on a different basis to previous editions of *The Reality of Aid*. Up until this year, government expenditure has been calculated on the basis of government consumption. These data on government outlays give a more complete picture of government spending as they include investment as well as consumption and local as well as central government;

per capita source: a calculation of total ODA divided by total population. ODA volume (1998) from OECD DAC press release 10 June 1999 and population from DAC Report 1998, Table 39 (1997 figures).

Is it going up or down?
volume source: for 1998 volume compared with 1997: OECD DAC Press Release 10 June 1999. The figures are in current prices, that is they have not been adjusted for inflation and exchange rates. The percentage is in real terms, namely, taking inflation and exchange rates into account;

percentage source: for 1998 percentage compared with 1997. The 1998 figures for ODA as a percentage of GNP are taken from the DAC Press release, issued in June 1999. The 1997 figures are taken from the DAC Report 1998, issued in January 1999. Figures issued in the press releases in June of each year are subsequently adjusted and a revised figure is given in the DAC report. This adjustment accounts for the difference between figures for 1997 quoted in this year's and last year's editions of *The Reality of Aid*;

outlook source: Reality of Aid Questionnaires.

How does country X compare to the other 20 donors
source for ranking volume and GNP: OECD DAC Press Release 10 June 1999 (1998 figures);

source for low income countries: (1997 figures): OECD DAC Report 1998 Table 34 (includes LLDCs and other LICs) except for World Aid: OECD GDFF 1993–1997, "Net Disbursements of ODA from all Sources combined to individual recipients" p67;

source for private flows: OECD DAC Report 1998 Table 13 (1997 figures). This includes flows through NGOs. Swiss data comes from the Swiss Government Statistical Service;

source for total flows: OECD DAC Report 1998 Table 13 (1997 figures) Swiss data comes from the Swiss Government Statistical Service.

How much does country X spend on basic health and basic education?
source: OECD DAC Statistics. Data is for 1997. Please note that these figures show commitments made during the year. Commitments may vary quite sharply as they will include multi-year projects.

How important are commercial interests in aid?
source for fully tied aid as a percentage of total ODA: OECD DAC Report Table 23. 1996 figures except for Belgium, where a 1997 figure is reported.

Icon graphs sources
GNP Percentage bar graph source: OECD DAC Reports, various years;

where is country X aid spent source: OECD DAC Report 1998, Table 34; Data for 1996/7;

how much country X aid is spent through multilaterals source: OECD DAC Report 1998, Table 13; Data for 1997;

what is country X aid spent on source: OECD DAC Report 1998 Table 19; Data for 1996;

how much country X aid goes to the poorest countries: OECD DAC Report 1998, Table 34; Data for 1996/7.

Source notes

A note on weighted and unweighted averages

Donors often refer to the DAC average when discussing their aid as a percentage of GNP. They usually mean the 'weighted average', that is the total of DAC donors' aid as a share of the total of DAC members GNP. This skews the average towards the bigger countries (Japan and USA) which have had poor ratios of aid: GNP.

NGOs believe that the 'unweighted average' (referred to in DAC reports as 'average country effort') is a fairer measure. This takes a simple average of the percentage of GNP achieved by all DAC members. Norway and the USA are both treated equally in terms of their share of national wealth. On the bar charts used in *The Reality of Aid*, both averages are shown.

A note on Portugal

At the time of producing most of the text and charts for this report, 1998 data from Portugal was not available. So most comparisons given do not reflect Portugal's 1998 figures. However, the Portugal charts on page 151 and the World Aid at a Glance charts on page 5 do reflect the latest figures including Portugal.

Exchange rates

Exchange rates used are the OECD annualised exchange rates – see page 288.

For more information on any of these data please contact: Development Initiatives, Old Westbrook Farm, Evercreech, Somerset BA4 6DS, UK or Email: di@devinit.org.

Exchange rates

Table 58 Annual average US dollar exchange rate 1998

Country	Currency	1996	1997	1998
Australia	Dollars	1.3496	1.3473	1.5923
Austria	Schillings	10.0820	12.1972	12.3758
Belgium	Francs	29.4972	35.7584	36.2976
Canada	Dollars	1.3728	1.385	1.4835
Denmark	Krone	5.6038	6.6041	6.6962
Finland	Markka	4.3666	5.1872	5.3453
France	Francs	4.9908	5.8373	5.8994
Germany	Marks	4.4338	1.7341	1.7594
Ireland	Punts	0.6245	0.6604	0.7030
Italy	Lire	1629.0000	1702.761	1736.3953
Japan	Yen	94.0700	120.9966	130.8945
Luxembourg	Francs	29.4972	35.7584	36.2976
Netherlands	Guilders	1.6050	1.9509	1.9845
New Zealand	Dollars	1.5240	1.5125	1.8685
Norway	Krone	6.3372	7.0723	7.5452
Portugal	Escudos	149.9300	175.1604	180.1491
Spain	Pesetas	124.6900	146.4122	149.3790
Sweden	Krone	7.1336	7.6346	7.9471
Switzerland	Francs	1.1823	1.45	1.4497
United Kingdom	Pounds	0.6336	0.6105	0.6036
European Union	ECU	0.7652	0.8824	0.8941